OPUS 3

For Roland John
with best wishes
from Bill J

Munich, 16.12.18

ALSO BY W. D. JACKSON

Then and Now:

Then and Now – Words in the Dark (Menard Press)
From Now to Then (Menard Press)

Selections from *Opus 3:*

Boccaccio in Florence and Other Poems (Shearsman Books)
A Giotto Triptych (Shoestring Press)
Afterwords. Or: *Occupying No-Man's-Land* (Shoestring Press)

THEN AND NOW

OPUS 3

W. D. JACKSON

Shoestring Press

All rights reserved. No part of this work covered by the copyright herein may be reproduced or used in any means—graphic, electronic, or mechanical, including copying, recording, taping, or information storage and retrieval systems—without written permission of the publisher.

Printed by imprintdigital
Upton Pyne, Exeter
www.digital.imprint.co.uk

Typesetting by narrator
www.narrator.me.uk
info@narrator.me.uk
033 022 300 39

Published by Shoestring Press
19 Devonshire Avenue, Beeston, Nottingham, NG9 1BS
(0115) 925 1827
www.shoestringpress.co.uk

First published 2018
© Copyright: W. D. Jackson

The moral right of the author has been asserted.

ISBN 978-1-912524-11-2

Cover image: Arturo Di Stefano, *Gallery of Modern Art, Palermo,* 2016
Oil on linen, 208.3 x 152.4 cm
Image courtesy of Purdy Hicks Gallery, London
© Copyright Arturo Di Stefano, 2016
Reproduced by permission of the artist.

CONTENTS

Opus 3, No. 1—The Death of Innocence		1
1	A Giotto Triptych	3
	i Left Outer Wing: Cimabue and the Sheep	3
	ii Right Outer Wing: Madonna and Fly	4
	iii Left Panel: Giotto and Forese da Rabatta	4
	iv Predella, Left Panel: The Workman's Coat-of-Arms	5
	v Right Panel: Giotto and King Robert the Wise	6
	vi Predella, Right Panel: The Poor Man and the Rich Man	7
	vii Central Panel: Giotto's O	7
	viii Predella, Central Panel: St Francis Praising God's Creatures	9
2	Boccaccio in Florence—Three Stories and a Dream	11
	i The Dream	11
	ii The Convent Garden	16
	iii Nastagio degli Onesti and the Necromancer	21
	iv Alibech and Rustico	28
3	François Villon: Two Extracts from *The Testament*	40
4	Jove's New World—A Post-Renaissance Picture Gallery	45
5	The Childhood and Song-Book of *Allerleirauh*—A *Kunstmärchen*	49
6	Heinrich Heine: From *Kühle Nacht* to *Matratzengruft*	60
	i "The night and the streets are still, as I go"	60
	ii Three Poems on the History of Religion	60
	Donna Clara	60
	Almansor	63
	Princess Sabbath	67
	iii "Like a storm in my brain, a flood of fields"	72
7	How Jack Got On in the World	76
8	Orpheus and Others—*ca.* 1375/1904	87
	i Song of Innocence: Sir Orfeo	87
	ii Song of Experience: Rainer Maria Rilke—*Orpheus. Eurydice. Hermes*	93
9	Gretl Braun Remembers Her Sister, Eva	96
10	A Brief Prelude. *Or:* Where He Came From (1)	107

11	The Death of Innocence		115
	i	The Curse	115
	ii	Rilke and Others	115
	iii	At Rilke's Grave	122
	iv	An Ordinary Day	123
	v	The Blessing	124

Opus 3, No. 2—Afterwords 127

1	A Brief Prelude (2)		129
2	Self-Portrait as a White-Collar Worker (4) *Or:* Occupying No-Man's-Land		137
	i	Working for the Enemy	137
	ii	Stephanskirchen (1)	138
	iii	after jandl	148
	iv	Death and Brandner Caspar—A True Story (after Franz von Kobell)	164
	v	Case Studies, 1941–1945	179
	vi	Stephanskirchen (2)	201
	vii	Mary and Martha (Working for Others)	213

Opus 3, No. 3—From Outsight to Insight 215

1	OT / NT		217
	i	The Death of King David	217
	ii	Pontius Pilate's Wife, Procula, Addresses a Group of Christians: Rome, AD 39	223
2	*Al Vescovo d'Assisi…*		233
3	Dante Alighieri: From *Dolce stil nuovo* to *Rime petrose*		243
	i	"*Per una ghirlandetta*" (To Fioretta)	243
	ii	"*Donne ch'avete intelletto d'amore*"	244
	iii	"*Così nel mio parlar voglio esser aspro*"	245
4	The Carpenter's *Cook's Tale. Or:* Blindman's Buff		248
5	The Dance of Death		268
6	Benvenuto *e gli altri*		282
7	Vitzliputzli (after Heine)		288

8	Shakespearean Sonnets	304
9	The Gift	325
10	Three Fables Ancient and Modern	328
	i Baucis and Philemon—A Pastoral Dialogue	328
	ii The Chest	333
	iii Tancred's Daughter	346
11	Peter Bell the Fourth	351
12	Fair's Fair	363
13	A Brief Prelude (3)	365
14	From Outsight to Insight	371
	i Nine Poems After Rilke—The Turn	371
	ii Siddhartha and Others	377
	iii Epilogue	386

ACKNOWLEDGEMENTS AND NOTES   **387**

Opus 3, No.1: The Death of Innocence

And the Lord God planted a garden eastward in Eden; and there he put the man whom he had formed.
Genesis II.8

*

Never such innocence again.
Philip Larkin, *MCMXIV*

*

It may be that universal history is the history of the different intonations given to a handful of metaphors.
Borges, *The Fearful Sphere of Pascal*

*

Each 'historical' fact…is nothing in itself. It operates only according to the way in which it is taken. And this way of taking it expresses symbolically the internal disposition of the individual… The foundation of [his] attitude must be an original choice. Furthermore, the choice is living and can be revoked…
Sartre, *Being and Nothingness*, IV.2.I

Giotto 1267–1337
Cimabue 1240–1302
Boccaci 1313–1375
St. F. Ascii 1181–1226
Dante 1265–1321

1   A GIOTTO TRIPTYCH

"Credette Cimabue nella pittura
* tener lo campo, ed ora ha Giotto il grido,*
* sì che la fama di colui è oscura."*
– Dante, *Purgatorio* XI. 94-96

"—but there is no competition—"
– T.S. Eliot, *Four Quartets*

i   Left Outer Wing: Cimabue and the Sheep

Beneath a gnarled old olive tree,
His back to its riven trunk, his eyes
Shaded by light-green foliage, he
Watches the rocks where his sheep graze.

Abruptly picking up a stone
Without unfixing his sharp look,
He then, with its lowered point—unthrown—
Sketches a ram with two ewes on a rock.

A boy of ten. Behind him stands
Giovanni Cimabue, who
Observes him mix black mud, red sands,
With *non-ti-scordar-di-me* for blue.

Astonished, the *maestro* asks Bordone
Of Vespignano if his son
Would care to join his workshop—only
A few miles off in Florence. The deal done,

Giotto left home—soon to be famed,
In the light of innocent Brother Sun,
For his sheep, rocks, mountains, monks… Untamed
By stone or saint, the wolf gnashed on.

ii   Right Outer Wing: Madonna and Fly

Unable to produce a smile,
He stumps off now to eat and drink.
It's his proud Byzantine stiff style,
Thinks Giotto, which can't feel or think.

The flat Madonna's bloodless lad
Yearns for rich milk. A fat green fly,
With a whiff of butcher's meat gone bad,
Blows in, zigzagging angrily.

But Giotto, the peasant's boy, can catch
A fly in flight. He pins it down
And paints a life-size, perfect match
On her nose beneath her baffled frown…

His master, back, swears—swats it off,
Smudging the paint—sees red—feels free
To teach him, low-born lout, to laugh!—
From whom in the end he learned to see,

Who in Padua painted the greyish smell
Of Lazarus, bandaged, still half-dead,
And the foul gawping mouth of Hell
With Satan gnawing a soul's head.

iii   Left Panel: Giotto and Forese da Rabatta

Returning from his birthplace in Mugello
    One hot dry summer, Giotto met a friend,
The hump-backed lawyer, Forese da Rabatta,
    Astride a hack, where rough hill-tracks descend

Through isolated grey-stone peasants' houses,
    Dark cypresses in rows and yellowing woods;
But as they crossed the Sieve down towards Florence
    Clouds formed, a wind rose, and rain fell in floods.

A peasant, old and poor, offered them shelter,
    Sharing polenta, bacon, last year's wine

With them as his guests; and, when the clouds looked lighter,
    Lent them a ragged cape, torn gabardine.

They ambled on through claggy mud in silence,
    Hoping the rain would stop—until, soaked through,
Forese turned to Giotto, whose bedraggled
    Profile amused him: "Giotto, looking at you,

Who'd ever guess you were the world's best painter?"
    Observing his friend's snub nose, wide mouth, long jaw,
"*Looks good, smells strong,*' my father said," said Giotto,
    Who'd painted Judas as a *bel signor*:

"It's what you do, not what you *have*, that matters.
    Wise judge and learned lawyer you may be,
My friend, but in those rags on that old pad-nag,
    Who'd guess *you* even knew your ABC?"

  iv   Predella, Left Panel: The Workman's Coat-of-Arms

Wearing a headpiece which he'd made,
A workman on a wall-eyed jade,
As if he were a knight or lord,
Asked Giotto would he kindly daub
His buckler with a coat-of-arms
And any other signs or charms
Which might protect him in the war:
He'd never been called up before
But hoped a coat-of-arms might scare
The enemy into taking care
With him and his stout-hearted steed.
Giotto thought, "Arms as charms indeed!"
And painted on his shield's bossed board
A helmet, battle-axe, lance, mace, sword—
Horns, teeth and claws to seize the day.
The insulted workman, refusing to pay
For Giotto's joke, declared he'd sue
For compensation. Giotto, who
Enjoyed a court-case, counter-claimed
For doing the job. Forese, famed
For impartial justice spiced with wit,
Ruled Giotto should be paid for it—

Awarding the workman and his horse
Exactly the same sum, of course.

v   Right Panel: Giotto and King Robert the Wise

Many years passed and Giotto, the farmer's son,
    Painted the world he found. His reputation
Grew—in Milan—Rome—Naples, where the court
    Of *Roberto il Saggio* led Renaissance fashion.

The king had raised a great Franciscan convent
    And church for royal burials. Giotto, requested
To fresco them, designed the Apocalypse—
    As Dante, his tough-minded friend, had suggested—

And scenes from *Job*, as when an anxious crowd
    Of peasants lament Job's loss of his sheep and cattle,
Or his weeping steward holding his nose in disgust
    At his leprous stinking master, on whom flies settle.

The king watched Giotto make him waft them off
    With his other hand till, moved by pride and pity,
He swore he'd make the painter the first man
    In Naples: "Since the main gates of the city

Are where I lodge, your Majesty, I am
    Already the first or last here," Giotto told him.
He sketched the kingdom as a saddled ass,
    Inspecting—as the king sat up to scold him—

A new, more splendid saddle with eager interest.
    Roberto laughed: "I'd take, if I were you,
A break, though, now that Brother Sun's so hot."—
    "And so would I," said Giotto, "if I were you."

vi   Predella, Right Panel: The Poor Man and the Rich Man

"And I will fetch a morsel of bread…"
— Genesis XVIII.5

Weary, benighted, a stranger on foot,
Caught in a storm between a stone hut
And marble villa, knocked at the door
Of the rich man's house: "You look too poor,"
It owner objected, "to work or pay…"
Sadly the traveller turned away,
Unwilling to beg from those who had
So little—but the peasant bade
Him make himself at home. His wife
Cooked *pasta*, made a bed: "Your life
Is harsh," their guest observed—and granted
Their daily bread. They also wanted
To depart this life together. Their third
Wish was to have their roof repaired…
The rich man's wife peeped out as the angel
Spread his bright wings: "I swear I'll strangle
You, husband, if he flitters away."—
He left at a gallop: "Sir, please stay
With us next time…"—But, alas, his first wish
Caused his shy, rearing horse to vanish!
He picked up its saddle. In the midday heat, it
Made him wish his fat wife was beneath it:
"Help me, you fool!" she cried—"What's so funny?"
"My dear, may all I mount turn to money…"

vii   Central Panel: Giotto's O

"…nacque al mondo un sole"
— Paradiso XI.50

The angel Giotto frescoed in the choir
Of old St Peter's, bearing an empty globe
In his right hand, his wings and swirling robe
Possessed by the energy of wind and fire,

Reached twice as high as even the tallest man.
His left hand weighed a pair of balanced scales,

Also containing nothing. The rounded sails
Of Giotto's *Navicella* were fuller than

The Church's tonsured domes… But the Pope had heard
His paintings praised—sent a court-monk to view
And choose examples of what he could do.
Mosaics were the art Rome still preferred,

And Assisi with its landscapes—legends—flowers
Of St Francis—failed to change the monk's cowled mind.
At Siena the only pictures he could find
Were proof of Duccio's seminal painting's powers…

In Florence, Giotto laboured in the heat.
Maria's halo shone among gold stars
Like angels showering peace on the world's wars,
While Sister Moon supported her bare feet.

When the monk described his mission, Giotto drew
In red a perfect circle on a board
And silently went on painting. Feeling ignored,
"That's nothing," scowled the nuncio: "What can you *do*?"

"Nothing is something—more, in fact, than enough,"
Smiled Giotto: "St Francis called himself God's fool—
Un tondo—no one." The monk, though an old mule,
Put Giotto's O in with his other stuff.

Puzzled, the Pope thought—looked again—and perceived
An attribute of Truth, the unblinking Sun.
True art unblinds—unbinds. And Giotto's was soon
Seen in old Rome, his gifts as well received

As elsewhere throughout re-born Italy.
To the things he'd seen on Sister Mother Earth
His maculate O thus gave miraculous birth.
Also to things of nothing no one can see—

But we know are present. Giotto loved his wife
And rued, when he came to die, his defective faith:
No life is—ever—perfect. But then death
Always perfects it. Death encircles life.

viii Predella, Central Panel: St Francis Praising God's Creatures

"O all ye workes of the Lord, blesse ye the Lorde: prayse hym, and magnifye hym for euer."
– 'Benedicite omnia opera domini domino',
The Boke of Common Prayer (1552)

Canticle of Brother Sun

Blessing and honour, glory and power,
Be unto Thee, and Thee alone,
My good, my most high Lord,
Who sitteth upon the throne,
Of Whom no man is worthy to speak a word.

Be praised, with all Your creatures, my good Lord,
Especially for our Master Brother Sun
Who brings the day: You light our lives by him,
And he is fair and splendid and adored
As if, Most High, his radiance were Your own.

Be praised for Sister Moon and the stars, my Lord,
Made beautiful, clear and precious by Your heavenly word.

Be praised, my Lord, for Brother Wind and the air
And the weather which sustains us,
Cloudy and cool or soft and fair.

Be praised, my Lord, for Sister Water,
Your most useful, humble, precious and pure daughter.

Be praised, my Lord, for Brother Fire,
By whom You illuminate the night,
For he is playful, handsome, vigorous, strong.

Be praised, my Lord, for our Sister and Mother Earth,
Who supports us and controls us—
Brings forth her varied fruits, her colourful flowers and grass.

Be praised, my Lord, for those who, because of Thy love, forgive
And suffer infirmity and tribulation:
Blessed are those who suffer in peace,
For they shall be crowned, Most High, by Thee.

Be praised, my Lord, for our Sister Death-
of-the-body, whom none alive can flee.
Woe to the unrepentant breathing their last breath,
Blessed are those who serve to the best of their ability,
For they shall not be harmed by the second death.

Now praise and bless the Lord of Immortality:
Give thanks and serve Him here with all humility.

2 BOCCACCIO IN FLORENCE—THREE STORIES AND A DREAM

i The Dream

"Al quale ella, quasi ridendo disse:
'Buono uomo, el mi par che tu sogni.'"
— *Decameron* II,v

May, 1348. The sun was sinking
Behind the campanile. Boccaccio knelt
Inside the still unfinished duomo, thinking
Of what he'd seen, and wondering how he felt
About the immortal Architect... Could He
Have *planned* this plague, this 'Great Mortality'?

Whole houses, great palazzi, emptied of
Their occupants, the dead piled up outside
With oozing tumours... Rat-packs freely roved
Deserted streets, where pigs and dogs had died
From mauling corpses or infected rags,
And looters staggered under bursting bags.

Abandoned children cried. The sick were left
To die alone, their bodies left to rot.
The stench of dead or dying people bereft
Him of all words. But some he knew were not
So easily shocked. All forms of strange excess
Flourished—helped stave off horror and distress.

Men dropped down dead in the street by day and night.
Coffins and grave-plots were a rarity.
Rough gangs of paupers dug deep plague-pits right
Across old churchyards, charging a fat fee
To stow the dead in tiers with a thin layer
Of soil between them. Priests charged more for a prayer.

But most were thrown in like dead goats or sheep...
Which stopped him trying to pray. Instead, he sat
And closed his aching eyes, and fell asleep,
And dreamt he'd travelled home to Naples—at

The market, where he'd come to buy a horse.
But all the horses were half-dead, or worse.

And all their grooms and riders were half-dead
And putrefying slowly. Stinking meat,
Alive with maggots, and the grinning head
Of a huge boar, were all there was to eat.
One stall had piles of figs, egg-plants, milk, honey,
But no one left alive to take his money.

And so he waved his bag, heavy with gold,
To bring them back to life: five hundred florins.
A pretty girl strolled past. From how she strolled
He knew she'd like to go with him to Florence.
She smiled and said she was his bastard sister.
I'm illegitimate too, he cried, and kissed her.

Safe in her rooms, she wore a veil-like dress
With living leaves and slowly opening flowers
Which he could see straight through. In less
Than no time he'd been there for hours and hours.
Her black eyes flashed. Fresh fruit and roasted meat
And wine appeared. OK, she laughed, let's eat.

And so they ate, drank, laughed, till very late.
As children we'd have shared a double bed,
She coyly giggled. Let's not curse our fate
But make up for it now. He gawped. She said,
Although we had one dad, a different womb
Had *us*... Or would you like a separate room?

My sweet, she whispered, now I've got you here
Locked in my soft white arms, within their pale,
I'll be a park and you can be my deer,
Feed where you want to feed, up hill down dale,
Graze on my lips, or if their slopes are dry
Look lower, where my rough moist-pastures lie.

At this he smiled and, since the night was hot,
They took each other's clothes off, kissed and groped,
And tried it standing up before they got
Into her bed. But, as she must have hoped,

He wanted to relieve himself before
Proceeding. Over there, she said. That door.

And off he dashed. Outside a loosened plank
Shot up and he shot down into the filth
Of many years. The next house was a bank,
In which his father sat, while his own wealth
Was counted by the old man's bastard daughter.
He closed his eyes. A stream of lukewarm water

Splashed off his chest. Shrieking with laughter, high
On the one remaining plank spanning the pool,
She squatted till she'd finished. That pig-sty
's the perfect place for you, she whooped—you fool!
He scraped away both fresh and ancient dirt.
No broken bones. But now his pride was hurt—

And, leaping the six-foot wall which separated
Back-street from sump, he found his sister's door,
Where he yelled and banged. In vain. Infuriated,
And feeling very nude, he banged and swore
At the blank windows. Till her sleepy bully
Opened one, dropped his clothes out, and said dully

Wake me again, friend, and I'll knock you cold.
The thick black beard and scars of this tough guy
Convinced his doxy's brother that the gold
Was gone for good. He raged. But, rather than die
On his sister's door-step, donned his shoes and shirt
And stumped off down the road, stinking of dirt.

But which, and where, was his inn? Beside the sea?
This was no town for wandering round at night.
Two hulks approached. Cut-throats perhaps. So he,
Exposed and helpless, side-stepped out of sight
Into a hut. But in they stepped as well.
By Christ, they huffed and phewed, what's that foul smell?

Holding his nose, one raised their dingy lamp,
Which lit up B., who, trapped and trembling, told
His tale of woe, inspiring them to thump
His dirt-caked back. You'd have lost more than gold,

They sniggered, if you'd dozed off in that bed.
Now come and help us crack a tomb instead.

The archbishop's dead, and buried in full regalia.
His ruby ring alone is worth five hundred
Florentine florins. B. noted, *inter alia*,
This ring could save his face. He also wondered
How much the bishop's vestments might be worth,
And all the other stuff he'd left on earth.

The only problem is, they groaned, you smell
Worse than a cess-pit, or like putrid flesh.
But halfway to the duomo there's a well
We'll let you down in. Then, if you smell fresh
Enough for church, we'll show you how to rob
Its rich to feed the poor. A damned good job!

So at the well they made him mount the bucket,
And wound him down until he hit the water.
Just then—a piece of filthy rotten luck—it
Chanced that the watch, checking that run-down quarter,
Felt like a drink. The fly-by-nights did a flit,
Leaving their new friend stuck once more in the shit.

As he knew, and didn't know. Once down he drank
His fill before performing his ablutions.
Up went the bucket. But the water stank.
The watch suspected poison or pollution:
Perhaps a murdered corpse. Then B.'s wet head
Popped over the rim of the well. They howled and fled.

B. scanned their lethal weapons. Could his inn
Be somehow *in* the duomo? His two friends
Smiled yes it could—began, then, breaking in
To where the bishop lay. To make amends
For running off, they grinned, they'd let poor B.
Enter the grave and say what he could see.

The vault had one immensely heavy lid
Of marble. Flights of stone-cold marble stairs
Faded to where a fetid darkness hid
The archbishop and the bones of his forebears.

B. reeled, and retched in horror. But they said,
You go in there alive, or go in dead.

Shaking with fear, B. squeezed into the hole
They'd levered open. First he stole the ring
And hid it in his pocket. Then he stole
The bishop's crozier, mitre, everything
Worth snitching he could strip or cut from the body.
Naked, Monsignor looked a proper noddy.

—But where's the ring? the furious bully-boys
Hissed down. It must be somewhere. Look again!
B. looked, until an unexpected noise
Of footsteps made the burglars change their plan.
Grabbing their swag, they scarpered quickly. But
First they dislodged their jemmies. The lid slammed shut.

B. couldn't budge it. Overcome with fear,
He fainted by the faintly glowing stiff.
Recovered, he was sure he'd starve in there
Or go stark staring mad. And even if
They disinterred him, he'd still come to grief.
The grave was robbed, and he'd be hanged as a thief.

Or could it be he was already dead?
The air was blacker than the blackest ink,
Drowning all words and blotting out B.'s head.
He cried out loud. His cry and the stifling stink
Of dusty death must mean he hadn't died—
As must whoever had arrived outside…

And then, within his dream, in some strange way
B. realized he was dreaming—only dreaming.
Which means that I don't really have to stay
In here, he thought. In fact, I'll try re-dreaming
These voices into—what? Another gang?
I'm not dead yet. Death's sickle can go hang.

And so the gang heaved up the heavy lid,
But no big bravo wanted to go in.
A priest among them sneered and sleekly slid
His legs through, jumping out of his snake's skin

When B. grabbed hold of them, and started to haul
Him down into the grave—legs, arse and all.

The priest began to kick and then to yell.
B. held on tight. The gangsters howled and fled.
Like a black flapping crow released from hell,
The priest fled too. Thus, very far from dead,
With the ring now on his finger, self-endowed
With life and luck, Boccaccio laughed out loud

And woke. Fat candles lit the thickening dark,
Where a group of girls were laughing with three men
About another girl called *Alibech*.
Boccaccio counted altogether ten,
As *Filostrato* begged *Fiammetta's* pardon
For telling one about a convent garden…

Boccaccio listened—couldn't help but smile…
Nastagio degli Onesti's heartless way
With women next beguiled them for a while.
Outside the plague still raged. Ten people. Say
Each told ten stories. Three plus one makes four,
To start with. Which makes ninety-six tales more…

ii   The Convent Garden

Not far from Florence lies a convent, whose
Nuns are devout, whose panoramic views
Are justly famous—but which we won't name,
For fear of spoiling so much well-earned fame…
Its ancient gardener, Nuto, who had come
From elsewhere, now felt ripe for going home
To doze beneath his neighbours' apple-trees
In gardens where no jumpy nuns could tease
Or tell him off or giggle and hide his tools.
—"They'd blare like ewes on heat. A flock of fools!"
He crudely croaked, once home, to anyone
Who'd listen: "Never cross a rutting nun."
Then Nuto died. One neighbour was a young
Mild-mannered man whose older wife's sharp tongue
Was often overheard hen-pecking him.
Masetto was his name—tall, strong, and slim

About the hips and buttocks. When they buried
Old Nuto, young Masetto had been married
For just two years. Two years which seemed two lives.
He stared at all the wrinkled, withered wives
Whose men were mouldering corpses. A last few
Were staggering under the bier. "There's nothing new,"
Masetto thought, "in heaven or earth. What fun
It must be, though, to do it with a nun!"
But now the dead man's brothers were in tears:
"A few more years they have, just a few years.
One woman brought them in. Another woman
Will see them out. Poor Nuto's case is common.
But not for me, no thank you, not just yet!
At break of day tomorrow, off I set.—
For though it's been no more than two short years,
God knows I've wept tin buckets full of tears
Since feeding at the trough of married life.
Some praise its pleasures, but my loud-mouthed wife
Has caused me nothing but expense and trouble.
Conjugal bliss? She's pricked that bitter bubble!
And yet, God also knows, the neighbours say—
Particularly the women, by the way—
My wife is true and steadfast, the best kind
Of cheerful helpmate you could hope to find.
But he who wears the boot knows where it pinches.
At first she praised me for my extra inches:
Too big for her I was, or so she claimed—
And humped me like a rabbit. Till, well-tamed,
I married her. But, only shortly after,
I was the butt of her and her friends' laughter.
The rows we've had! It does no good to curse her.
I'll knock her flat one day. Or vice versa.
She thought I was a big, soft, harmless brute.
High time I went! She'll like the extra loot.
When first I saw her hard face at our fair,
I thought she was a thief, if not a whore;
And though she can still fool me, the plain truth
Of the matter is: my wife's a bit of both."

Next evening, at the convent's kitchen door,
Masetto stood pretending to be poor
And begged with hand-signs, as if born deaf-mute.
The convent being a house of good repute,

This subterfuge, he hoped, would get him in
By prompting thoughts of virtue, not of sin.
The steward eyed his rags and read his signs,
But not his mind, and thought, "Before he dines,
I'll give this strong young lout those logs to chop
Which Nuto couldn't." Masetto chopped non-stop,
Hoicking huge bundles on his well-built back
And storing the wood in one long tidy stack
Against the kitchen wall beneath the eaves.
"There's more that he could do before he leaves,"
The steward urged the abbess. "Let him stay
For now," she trilled, "and get stuck in. In May
Hedges, weeds, lawns, need seeing to twice a week.
A deaf-mute shouldn't give the girls much cheek!
Be sure he gets a decent pair of pants."
Masetto eavesdropped, rubbing his red hands,
And laughed: "Your flowers and bushes shall be more
Thoroughly seen to now than ever before!"
First, though, he sought to please his two new bosses,
Clipped, weeded, mowed, scrubbed mosses from the crosses
Stationed upon the convent's Calvary.
At length the ageing steward left him free
To organize his work at his own pace.
One day, in a secluded shady place,
Masetto saw two very young nuns peeping
Around a bush, assuming he was sleeping.
The day before they'd laughed till they were puce
Using the sort of words nice nuns don't use—
Which he, of course, pretended not to hear.
The bolder one said, "I've had an idea
I'd tell you if I thought you'd keep it quiet—
To add some spice to our dull daily diet
Of fasting, Latin prayers and meditation.
The hottest spice, they say, is copulation.
This big strong lad's deaf, mute and also dim:
So why not try how hot it is with him?"
The other gaped: "But what about our vows?
And what if we got pregnant?"—"Use your nous,"
The younger scoffed: "As long as no one knows,
What difference does it make?" After three goes
With M. behind the tool-shed, she confirmed
The truth of all she'd heard. The coy one squirmed
And dithered, but then—not to be outdone—

Next afternoon she also had her fun;
And from then on they missed no chance to enjoy
The age-old pleasures of their big new toy.
Until one day an older sister, viewing
The Tuscan landscape, spotted all three screwing
Like mad down at the bottom of the garden:
Amazed by dumb Masetto's hefty hard-on,
Her eyes alone asked two more sisters—brought
To witness this *ménage à trois*—what ought
They now to do: inform the abbess—or...?
"Perhaps he'd welcome one or two nuns more,"
The shyest simpered, as they watched. And that
Knocked all their scruples into a cocked hat.
They waited till the three had finished dogging—
Giggling like adolescents, even snogging
A bit—and then went down to claim their share
In dim dumb strong Masetto: fair was fair.
The convent housed eight nuns in all, and so
Soon the remaining three were in the know.
Each took her turn at riding hell-for-leather,
While staunch Masetto braced himself to weather
This storm of nuns—unholy and unholier.
Asleep one morning by the great magnolia,
Whose lemon-scented blossom filled the shade
With sweet, narcotic perfume—newly laid,
Masetto was observed by the abbess
In an embarrassing state of some undress,
And, though she was a serious-minded nun,
When he began to stiffen in the sun,
Dreaming no doubt of what he'd just been having,
Her gawp became a gaze, till the same craving
To which her younger charges had succumbed
Grabbed her as well. Her Bible was well-thumbed—
But no help now. Plucking him like a flower,
She woke and led him to her cell, or bower,
In whose snug privacy she dared to savour
The vice she'd always viewed with most disfavour,
For several days. The nuns soon comprehended
Why work on their own gardens was suspended
And, bitterly complaining to their Mother
Superior, failed to comfort one another.
But she and he ploughed on. And even if
Masetto's tool was less than keen or stiff,

She still knew how to get the greens she wanted.
Her gardener dug, drilled, seeded, puffed and panted,
Though in the flabby end, afraid lest he
Should do himself some serious injury,
He blurted out, "Please stop now, ma'am. I've heard
One cock will do for ten hens. But, no bird,
You need at least ten men! And here am I
Also required to serve and satisfy
Another eight. It's heaven on earth. But, please,
To carry on, I need to stand at ease
A little."—"Ha!" she gasped. "Why aren't you dumb?"
"I was, ma'am. But, you see, the more I've come
With you and all the other nuns, the less
I've felt stone-deaf and tongue-tied." The abbess,
Recalling how the sisters had been miffed
To lose their gardener, feeling somewhat biffed
By all these revelations, sat down quickly
But, in a moment, started smiling slickly—
Painfully aware that what was happening here
Could terminate her promising career.
Masetto smiled as well: the steward had died
Not long before—perhaps they could decide
On some arrangement which would suit them all?
If no one knew beyond the garden wall,
What difference would it make? And so their neighbours
Were told Masetto's prayers and saintly labours
Of horticultural love, plus the nuns' fasting
And holy tears, had moved the Everlasting
To unlock his tongue and open his blocked ears.
Masetto worked as steward for many years,
Helped by the nuns, and helped them in return
To lead a pleasant life and not to burn.
He also sometimes visited his wife,
Who was not unimpressed by his new life
Of prosperous piety. The girls and boys
He fathered were the secret pride and joy
Of all the convent, cared for by the nuns'
Families. Masetto raced his riotous sons
Around the garden, gave his daughters cherries—
Showed them where they could gather nuts, plums, berries,
And played at hide-and-seek... Till, finally,
The good abbess retired, and so did he,
Discreetly bribed with a fat monthly pension.

His wife now welcomed his well-off attention—
A sweet reversal of their former roles
(But still involving neither of their souls)—
As keen and hot as she had once been cold,
"Though what," he wondered, "when she gets too old?"

iii   Nastagio degli Onesti and the Necromancer

In Trento, whose austere and gloomy church
Has weathered many centuries of strife,
Dispensing truth to souls afraid to search
For their own pathway through the woods of life,
There lived a youth who longed to have as his wife
A certain pious girl of noble stock;
But the more he told her so, the more she'd mock.

Rich as he was, this girl—a Traversari—
Treated him like a dog. His friends, appalled
At his declining health, declared it scary
To watch her tease him, till he cried or crawled…
Nastagio degli Onesti he was called.
He'd fallen in love, he said; and though it hurt,
You couldn't change your heart like you change your shirt.

As time went on, though, he became more bitter.
She grew as proper as a budding nun.
Not wishing to appear a fool or quitter,
He let offended pride sour all his fun.
His stubborn silence seemed to weigh a ton:
In fact, he looked hell-bent on self-destruction,
Dragged down by his love / hatred's swamp-like suction.

Secretly flattered but afraid and frigid,
She knelt in a chilly chapel, getting segs
On her bare knees. To her the rule seemed rigid:
Good works do not involve a youth who begs
To kiss you. *Re* the heat between her legs,
In which she was convinced her soul might burn, "O
Save me, dear Lord," she prayed, "from my own *Inferno*!"

Her girlfriends, getting married, asked her why
She treated him so harshly. With a cruel
Grin or grimace, she'd claim she'd rather die
Than marry a tin-pot commoner, the fool!
She often used a clyster when at stool;
Indulged in other nasty little habits;
And kept a stoat for hunting snakes and rabbits.

Sometimes she dreamt that she herself was hunted
By her father's howling pack of dogged dickers,
But always woke in time. Nastagio wanted
Above all things, she knew, to get his pickers
And feelers into what were not her knickers
Exactly but a sort of locking belt—
Where she herself quite often picked and felt.

After a year of so of this impasse
Nastagio, who had once been blithe and plump,
Felt like his nerves were stretched as thin as glass.
At last he puked his gripes in one big lump:
Unless she married him, he swore he'd jump
Into a romantic chasm in the Alps!
The hair stood up on both their prickly scalps.

"Then kill yourself," she shrilled: "See if I care!"
"My love," he bellowed, "if not consummated,
Will kill me anyway!" She swore: "I swear
Your love is nothing but brute lust, frustrated
By Jesus Christ, to whom I've consecrated
My life. I mean, my body and my soul
Are Jesus's, not yours. So shut your hole!

"You'll never have my body—not unless
You hunt me down with dogs and try to rape me.
My heart—unless you tear it from my breast—
Is His, not yours. I swear you'll never grope me.
Don't think your filthy fantasies escape me:
I know what men do. First of all you hump us—
And when you've had enough, you hate and dump us."

Speechless with shock, Nastagio left the town.
The Dolomites lay north and east of Trent.
His horse stopped in a wood where, dressed in brown

22

And vivid green, a young man stood. They went
Some way on foot: "My task is to prevent
You taking your own life," the stranger said.
"Life's short enough. We're all a long time dead."

It seemed that he could read Nastagio's mind.
He asked about old friends, but they were all
Long dead. They wept together. "Never mind
About the past, though. We survive or fall
Only here now. To belly-ache or bawl
Too much distorts the world under our noses:
Though all (or fate) proposes, each disposes…

But first some food and rest…" At once the trees
Became the doors and bookshelves of a room
Which opened into further libraries:
"My house is built of books—for some the tomb
Of history, but for me its brightest bloom.
The past is dead but should be with us, too:
I'll just call up a few dead souls for you."

—*Lucrece* came first, between her breasts the knife
Which might have done for *Tarquin*. With deep groans
She called on Jove to plague the rapist's life,
To make him moan: "Let no one hear his moans,
But stone him with hard hearts, harder than stones,
And let mild women lose their female mildness—
Wilder to him than tigers in their wildness.

"O give him time to think, and tear his hair!
O give him time to hate himself and rave!
Let him have time to wallow in despair.
Let him have time to groan as passion's slave.
Let him have time to beg, and cringe and crave,
And let the memory of his filthy crime
Have time to make his life a waste of time!"

—The next was *Troilus*, wishing he could die,
Looking so lean and feeble, pale and sick,
That no one knew him when he passed them by.
He felt so weak he used a walking stick.
Eating his heart out, drained and choleric,

If any old friend asked him where it hurt,
He answered it was in around his heart.

Nastagio heard him thinking. When he slept,
He saw his dreams: one afternoon he thought
That he was in a forest, where he wept
For her in whose hot snare his heart was caught.
And up and down he stalked and madly sought
Her in the sullen heat. But then he saw,
Asleep in the bright sun, a golden boar.

And in this big brute's arms, kissing his mouth
And silver tusks, lay lovely *Lady C.*,
As if the uncanny beast were her uncouth
Lord and master. When Troilus dreamt this, he
And poor Nastagio woke up suddenly:
"I'm dead already," each began to cry,
"Or, if not, why not?—Why can't I just die?…"

But next came that sweet peasant-girl, *Griselda*,
Waiting on her strange husband, *Marquis Walter*,
Who, testing her stoic fealty, cruelly held her
As helpless as a lamb on wedlock's altar.
But after all her trials he couldn't fault her.
Helpless, she helped herself. Powerless, her power
Was inwardly to bless and to endure.

Nastagio saw how, even as a marchioness,
Her soul was full of plain humility;
No expensive tastes, or over-touchiness,
No pomp, or imitation royalty:
Always benevolent and patient, she
Remained discreetly modest, full of kindness
Towards her powerful husband's wilful blindness…

—At last the necromancer clapped his hands,
Announcing that their revels now were ended,
Although he also issued soft commands
Resulting in a banquet, strangely attended
By magic shapes; the whole thing seemed suspended
By music in mid-air. He smiled at his guest:
"Lovers should try to eat, and also rest…"

After their meal Nastagio fell asleep,
And slept and dreamt of nothing all that night
And all the following day. As for the leap
He'd planned to take—to put himself in the right—
Into some dark abyss, when it grew light
On the third day, he woke and—lighter, too—
Asked his new *alter ego* what to do.

The necromancer told him he should bring
The girl to where his house and library stood,
Where she'd receive a valuable thing
Which he'd invoke in that enchanted wood:
A thing of more than usual flesh and blood,
And worth as much as they themselves were worth,
But buried, like their futures, in the earth…

At first, of course, she didn't want to come
But, in the end, sheer curiosity
Tempted her from her safe, ancestral home
Into the dirty wood. What might it be,
This precious thing she was to get or see?
Nastagio said he didn't have a clue:
Their host, no doubt, would tell them what to do.

When they arrived, both house and host were gone.
The girl accused him of a filthy trick
To get her in the wild woods on her own,
Confirming her belief that he was sick:
Just let him try, though—she could scratch and kick!
Needled, Nastagio finally lost his temper
And yelled at her to shut up or he'd thump her.

Instead of which she took a great deep breath
And started screaming madly. But then stopped.
The woods had turned as cold and dark as death.
Another woman screamed. Their hot hearts quopped
As, in the nude, the screamer flipped and flopped
Towards them through the undergrowth. A veil
Concealed her face. Her skin was torn and pale.

She seemed to be pursued by (invisible) hounds,
Whose teeth and claws she strove to push away
But which inflicted further gaping wounds

25

On back and legs while, shocked and helpless, they
Were forced to watch. She knelt and tried to pray
Just as a knight came crashing through the trees
On his black horse, and knocked her off her knees.

Swinging his axe, he seemed about to chop
The girl in pieces, when a virile shout
Clanged through the turgid air and made him stop.
Nastagio bravely clamoured: You great lout!
Try picking an opponent who can clout
You back! But he replied: Nastagio, look
In the black mirror of your life's closed book.

Nastagio looked, but couldn't see his face:
He wore an executioner's black hood.
He named a recent time and nearby place
Where he'd chopped off his hand and let the blood
Soak back to earth. Thrilled, the girl understood
How much he'd loved her. Ailing but satisfied,
Her ecstatic soul praised God, fell ill and died.

She'd hoped to go to heaven, whereas their hell
Was as Nastagio and his girl could see…
With that he raised his axe again. It fell
As if he were the girl's arch-enemy,
Splitting her bare back open. Groaning, he
Thrust his mailed fist into the darkest part
Of the huge wound, and grasped her pumping heart.

She died in terror, watching him pluck out
Heart, lungs and acrid entrails. He then threw
His dogs the whole hot heap. And she lay quiet
While he, in tears at what they had to do,
Waited and watched. The other pair wept too,
Until the dead girl sprang to her dead feet,
And the ritual time-loop started to repeat…

She raced off through the woods, pursued by the hounds,
The knight remounted and gave furious chase…
At last their host appeared, between two mounds
Which were their future graves. With gentle grace
He wiped the tears from her face and his face:

"Unless you want to die as hunter and quarry,"
He smiled, "agree to part in peace—or marry."

The Clouds dispell'd, the Sky resum'd its Light,
And Nature stood recover'd of her Fright.
But Fear, the last of Ills, remain'd behind,
And Horror sat on his Mind and her Mind.
She thought herself the trembling Dame who fled,
He thought himself the Ghost that spurr'd the Steed:
The downfal of her Empire she divin'd;
And his proud Heart with secret Sorrow pin'd.
Home as they went, the sad Discourse renew'd
Of the relentless Dame to Death pursu'd.
At ev'ry little Noise they look'd behind,
For still the Scene was present to their Mind…
Return'd, he took his Bed, with little Rest,
But in uneasy Slumbers dreamt the Worst:
She, forc'd to wake because afraid to sleep,
Her Blood all Fever'd, with a furious Leap
Sprung from the Bed, distracted in her Mind,
Till, desp'rate any Succour else to find,
She ceas'd all farther hope; and now began
To make reflection on th' unhappy Man.
Rich, Brave, and Young, who past expression lov'd,
Proof to Disdain; and not to be remov'd:
Of all the Men respected, and admir'd,
Of all the Dames, except her self, desir'd.
This quell'd her Pride, yet other Doubts remain'd,
That once disdaining she might be disdain'd:
The Fear was just, but greater Fear prevail'd,
Fear of her Life by hellish Hounds assail'd.
The welcom Message sent, was soon receiv'd;
'Twas what he wish'd, and hop'd, though scarce believ'd;
But she with such a Zeal the Cause embrac'd,
(As Women where they will, are all in hast)
That Father, Mother, and her Kin beside,
Were overborn by fury of the Tide:
With full consent of all, she chang'd her State,
Resistless in her Love, as in her Hate.

iv Alibech and Rustico

"To Carthage then I came…"
– St Augustine

In the town of Fano, south of Rimini, there once lived two friends called Guidotto da Cremona and Giacomino da Pavia. Notorious in their youth for running wild, they had spent much of their lives as mercenary soldiers, most recently in and around Faenza, where Guidotto, though wounded, had rescued from a burning building a two-year-old child, whom he had since cared for. After Faenza, Guidotto's condition gradually worsened and, as he lay dying a year or so later, he committed the little girl to his comrade's care, together with his worldly possessions. Thinking it was high time to give up soldiering, Giacomino became a merchant, trading eventually between Sicily and North Africa, where he and the growing girl settled for a time in Sousa—about a hundred miles from all that remained of Rome's great rival, Carthage, one of whose former inhabitants, Aurelius Augustinus, a pagan student of rhetoric who later became Bishop of Hippo, had written (unbeknown to Giacomino and his pubescent ward) in his famous Confessions *of about the year 400, "For in my youth I did sometimes burn with a kind of hellish desire, and I dared to run wild in many luxurious pleasures… I fell from thee, O my God, … in that youth of mine; and became unto myself thereby a land of want and misery…"*

>Tunisia seemed an inhospitable land
>At first to both of them—as arid a waste
>As war had become to Giacomino, and
>His youth to St Augustine—but, well-placed
>For catering to the insatiable demand
>For silks and leather-goods to flatter the taste
>Of rich Italians, Sousa had, at least, a
>Catholic church—for Christmas and for Easter…

>The girl had said her name was "little Agnesa",
>When "Papa"—viz. Guidotto—saved her neck.
>Her Arab friends in Sousa, though, to please her,
>Gave her the soubriquet of Alibech.
>Her chauvinistic guardian liked to tease her
>By calling her his little *At-my-beck!*
>Until she grew too pubic—svelte and wildish—
>To vex by methods now dismissed as "childish"…

>When Alibech was fourteen years of age,
>She sometimes felt more—sometimes less—religious.
>She studied the Catechism page by page;
>Devoured the lives of martyrs—whose prodigious
>Feats of devotion foiled the Devil's rage,

Gaining them places more or less prestigious
Among the angels and the saints on high—
And almost wished she'd had the chance to die.

Instead, when Giacomino was away
One Easter, she was thrilled to bits in church
By a desert monk, who'd come to preach and pray,
Exhorting Christ's elect not to besmirch
His name with mortal sins on Easter Day,
But rise above their worldliness and search
For ways to serve Him. Such was the high aim
Of his brother hermits. Lay-folk should do the same.

Misunderstanding, Alibech set out
Early next morning—driven by adolescence,
If not by holier urges—in no doubt
She'd find some way (lit by the incandescence
Of her ignited faith) to flee and flout
World, flesh and Devil, in the helpful presence
Of some such handsome monk as she'd adored
In church, but in the desert, like Our Lord.

For had He not been tempted by the Devil
And, fasting forty days and nights, prevailed?
Hungry and hot, she approached a hermit's hovel,
Whose owner took one look at her and quailed.
The next pronounced her wicked, if not evil,
And shooed her off before he foully failed
To hold his own. The third, in finer fettle,
Allowed the temptress in—to test his mettle.

Her brow was overhung with coins of gold;
They sparkled in the auburn of her hair,
Which clustered thickly, with its bright locks rolled
In braids behind; and though her slim legs were
Long for a European fourteen-year-old,
It might have reached her heels. Her general air
Was of a partly pious, rather naughty
Tuscan Madonna, *ca.* 1440.

Rustico was this hermit's name, Augustine
His favourite author. He believed the Fall—
Or love of self—caused Adam's fleshly lusting

After what drags us down; whereas, since all
Uncontrolled bodily passion was disgusting,
The ascetic with his rosary and bowl
Reversed, by the grace of God—not works or merit—
The perverted will's revolt against the spirit…

The girl's fine skin was white. But her large eyes
Were black as midnight; lashes the same hue,
Lowered and long, in whose silk shadow lies
A deep attraction: shooting into view
From behind their half-raised veil, a black glance flies
As straight as the fastest arrow ever flew…
Rustico thought of snakes, pouring their length
From earth through air to bite with sinuous strength.

Sermons he'd read, and lectures he'd endured—
Perused the lives of chaste, abstemious saints
From Chrysostom to Ambrose. Long inured
To study, he now welcomed its constraints;
But how faith is acquired—and how secured—
He found no other theologian paints
Like St Augustine in his fine *Confessions*,
Which almost made him envy his transgressions.

But only "almost". Which was why he dared
To share his roots and berries with this girl,
Who wanted to serve God. He felt prepared,
Felt 'chosen'. But his will began to whirl
When in the night her bed-clothes slipped and bared
Pale curves and perfect skin that shone like pearl…
Rustico, moon-struck, sat in a dark corner,
Feeling like *Adam*, not much like *Jack Horner*,

And not at all like one of God's elect.
Which cast him down and cooled his spirit's ardour.
But not his body's, which was so erect
He felt as though it hardly could get harder.
By midnight his sole thought was to direct
This *Eve* away from scruples which might guard her
Innocence from his new—re-lapsed—intention,
Whose name and nature we need scarcely mention…

He staggered out. The desert night was cold
And the moon whiter than he'd ever seen it.
His body, though, was burning. Brash and bold,
He wasted water trying to cool and clean it.
The star-blue sky turned orange and then gold
As a huge red sun, so bright he had to screen it,
Rose and awoke, from its distant, low horizon,
The hottest thing he'd ever fixed his eyes on.

He first of all delivered a long speech
On how the Devil was the enemy
Not only of the Lord but, naturally, each
Who longed to serve Him. Therefore one way she
Could please their heavenly Father, which he'd teach
Her if she took her calling seriously,
Was, when the Devil's pride began to swell,
To thrust him back where he belonged—in Hell.

"Just do whatever I do, if you want
To work the miracle for which we're born!"
He cried, and threw his clothes off. "If you don't,
Beware the fiend!" So, naked in the dawn,
They knelt, facing each other, till in front
Of Rustico she saw a sort of horn
Arise and point at her. "Oh help, what's that?"
She gasped—and smiled—and hid it with her hat.

"My daughter," he explained, "this is the devil
I told you of. He's hurting me so much,
The spit-fire, trying to pump me full of evil,
That I'm about to burst. So please don't touch,
But help me turn his fire to harmless dribble
By stuffing him in Hell." He spoke with such
Conviction that she gazed into his eyes—
And asked him was that Hell between her thighs.

Somewhat perturbed, the hermit blinked and said
How did she guess? Because, she grinned, it's hot.
And so he hotly laid her on the bed
And showed her what went where and who did what.
The first time hurt a bit. She also bled
A teaspoonful, which made a pretty blot:

"If that's the only harm the fiend can do,
  Quick, put him in again," she whooped. "Yoo-hoo!"

To serve the Lord had been her only aim—
She'd hardly hoped for such ecstatic fun.
They added to their first and favourite game
A glut of variations. Doing and done,
Each gave and got at first about the same,
Though (as Tiresias said) of any one
Extended uninhibited bout of sex
A tenth was his, nine tenths were Alibech's.

As time slipped by, they played their games too often
For Rustico, though not enough for her.
The twinkle in his eye began to soften,
His blood turned cool, then cold. In one nightmare,
He lay alive and starving in his coffin.—
His diet of roots was hardly wholesome fare…
Alibech quipped they needed now to quell
Not his rebellious Devil but her Hell.

Which prompted sudden pricks of sharp remorse.
His other hero was St Anthony,
Tempted by flesh-pots, luxury and, of course,
Pudenda… But the trouble was that he
Had tempted her! Which made it even worse…
Alibech yawned and, stretching, whispered, "We
Are failing to serve God…" He brightened: "Another
Way is: *Honour thy father and thy mother!*

In other words, my dear, *Where do they live?*"…
Soon two small forms, lit by the moon's chaste glow,
Crossed the bare coastal sands. "God will forgive
Us. It's His job," thought rampant Rustico,
As he and she took one last chance to relieve
Her Hell, his Devil—as if to spray or sow
The dunes with seed. Beneath the flashing sky,
Her naked buttocks gleamed. He thought he'd die!—

But didn't. And, with little cause to grieve,
The following morning they arrived in Sousa,
Where Giacomino had begun to give
Her up for lost. Too happy to accuse her—

Uncertain, also, what to accuse her *of*—
He smiled and wept until it seemed to amuse her.
She would have come back sooner, she said prissily,
But had imagined he was still in Sicily.

Rustico'd dropped her at her guardian's door:
No need for them to meet each other, lest
His looks betrayed some guilty secret—or
Her blushes—and the ex-soldier guessed the rest.—
"Goodbye. And thank you."—"Thank you too, you bore!"
She'd mouthed as he walked off… The priest who confessed
The hermit, though—alarmed—chose not to faff
But, being the merchant's confrère, blew the gaff.

As guardian, he indulged in righteous anger
To start with, loudly threatening to pursue
The lout who'd lewdly dared to abuse and bang her—
How often had he said?!—and so undo
In weeks her whole upbringing!—*Blast and hang her,
Whatever did she think he was up to?…*
At last, though, he stopped marching up and down
Their garden, which the sun had burnt light-brown:

"Well, nothing's new, of course—though I must say,
 It's all the fault of this indecent sun,
Which cannot help but fire our helpless clay—
 And will keep baking, broiling, burning on,
Until, no matter how we kneel and pray,
 The flesh is weakened and the soul undone:
What men call gallantry, and God adultery,
Is much more common where the climate's sultry.

"Italy at least is somewhat further North—
 And so more moral, since the winter season
Cools their hot heads and livers, and so forth.
 Snow even brought St Anthony to reason!…"
In short, the virtuous country of their birth
 Soon seemed a better place to guard Agnesa in—
Also, perhaps, to get her off his hands
By tying her up in good strong bridal bands.

Meanwhile, young Rustico had heard some news
About his father, who, it seems, had died:

33

A Spanish merchant whose old-fashioned views,
  Politic, worldly, never could abide
His son's ascetic ways, who, free to choose
  A bishop's or an abbot's mitre, shied
Away from any sensible position—
  For instance, in the Holy Inquisition…

"My father was an honourable man,"
  Rustico told the priest, "not always well-
Advised, with flaws we scarcely now need scan.
  He lived his life. There's not much more to tell.
And if his feelings now and then outran
  Discretion, and were not so peaceable
As others' who remained more supercilious,
He had been brought up proud and was born bilious."

His father's death had left him rather wealthy,
  And prompted his return to Aragon,
Where (he well knew) a somewhat less unhealthy
  Life than beneath the hot Sahara sun
Awaited him. His rags were torn and filthy,
  So, wanting now to look the paragon
Of virtuous living, he scrounged some clothes from the priest
And sailed off feeling clean again at least.

So much for Rustico. While he was waving
  Goodbye to Africa on one ship, two
Travellers sat primly on another, moving
  North up the Adriatic's blinding blue.
When they touched land, "We'll go no more a-roving
  So far, my dear," old Giacomino, who
Felt glad to be back home, fondly reflected.
The girl was better pleased than she'd expected.

But nice is often nastier than it seems.
  Fano reminded Giacomino of
The Emperor Frederick's army. Like bad dreams,
  While visiting Guidotto's simple grave—
Or like harsh variations on mad themes—
  Unwanted memories surfaced. Youthful, brave—
And careless—they'd been paid to fire or pillage
Everything from rich city to poor village.

Most towns were taken part by desperate part,
With both sides drunk on blood. Street after street,
Some band of hopeless, lacerated hearts
Fought to the last, until they ceased to beat;
And pointless acts of heroism on their part
Inflamed the raging victors, till the heat
Of carnage, like the Nile's sun-sodden slime,
Engendered every form of monstrous crime...

One night he dreamt that, as he marched, he trod
Over a heap of dead, and felt his heel
Gripped as if by the monstrous serpent's head
Whose fangs Eve taught the rest of us to feel;
He kicked in vain, and cursed, and writhed, and bled,
And howled for help as wolves might for a meal:
The grinning teeth still kept their horrid hold,
Like a steel gin. His blood ran hot and cold.

His friend, Guidotto, feeling someone's boot
Crushing his face, had snatched at it and bit
The tender tendon just above the foot
(The one some ancient Muse or modern wit
So aptly named) till, working his way through 't,
He made his teeth meet—nor relinquished it
When Giacomino lunged and hacked the head
Quite off, which hung there like a lump of lead...

He woke up kicking—wondering, briefly, why
The idea of travelling home had seemed so good.
The wars were over, though, since Emperors die
Like other men. Why not then, since they could,
Continue to Faenza, where he'd try
To find Agnesa's family, or some dude
To wed her, in the town Guidotto got her—he
Might even wheel and deal a bit in pottery.

In *Fayence* they soon found that no one knew
Whose child the girl might be. Old Giacomin
Reflected that she'd been no more than two
Years old when rescued. He himself had been
Doing the things victorious soldiers do
Down by the river. To preserve his skin,

He didn't tell (why should he?) the whole story,
Which was, as well as risqué, far too gory…

They took a villa by an old piazza.
In next to no time A. had two admirers
Competing for her heart and hand. But that's a
Pleasant enough cleft stick for girls desirous
Of masculine attention. She said *grazie*
For such good-looking, keen, well-off inquirers
Each evening in her prayers to the saints and Cupid:
To thank the men themselves would have been stupid.

Giannole and Minghino were their names.
The former made more progress than the latter,
Fulfilling one of most young men's main aims
(And one of his sweet girl-friend's, for that matter)
By playing *The Devil in Hell*—and other games
She hadn't played before. Her idle chatter
Seemed to enthral and even thrill the other,
Who saw himself more as her spiritual brother.

Her guardian couldn't guard her day and night;
Both youths had bribed the maid who did the cooking:
He kept on hoping A. would be all right;
They kept on entering while he wasn't looking—
But met, of course, and in the ensuing fight
A candle set the house on fire. A.'s shrieking
Brought neighbours with big buckets of cold water.
She jumped from her bedroom window, and they caught her.

The bobbies of the *podestà* arrived,
And dragged the brawling rivals off each other.
Breathless, bruised, bollocked, bleeding, each derived
Much manly satisfaction from this pudder.
The girl was thrilled but, seeing both were knived
Quite nastily in places, started to shudder.
Fire hissed and spat, and their shambolic cock-up
Landed this brace of *bravi* in the lock-up.

When Giacomin came home, his ward swore blind
She'd no idea why *both* were in the house—
Hoping, no doubt, her guardian wouldn't mind
So much if only one had smelt her rose…

The following morning they awoke to find
The piazza crowded with both Romeos'
Apologetic friends and close relations,
Anxious to counter "these false allegations".

Giannole's family came from the next town,
To where they'd fled about twelve years before,
When Kaiser Friedrich's soldiers had burned down
Their villa in Faenza. Since the war,
They'd serviced and paid off a largish loan
But would be happy now to borrow more
To help Giannole: "Nothing could… be easier…,"
The father stammered, staring at Agnesa.

Minghino's family similarly offered—
Rather than have a court decide the case—
To double the damage Giacomin had suffered,
Also to compensate his loss of face…
Agnesa, having heard more than enough, 'd
Withdrawn so as to avoid the embarrassing gaze
Of her new lover's father—who now dragged
His fat wife up from where she'd plumped down, fagged.

Fat Agnes was her name—her stock Germanic,
Her features coarse: yet, placed beside Agnesa—
One slim, the other dumpy—an organic
Likeness emerged, as of two garden peas—a
Kinship which might have made the prettier panic
Or caused, perhaps, some symptoms of amnesia;
Instead of which, she murmured, "Father! mother!
But where's Giannole?—where's my long-lost brother?"

He was, of course, still under lock and key.
Agnes cowily wept. Agnesa's father
Proudly confirmed her true identity
By hinting at a birthmark—one she'd rather
Not show but which her guardian jested he
Had seen as well. To stem this flood of blather,
Agnesa volunteered to tell their story—
Unexpurgated, risky and (yes) gory—

Although, as Giacomino now confessed,
The day Guidotto had contrived to save

The crying child, they'd tried their very best
Not only to avoid an early grave
Themselves but to harm no one. Long oppressed
By war, the families bridled…, but forgave
Him, after all, when A. claimed one who had
Thus brought her home must be more good than bad—

Prepared, as he also was, to drop all charges…
This news was carried to the *podestà*,
Whose comment was that one large heart enlarges
The hearts of others, even during war,
And that a deed's full nature only emerges
From time's dark womb. Man makes his future, or
Destroys it. He himself would let theirs grow—
Provided that A. married Minghino.

Giannole grinned to hear he'd got a sister.
His new-found sister gave a rueful shrug.
Her parents laughed and cried how much they'd missed her.
Minghino gave his *sposa* a soulful hug.
Giacomin gave the bride away and kissed her,
Returning, relieved, to Fano—till they dug
His grave beside his friend's. So much for them.
Rustico later wrote a sort of hymn:

Rustico's Ottave Rime

My wife and children sleep. The orange-tree
Is hung with aromatic winter fruit
Above the warm dark courtyard. I can see,
Through dark-green leaves, the moon- and star-light shoot
From nowhere into somewhere endlessly.
Goats bleat. A distant goat-herd plays his flute.
Any regrets? My father died while I
Sought God beneath an unforgiving sky.

"The love of self extending to contempt
   For God" *described him; whereas the chosen few,*
   God's sheep, abased themselves. No goat's attempt
   To save his soul by works could work. I knew,
   Or thought I knew, no meretrix could tempt
   A soul elected to tell false from true!

But, then, I chose (and choose) an ordinary life:
I live, let live—like food, and like my wife…

As long as he serves God no man is free.
And clerics sow the seeds of endless war:
For God-creating man, no orange-tree
Is ever enough—he wants it all, and more.
God takes omniresponsibility:
Our After's *His omnipotent* Before.
I know all this, but choose to hold my tongue:
God's right—His church will burn you if you're wrong.

Self-punishment takes many twisted forms.
Our futile passions fail. To forget and forgive
Absolves crazed minds of (self-)destructive norms,
Empowering others too to live / let live.
And more than that? Until we're food for worms,
What we receive will mirror what we give:
Seeking false gods beneath an angry sky
Finds nothing—but a place to die / let die.

3   FRANÇOIS VILLON: TWO EXTRACTS FROM *THE TESTAMENT*

Ballade

("Dictes moy ou, n'en quel pays")

O tell me in which country now
Is Flora, the lovely Roman?
Or Alexander's Thais who
Was Alcibiades' cousin;
Echo who spoke—poor tongue-tied woman—
Where babbling waters pool or flow,
Whose beauty was more than human?—
But where is last year's snow?

Where is the learned Heloise,
For whom they gelded Abelard?
Made him a monk at Saint Denis—
Love pained him long and hard!
And where's the queen who ordered her guard
To tie up Buridan and throw
Him into the Seine like a tub of lard?…
But where is last year's snow?

Queen Blanche who sang—sweet fleur-de-lys—
Like a Siren come again;
Big-footed Bertha, Beatrice, Alice,
And that Amazon who held Maine;
And Jeanne, the good girl of Lorraine
Burnt by the English… Where are they? Oh,
Sweet Virgin Mary, long may you reign:
But where is last year's snow?

If any should ask this week, this year,
Where are they? Where did they all go?
This same refrain is all you'll hear:
Where is last year's snow?

*

("*Puis de papes, roys, filz de roys*")

The same thing goes for kings and popes,
Their fecund queens, and all their sons—
Buried together with their hopes,
Their power and glory gone.
And won't *I* die, a poor bag-man
From Rennes? Oh, yes. If it please God,
As long as I've had my fun,
I'll rest under any sod.

This world won't last for ever,
Whatever the thieving rich may think—
We're all of us under fate's cleaver,
Any old crock on the brink
Will tell you. Young and in the pink,
He'd josh his wife—his friends—his folks—
But, now, would cause a social stink
If he started cracking jokes.

Obliged to beg or steal or borrow
By heartless Mother Necessity,
He gloomily hopes today that tomorrow
His death will set him free—
And, but for God's commandment, he
(With his back to yet another wall)
Often might have horribly
Put an end to it all!

For if in his youth he made them laugh,
Nothing he says now can or will:
An ancient ape's a horror-and-a-half;
His sour face sucks life's bitter pill.
If he's silent they think he's ill,
Or finally going gaga.
If he speaks he's told to be still:
Who cares for his second-hand saga?

And as for poor decrepit biddies
Without a sou, or fish to fry,
Who see young things with plumped-up diddies
Taking their place on the sly,
They importune God to tell them why

And by what right they were born so *soon*!
But our Lord declines to argufy,
Knowing he'd get the wooden spoon…

I seem to hear the beauty who
Was once an armouress
Wishing their wish which can't come true—
For youth again—like this:
"Ah, why has age crept up, like a fierce
Thief, so soon, to crease my skin?
What stops me now, in my distress,
From doing myself in?

Old age has left me in the lurch
And stripped my beauty of its power
Over merchants, scholars, men of the church:
There wasn't one who wouldn't shower
All that he owned, his widow's dower—
No matter what—on me
For an hour or less than an hour
Of what tramps won't tickle now for free!

I refused it to plenty of men,
Which wasn't especially smart of me,
For the love of a young ex-con
Who never paid my fee.
He fooled me. But—I swear it—he
Was my sweetest taste of honey.
Who cares if he mainly seemed to be
In love with my hard-earned money?

Who cares if he dragged me round the floor
Or kicked me a bit? He couldn't kill
My love. If he'd broken my back or my jaw,
Then asked for a kiss, I'd still
Have given him one with no ill will…
A fat lot *I* got, all the same.
The greedy bully screwed me, until
There's nothing left but the sin and shame.

And he's been dead these thirty years.
But I live on—old, grey and glum.
When I think of the good times—remember, in tears,

What I was and what I've become—
When I look at my naked breasts and bum,
And see my body so very changed,
  Poor, dry, meagre, gnarled and numb,
  I think I must be completely deranged.

What has become of that lucid brow?
That golden hair, those eyebrows raised
Above my wide-set eyes, aglow
  With pretty glances which amazed
  The shrewdest; and my straight nose, praised
Together with my shapely ears
And dimpled chin; my face which gazed
With hope into the coming years?

My slender shoulders—oh, and those lips!…—
Long arms, slim fingers, skilled at their trade,
Small boobs, full buttocks, swinging hips—
  A fine high arse, as good as made
  For the fine art of getting laid;
Those marble loins, that tiny V
Between my powerful thighs, in the shade
Of its own sweet-scented shrubbery?

My forehead's wrinkled, hair's gone grey,
My brows are scurf and my eyes dull
Which flashed hot looks and smiles in their day
  At many a lecherous fool;
My nose is hooked like the beak of a gull;
My pendulous ears sprout moss;
My drab skin hardly hides my skull;
My chins are puckered, lips a dead loss.

This is the way our beauty ends:
My arms are short, hands cramped and lean;
My shoulders hunch as my spine bends;
My tits are—*pah!*—just shrunken skin,
My buttocks as slack, all fallen in.
My cunt? A horror! My thighs? The truth is
Their bones are sticks, not thigh-bones—thin
And blotched with spots, like sausages.

—And that's how we mourn the good old days
Among ourselves, poor senile crones
Who squat on our hams by a small blaze
Of twigs and straw, like bundles of bones
And rags. The fires which light our groans
No sooner flare than they go out…
And we were all so lovely once.
But that's how it is for tart and tout."

4 JOVE'S NEW WORLD—A POST-RENAISSANCE PICTURE GALLERY

"Men say that Giantes went about
   the Realme of Heaven to win,
To place themselves to raigne as Gods
   and lawlesse Lordes therein…
The which as soone as Saturns sonne
   from Heaven aloft did see,
He fetcht a sigh…"
– Ovid, *Metamorphoses* I

In most Renaissance paintings of classical subjects—with famous exceptions such as the rape of Chloris in Botticelli's Primavera *or Titian's* The Flaying of Marsyas—*the gods, when they appear, are not only beautiful but seem, in the main, to be benign. And yet in the myths themselves, as recounted in even the better-known ancient literature, Zeus/Jove—or "Saturns sonne"—for example, frequently behaves like a tyrant whose power has gone less to his head than to his organs of reproduction. In fact, reproducing himself in one shape or another seems to have been one of Jove's main ways of passing the time or, in his case, eternity. In the above lines from Arthur Golding's translation of Ovid's* Metamorphoses *(1537), Ovid seems to compress allusions to Saturn and the Titans' attack on their father Uranus, and Jove's attack on Saturn, into an (unsuccessful) attack on Jove himself. Ovid briefly describes an imaginary "golden age", which he brings to an end after a mere thirty lines with the thrusting of Saturn into Limbo by "Jove unjust"—after which men misbehave to the best of their ability. Jove attempts to do something about this by flooding the world and drowning everyone except Deucalion and his wife—but the gods then get up to no good themselves, with Apollo chasing Daphne, and Jove (quickly forgetting his indignation) transforming Io into a white cow so as to conceal her from the jealous Juno… In other versions of how the world began, Saturn's son, having seized power from his father, at once set about consolidating it—in ways not unfamiliar to later despots and politicos great and small. For example, Niccolò Machiavelli, in* The Prince *(1513)—taking it for granted that "The wish to acquire more is admittedly a very natural and common thing, and when men succeed in this they are always praised rather than condemned"—says of rulers in general, "It is far better to be feared than loved if you cannot be both" since "the bond of love is one which men, wretched creatures that they are, break when it is to their advantage to do so; but fear is strengthened by a dread of punishment which is always effective." And so "when he seizes a state the new ruler ought to determine all the injuries that he will need to inflict" and inflict them with the utmost cruelty. According to Machiavellian statecraft, this constitutes "cruelty used well". But "cruelty badly used is that which, although infrequent to start with, as time goes on, rather than disappearing, grows in intensity". The new ruler is then hated more than feared and "cannot possibly stay in power"… Although myths of the sort adapted in the following Petrarchan—and also Shakespearean—sonnets were often painted during the 15th and 16th centuries in Italy, the artists were paid by those in power. Their cruelty therefore tends to disappear into representations better suited to the public or private chambers of wealthy patrons eager for the respectability which the fine arts as well as the theories of humanism helped to confer on the great shift in moral values from the world of Giotto and St Francis, say, to that of the princes and merchants of the Renaissance with their ever-growing "wish to acquire more":*

i

To start with, Jove pursued his proud twin-sister
Juno, who only yielded to his charms
When the bedraggled dove she'd rescued kissed her—
And forced its way between her legs and arms.

His mother Rhea knew that, if Jove married,
Women were bitched. He raged. She hissed—and grew
Into a snake to scare him. Which miscarried:
Her son out-snaked her snake; and forced her too.

Some say that Venus was Jove's foam-born daughter
(Her mother's parents were the Air and Earth):
Jove watched her perfect body rise from the water,

And rose as well. Thus out of his full horn
Poured gods and men. And Venus soon gave birth
To the god whose bolts caused billions to be born.

ii

Acrisius, Danae's father, should have begged
Great Jove for mercy, rather than have locked
His only daughter—moon-pale, blonde, long-legged—
In a tower of brass. But God is not mocked.

So, rising to the challenge, macho Jove,
Ejaculating sun-light, showered like gold,
Or like a fountain, into his dry love:
Oh, he was more than she could hope to hold!

She'd want no other lover after that.
Their son would lop Medusa's snake-haired head,
And save Andromeda. Jove's lust begat

Blessings on all predestined to enjoy him.
The wimp her father, though, deserved to be dead:
Who better than his grandson to destroy him?

iii

Jove's favourite was the pretty Trojan boy
Who fetched his nectar: honey-skinned, well-hung,
Ganymede blushed like a girl. No human toy,
He'd sulk and fidget. Jove preferred them young.

Juno was jealous, and/or envious. He
Was sure she fancied sexy G. as well.
Hebe, his ex-cup-bearer, chafed. But she
Was Juno's tattling pet. And boys don't tell.

King Tros, his father, cried. The girls all loved him.
As terrified as a child, he'd burst into tears
And pissed himself when Jove the Eagle removed him
From chasing pig-tails, horny beyond his years…

So Jove sent horses and a golden vine
Of Vulcan's. But Tros smashed it. Pearls before swine.

iv

Juno would sometimes groan, "Oh god, you *bull!*"
Which set him thinking. Soon he proudly trotted
Up to Europa, where she walked, arms full
Of flowers, along the sands. They played; he plotted—

Demure and little, with horns as soft as wax—
To lure her off to Crete, where they'd have fun…
And made, for years, the beast with two humped backs.
Lewd girl/boy-humping Minos was their son.

Years later, Pasiphae groaned, "You son of a—*bull?*"
Which set her thinking. Neptune's lightly trod
The waves. Sly Daedalus helped. She felt so full
She thought she'd split, and shrieked, "Oh bull, you *god!*—"

So one bull led to another—bearing fruit
From Jove to man-made, roaring, man-eating brute.

v

The swan great Jove had entered in his need
Flattened and raped the girl. Later, he watched
Her—grunting—bear huge eggs. More blood would bleed—
More guts be split—than Leda's, when they hatched.

Jove claimed Tyndareus had inseminated
Her womb already. Helen was Jove's, of course,
But not sour Clytemnaestra. Pollux—fated
To star among the Immortals by the force

Of his straight right, left hook, and upper-cut—
Invented the Spartan war-dance. Victorious, he
Loved bellicose bards and music. But,

As for that loser Castor, who'd dare claim
That he was Jove's?... His mother? Ah, but she,
After Jove trod her, never spoke again.

5   THE CHILDHOOD AND SONG-BOOK OF *ALLERLEIRAUH—A KUNSTMÄRCHEN*

i

Mr Fox is in his lair,
Weeping and wailing it isn't fair
That his coat is red:
Mrs Fox is dead.

      *

Cuckoo, cuckoo, tell me true
    How old will I
    Be when I die?

And write with your beak
    On the tip of my knife
    How old when a wife?

      *

Mr Wolf, don't wolf me down!
I can't give you half-a-crown,
But a penny I can give
If you'll only let me live.

      *

An angel sat on a branch in a tree
With a chicken for you and a chicken for me.
He would have liked to gut them,
But had no knife to cut them.
A knife dropped down from the clouds above
And chopped the angel's head right off.
The milk-maid ran to the barber's shop
But no one was there to bandage it up.
In the kitchen the cat was sleeping,
From the window a mouse was peeping.
On the roof the chickens—still unplucked—
Ruffled their feathers and squawked and clucked.

      *

Fixy foxy, foxy fix,
Don't you chase my hen or chicks!
If you harm my chicks or hen,
May the cuckoo chase you then—
On the kitchen table put you,
Gut you like a fish and cut you
With his beak in very many
Bits no bigger than a penny!

ii

My mother died. The King my father
    preserved her golden hair
In a large vitrine beside his bed.
    My hair was like her hair.

She'd made him swear he'd only marry
    again if he could find
A head of hair as golden.
    He must have been out of his mind

To tell them all he'd marry *me*
    when I was old enough.
Never, I said. Or not till three
    gowns of witch-woven stuff—

The first as golden as the sun,
    the next as bright as stars,
The third as silvery as the moon—
    and a coat cut from the furs

Of each and every creature in
    his whole wide kingdom were
Brought to me packed in a walnut shell.
    I also cut my hair

And shaved my head, rubbing my face
    with earth and ashes and soot;
But nothing helped. The gowns and coat
    were sewn. I fled on foot—

Dressed in the coat—with the gowns concealed
    in its pocket. Far away
In another land some huntsmen found me
    asleep in a hollow tree.

They called me *Patchwork*, carried me off
    to slave in the royal kitchen.
I made up songs to amuse the cook—
    and slept where no one could see me.

iii

Pitchy patchy Peter
Hides behind the heater,
Darning socks and shining shoes,
Till the old cat miaows and mews:
    She's a greedy eater!
Eats the shine and eats the shoe,
Then she eats up Peter too.
Eats the shoe and eats the shine,
Eats your dinner, then eats mine.

    *

Chop the tom-cat's tail off,
But don't chop it all off.
Put it, when you dock it,
In the vicar's pocket.

    *

A fox sat in the green plum-tree
Plucking yellow plums for tea.
I said he'd better give me one,
He said he'd throw me down a stone.
I took up my white stick instead—
And knocked off his red head.

    *

Mr Crow, don't mop and mow,
Grieving still for Mrs Crow

In the rain and mud.
Can't afford a pair of boots,
And you'll spatter your black suit
 In the rain and mud.
If you'd also lost a leg,
One boot you could beg
 In the rain and mud.
But you're proud as well as poor,
Stalking round outside my door
 In the rain and mud.

 *

The Hungry Child

Mother, oh mother, I can't get my breath,
Give me some bread, I'm starving to death.
Be brave and don't cry now, my little man,
Tomorrow we'll sow as fast as we can.

And when they'd sowed the corn,
The child was still forlorn.

Mother, oh mother, I can't get my breath,
Give me some bread, I'm starving to death.
Don't cry now, have patience, my little man,
We're cutting the corn as fast as we can.

And when they'd cut the corn,
The child was still forlorn.

Mother, oh mother, I can't get my breath,
Give me some bread, I'm starving to death.
Be patient, be patient, my little man,
We're threshing the corn as fast as we can.

And when they'd threshed the corn,
The child was still forlorn.

Mother, oh mother, I can't get my breath,
Give me some bread, I'm starving to death.
Be patient and wait now, my little man,
We're grinding the corn as fast as we can.

And when they'd ground the corn,
The child was still forlorn.

Mother, oh mother, I can't get my breath,
Give me some bread, I'm starving to death.
Wait, oh wait, my little man,
We're baking the bread as fast as we can.

But when they'd baked the bread,
The child was dead.

iv

And then my father died—I heard
    them talking. To my relief
And sorrow, it seemed he'd pined away
    and died at last of grief.

I was now twelve years old. My hair
    had started to grow again.
The cook was not unkind. My bed
    was under the stairs. In my den

I sang my songs while brushing my hair
    and wore my dress of stars,
Which glowed in the darkness. But elsewhere
    I wore my coat of furs…

In April the King our master held
    a ball. I pestered the cook
To lend me a decent pair of shoes
    and let me go and look.

I washed my face and let down my hair.
    The King asked *me* to dance.
Wearing my dress of lucky stars,
    I blushed but leapt at the chance.

I'd only danced before as a child,
    but now my body and feet
Knew what to do. When he looked I felt
    a different sort of heat—

But, later, when he asked my name,
    I ran away and put
My coat of many furs back on,
    and rubbed my face with soot.

I shoved my hair back into my hood.
    He'd looked as my father looked
On the day he said he'd marry me…
    I sang—scrubbed—chopped—cried—cooked…

v

Croak, croak, croak!
If I'd had a bloke
When I was young and lovely,

I wouldn't have to sit
In a pond or a pit
Looking plug ugly.

*

About Schlaraffenland

Schlaraffenland's a wondrous place
Where lazy lumps can feed their face
Behind Rice Pudding Hill.
But if you want to get there, you
Must munch much more than your fill.

The hill is more than three miles long—
Just chomp and chew, you can't go wrong.
Unless you become too sick,
You'll find the houses there are built
Of cake instead of brick.

The fence around the garden is
Made up of huge fried sausages,
And anyone who wants
Can eat them, and the cake-house too—
There are no Do's and Don'ts.

Roast geese and ducks and pigeons fly
Like real live birds across the sky.
Nothing you've seen can match it.
And if you want to eat one, all
You've got to do is catch it.

Sometimes they land on the kitchen table,
While roasted porkers there are able
To run around with knives
Stuck in their tender meat, to carve it.
You'll have the time of your lives!

There honey falls instead of rain,
And almond flakes snow slowly down.
Doughnuts, and ice-cream cones,
Grow on the trees in Lollipop Wood.
Milk-streams have chocolate stones.

All sorts of women, children, men,
Lie idling there. Whoever can
Do nothing's made a lord.
The laziest of the lot's their king.
His fat knights were born bored.

Now, if you'd like to set off, but
Are still unsure which way to trot,
Ask anyone who's blind.
The deaf and dumb will also tell
You where to go, you'll find.

>   Red, white and blue,
>   A shame it's not true.

*

The Crooked Hunchback

If I go into our garden,
When I want to hide or play,
There's a crooked little hunchback
Who keeps getting in my way.

*If I go into our kitchen,
When I want to ask for more,
There's a crooked little hunchback
Knocks my porridge on the floor.*

*When I go into our cellar
Where it's always damp and dark,
There's a crooked little hunchback
Puts the light out for a joke.*

*If I go into my bedroom,
When it's time to make my bed,
There's a crooked little hunchback
Laughs till he's nearly dead.*

*When I go into the church
Where I sing or kneel and pray,
There's a crooked little hunchback
Who says what he said today:*

Little child, I beg of you,
Pray for the crooked hunchback too.

*

*Butterfly, butterfly, sit on my hand:
     To sit a bit won't hurt.
          Don't worry or hurry
               Away!*

*Your soft wings twinkle when you land,
     Like sunlight on a silken skirt
          Or shirt,
     Or moonlight in May.*

*

*Ladybird, ladybird, fly past my door.
Your mother's gone to Hamburg town,
Your father's gone to war.
Hamburg town is all burned down.
Ladybird, fly past my door.*

vi

I laughed and cried for no good reason.
    The cook prepared a stew
Of meat and herbs for love-sick girls
    and gave me work to do.

In May there was another ball.
    She warned me not to lose
This chance to change my life. When I quailed,
    she fetched her dancing shoes

And told me to wear the silvery dress
    which shone like a full moon.
Nothing could hide its light. My hair
    was long now. And so, soon

The King and I were dancing. He
    refused to let me stop.
We danced and danced. I laughed and cried
    until, about to drop,

I slipped away to hide in my coat.
    At the next ball in June
I wore my dress which blazed like the sun
    in a clear sky at noon.

Will you or won't you marry me,
    with the sun in your hair and dress?—
I lost one shoe as I turned and ran,
    unable to say yes.

The King picked up the shoe and searched
    his palace from attic to cellar.
He found the other—and me—in the kitchen,
    like a patchwork Cinderella,

Except that the cook—who burned my coat—
    had been a good step-mother.
In July the King and I were married.
    At times I think of my father…

vii

As I sat in an apple-tree
Merrily crunching carrots,
The farmer and his wife rode by
And took them for pretty parrots.

Aha, you rogue, you chicken thief,
How dare you scrump my nuts!
But I had never in my life
Tasted such juicy tarts.

A cow sat in a swallow's nest
With twenty bleating kids.
A donkey, bearing gifts, came flying
Over the moon though the clouds.

I slapped the eggs in a frying pan
And soaped his whip and boots.
See how the dancing donkey whistles
When bitten by fleas, the brutes!

*

Sleep, baby, sleep!
Can't you hear the sheep?

Some are black and some are white,
Some like babies and some bite.
The green ones, if they catch you,
Will smack your bum and scratch you.
The fat ones eat the thinner
And babies for their dinner.

Can't you hear the sheep?
Sleep, baby, sleep.

*

There were three beggars chased a hare,
They came on stilts and crutches.
And one was deaf and one was blind.
The mute one said, "I think you'll find
The tame sort live in hutches."

The deaf one heard a jenny call,
The mute one whooped and hollo'd,
And when he spied the boxing buck
The blind one cried, "Oho, what luck!"
Where the hare led they followed.

    *

    Hush-a-bye, baby,
    Who's rustling the hay?
The old cat's dead, and the mice play.

    Your father's in Norway,
    Your brothers—who knows?
They come and they go as the war comes and goes.

    Hush-a-bye, baby,
    Who's rustling the hay?
When the cat's dead, the mice play.

    *

Where have you been all winter, my son?
Where did you live and what have you done?
I built a house in Schlampampenland.
That's good. What's good? It was built on sand,
And a wild pig came and knocked it down.
That's bad. What's bad? I took my gun,
And shot the pig for its sausage-meat.
That's good. What's good? Two feet and four feet
Stole my meat in the thick of the night.
That's bad. What's bad? I cut off their flight.
Four feet is now my friend for life,
And two feet my wife.

viii

My *Märchen* is done.
See how the mice run.
    With their fur I could make
A hat for my son.

6 HEINRICH HEINE: FROM *KÜHLE NACHT* TO *MATRATZENGRUFT*

"...innocence is the last thing that can be sustained naturally"
– Joseph Brodsky

"Death is the coolness of the night,
Life is the sultry heat of day.
As darkness falls, I'm drowsy—
Tired of the day and its light.

Over my bed there grows a tall tree.
In the tree a youthful nightingale
Jug-jugs of love. Though I'm dreaming,
The song still reaches me."
– Heine, *Der Tod ist die kühle Nacht*

i

The night and the streets are still, as I go
To take a look at the house where she lived.
She left this city years ago.
But the house itself still stands where it did.

And a man stands, as if in my place,
Wringing his hands in constant pain.
It gives me a shock to glimpse his face:
The moon shows me myself again.

You there, my double! Looking so sick,
Why do you ape the ridiculous plight
In which I was cut to the very quick
In times gone by here, night after night?

ii   Three Poems on the History of Religion

Donna Clara

Heine claimed in a letter to his friend Moses Moser, who had helped to found the Berlin Verein für Cultur und Wissenschaft der Juden *in 1821, that* Donna Clara *represented a scene from his own life, with the Berlin zoo replaced by an Andalusian garden, a baroness by a señora and himself by "a holy George or even Apollo"… Although born into a Jewish family, Heine's upbringing had not been strict. In 1823, however, when the poem was written, he had spent some time working for the* Verein, *thus becoming better acquainted with the history of Jewish persecution and emancipation. In particular he became interested in the Middle Ages and in what his biographer, J.L. Sammons, calls "the glorious and tragic age of Spanish Jewry". Heine informed Moser of his intention to publish the poem in his next book but cautioned him to take all possible care in the meantime not to let it fall into Christian hands, explaining somewhat dramatically that he had "very important reasons" for this:*

    Strolling in the judge her father's
    Moonlit garden, Donna Clara
    Hears the castle drums' and trumpets'
    Rat-a-tat and tarantara.

    "What a drag it is, this dancing—
    And the stupid things they say,
    Knights and courtiers. One compared me
    To the darling buds of May!

    What a total drag it all is
    Since I've watched that other knight
    From my window, lit by moonbeams,
    Playing lute-songs night by night.

    When he stands there—slim and fearless,
    Like St George, with pale and dashing
    Features—I can see his eyes
    Shooting looks…" With dark looks flashing—

    Lost in thought—sweet Donna Clara
    Shyly drops her eyes. But then,
    Raising them, she finds the handsome
    Stranger standing there again.

    Soon they're holding hands and whispering.
    Roses nod and greet them. Soon
    Soft winds flatter, soft hearts flutter
    Underneath a *Märchen*-moon.

    And they stroll beside the roses,
    Warm and glowing in their bed:

"Darling, tell me, though, why have you
   Suddenly turned quite so red?"

"Stinging midges and mosquitos
   Every summer, dear, refuse—
Pah!—to spare me. *Pah!* I hate them
   Like a swarm of long-nosed Jews."

But her lover whispers softly,
"Never mind the Jews or midges…"
   Almond petals fall in thousands
   Forming snow-white heaps and ridges.

Almond petals fall like snow-flakes
   Pouring forth their lovely scent:
"Darling, tell me, though, how truly
   Your true love is really meant?"

"Oh, I love you, and I swear it
   By the Mass, whose pyx and chalice
Raise the flesh and blood the Jews
   Killed with god-forsaken malice."

But her lover whispers softly,
"Never mind the Jews or Jesus…"
   In the distance, swaying lilies
   Dream of where the darkness ceases.

In a stream of light, white lilies
   Contemplate the stars above:
"Darling, tell me, are you certain
   What you've sworn is not false love?"

"There's as little falsehood as
   Moorish blood in my white face,
Or as dirty Jewish blood
   In the pure blood of our race."

But her lover whispers softly,
"Never mind the Jews or Moors";
   Leads her to a myrtle arbour
   In the garden, where they pause

While he softly weaves a love-net
Round her body, under cover
Of the leaves—brief words, long kisses—
Till their heated hearts boil over.

And the nightingale sings sweetly
Songs of liquid love, non-stop;
As if in a dance with torches,
Little glow-worms seem to hop.

In the arbour one hears nothing
But a sort of silent seething—
As of myrtle bushes whispering
Or of furtive flowers breathing…

Waking in her lover's arms,
All at once sweet Donna Clara
Hears again the drums' and trumpets'
Rat-a-tat and tarantara.

"Listen! we must part soon, dearest,
But you haven't told me yet
Your beloved name. Please tell me
Now, before we both forget…"

And her lover, smiling brightly,
So as not to seem too horrid,
Kissing first his Donna's fingers,
And her lovely lips and forehead,

Simply says he is the son—
Not unwilling, now, to cross her—
Of the great and learned Rabbi,
Israel of Saragossa.

*

Almansor

In Heine's great Buch der Lieder, *'Donna Clara' is immediately followed by 'Almansor', which takes place in and around Córdoba in Andalusia, some time after about 1530… When Granada fell to the Christians in 1492, the mosque at Córdoba was the largest in the Western world—too big (and perhaps too impressive) to demolish. The erection of the present cathedral in the middle of the mosque itself was begun in 1523, as a sign of Christian supremacy. In 1825, not long before his poem was published, Heine was baptized as a Protestant Christian, and Almansor's apostacy is presumably related to his own. Heine changed religion for purely practical reasons (Jews had limited rights in nineteenth-century Germany), and he perhaps fancied it didn't matter. But it seems to have rankled for the rest of his life:*

(i)

Córdoba's immense cathedral
Stands on thirteen hundred columns:
Under that almighty dome you
Either feel oppressed or solemn.

Verses out of the Koran
Twine like plants in Arabic
Down its mihrab's walls and pillars—
Flowers for pious souls to pick.

Moorish kings once raised these arches
As a mosque to Allah's glory.
But the times have changed. Who lords it
Here is now another story.

Melancholy bells now toll,
Calling Christians from the tower
Where the imam called the Moslems
When the Moslems were in power.

Where the faithful sang the Prophet's
Words and wisdom, chanting prayers,
Tonsured priests now raise their blander
Host from further up the stairs.

And they twist and twirl in front of
Gaudy dolls and holy relics,
And there's smoke and bells and bleating,
And their big dumb candles flicker.

Silent in that huge cathedral
Stands Almansor ben Abdullah,
And observes the many columns—
But no mufti and no mullah.

"Oh, you pillars, once so holy,
  Built to march in Allah's praise,
  Now you serve our Christian masters'
  Hated and unholy ways!

"Moving with the times, your un-moved
  Patience helps you bear their cross.
  Weaker vessels should be able
  Likewise to contain their loss!"

Over the cathedral font,
  Thus Almansor ben Abdullah
  Primly bends his proud neck, hoping
  Soon his life will be cheerfuller.

(ii)

Hastily he leaves the building,
  Racing off on his black mare;
  In his cap a cocky feather
  Braves the blast which dries his hair.

On the way to Alcolea,
  By the blue Guadalquivir,
  Where the almond blossom whitens
  And the orange scents the air,

Like a Christian knight, he gaily
  Hunts and whistles, laughs and sings,
  And the birds join in, descanting
  On the river's mutterings.

On a hill near Alcolea
  Stands the castle. Donna Clara
  Smiles to think the duke her father
  Is off fighting in Navarra.

And Almansor, from a distance,
  Hears the drums and trumpets braying;
  Sees beneath the trees' dark arches
  Flashing lights, musicians playing.

And a dozen ladies dancing
With a dozen knights, all dressed
Up to kill. But, freshly christened,
Don Almansor danced the best.

Treading air, he whirled and flirted
Like Don Juan round the hall;
Knowing how to tease and flatter
Twelve young girls, he pleased them all:

Kissing Isabella's fingers
Lightly, on he lightly danced;
Shyly flirts with shy Elvira,
Eyeing her as if entranced;

With a laugh, asks Leonora
Is he better-dressed today?
Making sure his cloak's embroidered
Golden cross is on display;

Tells each one how much he loves her—
And, to stop them taking fright,
Swears "—as true as I'm a Christian"
Thirty times at least that night.

(iii)

In the hall at Alcolea
All their revels now are ended.
Shadows gather. One last couple
Sit in darkness, unattended.

Donna Clara and Almansor
Sit alone beneath the glimmer
Shed by one last lonely candle,
Which makes solid bodies shimmer.

Clara, shimmering in her armchair,
Holds Almansor's sleepy head,
Which he lays on her sweet knees.
He's so tired he feels half-dead.

Pensively, she pours an attar
Of red roses from a golden
Bottle on his dark-brown hair,
Till his heart-felt sighs embolden

Her to kiss him—press the softness
Of her red lips, pensively,
To his dark, rose-scented curls;
But he frowns so darkly she

Weeps hot tears from her bright eyes,
Pensively, and lets them fall
On Almansor's oily hair,
Till his twitching lips appal

Her red lips, as now he dreams—
Head bowed, weeping, back at home
In among a crowd of voices
Under that almighty dome

Where, in Córdoba, the columns,
Muttering darkly, seem to say
They can't stand it any longer!
Tremors shake the walls—and they

Totter, crack, and start to tumble.
Priests and people cower, turn pale.
With a crash the dome collapses—
And their gods cry out and quail.

*

Princess Sabbath

"*You call'd me dog…*" – *Shylock*
– *The Merchant of Venice*, I.iii.123

*The relationship of Heine's poetry to the social and political history of his time was virtually always confrontational—whether directly and specifically, as in '*The Slave-Ship*' and much of '*Germany. A Winter's Tale*' (see* Words in the Dark*), or more obliquely, as in* Donna Clara, Almansor *and* Princess Sabbath. *Whichever approach he took, though, Heine had the gift of grasping the permanently relevant amid the turbulence of the 'Age of Revolution'—as Eric Hobsbawm called the period from 1789 to 1848—so that what he wrote still matters, and not only as poetry. As the* *concluding section of the last full-length volume of poems that he published,* Romanzero *(1851), Heine—always a thoughtful arranger of his work—chose three long and complex pieces on Jewish themes, which he entitled* Hebräische Melodien. *J.L. Sammons, comments, "The first and most compact of them is…'Prinzessin Sabbath', which with distanced and ironic sympathy captures the transformation of the poor, servile workaday Jew into a prince on the Sabbath"* (Heinrich Heine: A Modern Biography, *1979). But the poem (as often with Heine) is not easy to pin down, and Peter Branscombe (in his 'Introduction' to* Heine: Selected Verse, *1967) describes it as "perhaps the most beautiful of Heine's poetic tributes to the religion of his fathers…". Branscombe goes on to say that "the tone of the poem is predominantly one of nostalgia, of a quiet exultation which makes life for all its sufferings worth living". No doubt Heine gets it both ways. Moreover, in the context of nineteenth century anti-Semitism—and with the benefit of hindsight—the disenchanted, as well as enchanted, irony with which Heine invests his subject appears clear-sighted to the point of prophetic. In* The Destruction of the European Jews *(1985), Raul Hilberg describes the sort of isolation or expulsion which the poem adumbrates (ranging in the real world from the barring of Jews from certain professions to ghettoization to enforced emigration) as the second anti-Jewish policy in European history, the first having been conversion to Christianity. Heine himself had endured both and, if he had lived a century later, might have experienced the third, which was annihilation:*

>Sometimes in Arabian folk-tales
>There's a prince who—though enchanted—
>In his handsome human form
>Gets to woo the girl he wanted;
>
>And a king's son nobly swaggers,
>Back from being a hairy brute,
>Dressed in rich and brilliant garments,
>Playing love-songs on the flute.
>
>But the magic respite passes,
>And His Royal Highness stands
>Once again a shaggy monster
>With the flute in his huge hands…
>
>Long ago a witch's Evil
>Eye turned one prince, Israel,
>Into a stray dog—although he
>Keeps on trying to break the spell.
>
>All week long, with doggy thoughts,
>Eating refuse, sniffing turds,
>Through the streets he runs, enduring
>Urchins' stones and, worse, their words.

But at dusk on Friday evening
Suddenly the spell grows weaker,
And the dog's a man again—
Princely lover, earnest seeker

After truth, with thoughts and feelings,
And his human head held high,
Entering then the king his father's
Doorway, dressed-up festively,

Washed and brushed, and greeting proudly
Those familiar halls: "Once more,
Jacob's tents, I kiss the sacred
Door-posts of your sacred doors!"

Through the house mysterious whispers
Weave the history of the Word:
Awesomely, amid the silence,
Breathes the house's unseen Lord.

Silence! Only the Lord's steward
(*Vulgo* synagogue attendant)
Hops about there, lighting lamps:
Some are standing, others pendant,

All convey religious solace,
Shining, gleaming, deep in shade,
While the candles proudly flicker
On the almemor's balustrade.

By the shrine in which the Torah
Rests, and which is decorated
With a costly silken cover,
Gilded, jewelled, illuminated,

Stands the cantor, at his prayer-desk—
A coquettish little man,
Who adjusts his smart black coat as
Noticeably as he can.

Showing off his soft white hands, he
Fingers first his neck and then,

Index-finger to his forehead,
Places thumb to throat again

In a curious gesture, humming
Quietly to himself, until
Lecho Daudi Likras Kalle!
Rings out loud and clear to fill

The entire hall with jubilation—
"Come, beloved, to the place
Where thy waiting bride unveils
For thine eyes her timid face."

This high-minded song was penned by
Don Jehuda ben Halevy,
Who—a troubador—was one of
The most famous sons of Levi.

In his song is celebrated
Israel's marriage to the peerless
Princess Sabbath, still and silent,
And as flawless as a pearl is,

Or a flower of perfect beauty—
Lovelier, for example, than
That great Queen of Sheba, brightest
Confidante of Solomon,

Who, blue-stockinged Ethiopian,
With her brilliant quips and/or
Cunning riddles, set to dazzle,
Soon became a crashing bore,

While the Princess, as the very
Personification of
Peace and quiet, detests all showy
Intellectual push and shove,

Not to mention all excited
Loudness, stamping or declaiming
Grandly, storming in with hair
Wind-blown and in need of combing.

And she covers, with a bonnet,
Her own chastely plaited tresses,
Blooming like a slender myrtle,
With gazelle-like eyes and lashes,

Though she lets her princeling do
Anything but smoke—would say
"Darling! Smoking is a no-no
On the holy Sabbath day—

But, instead, today at lunch-time
You'll find steaming on the table
Heavenly schalet. And you may
Eat as much as you are able."

Schalet, schöner Götterfunken,
Tochter aus Elysium!
That's how Schiller's anthem would have
Sounded if he'd tasted some.

Heavenly schalet is the food
Which our dear Lord God himself
Recommended for the Sabbath—
On Mount Sinai's topmost shelf,

Where He wrote the Ten Commandments
And the Law, as in His book,
Teaching Moses in the storm-cloud
How to judge and what to cook.

Schalet is the Lord our God's
Genuine ambrosia—
Blissful food of Paradise—
And so far beyond compare

That the ambrosia of those spurious
Heathen gods of ancient Greece
Seems like devils' excrement:
Weren't they devils in disguise?

Which is why, when eating schalet,
Israel's princely eyes start gleaming.

He unbuttons his best waistcoat
And intones, as if day-dreaming,

"Once again I hear the Jordan
Streaming and the rumbling springs
Of the palm-filled vale at Bethel,
Camels, distant ting-a-lings

Rung by herdsmen's fat bell-wethers
As they lead their lambs and sheep
Evenings down Mount Gileath's slopes to
Fields where they can safely sleep…"

But the Sabbath will be over
Soon. As if on shadow legs,
Like a dog, the hour comes running—
Israel's courage sighs and sags,

As he feels its mocking, ice-cold
Eyes transfix his heart of hearts.
And a shudder runs right through him
Now, in case the dog-change starts,

Till the princess kindly hands him
Her nard-box of solid gold.
Slowly he inhales it, hoping
That its airy charm will hold…

Quickly the sad princess pours him
One last goblet. Once again,
He as quickly drains it. Only
A few drops of wine remain.

These he sprinkles on the table
In the flickering candle-light.
Dips the candle in the puddle,
Where it sputters and goes out.

iii

As already noted in Then and Now, *for the last eight years of his life (from 1848 to 1856) Heine was painfully and increasingly paralysed by a disease of the spinal cord which confined him to his 'mattress-grave'. He was also chronically short of money, having lived by his wits in political exile in Paris since 1831… In 1848 he spent from February to April in a hospital. After mid-May he was never to walk again. In September, he wrote to his brother Max: "Even if I don't die straight away, life is still lost to me for ever, and yet I love life with such ardent passion…" The paralysis would affect sometimes one part of his body, some-times another: "My lips are lamed like my feet, my eating tools are lamed, as well as my excretory organs. I can neither chew nor crap; I am fed like a bird. This non-life is not to be borne." But bear it he did, with a stoicism which surprised even himself— and with practically no reduction in his creative output. Some of his most famous poems were written at this time—for example, his two 'Lazarus' sequences (see* From Now to Then*). The following is a translation of "Mir lodert und wogt im Hirn eine Flut", which Branscombe called "the apotheosis of his* Doppelgänger *works":*

> Like a storm in my brain, a flood of fields—
> Hills—forests—flashes and surges!
> Until, from the mad confusion, a scene
> With firmer contours emerges.
>
> The town is Godesberg, I think,
> Whose hovering forms now harden.
> And under the limetree here I sit
> As of old in the tavern-garden.
>
> My mouth is as dry as if I'd sucked
> The sun—which now is setting.
> Landlord! Landlord! A bottle of fine
> White wine! My throat needs wetting.
>
> The blessed vine-juice, swirling down
> To my soul, begins to lull it—
> And on its way extinguishes
> The sunburn in my gullet.
>
> Landlord, a second bottle! I drank
> The first in a fit of distraction.
> O noble wine, forgive this crass
> And middle-class reaction!
>
> I gaze at the rose-coloured Drachenfels
> And the highly Romantic ruins
> Of a castle mirrored in the Rhine—
> A landscape worth reviewing.

I hear the far-off wine-grower's song
And drink my wine while thinking
How gaily the finches chatter and cheep—
Not thinking what I'm drinking.

But now I stick my nose in my glass,
Inspecting its contents closely
Before I drink; or sometimes I
Just take a swig morosely.

And, strangely, as I drink, I seem
To be joined by my own double.
Another wretched sot! We make
A most peculiar couple.

He looks so sick and miserable—
So pale and emaciated—
And stares with such pained scorn—that I
Start to feel irritated.

This person claims that he's myself—
We two one perceived perceiver—
A weak, self-alienated wretch,
Sick of a raging fever.

He claims we're not in Godesberg
At the tavern. But in a distant
Sick-room in Paris. Until I shout,
"Stop lying! Stop it this instant!

"It's you that's sick. Like a blood-red rose,
I'm fighting fit. And, further,
I'm very strong. So shut your mouth—
Or else there'll be blue murder!"

He shrugs his shoulders, and sighs *"You fool"*,
Which makes me boil with anger,
Until at last I start to thump
My own damned double-ganger.

But, strangely, every time I land
A punch on the other fellow,

I feel it bruise myself, until
I'm blue and black and yellow.

And during this unhappy brawl,
My mouth gets drier and drier.
When I try to call for wine, I can't.
It's as if my throat's on fire.

My senses fail. In a dream I hear
Voices, prescribing sourly
A poultice. The Mixture. A dozen drops
In a tablespoonful hourly.

7   HOW JACK GOT ON IN THE WORLD

"There is no bloodless myth will hold"
– Geoffrey Hill

At the beginning of 'The House That Jack Built' in From Now to Then, *Jack's father—embarrassed by his fool of a son—gets rid of him by apprenticing him to a goldsmith. When Jack eventually returns home, he has lost all his earnings through happy-go-lucky naivety. He finds that his father has died, but he and his mother are reconciled. After some years, during which Jack grows up and begins to lose his innocence, his mother dies as well:*

i

"For dust thou art..." Jack heard the holy words
 Over the grave in which his mother now
 Rejoined his foolish father. Brooding birds
 Called quietly in their nests from lake and bough.
"Enough's enough," thought Jack. "Now let's see how
 I get on in the world." He took some bread
 And wine—and left. Let the dead bury their dead.

The April twilight faded. Deep in a wood,
 Jack stumbled across a hooded, pallid man,
 Hunched on a tree-stump. Having shared his food,
 He watched amazed as hood and cloak began
 To bristle into muzzle and brush: "You can
 Summon me if you need me," the fox said.
"I'm not that daft!" thought Jack. And, thanking him, fled.

"Foxes have holes," he rued, though—as cold rain
 Dropped through black boughs. On a rock by a dried-up stream
 A fair-haired woman writhed as if in pain,
 Silently begging for help. As in a dream,
 Jack gave her wine. The rain began to teem.
 A flashing salmon thrashed a pool: "I'll take
 You up," she seemed to grunt, "to a silent lake..."

"Well, you go your way, I'll go mine," thought Jack,
 And hurried on. At once, the moon's mad light
 Revealed a crying child, where the narrow track
 Stopped at a broken bridge. Green-eyed, but white

And sickly, soon she sang—a bird in the night,
Fed on Jack's crusts—and offered to show him lands
Across the sea. But Jack clapped grubby hands,

Till the bird flew off. He slept. And when he woke,
A fair-haired, pale-skinned girl with eyes as green
As May beneath an ancient sunlit oak
Sat by him in the dawn, as bright and serene
As if she were his long-lost sister, seen
Now for the first time... Dark, black-haired, brown-eyed,
Jack wondered whether he might not have died

And gone to heaven: "My friends, the fox and fish
And bird have sent me, seeing you're on your own
With nothing left," she smiled. "I only wish
I'd brought more bread," thought Jack: "you're skin and bone."
She said, "I cannot live by bread alone."
"And I," he laughed, "can't walk for long on air.
Let's beg together. What we get we'll share."

"No need to beg," she smiled again: "I know
Enough of herbs and medicines to ensure
We'll be invited in. And if, as we go,
There are the usual hardships to endure,
You'll find there's not a lot which I can't cure..."
With that they started on their common way,
And came to a large farm later that day.

ii

The cows had not been milked. The farmer's wife
Answered their knock with tears in her cold eyes.
Her husband lay in danger of his life
From a strange, unhealing wound. The stench and flies
Made Jack feel sick. They heard a lamb's death-cries
And fox's bark. His sister mixed lamb's blood
With earth to make a poultice of thick mud.

Next morning, when the wound began to heal,
The farmer offered them the rest of the lamb.
"Our fee," Jack's sister said, "is one square meal."
But Jack gasped, "What? If you aren't starved, I am!

Let's take the meat. Or is the mud a scam?"
She smiled, relenting: "Since my brother Jack
Is hungry again, please put some in his sack."

And so, that evening, deep in a dark wood,
Jack stoked a fire to broil their cuts of meat.
His sister gathered herbs. A dog-fox stood
And watched him. When the roasting was complete
Jack waited. But then he began to eat.
He slipped the fox a leg- and shoulder-bone,
And quickly ate the rest up on his own.

His sister brought sweet mint. So Jack explained
A fox had crept up, just as the meat was done,
And snatched it. He'd resisted, but in vain:
It was a vicious sharp-toothed hungry one.
They'd have to find another ailing man.
Nor was there any point at all in running
After a fox so very fast and cunning.

"The lamb was yours, not mine. But as to whether
We chase the fox," Jack's sister quietly said,
"If we two are to travel far together,
You must tell me what happened." Turning red,
Jack swore the greedy fox by now had fed
To more than satisfaction on their dinner,
While he for one continued getting thinner.

She sighed. He shrugged. At last, they went to sleep
Beside the dying remnants of their fire.
Next day Jack's strange twin-sister could hardly keep
Up with him. Paler, sadder, she seemed to tire
Before she should. "I may be a white liar,
But that roast lamb," thought Jack, "has done me good.
Who knows what we might meet in this wild wood?

And, if she's ill, I'm strong enough for two."
Between the trees, Jack glimpsed a fertile land
Of fields and hedges. Then a horseman, who
Was one of several sent to find them and
Convey the worried King's urgent command
That they should heal his Queen. But if she died,
They died as well. Jack shrugged. His sister sighed.

iii

Jack's sister's fame had spread. But, sick at heart,
She only slowly reached the Queen's sick-bed,
And before the frantic King could even start
To blame them, his beloved Queen was dead.
"Oh, damn and blast, we're for it now," Jack said.
But his sister told the King he needn't grieve,
Requesting him and all his court to leave.

She also asked them for their largest pot
And, filling it with water, took a knife
With which she swiftly and expertly cut
The King's still warm, white-skinned and loving wife
Into six pieces. The heart, still red with life,
She cradled in her hands. And then she sat,
Surrounded by the body, in the vat.

The bloody water swirled. A powerful fish
Thrashed in the brew, and quickly disappeared,
As did the limbs and torso. Jack's one wish
Was ditto. But he rubbed his eyes as he peered
Into the bubbling cauldron—whooped and cheered
As, first his sister, then the smiling Queen
Rose from the limpid water, fresh and clean.

The women laughed and dried their hair, while Jack
Was sent to fetch the mourning King and court,
Who entered with long faces, dressed in black,
Then gaped at what Jack's sister's skill had wrought.
The ecstatic King declared such doctors ought
To be rewarded with their weight in gold,
Or all the gems their healing hands could hold.

"Just bed and board," Jack's bright-eyed sister said,
"And tomorrow morning we'll be on our way."
Jack hissed, "You must be mad! The Queen was *dead*.
Let her rich husband pay what he wants to pay."
"But *not* in gold," she whispered. The next day,
Confiding in the King, Jack coolly told
Him they'd accept a rucksackful of gold.

But where to hide it? Joking, Jack explained
To his sister that although the spirit was willing
His body not infrequently complained
Its feet were cold, its belly needed filling—
Now they'd no longer be reduced to killing
Foxes or fish or birds to clothe or feed
Themselves. The gold would pay for every need.

In any case, they'd earned it, hadn't they?
"Your choice," she seemed to sing: "You're on your own."
Then turned into a bird and flew away.
"A strange young girl," thought Jack, "I'm glad she's gone.
She'd no idea at all of getting on."
He set off boldly. When the last of the light
Faded, he found an inn and stayed the night.

iv

This inn was Jack's first inn. He soon found out
How many ways there are to blow one's gold:
The drink, the gambling table, the smart tout
With gilt-edged bonds, his girl-friend with her bold
Come-hither look, her body you can hold
For as long as you can give what hookers take—
The wherewithal that tells them you're a rake…

Sometimes a silent bird sat watching him.
His wealth, in any case, was quickly spent;
He also gave a lot away, as the whim
Took him. One day a well-off merchant sent
To hire Jack's sister's skills. And so Jack went
To try and cure his daughter. But she died
While Jack was on his way to her bed-side.

The merchant warned him: "You could raise the Queen,
So raise my daughter." Jack thought, "Well, why not
Give it a try? And what I make I mean
To save this time!" He said, "I need a pot
Or, better still, a bath of fairly hot
Water. And with the help of a sharp knife,
I'll bring your stone-cold daughter back to life."

Soon Jack was sitting in the bloody water,
Sick in his stomach, sicker still at heart,
Beside the merchant's dead, dismembered daughter,
When in his sister flew: "You're not so smart
As I'd have hoped, dear brother. For a start,
You cannot buy or sell the gift of life:
Faith, hope and love revived the King's dead wife.

"Now let me clean up this unholy mess.
But woe betide you if you ask for money."
With that, before Jack could say no or yes,
The daughter was as gay as May is sunny.
They laughed so much he wondered what was funny.
The female mind and nature were of a sort
To which Jack had not given a lot of thought.

—A bird again, his flighty sister flew
Into the woods. The merchant's daughter ran
To fetch her dad, who asked what he could do
For him. The mind and nature of this man
Made sense to Jack, who sensibly began
By asserting that he wouldn't ask the earth—
But how much did he think his child was worth?

The merchant liked to show how rich he was
And doubled what the King had given Jack.
It didn't last much longer, though, because
He'd twice as many friends now, and no lack
Of borrowers who declined to pay him back.
And Jack was careless. Only six months on,
In spite of his resolve, the gold was gone.

v

His friends soon went as well. And for a time
Jack was reduced to begging, and then stealing,
From markets, farm-yards, inns… A life of crime
Beckoned. Until one night, when he was feeling
If things got any worse he'd soon need healing
Himself, he saw his sister in a dream,
Who told him things are only how they seem.

To make his empty haversack seem full
He only had to look around and wish
The things he named were in it. I'm no fool,
Thought Jack. But, then, he tried it. Like a flash,
Two roast geese with potatoes in a dish
Had flown into his bag from an inn-garden,
And Jack was gone, without a beg-your-pardon.

You see, it works, his sister seemed to say,
While Jack was gorging on the larger goose,
As if beneath the light-green leaves of May:
Just put your rucksack to its proper use
And all your trials are over. Take your choice
Of what you want. Just say the word. Feel free,
He seemed to hear her say. It works, you see.

The light grew stormy, and his sister's words
Swirled as a cold wind rose among the trees.
Jack had already golloped the first of the birds
When a gruff voice growled, That other of them geese
Belongs to us. Or else we'll smash your knees.
Two looming hulks. You're welcome, gents! gulped Jack,
Stashing the bag itself behind his back,

And if you'd like some grog to swill it down,
You'll find a nice dry inn along the lane.
The bullies grabbed the goose. Jack feigned a frown,
Then crept behind them in the teeming rain
To eavesdrop. Through a dirty window-pane
He watched the landlord and his bouncers beat
The goose-thieves till they knocked them off their feet.

Afraid in case the landlord should suss out
Who'd scoffed the bigger goose, and get his men
To bounce him as another thieving lout,
Jack slunk off through the storm-tossed woods again;
Soon lost, he stopped by a dark hole or den
But dared not enter. Trembling now with dread,
He knew whatever was inside was dead.

Instinctively, he cast about for his sister.
Beneath a castle's walls another inn
Quickly persuaded him he'd hardly missed her.

But all its rooms were full. The merry din
Came from the lord and lady's kith and kin,
Who'd left the castle, with their noble hosts—
Besieged, it seemed, by very dangerous ghosts.

vi

Just ghosts? Jack smiled, who, feeling brave again,
Was also keen on somewhere warm and dry
To sleep. The landlord claimed that many men
Of proven worth had been prepared to try
And drive the poltergeists away or die:
Most lost their nerve, but some their lives. The lord
Had now stumped up a very large reward.

A large reward? Jack smiled again. Please give
Me first some food and drink, though—then the key.
Not being a ghost, if I'm to stay alive
I need to keep my strength up. Later, we'll see
Who'll lord it at the castle, them or me.
I'll have you know that I'm not easily daunted:
I've slept in lots of houses which were haunted.

The landlord warned him some had gone as mad
As rabid dogs. Jack bared his teeth and cried
It's only in your thoughts that things seem bad!
And instantly he found himself inside
The richly furnished castle, viewing with pride
The carpets, dark-red curtains, gold and white
Panels, the stucco marble, lustrous lamp-light,

And, then, the master-bedroom with a tall
Four-poster. Just the thing for me, thought Jack:
This chamber's big enough to hold a ball.
What lamps, what chandeliers! His haversack
Was loaded with the landlord's generous snack.
Jack munched with gusto, drinking long and deep,
Then lay down on the bed and fell asleep.

He woke—or seemed to wake—in total blackness.
Or was he blind? Or dreaming? Or now in
The castle's dungeon, whose foul-smelling dankness

And eery silence started slowly to spin
Around him—but, abruptly, then began
Filling with sound and fury, tails and horns
Of jeering apes, or hairy leprechauns.

These naked, crazy creatures danced about
Jack's bed, long-haired, long-fingered, black, brown, grey,
In smoky, sulphurous light. Stifling a shout,
He thought, Ignore them and they'll go away.
But still they danced and jeered. All right, I'll stay
Here quietly till the dawn, decided Jack.
But then he wished all seven into his sack.

For seven they seemed to be. And in they went.
Once more black silence reigned. Jack told the lord
The following morning that he'd caught and sent
The ghosts to hell for ever. Bed and board
Were clearly an inadequate reward,
The lord insisted… Jack accepted cash
And (feeling the devils kick) said, Thanks, must dash.

vii

And dashed at once to a nearby blacksmith's shop,
Where he employed the smith's apprentices
To hammer at the haversack non-stop
Until the devils were all dead: that is,
Until their kicks and cries ran out of fizz.
But one lay doggo. Later, when he could,
His black back disappeared in the black wood.

Jack thought he saw him slip down that dark hole
Of death. And, come to that, he felt quite ill
And older now himself, as if his soul,
Weary of slowly climbing life's long hill,
Were starting to descend it—till
One evening he stood undecided where
The path became two paths, one foul, one fair.

Then, suddenly, in a flash of golden light,
A firebird with green eyes appeared, and explained
In flame-like words which flickered through the night

One path led on to hell, the other gained
The heights of heaven. But which went where? Jack feigned
Confusion in the hope the bird would tell
Whether the fair path led to heaven or hell.

Instead, its green eyes blazed. Jack snatched a feather
Of fiery orange from the bird's long tail,
And chose the broad and primrose way, wherever
It led. He knocked and knocked. The Devil turned pale
And, warned by the 'ghost' who'd lived to tell the tale,
Told him to go to hell—or, rather, heaven,
Where he could cull six *angels* out of seven!

No hope in this place, Jack thought: Better try
The other path. But the feather turned to dust
As he saw his sister, like an angel, fly
Onto the gate which neither moth nor rust
Corrupts. And yet, I'll get in here or bust,
He thought: *Just say the magic word. Feel free.—*
It worked for seven devils. Let's try me.

His sister beat her wings and seemed to cry
How could you? But go on. And don't look back.
Jack called, In that case, if I live or die,
I'll do without your magic haversack!
And over the gate it went. As soon as Jack
Had heard it land, he wished himself inside it.
I'm in! he whooped. A softer voice denied it.

Before he could get out, though, to make sure,
He felt the bag being hammered, and awoke
To find an angry farmer and two or more
Farm-hands—his 'bouncers'—beating him till they broke
Their clubs across his back. The farmer took
His stolen goose. The soft voice said, "They've gone.
Get up again. And don't look back. Go on.

Coda

For dust thou art…" Hearing the holy words
Reminded Jack of his parents. Also of how
Ill they had fared. "And I?" Black carrion-birds

Cawed in the rain from an overhanging bough.
Jack's brown eyes blazed, but softly: "Let's see *now*
How I get on." As if his sister led
The way, they went—among the quick and the dead.

8 ORPHEUS AND OTHERS—*ca.* 1375/1904

> *"They tooke*
> *a path that steep upright*
> *Rose darke and full of foggye mist.*
> *And now they were within*
> *A kenning of the upper earth,*
> *when Orphye did begin*
> *To dout him, lest she followed not…"*
> *–* Ovid, *Metamorphoses* Bk X

i   Song of Innocence: Sir Orfeo

Sir Orfeo was a Celtic king
who loved, above all things, to sing
while playing the lyre or harp.
                              And he
had learned to play so skilfully,
none better. When he sang and played,
the Apollonian sounds he made
in Winchester—a holy place
known also at that time as *Thrace*—
were such that by some rare device
you thought you were in Paradise…

His wife was called *Eurydice*.

One day, beneath a grafted tree
in May-time, this much-loved May Queen
fell fast asleep in its shade. The green
was white with blossom. When she woke,
she cried out loud—and coughed and choked—
rubbing her lovely hands and feet,
scratching her face till it bled wet,
and tearing her hair and clothes. Her maids
were close at hand but, too afraid
to try to touch or help her, ran
straight to the palace, and began
crying to knight, lad, lord and lady
their Queen had gone completely crazy.

They found her in the orchard where
her flashing eyes and floating hair
alarmed and repelled them.
                            The strongest caught
her up in their arms and gently brought
her home to bed. When she screamed, they held
her body down. But she kicked and yelled
in pain, as if an unseen knife
were cutting out her very life—
and tried, again, to run away.
Nobody knew what to do or say—
till Orfeo begged his wife to be still
and, after one last angry shrill
scream, she started crying.
                         Tears
loosened her tongue: "So many years!—
now, to be raped—torn—forced apart…"

"Never!" cried Orfeo: "Heart in heart,
Where you go I go, where I you!"

"My love, there's nothing we can do.
The crown he wore was neither gold
nor silver but—a thousand-fold
more dazzling—made of precious stone,
whiter and brighter than the moon…"—

And, shimmering, she started to disappear,
sighing, "I'm neither there nor here…
From under that grafted apple-tree
their King sprang up—and hideously
removed my heart and brain. What's left
is lifeless matter—my body, bereft
of freedom or the power to choose—
a thing, with nothing more to lose
but pain and shame—so weakened, so hollow
that all I can do now is follow
what's gone…"—And, dragged away, she faded
before their eyes.
                Amazed, but persuaded
his wife's strange tale was true, the King
furiously swore to find and bring
her straight back home.

                         His counsellors, lords
and ladies, hearing these wild words,
looked worried.
              His steward—privately—pleaded
with him to stay where he was needed:
the people worshipped him but he
had been informed that, secretly,
others were tired of holy singers
and couldn't wait to get their fingers
on greater power and wealth than was
allowed by law in Orfeo's Thrace.
The King took up his harp and left
this man in charge.
                    The people wept
to see him hike off on his own
with nothing, leaving palace, throne
and wealth behind him, in the guise
of a poor minstrel.
                   Many eyes
observed him penetrate the wood
beyond the city walls. "No good
will come of this," the merchants said:
"soon King and Queen will both be dead…"
And met behind closed doors to consider
selling the throne to the highest bidder.
Among them sat the steward's spy…

Sir Orfeo sat in the wood, where shy
creatures approached to hear him play,
and birds which whistled their wild *lais*
in tune with his artful harp and voice—
where even the trees and flowers rejoiced,
or so it seemed, to hear his song…

And, sure enough, before very long,
swarms of bright forms appeared and listened,
leaving a trail of dust, which glistened
briefly behind them when they fled.
Orfeo followed as far as it led…

That night he played again.
                           Between
bushes and trees, a King and his Queen

rode out to hunt on unicorns
like shifting shadows. Their huntsmen's horns
silenced his harp.
            But not for long:
the whole hunt stopped to hear his song.

The forest was lit by a full moon,
which blazed as white as ice at noon.
But when he paused to look, they were gone.
Into the dark their dust led on
like stars, whose sky then curved underground.
West of the dawn, Sir Orfeo found
a cavern, then a sunless sea.

Their dwelling-place was fetid.
                          He
could see things if he looked away,
and glimpsed, as if on a dull day,
his wife amid a lifeless lot
of women and children, who could not
look, but seemed merely looked at. Blank
eyes stared unblinkingly. Some stank
of rotting flesh—condemned to decay
in herds.
           Sir Orfeo tried to play,
but only caused them all to groan.

He moved away and, seated alone
on the bare shore whose bitter waves,
as grey as lead, lapped rocks and caves
listlessly, played again...
                      And soon
they appeared, in pairs, to listen. Then
began to sway and dance and hop
as if they had to...
                A cry of *Stop!*
brought dance and music to a halt
as, out of a cave, glinting like salt
their King and Queen emerged. Their crowns
And other jewels and glowing stones
lit up that dismal land and sea.

—Who are you?
                    "Lord, my minstrelsy
seemed to divert your hunt by night.
I followed by the blinding light
of a mad full moon."
                         *Our goddess—who
has granted power over such as you
to me. But play now.*
                    Orfeo played
until that whole dark world was swayed
like trees in a wind…
                    *As Hades' king,
I give and take. Choose anything,
here or above, as your reward.*

So Orfeo fetched his wife: "My lord,
give me this woman."
                    *This woman is dead!
I claimed her bleeding heart and head…
But take them back. The gods are kind
to those that help themselves. She's blind,
so lead her by the hand—to the tree
I took her under. You are free
to do this thing. This place is lit
by the hearts and minds we bring to it,
which here turn into precious stones
as bright as stars or dying suns:
take hers, which—with your harp—will light
your way through our unending night.
No earthly life here stands a chance…
But, first, more music and more dance—
then seize the day! …"*
                    Later, beneath
that grafted tree, the Queen's sour breath
became as sweet as a flower or an apple.

King Orfeo made of two a couple
almost before his wife awoke.

She sighed, and peered about, and spoke
uncertainly, as if afraid:
"My love, I fell asleep in the shade,
but dreamt I woke up here again

trembling with fear, in terrible pain,
because I'd lost my heart and my mind
and could not act to help you find
the King who'd trapped and ravished them..."

And so she told him her bad dream
of having lost her power to choose,
which left her nothing more to lose—
already fading, as dreams do
by the light of day, like honey-dew...
She hardly remembered now the strange place
she'd dreamt of, or that blinding face—
as if she'd really been half-dead,
or more than half...
                    Sir Orfeo said,
"Where you go I go: nothing could ever
divide our minds or finally sever
your heart from mine... Before you forget,
with your permission, love, I'll set
your dream to music, adding what
your absent mind, let's say, forgot
at once—or never noticed."
                         "Yes...
I dreamt I died, you see—no less...
But sing me a *lai* to heal my heart."

"Since ends are where all things must start—
since night must always end in day
or sweet soil come from sour decay,
and fallen leaves and rotted fruit
are where the sprouting seed must root—
as Spring from Winter, New Year from Old,
so art and alchemy make gold
from life and rubbish. Therefore, again
here *now*, let me begin with *then:*

*Sir Orfeo was a Celtic king
who loved, above all things, to sing
while playing the lyre or harp.*
                    And he
*had learned to play so skilfully,
none better. When he sang and played,
the Apollonian sounds he made*

in Winchester—a holy place,
known also at that time as Thrace—
were such that by some rare device
you thought you were in Paradise.

His wife was called Eurydice..."

(da capo)

  ii Song of Experience: Rainer Maria Rilke—*Orpheus. Eurydice. Hermes*

A strange dark mine of souls. As still
As silver ore, they silently pulsed
Like arteries through its darkness. Blood
Welled up through roots, flowed off into people,
Seeming as heavy as porphyry.
Otherwise no red—

Only rocks
And unreal woods; bridges over nothing;
And that great grey blind lake which hung
Above its distant bed like clouds
Of rain above a landscape. But also,
Between soft meadows full of patience,
A single path—like a pale strip
Of linen laid in the sun to bleach.

And on this single path they came.

In front the slender man in blue—
Wordless, impatient, staring ahead,
With steps which took great bites of the way,
Swallowing them whole. His heavy hands
Hung clenched among his garment's folds,
No longer aware of the light lyre
Twined round the left, a climbing rose
Growing in the boughs of an olive.
His sight and hearing seemed to divide,
In that the first, like a dog, ran off
Ahead—turned round—came back—stood waiting
Again in the distance by the next
Turning, whereas his hearing hung

Behind like an odour, almost as far
Back as the footsteps of the two
He hoped were following him on up
The slope. But only distant echoes
Of his ascent, his cloak's swish, reached
His ears. *They're coming, though*, he said
Out loud—hearing his words re-echo…
And so they were. But terribly,
Terribly quietly. Had he turned then
(And with that single backward look
Ended this work), he might have seen
Them, seen how quiet they were, unspeaking:

He—the message-bearing god of travel,
His hood pulled over his bright eyes,
With wings that fluttered round his ankles,
Raising his slender staff of office—
And, guided by his left hand, *she*.

So greatly loved that, from his lyre,
More mourning issued than from wailing
Women—a world of mourning, in which
All things were present: wood and valley—
Village and road—field, river, beast;
And even—to make this world of his
Just like the other Earth—a sun,
And a still and starry sky which wheeled
And wailed: a sky with disfigured stars…
So greatly loved.

She, though, hand in hand with the god,
Her short steps hampered by her shroud,
Uncertain, gentle, and without impatience,
Sunk in herself, in her gravid being,
Gave no thought to the man in front
Nor to the pathway leading to life:
Sunk in herself. Her presence in death
Utterly fulfilled her.
She was as full of her great death
As a fruit is full of sweetness and darkness:
A death so new that she grasped nothing.

She had become a girl again
And was not to be touched. Her sex had closed
Like a young flower at dusk; her hands
Had grown so unaccustomed there
To marriage that even the weightless god's
Infinitely delicate guiding touch
Seemed too familiar, seemed offensive.

She was no longer that blonde woman
Echoing sometimes through his poems:
No more their broad bed's scent, its island,
And that man's property no more:

Loosened already like long hair,
Dispersed like fallen rain, and shared
Like an abundant hoard, she was

Already root.

And when the god
Stopped her abruptly, pained and blurting
The words, *He has turned round!* she still
Grasped nothing but asked quietly, *Who?*

Far off, though, dark in the bright way out,
Somebody stood, whose countenance
She could not see. He stood and watched
How on a narrow path between meadows
The message-bearing god, with grief
In his look, turned quietly round and followed
Her form returning now the same way,
Her steps still hindered by her shroud,
Uncertain, gentle, and without impatience.

9   GRETL BRAUN REMEMBERS HER SISTER, EVA

"Ich bin nicht schuld"
– Eva Braun (diary entry, 28 May, 1935)

i   We Had No Garden and No Rose-trees

Mother called us her rose-buds—*Snow-white*
and *Rose-red*. Father was often AWOL.
We punched him with our little fists
when he came home. But he just bared
his teeth and laughed. Our eldest sister
soon left, and kept her distance. We
took care of Mother and she us.
We had no garden and no rose-trees.

On Sundays, though, we'd go for a walk
along the Isar, as far as Munich's
most beautiful rose-garden. Mother dozed
in the sun. We fed the birds, which weren't
afraid of us, and took some crumbs
of cheese to coax the mice from their mouse-holes
in the forest of roses. In one dark corner
were beds of poisonous plants. *Verboten.*

Our Grandpa, a vet, lived in a small cottage
in a wood. He told us *Märchen*. We played
at horse and carriage. Evi drove
us further and further. We slept on dry leaves.
Grandpa's dog found us. Mother was worried
stupid. But Evi said we'd seen
the beautiful child in shining white
who Grandpa had told us guards good children.

At home we were really good—to help
poor Mother. Father had fought in the war.
After the war he left us (he came
back later). Mother sewed—to make
ends meet. We kept things very clean
and tidy, pretending a prince would knock
one day at our door. Or a bear. We knew
bears meant no harm. But if a wolf came…?

ii The Grandfather's Tale (1): The Child in White

A widow lived in a lonely cottage
  beside a Märchen-*wood.*
Her daughters grew like two young rose-trees,
  one white, one red, both good.

They shared the housework. In the summer
  picked flowers, then gathered fruit
And shared it. Safe by their fire in the winter,
  spun wool. No man or brute

Troubled their dreams. A lamb and rabbits
  ate from their hands. Snow fell
As soft and white as a dove's feathers.
  On the hob shone a brass kettle.

Their mother read them stories, in which
  the brave and loyal thrive.
They promised never to leave each other:
  "Not for as long as we live."

In the spring they ran about in the wood.
  Animals did them no harm.
The roe grazed by their side, the hare
  showed them her secret form.

Sometimes they stayed out late. When darkness
  approached, they nestled down
Next to each other beneath the tall trees—
  slept on soft moss till dawn.

But then one night they got lost in the dark
  and might have slipped down a cliff:
A blaze of light prevented them
  and showed them the path, as if

An angel had been sent to guide
  them home. Another night
Someone or something knocked. Then growled.
  There was no light but their firelight.

iii   What's In a Name?

To salve his conscience, Father paid
for Evi to study typing and book-keeping—
at a convent across the Inn from *Braunau*.
Well, what's in a name?...—A whole year away
from home! She landed her glamorous job
at the *Photohaus* shortly after. One evening
Evi fetched beer and wurst for the boss
and a client who said his name was *Herr Wolf*.

Hitler devoured her with his eyes.
She liked to be looked at—posed for photos.
All good clean fun, of course. A platonic
affair to start with: Adi's Evi.
He was old enough to be her father.
But he remained her ideal man. She loved
to be in love. When Mother frowned,
he charmed her. Dogs and children adored him.

In the boss's idyllic garden beside
the Isar he lay on the grass in his shirt-sleeves,
photographed by Evi. But soon the Party
took almost all of his time. His first love
was *Deutschland*, we all believed. She waited
and wilted. Then tried to kill herself
with Father's pistol... And three years later
again—with sleeping pills... Until

at last he relented: "I must take care
of the poor child..." And so she became
the Berghof's mistress, where he led
an almost bohemian life! She loved
the mountains—felt free to sunbathe, ramble,
swim, sleep, ski, skate. I loved it, too.
Our paradise on earth. Blue sky,
wild flowers, small children. Fashion, films...

iv   The Grandfather's Tale (2): Their Black Friend

Snow-white had met the bear in the forest
       while gathering cones and wood.
She asked her frightened mother and sister
       to fetch the bear some food.

He seemed half-frozen. So they suggested
       he warm himself by the fire.
He asked them to sweep the snow from his coat.
       Soon he began to snore.

In the morning the bear was gone, but appeared
       again the following night.
He growled in contentment. Both girls played
       with their big black friend. But Snow-white

Rode through the woods on his strong broad back.
       Later she stayed away
For a night or two. He must have had
       a place for her to stay.

He came to their cottage by day or night.
       He carried her far and wide.
She skated and ski-ed. And Rose-red played
       as well with the bear outside.

When the ground grew softer, though, he left them—
       to recover his rightful treasure
From a wicked tribe of long-nosed dwarfs
       who were greedy and sly beyond measure.

Snow-white unbolted the kitchen-door.
       In his hurry, he caught his coat,
Revealing a patch of gold. She stifled
       the cry that rose in her throat.

But as he loped away through the trees
       she softly started to cry.
And cried so much in the weeks that followed
       Rose-red was afraid she might die.

v   All True Romantics

He also bought her a house of her own
in Munich. We lived there together. His flat
was just across the river. The Berghof
was our Grand Hotel. He liked to hold forth
at dinner—on politics, his great triumphs,
Germany's future. *Re* painting and music
he detested the Moderns, loved rural landscapes—
could paint them, too. Played Beethoven, Brahms,

when he had time. The greatest was Wagner.
—All true Romantics, like himself,
or like old Fritz with his *Castel del Monte*...
He could be charming and even *gemütlich*,
but liked to be known as well as a *Schlitzohr*
like Brandner Caspar—a favourite tale—
who cheated Death by getting him drunk
and winning a bet with him at cards.

As for the Jews, if you offered your finger
they'd take your arm—and hate or despise you
for letting them. Look at Eisner, shot
in the street—and rightly. All Eastern Europe,
from Riga to Odessa, was riddled with Jewish
Bolshevists. To clear all that away—
make *Lebensraum* for the master-race—
and retire with Fräulein Braun to Linz

was all he wanted from life. But they
were highly organized—and after
not just our gold but our blood. He knew
so much that ignorant weakness—crippled
minds or crippled bodies—disgusted him.
Karl Brandt once mentioned Kaspar Hauser:
"Poor innocent child," said Evi sadly.
"Yes, yes," he explained, "but better dead."

vi   The Grandfather's Tale (3): The Three Dwarfs

At last Rose-red and her anxious mother
  got poor Snow-white out of bed
And then out-of-doors. In the wood they met
  not the bear but a dwarf, who said

"My dears, my dears, assist a poor bag-man.
  The wedge sprang out—my beard
Is trapped in this log for my fire." When they managed
  to cut it, he snapped and sneered

"You stupid geese!" With a clink of gold
  he shouldered his knapsack—which
Was large and heavy. So was *he poor?*
  Or were he and his ilk really rich?…

By the river another was counting something.
  "My dears, I know I'm a clown,
But I've tangled my beard in my fishing line.
  If this eel pulls me in I'll drown!"

As he hopped about, a pearl or two
  plopped in. They managed to sever
His long grey beard. Well, was *he a fool?*
  Or was he rich and clever?…

Behind them another screamed—a great eagle
  had grabbed him. Full of pity,
They hung on tight. His idiot's face
  and crippled legs weren't pretty.

The eagle dropped him. Burbling, he hobbled
  away. As they watched him go,
He hauled a huge bag from a bush. A cretin,
  but rich, it seemed, even so…

By the bush a pile of precious stones
  confirmed that the dwarfs were stealing
Their black friend's treasure. They stole it back—
  but with a sinking feeling.

vii   By the Fireside

One evening Evi overheard
Karl Brandt complain to Morell, of all
people, about the swarms of psychiatrists
deserting their posts, "like rats"… So know-all
Morell said, "Are you surprised?—But hasn't
T4 been scrapped?"—"Officially. But
we still use Luminal. *And*, of course,
the Munich diet…"—I said, "Ask Adi…"

but she replied, "I'd rather trust him,
he's my *Führer*." Once, at another soirée,
the boss's daughter—an old flame—brought up
the mass 'resettlement' of Jewish
families from Holland: some friends had gone
to live there, brilliant musicians… Hitler
attacked her—slapped her down so hard
that none of us ever mentioned the Jews

again. There were rumours, of course. But secrets
of that sort weren't for the fireside—would
be almost like asking him to take
his clothes off. Evi told me not even
his doctors examined him naked—although
he was perfectly normal, she said. A bit of
an old maid—an eccentric—a vegetarian.
Obsessively clean and prudish. Like

herself. But very, very strong.
Even when Munich was battered by air-raids
and Evi's house and his flat were in ruins,
he never lost faith in the final victory.
So many people died for their *Führer*.
And so many died against him, including
close friends, like Röhm. Or Hermann, my husband—
almost a relative. But that was later…

viii The Grandfather's Tale (4): Follow-My-Leader

One Sunday the girls were walking home
    from church. They surprised all three
Dwarfs in front of a cave, defending
    their loot obstreperously.

The idiot pointed. All at once,
    like wasps, they flew at Rose-red,
Who was closer. She screamed and flailed as they clawed her,
    then seemed to fall down dead.

Snow-white was terrified. They dragged
    her sister towards their cave,
Leering and laughing. One got out his knife.
    She shrieked a prayer—"God save

Our innocent souls!" A furious bear
    crashed through the bushes and towered
Roaring and growling on his hind legs.
    The dwarfs grovelled and cowered.

They hid behind Rose-red and blubbered
    "Eat her, not us! And her!
They're fat and juicy. Take your treasure,
    but let us live!" The great bear

Crushed the skull of the idiot first,
    as if he hated him most;
Then brained the clever 'foolish' one
    against their cave's door-post;

Then wrung the neck of the first the children
    had helped. Rose-red gave a groan,
As he wolfed all three of them down. They were
    nothing but skin and bone.

By now the sisters were almost as frightened
    of the bear as the dwarfs he'd fed
His face on. They ran away. But he
    refused to follow. He led.

ix   Dreams and Nightmares

When Barbarossa failed, we knew
the war had failed. Some started to question
the *Führer*. And all too soon our *Märchen*
was history, our dream a nightmare. He
fought on to the end. Why marry? But I
was married. To Hermann, Himmler's liaison
officer. After his boss's treachery,
Hermann was AWOL. Hitler ordered

that he be shot. I remember thinking
at the Berghof that maybe he and Evi
and even the *Führer* himself had retreated
from Berlin at the very last minute, and/or
were still alive. Well, I was pregnant
and full of hope. Whereas they knew
their 'castle of castles' at Linz was never
to be. The officers' attempted murder

had shaken us all—left Hitler ill.
He had at least two hundred hanged—
with piano wire. The hangings were filmed
and photoed by the SS. My Hermann
showed me. I think that was when Adi
lost all real hope. But Speer and others
kept working on Linz—his 'German Rome',
his 'Acropolis'—right to the end. And so

did Evi. The look of the parks and proms,
kitchens and business districts—all
were Fräulein Braun's affair. Huge models
were built, unveiled on his birthday. Their private
residence overlooked the city…
But more and more people died in the war.
And more and more Jews—as we discovered
later. But we were innocent of all that.

x   The Grandfather's Tale (5): What the Bear Said

As the girls ran off, he roared. Then silence.
    When they reached the trees they stopped:
No bear, but a man in gold—the son
    of a king. Their hot hearts quopped.

He told them the dwarfs had kidnapped him,
    and made him work like a beast
Until he almost was one. The girls
    had helped his escape. Released

From the dwarfs' sick magic by their blood
    and in possession again
Of his lands and treasure, their friend was free—
    as a super-man among men,

A pure-bred leader—to ask Snow-white
    to live with him as his queen
In his castle of castles, which the dwarfs
    had intended to make their own.

After the marriage, both were crowned.
    The King invited her mother
And sister to live with them. Rose-red
    married his younger brother.

In the palace, not a single cloud
    nor even a family squabble
Darkened their lives—till the Bone-man knocked
    at its drawbridge. Accustomed to trouble,

Their mother cheated him for years.
    She asked them, when she was dead,
To plant two rose-trees on her grave,
    one white and one blood-red.

At last she faded away, amid
    her grandchildren's innocent laughter.
The roses grew beside her black stone,
    bloomed there for ever after.

xi   A Beautiful Corpse

Imagine the way it might have been.
Imagine living happily. Imagine
how wrong we were. Real life with Hitler
was hypochondia, bad nerves, no smoking,
no meat, no drink. As 'Patient A',
he swallowed enormous numbers of pills—
uppers and downers. The ultimate downer
was downfall—"a bullet in the brain".

Till then, though, Evi's carefree, calm,
bright view of things was more and more
of a help. The Berghof *was* her palace.
At the Chancellery, as his 'secretary',
she used the side way-in. When he led
from his 'Lair' in Prussia, they phoned. She changed
her outfit, put on make-up, threw
the occasional party. Waited for air-raids.

Their last retreat was the Bunker. Berlin,
Munich, the *Reich*, and half of Europe
were rubble. Hitler's "fight to the death"
only increased the wreckage. He knew
it was over—told the women to leave.
When Evi stood firm, he kissed her in front of
his assembled staff. At last he made her
his wife. And she stayed loyal to the end.

She wanted to be "a beautiful corpse"—
chose poison. He blew his head off. People
who yearn—hope—lust for more from life
than life can give, who cannot live
with less than that, must either deceive
themselves and others or die. No life
is perfect. There never was or will be
a *Märchenwald*. I know that now.

10 A BRIEF PRELUDE. *OR:* WHERE HE CAME FROM (1)

"—Ego credo ut vita pauperum est simpliciter atrox, simpliciter sanguinarius atrox, in Liverpoolio."
– Joyce, *A Portrait of the Artist as a Young Man*

*"… And came, as most men deemed, to little good,
But came to Oxford and his friends no more."*
– Matthew Arnold, *The Scholar-Gipsy*

i Past and Future

The place they lived until he was, what, twelve
years old (if I remember rightly) was
uglier, dirtier, smellier and more dangerous
than any other place he left or came from.
Which may be why he later thought of the arts—
books above all, but also paintings, music—
then roses, orchids, apple-blossom, girls'
amazing eyes, lips, softness—as what offered
his squalid past a future, as if beauty
were always truth, and truth a sort of beauty.

ii Head in the Clouds (1)

*I died in harness. While I was still headmaster
I picked him as headboy. Though rather young,
he'd worked at rugger and in class to prove
himself a leader. A conscientious, strong
Christian, he'd pull his weight… My Sixth Remove
got them to college faster—
and on to their careers. I thought he'd make
a civil servant or perhaps a police
officer, even a bishop. Elbow-grease
he had in plenty. But leaving was a mistake.*

iii From School to Church

At Grove St Primary School no one did well
on principle. Discovering to his surprise
at grammar school a knack for passing exams
shortly began to look like a way of escaping
the violent chaos of too big a family
trapped in their back-to-back. Sundays were hellish—
clean clothes, no playing out—until he found
a sanctuary in St Mark's, whose Low Church vicar
insisted on the Prayer Book. Word by slow
and peaceful word, it soothed his vexed attention.

iv The Vicar

I'd drop broad hints—but every Sunday he
and one old biddy or penitent husband would
turn up inside the porch at five-to-eight
for early Communion. Yawning did no good.
My wife, still half asleep, would have to wait.
If fewer than "two or three",
I'd grin and send him home. But he'd be back
for Matins, Evening Prayer and Sunday School.
He might have taken orders but—the fool—
at Oxford he went off the beaten track…

v That Summer

At church there was a girl in the pew in front
with long blonde ringlets—lightly downed pink cheeks—
ears pierced by ear-rings. Coyly kneeling to pray,
she'd show a naked strip of gartered thigh.
He put her hand in his trouser-pocket. But
she panicked. Like the milkless cow the farmer
fenced off until the butcher's van arrived.—
That summer's job. She crashed barbed wire, stampeding
the herd—he couldn't stop them—till they stopped
in the corn three fields away. And there he left them.

vi   Catholic and Protestant

We met as Freshers. Older, I saw at once
he needed guidance. Graceless, and too young
to be away from home, he'd no idea
of social life—went puce or lost his tongue
in company—drank neither wine nor beer
nor sherry. Though no dunce,
his dress-sense verged on zero. Imbibed too much
Lawrence—and might have failed Prelims proclaiming
Milton a pious fraud. He needed taming...
His unkempt poems raved. We've long lost touch.

vii   Literature and Dogma

So far so good. At last a room of his own—
at eighteen-years-of-age a first-time-ever.
The nosey homo his scout looked frankly miffed
when he joined the Christian Union. Soon a girl there
was shielding her puritanical suspenders.
Milton (for two whole terms) viewed Christian dogma
as a form of 'science'. Even Comus had more life
in him than God. God gave despotic power
to men (according to Samson) over their females.
But chastity, clearly, meant obedience later.

viii   Theologian

His friend and mine once told me they'd been reading
Arnold and Wordsworth. The former said the latter
cut himself off from half of life—withdrew
as if into a monastery. The matter
with both, I'd say, was that we cannot do
without our Lord, nailed bleeding
where he'd been nailed for nineteen hundred years...
I taught, then, Latin, Greek, Divinity.
Our friend was 'one of us'. But—godless—he
left and was on his own with his hopes and fears.

ix   Mud and Music

Still well-behaved, he thought he'd better ask
permission to stay out late (no girls in college
post-10 pm). Brusquely ignoring his question,
the Dean asked *why*, though, leave a trail of mud
across the Music House's polished floor
at last night's concert… The thing to do, it seemed,
was bribe one's scout. But how? He found he cared
and didn't care about do's / don't's—what when
to ask, wear—not ask, not wear. But he cared
always for art, girls, tulips… The rest was mud.

x   Just Friends

I told my future husband not to worry,
no one could be less forward or more shy.
I suggested going to see The Sound of Music.
I have to admit he seemed to wonder why,
but laughed "If you're quite sure it won't make you sick,
it won't make me!" Seemed very
amused as well by Beecham's "Madam, you
have that between your legs which could give joy
to thousands…"—begged me, blushing like a boy,
to play my cello. I never did, though I do.

xi   Love-Sick

She seemed to find his words and ways more innocent
than *I* remember them! And yet it's true
that prettiness enticed him… One sultry Sunday
she sent him packing when he came for tea:
a big red spot had burst on her pale chin
shortly before her boyfriend's weekly visit.
Tears—tweezers—lint! Retiring to the Ashmolean,
he stared at neither Raphael's battle scenes,
nor even Uccello's *Hunt*, but Pinturicchio's
yellow-faced love-sick youth in an Umbrian landscape.

xii   The Voice of the Staircase

We noticed straight away he didn't fit.
His accent told us where he went to school.
Rumour had it he worked eight hours a day.
We'd visit one another as a rule
for tea. But he was obstinately 'grey'.
He'd never stop to chat
outside his room or on the stairs, as we did.
And the moment term was over, off he'd hitch
back North. We knew, of course, his sort aren't rich.
To get on here, though, more than graft is needed.

xiii   In/Out

Yoga was not yet in. He'd never liked
closed curtains. But he closed them when, one night,
while he was standing on his head or balanced
in some outlandish posture, he suddenly heard
beyond his open window, which looked out
on Iffley Meadow, a burst of stifled laughter—
then whispered words—then footsteps… Having thus
survived two years—as required—on Staircase 8,
he left and rented a room in the ordinary house
of an ordinary kindly working-class elderly couple.

xiv   M.A. (History), Dip. Ed.—The Best Man

My dad had been a process-worker. I
felt privileged living in. But he moved out
into digs as bare as a monastic cell.
No visitors. Later he effed about
in a big cheap grotty bed-sit. You could smell
his need to shog. But why
not stay and use your contacts, if you can?
He wrote bad poetry—sketched his girlfriends nude
(some of his 'art', I'd say, was just plain crude)—
played the recorder. I was his best man.

xv The Kiss of Life

Jude was insatiable—a huge relief,
and in more ways than one—after the one
who nearly drove him mad with one long kiss
had asked him *not* to see her. Well, she'd suffered
a breakdown—always had the lights on (no
poetry, but philology—no love, but sex—
her analyst advised)—turned pale once when
her boyfriend, walking in, inquired *Who's this?*...
After Jude, though, he'd felt completely emptied—
in body, heart, mind, soul—of love, of hate.

xvi What We All Did

Straight after Finals on to a quick B. Phil.
Then the career, what else? That's what we all did.
I signed him in for dinners. I swear he ate
more tuck than any trencherman in hall did!
No money, so he'd bath—drink—fill his plate
for free in college... Still
a child in some ways—careless, naïve, romantic—
at times he'd get so drunk he couldn't stand.
Then Florence. Telling him Clough—who bit the hand
of Oxford—died there was, *I suppose, "pedantic"*...

xvii Art and Nature

Though Wordsworth crossed the Alps to Italy,
he stopped at Como. Ten years later, *The Prelude*,
describing his 'epic' journey, made no mention
of church or painting, sculpture, music—even
of Italian poetry. The mountains had, it seems,
been awful—they'd got lost—the lakeside woods
were alien and unfriendly, loud with insects
which buzzed and stung, with cries of unknown birds.
Nature—was Grasmere... Whereas, to him, Italian
landscape appeared to *be* a work of art.

xviii   The Armchair Romantic

I wish I'd taught him. But, as Research Fellow,
I watched while others did it rather poorly.
The better way in life as well as art
is knowledge and *ideas, Slowly, but surely,*
heart learns to work with head. And head with heart,
or one is bright but shallow.
My armchair's deep. He'd laugh. "I disagree"
his T-shirt should have shouted. His abhorrence
of Oxford may yet sweeten. As for Florence,
perhaps he really was *a scholar-gipsy.*

xix   *Grüße aus 'Monaco di Baviera'*

Two years of post-grad grant were what attracted
him back to *Alma Mater*. How to write
in verse was his real project. Metrical rhythm—
Mozart (*K.201*) in New College Chapel—
and sex—had what in common? The girl in his bed
was not the right one, who, in her red bikini,
had walked along the sunlit colonnade
in the *ostello* where he'd worked, to whom he'd sold
his dinner (part of his pay) half-price—beneath
the former villa's great magnolias' blossoms…

xx   The Supervisors

"You bore," *I thought,* "with your senseless prosody!"—
but murmured, "It's all iambic, is it not?"
He disagreed. I pondered how (and why)
I might get rid of him. Well, I mean, what
a waste of public money! And was I
the published poet, or he?

                    …

We'd moved. Our frightened cats hid up the tree
of our big cupboard. How to get them down?…
I chain-smoked, I'm afraid, which made him frown.
He left without as much as telling me.

xxi *Nach Gardasee*

Lawn Tennyson had taught him all he could.
Likewise the oral / anal American girl
from Florence who came to Oxford. Was it right
or wrong of him to let her stay? And did he,
or did he not, intend to follow her
to far-off California? Changed his mind
perhaps? Or lied? He saw her off… No money
then for the meter, he froze. The red bikini
had moved to Riva, where sub-zero winds
amazed him. As did she. And so he stayed there.

11 THE DEATH OF INNOCENCE

i The Curse

"Enough! or Too much"
– Blake

The apple grew like any other fruit
In that ecstatic garden. But they knew—
Or thought they knew—its knowledge was the root
Of greatness. Till in their growing minds it grew
Like nothing else. The snake's experiment
Was programmed to pollute the atmosphere:
The only knowledge gained was fear
Of losing. And in ways they'd never meant
They now seemed bound to suffer. Since their choice
Would only double-bind them if reversed,
They claimed God's blessing—who were clearly cursed—
And soldiered on, attempting to rejoice
In their achievements. And their fate was such
That their first were last and their last were at least
An unsatisfactory, discontented beast
Condemned, by wanting too much, to *want* too much.

ii Rilke and Others

Early Apollo

As sometimes, when the woods are dry and leafless,
A dawn looks through them that's already bright
With Spring: so there is nothing in this griefless
Face which could shade the almost fatal light

To which all Poetry might here expose us.
For there's no shadow yet in how he sees,
His head's too cool for bay-leaves, and the roses
Will only later grow as tall as trees

And form a garden out of his old brows
Whose single, fallen leaves, when song or hymn
Bursts from his lips, will move where his mouth blows,

Which is still silent—pristine and still gleaming—
And, smiling, drinks in something which comes streaming
As if all song were entering him.

*

Leda

The swan the great god entered in his need
Shocked him—or almost shocked him—by its beauty;
Confused, he disappeared in it completely,
But then, concealed, was driven to the deed

Before he'd even tried to probe or plot
Its unknown *Dasein*. And she—the opened one—
Realized at once who'd come disguised as a swan,
And knew at once: he wanted what—

Confused, unable to withstand
His will—she couldn't cover. Moving lower,
And necking past her weakening hand,

Into his love the god released soul's sap—
And, only then at one with its white power,
Became pure swan in her loved lap.

*

Abishag

"*Now David was old and stricken in years; and they covered him with clothes, but he begat no heat. Wherefore his servants said unto him, Let there be sought for my lord the king a young virgin: and let her stand before the king, and let him cherish her, and let her lie in thy bosom, that my lord the king may get heat.
So they sought for a fair damsel throughout all the coasts of Israel, and found Abishag a Shunnamite, and brought her to the king.*"
– 1 Kings I.1-3

I

She lay there. And her child-like arms were made
Secure by servants round the withering man—

On whom she sweetly lay as time dragged on.
He was so old she almost felt afraid.

And now and then she'd turn and push her face
Into his beard, whenever an owl hooted;
And all that Night was came, crowding the space
Which terror and desire had now transmuted.

The stars were trembling just as she was trembling.
Across the chamber wafted a curious scent.
The curtain moved by itself, like something resembling
Something in search of which her quiet look went.

But she held on tight as he grew darker, older;
And, out of reach of quintessential night,
She lay, feeling his kingly limbs grow colder,
A virgin and as light as a soul is light.

II

He sat enthroned and thought the whole dull day
Of things he'd done, of pleasure and frustration,
Indulging his favourite bitch's wish to play.—
But, in the evening now, Abishag swayed
And arched above him. His crazy life lay
Like a coast abandoned to its reputation
Beneath her silent breasts' curved constellation.

And sometimes, as the lover of many women,
He'd recognize through brows which needed trimming
Her unexcited, kissless mouth. He found
Her callow feelings' green divining rod
Was not to be tugged down to his deep ground.
He shuddered coldly; hearkened like a hound,
And sought himself in his last blood.

*

Saint George

On her frightened knees all night,
Weak and wakeful, "Look," the virgin

Called, "a watchful dragon,"—urging
  Him to come and solve her plight:

"Why guard *me*?" On his pale horse,
  In his glorious suit of armour,
  Bursting forth, to cheer and charm her,
  Like the dawn—a brilliant force,

Up to whom, still kneeling, she
  Gazed: along the downs he thundered
  Brightly, raising his two-handed
  Weapon, much too dangerously,

And too dangerous, even though,
  Praying harder, as a woman
  On her helpless knees, she'd summoned
  Him to save her—could not know

How her heart, so pure and willing,
  Dragged him down from God's heaven-filling
  Light. Her prayers, while he was killing,
  Grew as tall as towers can grow.

*

The Unicorn

The saint looked up. And prayer slipped from his mind
  As a helmet falls from the head—distracted
  By the silent, unbelieved-in, never-expected
  Animal drawing near like an abducted,
  Helplessly pleading, all-white, wide-eyed hind.

The creature's long, stiff legs of ivory-white
  Moved forward with an easy, balanced tread;
  A blessed gleam went gliding through its coat,
  And on its lucid, peaceful, beast's forehead
  Its horn shone like a tower in bright moon-light,
  And rose as each step forward raised its head.

The mouth, beflecked with rosy, greyish foam,
  Was puckered, and the white teeth, shining through—
  Whiter than all—gleamed in the glade's pale glow.

The slightly panting nostrils noticed who
Was there, whereas its gaze, which no
Object restricts, cast visions on the gloom,
Weaving a saga cycle in deep blue.

*

The Carousel

    (Jardin du Luxembourg)

Rotating in the shade of its bright roof,
For a little while this gaily coloured stand
Of horses from the slowly vanishing land
Of childhood moves, though they don't move a hoof.
Though some are hitched to coaches, they don't pant;
But all of them have brave and eager faces.
A fierce red lion puts them through their paces,
And now and then a pure white elephant.

As if through trees, a stag swings into view,
Wearing a bridle, reins and saddle, where
A little girl is buckled, dressed in blue.

And, on the lion, a boy—not yet a youth—
Rides white and holding tight with one small hand.
The lion itself exhibits tongue and tooth.

And now and then a pure white elephant.

And, on their horses, riding through the air
They come; and fair-haired girls who—if the truth
Were told—are too mature for such uncouth
Horse-jumping, looking here, there, anywhere—

And now and then a pure white elephant.

And so it hurries past to its conclusion,
And whirls and circles on without an aim.
Reds, greens and greys in colourful profusion;
A profile, hardly worthy of the name;
Sometimes a smile, as if in sweet collusion,

Still dazzling—blessed—and wasted on the illusion
Of this blind, breathless game…

*

Portrait of my Father as a Young Man

The dream-filled eyes. The brow's strong predilection
For far-off things. About the mouth enorm-
ous youth, and unused smiles of seduction,
And—posed before the braided, laced perfection
Of the tightly fitting, noble uniform—
The sabre's knuckle-guard and both hands, which
Are quiet and wait, not pushing and not pushed—
And, now, almost invisible. As if such
As touch the distance vanish. And
The whole is veiled within itself—and hushed—
And dimmed as if we couldn't understand;
And its deeply clouded depths hold out no hope.—

You quickly fading old daguerreotype
In my more slowly fading hand.

*

Spanish Dancer

As in the hand, before it really burns,
A match's sulphur head, from all sides, sends
Out white-hot, flickering tongues, so now she turns
In quick, bright, flickering circles, hotly warns
Her audience back to where the dance extends.—

And suddenly the whole full flame is there.

And, with a single look, she lights her hair;
Abruptly turns, and sets her dress alight
With daring art, and heated appetite;
And raises naked arms like rattling snakes,
Which her fire-dance alarms—and now awakes.

And then, as if the fire were burning low,
She gathers it all up—only to throw

It proudly down, and gestures proudly, glaring
At where it hits the ground, still madly flaring
And raging on, consuming time and space...
But now, assured of victory, with a sweet
Familiar smile, she raises her fine face,
And stamps it out with powerful little feet.

                    *

The Panther

    (In the Jardin des Plantes, Paris)

Bars pass and pass. His stare no longer rages
But, utterly tired, can't hold things any more.
He sees a thousand bars. Beyond his cage's
Bar after bar, no other world is there.

His soft lithe slouch hunts down no weak tormentor
But, circling on and on with short sharp turns,
Is like a dance of power around a centre
In which his great dazed will no longer burns.

Sometimes, the curtains of his pupils sliding
Open, a silent image soothes his eyes—
Enters his tense, still bulk. Till, swiftly gliding
Into his heart, it dies.

                    *

Morgue

They lie here, as if waiting to be told,
Belatedly, some tale to reconcile them
To one another and to this deep cold,
Some plot or plan to enliven or inspire them;

For nothing here has ended, nothing has changed.
What sort of names—for which undying truths—
Are found in inside pockets? Someone has washed
The worn-out sadness round their mouths,

But failed to shift it; cleaned it, anyhow.
Their beards still sprout, the bristles somewhat harder
But tidied up—whose conscientious warder

Spares starers any sickness or surprise...
Behind their weary eyelids their cold eyes
Have turned, until they're looking inward now.

iii   At Rilke's Grave

> "... *This time the examination showed that he had leukaemia in a rare and especially painful form that first manifests itself in the intestines and in the final stage produces black pustules on the mucous membranes of the mouth and nose. These burst and bleed, making it difficult for the patient to drink, so that he is plagued by thirst as well as unremitting pain.*"
> – W. Leppmann, *Rilke: A Life*

"*Rose, oh reiner Widerspruch, Lust,
Niemandes Schlaf zu sein unter soviel
Lidern*"

*

Rilke's Last Poem—Sanatorium Val-Mont, December 1926

Come then, you last—incurable—amazing
Torment: I feel you spreading through my body.
I blazed in spirit—whereas now I'm blazing
In you. The wood resisted, but is ready
To accept your flames now—cease to try to quell
You—feed your furious presence—nurture you.
My earthly mildness turns to a final hell
Of pain, like fire which has no then—no now.
Free of all futures, planless, and quite pure,
I have ascended this chaotic pyre,
Certain that nowhere, for my hoarding heart—
Now silenced—can a future still be bought.
Is it still I who burn? No memory shows me
Who I once was. Fire turns all memories
To ash. O life, o life—outside of this.
And I in raging flame. Here no one knows me.

*

Consumed at last by pain like fire,
Rilke composed for his own or any
Gravestone:

"Rose, oh pure contradiction, desire
To be no one's sleep under so many
Eyelids"

    iv   An Ordinary Day

As if you dreamt you were lying
On a beach in the summer sun.
But abruptly started crying
For help as the tide came in.

As if your cries were silent:
How *could* anyone help?
Electric terror jangled
From your knees through your groin to your scalp.

And the ice-cold sea came crunching
  Closer. Soon its grey waves
Would bundle and lock your body
  Into an unmarked grave.

"Not fair! Why me?" you spluttered.
"I've always done my best
  To write about what mattered;
  I'm a cut above the rest…"

As if the salt and bitter
Water could really drown
Your spirit. As if its current
Could drag you down and down.

Until, in your dream, you were watching
  Your burbling face turn blue;
  Until, absurdly, you realized
That all you needed to do

Was stand and walk out of the water
To where the beach was dry.

Which you did—and awoke. To the quietness
Of an utterly ordinary day.

v   The Blessing

   (after Chuang Tzu)

   "Who knows that life and death, existence and annihilation are a single body? I will be his friend!"
   – Chuang Tzu, ch.6

(i)

The Chinese Masters Yü and Ssu
Agreed in their hearts with Li and Lai
That all a Master has to do
Is be content—to live, to die…

When Master Ssu's white horse ran off,
His neighbours blamed it on bad luck.
But the horse returned with three wild mares:
Ssu thought, "What's bad? What's good?"

While breaking in the mares, Li's son
Fell and injured his back.
But imperial army recruiters took
His neighbours' sons: "Good? Bad?"

Li's son lay helpless on his bed.
Enemy soldiers came
And burnt the village. Now Li wept,
Even *if* all luck is the same,

For his only son… "But who can own
The stars, which take and give?
Things merely happen. I alone
Must make them die or live.

"And man alone, of all that dies
Beneath the silent sun,
Is blessed with procreative eyes—
To make things, or undo what's done…"

(ii)

Suddenly master Yü fell ill.
His body, twisting in a knot,
Grew crippled. Unconcerned and still,
Yu smiled on this and smiled on that.

When Master Ssu inquired if he
Was content with crawling on the ground,
Yü wrote in the dust: "To let life be"—
And he laughed—"is Freeing-the-Bound."

The next to ail was Master Lai,
Writhing and wheezing at death's door.
His wife and children raised a cry.
But Lai praised *Less* like praising *More*.

When Master Li inquired if he
Was content to draw his final breath,
Lai smiled: "Life's not at fault. To free
The bound, I praise my death."

Then Ssu and Li burst into song:
Sick Yü and dying Lai were right,
Content with change in the changeless Night.
How could the Way itself be wrong?

Opus 3, No.2: Afterwords

All that we are *is the result of what we have thought; it is founded upon our thoughts, it is made by our thoughts.*
Dhammapada 1

*

You will not be master of others or their slave… I want his life still to be his, mine to be mine.
James Joyce, *Ulysses*

*

… if way to the Better there be, it exacts a full look at the Worst.
Thomas Hardy, *In Tenebris II*

*

I am responsible for everything, in fact, except for my very responsibility, for I am not the foundation of my being… I am responsible for my very desire of fleeing responsibilities…
Sartre, *Being and Nothingness,* IV.1.III

1   A BRIEF PRELUDE (2)

"I remember ten or twelve images from my childhood, and I try to forget them. When I think of my adolescence, I am not resigned to what I was; I would have preferred to be someone else. At the same time, all this may be transmuted by, may become a subject for, poetry."
– Borges

i   Words Mattered

Miss Philips had big teeth *("All the better*
to bite you with, my dears!") but seemed quite kind
the day his mother came to school as well.
They talked about his writing: he'd spelt "and"
adn (and so on)—but why was that so bad?
His mother was very clever, but had failed
the grammar-school exam because of illness—
her mother's fault who'd sent her, ill, to sit it…
He copied reams of *Lollipop Wood* to try
and please her. She never read his writing again.

ii   Infants' School Headmistress

I remember the Jackson children. I told the eldest—
a two-faced smiler, or I'm much mistaken—
he'd miss his special treat because his birthday
fell in the hols. Next year it mightn't. So
Watch out… *One pull for every year—the bad kids*
harder and by the short hairs. Up on the stage,
*during Assembly. Then—*Hands together, close
your eyes. "Our Father, which art in heaven…" *I kept 'em*
standing to attention. No need for caning. My methods
caused tears, but left no welts or swollen fingers…

iii   Apron-Strings: Guilty Until Proven Innocent—

Or: *if you're good, you're bad* ("Who do you think
you are?"). Or: *if you can't, you must* (say, *write*
this sentence / *name this thing*). Or: *if you want to,*

you mustn't (look, or cuddle, or cry—"There! Now
you've something to cry about!"). Or: *if I'm wrong,
I'm right (I'm always right)*. Or: *if you did,
you didn't* (and: *if you didn't, you did*). Or: *if you
don't try, you're lazy*—*useless*—*bad*. And: *if you
try, you'll be laughed at, then be laughed at if you
fail*—*or succeed…*
                      I think this marred him / made him.

iv   Sunday School

*Their father sold me a worthless life-insurance
and something that failed to cover my stolen bike…
After his Sunday dinner he wanted a snooze,
so all five children went to Sunday School—
I taught them. I'd see them sometimes crossing the bombsite
or 'field', where scruffy neighbours' kids were booting
a ball—dolled up in their clean clothes and carrying
Bibles, a little group of martyrs—despisèd
and rejected. Four learned nothing. The eldest "dared
to be a Daniel"—loved the songs, the texts, the stories…*

v   Stiff as a Poker

Some things were clearly sinful, others not.
But this? Or was the way that God had made him
somehow not right? St Paul said *Better not burn.*
But God himself appeared as a burning bush
and spoke with Moses… One job he'd always liked,
early on cold dark mornings, was lighting the fire.
Starting from underneath, some glowing embers
from yesterday, perhaps—then paper, firewood—
firelighter, coal. The poker let in air.
If left, it sometimes turned red-hot. So did he.

vi   Head in the Clouds (2)—Speech Day

*The Headboy's Speech on Speech Day was pro forma,
but he surprised us all—even me—by, firstly,
having the amused / amusing nerve to admit*

he was as nervous as Belshazzar, weighed
in the balance—thoughts troubled, joints loosened, knees smiting
against each other. And then by making a plea
for friendly cooperation, order, effort,
in the microcosm a school's best seen as. The speech
was cheered and applauded. We'd read The Problem of Pain
in class. I briefly forgot my pain, my problems.

vii   The School Chaplain

"The mountain snob is a Wordsworthian fruit"
– Auden

His friend the process-worker's son, who'd won
a place at public school, then Oxford, told him
they'd nicknamed him *Big Dick*. Blinded, misled
by his dog-collar, his parents never noticed
what he, misled as well, found puzzling—then queer.
His brother went to that school, too. The Chaplain
loved lakes and mountains. Pig-like, greedy eyes
in the rear-view mirror. They stayed at a cottage in Wales.
Its (single) owner leered—the Rector chatted…
"Boy Smashes Rector's Skull with Cue" came later.

viii   The Oxford Blue

Though captain of Wirral Seconds for two years—
First team when their scrum-half was playing for England—
he claimed he'd become 'unclubbable'. Wouldn't train
at first—then play… As head of our Christian Union,
I tried as well to stop his Eastward drift.
He came for weekends to North Wales. We walked
and talked. But then he dropped us. Something was wrong
with how he couldn't conform, join in… To try
and win is human nature. "But competition,"
he insisted, "is self-destructive." *I said,* "You loser."

ix   Byron *et al*

Playing Romantic Poet was no help.
Nor getting drunk—nor smoking dope—nor drugs.
Politely—quietly—dropping people who *would* not
live and let live but strove to put down others
made a real difference. And reading—that classic mode
of meditation—made another: Byron
discarding his former snake-skins—Lawrence, who mocked
the Oxford voice, who knocked great holes in how
we'd come to see things—Joyce, with his "silence, exile
and cunning"—Shakespeare's, Chaucer's *"gentil herte"*...

x   William Brown and Father Michael

I learned to cook at sea, while running away
from home. When I was young, poor Oscar's trial
was recent history... My family was deeply Catholic:
I was quite sure I'd go to Hell, but couldn't
help how I was... I cooked for the Duke of Marlborough
later, where half the staff was cock-eyed. Michael
was my confessor. He told me, "Listen, Bill,
God made you that way: how can it be a sin?"
Deeply relieved, I retired to my birthplace in Oxford.
He weeded my garden. Nice boy. I made tea, told stories...

xi   Wm Shagspere

By Summer '68 he'd finished reading
Shakespeare from start to finish for the first
time—not the last—missing the demos, less so
the girls... In '69 he cycled to Florence.
Shakespeare knew how to get by boat from Padua
to Venice—how Jews and blacks were seen there. Saw
Titiano's *V & A*, perhaps—or *Lucrece*—
and *Marsyas?*... Knew in the end—had always known—
if William the Conqueror came before Richard III,
He who had conquered no one came before both.

xii   Cambridge Lawyer

They thought I'd had a breakdown. Psycho-babble
presumed that wearing black meant 'deep depression'…
My back was killing me—took too much codeine
and fainted, I think… "I have a rare rheumatic
condition," I neglected to tell them—I told them nothing.
Playing 'my brother's keeper', *my Christian brother*
dashed straight from Oxford, sod him: he thinks he's Jesus…
The shrinks prescribed a year at home, which served
'home' right. They fetched me. Mother kept on puking
beside the car. Was that supposed to be my *fault?*

xiii   From *Liverpoolio* to Florence

Tired of familial binds and clinches—*live*
and let die—you lose if you win / you win if you lose—
of Oxford's superior voices: why not leave them?
To stay would mean more compromise than he
could freely handle. Italy meant new faces
as well as places. Like Jonah, he took
his demons with him. But not to play the game
cancels the game. To cycle there alone
against the Mistral, along the *Côte d'Azur,*
defying old / new fears, lightened his darkness.

xiv   Letters Home

   "[He] was morally duplicitous, as all men are."
   – Borges

He'd always had bad habits—wrote his letters
in barely legible pencil on scraps of paper…
Such nonsense too. Here's one advising me
to read more—watch the telly less—as a help
against old age: I must have been forty! Another
from Florence to tell us Italy's the most
"gloriously beautiful country": I and dad
must see it all one day—we could stay in hostels…
Too much about too many stupid girls…
He'd ask for family news. But did he want it?

xv   Red Light—'Make Love, Not War'

"Was it a vision or a waking dream?"
– Keats

Florence was full of young Americans who
had left *their* homes to dodge the risk of dying
like dogs in Vietnam. An artist friend had a studio
in town. Out late one night with a foot-loose girl
from London, having kissed and groped for an hour
behind Medusa's head and *The Rape of the Sabines*
at the back of the *Loggia,* they called and were offered
a mattress in a small hot windowless store-room…
Beneath a bare red light-bulb, as never before
or since, the world was changed… Or did he dream it?

xvi   Landscape Painter

I thought we were good friends. There was something false
about his niceness. That girl he had in the store-room
was mine. He helped himself—as he did to wine
from the kitchen where we worked. Got drunk in the campsite—
some girl again—flaked out on the grass—was caught
by the cook, breaking and entering, bottle in hand,
through the back way in at dawn. No big offence there—
the boss's daughter stole from the hostellers' clothes-line.
But his sense of right and wrong was barely adult.
I work hard still—paint dogs now, too. Good business.

xvii   A Wordsworth Editor

"And so we all of us in some degree
Are led to knowledge"
– Wordsworth

Returning to *Alma Mater,* he remembered
the friendly don he'd met on the grass at Stratford
while sunning himself in cycling shorts in front of
the Shakespeare Theatre. He'd failed to get his First,
but this nice white-haired gent was so impressed
by his knowledge of Wordsworth (he thought) that he'd arranged

a grant… The note said "Come to tea at Balliol…"
But nice turned nasty when he firmly removed
don's hand from cyclist's thigh. Soon threatened, the grant
looked lost . He rallied. Read and wrote—regained it.

xviii   Fresher

My school was an old-fashioned boarding school.
Some girls got into trouble. Most knew nothing,
outside of dreams or nightmares, about boys…
My parents warned me: Oxford men had changed.
Since 1968, sex, drugs and drink
were all the rage. At school my favourite teacher
told me Take care… *Though lovelorn, I was slow*
to fuck—and so he dropped me. No note, no phonecall,
nothing… I had a breakdown. Later, I passed him
on Banbury Road. No greetings. I looked at the pavement.

xix   Shopping in Oxford

The oral-anal 'Sunshine Girl' was no
shop-lifter. Nearly nabbed once, they ran off
through the crowd outside… He had, perhaps, been made
to feel so vaguely guilty at all times
that kicking against the pricks could easily lead
to harming others: *live* forgot *let live*,
reaction forgot *free action*—and *forget*
forgot *forgive*. In Florence, later, he stole
a toothbrush. *Handcuffs!* the manager mimicked, laughing.
Humbled, he laughed as well—and dropped that game.

xx   Intensive Care

He's been to visit, briefly, from Munich. My eldest—
most useless—son…

     But this isn't for Oxford cissies…

—*St Paul's still stood. There was a service there.*
Some of them had one leg, as I have now.

*I also have bad dreams. Of messmates wounded
and screaming—one in my arms—on Crete. Of coal-mines—
lost in the dark, our lamps kaputt—feet frozen
in rags. The camp ran out of socks, clothes, everything…
Still, the black market flourished—chocolate, ciggies
for cheese, ham, bread. And that nice girl in the village…*

xxi   Blame and Responsibility

Blaming one's parents is always a mistake,
perhaps. But how responsible *is* one / *was* he—
then a mere child—for feeling terrified
by terrifying behaviour? His father—veins swollen
with rage—loud shouting—hatred—big hard heavy
hands… Afterwards, guilt, withdrawal. No words, no love.
Just as if nothing had happened. Just as if!…
And still the question nags. Can such old wounds
be healed by my responsibility here
and now for how I say them? *Is* thought free?

2 SELF-PORTRAIT AS A WHITE-COLLAR WORKER (4). *OR:* OCCUPYING NO-MAN'S-LAND

"The poetry doesn't matter"
– T.S. Eliot

i Working for the Enemy

No work on "our side" meant that he—"like a spy"—
Felt forced to slave for umpteen years on "theirs":
For the sake of his art, he claimed—to leave it free
Of markets, fashions, cliques, to do or be
Whatever it needed. At last, the job and its cares
Silenced him. Left him puzzling over why.

He thought he'd grown, perhaps, to believe his lies:
At first we act them, then we act on them.
Once an escape from the gold-and-ivory tower,
"Useful experience" had gradually assumed more power
Over his heart and mind—by guilt and shame
As well as muddied, muddled compromise—

Than he'd ever expected. Though he held that art
Can swallow any subject—even the pride
Of the wounded artist—he knew as well that he ought
To have left that place where bodies and souls are bought,
Whose ways are all dead ends, where he might have died—
Of stomach cancer, say, or a stricken heart—

But, dully, suffered on. Self-punishment
Takes many forms. A more or less settled gloom
Grew slowly thicker, rarely now relieved
By doing things in which he still believed—
By looking forward to less fear, less boredom—
Or saying, for instance, what he really meant.

Disgusted, insecure, self-alienated,
Yet still condoning corporate power and greed,
He also told himself such sacrifice—
Which only went to show how little choice

We really have—was needed if the needs
Of his family were to be accommodated…

And so he managed. While others managed the world.
But art needs deep slow truth, the spiralling peace
Beyond all understanding. Not, of course,
As therapy, or some hermeneutic pause
In the race for gold. Or even here. But at least
As an end—in view or not—whereto we're swirled

Like eddies in a stream. We write to live;
He lived to try and find the time to write:
"What poets need above all things is luck!—
Plus native wit, perhaps, or witless pluck—
To help them through this fight that's not their fight,
This give-and-take that's only *take* not *give*…"

And yet, when he retired, he wished he'd done
Something to try and curb the booming harm
To human nature and/or the Nature we share—
Their actual earth and water, fire and air—
Instead of (in secret) sounding a quiet alarm
In ever fewer words. The enemy won.

ii   Stephanskirchen (1)

> *"The moment that his face I see,*
> *I know the man that must hear me."*
> – Coleridge, *The Ancient Mariner*

Although he thought he'd get what he deserved—
An unfulfilled, dull, unfulfilling life—
"The observer must be more than the observed,"
Observed his undefeated, German wife…

*

Today, they were revisiting the church
Of a tiny village—*Wirtshaus,* school, two farms—
Which an Allied bomber (lost perhaps) in search
Of other targets, riding an Alpine storm,

Hit and destroyed one black and blinding night
In mid-November, 1944:
Re-built on its green hill, and gleaming white
In the Easter sun, the church outlives the war…

Below it, the German landscape Primo Levi
Found "rich and civilized"—vast fields, thick forests,
Geraniums on house-fronts—flourished under the heavy
Aura of the history sun and church forget.

Their last time here—an outing with the firm
The previous summer—an eighty-year-old man,
Or so he claimed, addressed them in a firm
And interested voice, as they began

To read—as visitors will—the fading names
And ages of the local dead, whose graves
He tended—simple epitaphs, brief rhymes,
German for *Rest in Peace* or *Jesus saves:*

"It's nice up here," he'd grinned. "But not down there"—
Where wilting flowers and wreaths half-hid a mound:
"Bavaria's known for *Föhn*—blue skies—clear air—
But you don't get much of that beneath the ground…

Look at this family here, for instance." They'd
Paused by a plain black stone, commemorating
Four fallen sons. Beside them their parents lay—
Rosa and Franz—who'd died a short time later.

One son lived on for thirty years and more.
"Their youngest was my schoolfriend. Here's our teacher.
At over seventy, he taught right through the war.
His daughter was a very pretty creature.

But after I'd gone missing, presumed dead,
She married my best friend. Left in the lurch,
I married hers." And, with a laugh, he'd led
Them both inside the perfectly restored church—

An early Gothic structure with baroque
Statues and gaily painted ornamentation

Which also displayed, no larger than a plaque,
Evidence of almost literal decimation:

Thirty-three *Sterbebilder,* in a frame,
Of Hemhof's war-dead—some no more than boys,
Others not even wearing uniform,
A Nazi or two: *"God gives and God destroys…"*

He'd jabbed a grubby finger: "That one's me.
I turned up later, long after the war
Was over. So they left me. As you can see,
The English dropped in on us once before":

A photo of the church minus its spire
And half its nave. Old Rumpelstiltskin smiled
With teeth askew: "Well, no hard feelings. The fire
That stormy night, though, could be seen for miles.

Or so they say. I was a long way east
Of here by then. And didn't see a thing…
The work's my pastime. Tiring now. At least
Our modern bells aren't difficult to ring"—

And he'd flicked a switch to show them what he meant…
Now, in the unnaturally hot Easter sun,
The six-year winter of war's discontent
Was hard to imagine—and had been so then.

Facing the cemetery, across the lane,
Under an ancient wooden barn's wide eaves,
Six beehives, as in Brueghel, still looked down,
Long empty of their bees, baking beneath

The dazzling, deep-blue sky. The church and woods
And *Wirtshaus* slept in their old Sunday silence…
"There's nothing like the sun—until you're dead,"
He'd grinned again, and gone about his business.

*

Mid-day. And not a sound on either farm.
They entered the old *Wirtshaus* with its thick

Walls and small windows—cool in summer, warm
In winter. Painted eggs, to 'peck' and crack,

Filled nest-like baskets on each table-mat.
The *Wirt,* a former colleague's uncle, brought
Beer and fresh *Bretzeln*. Three or four locals sat
Drinking around their *Stammtisch,* or sunk in thought.

"Last summer," he asked his wife, "do you remember
The 'modern' bells, while the others strolled ahead?—
Our very own Tiresias telling the number
Of the ancient parish church's young war-dead?"—

"Then, after dinner, when he hobbled in,
You joined him—"
                    "Having ordered *zwei Maß Bier*—"
"While the others talked dull shop."
                                    "Ah, well, you win
Some and you lose some. As he said. In here,

Behind you, in that corner, on His cross,
He praised the Son of Man, who lost *and* won,
Like war-torn Germany—which healed its loss
By spinning gold from straw… Well, I've begun

Trying to remember what he said—thought—saw—
And making notes for a long poem on why
So *many* goose-stepped off to Hitler's war…
I went to work—but not, I hope, to die!

He laughed when I said that. He himself knew
He wouldn't die. He'd volunteered before
Being press-ganged by the *Waffen-SS,* who
Did Hitler's dirty work. When asked what *for,*

He seemed less certain: 'Everyone went who could…
Not only because they had to. Many believed
Their solemn duty was to fight for the good
Of *Reich—Volk—Führer*…' Some were less deceived,

Perhaps. But Nazism somehow left you no words
To think with… He—was young and tired of home,

Of farm-work—enclosed by mountains, endless woods—
Of waiting for some change, for things to come…

So why not go, he'd thought—*and* make *things change!*
No one could ever have imagined how
Bad it would get.—*Over that mountain-range*
Life must be better… He knew better now.

As for the crassest fascists, those in thrall
To Hitler's crazed illusions, 'We Germans love
To lead and be led, you know. And *Over all*
Was *Deutschland, Deutschland'*—led from the front and above,

In bold defiance of the League of Nations,
The Amis and the Brits, the French and Poles,
Who'd revelled in the Reich's humiliation,
The injury and the insult of Versailles,

With words—words—words that drove ecstatic crowds
Like herds to roar and bellow, shed hot tears,
Rage, groan, laugh, hiss as one—all armed, all proud
To lose their individual minds and fears—

By someone who, he'd thought, was hardly sane
To start with, and in time became unfit
To lead at all. But they slaughtered and were slain,
Their most inviolable slogan being *Macht mit!*—

First mobbed, then murdered (scapegoat-like) the Jews,
Their 'enemy within', for plotting what
Would further *them.* The Slump was front-page news;
But storm-troopers got good boots, and shirts, and hats.

The Jews were *different*—foreign—self-employed—
Agreed / refused you credit—paid your employer:
'The socialism of idiots' marched to destroy
Their 'threat' to international German power.

The SS motto's counter-threat—*'My Honour*
Is total and unquestioning *Loyalty'*—
Later assigned crack squads the role of goner:
Theirs was to do, theirs not to reason why—"

"He didn't say that."
                              "No. But, towards the end,
The Nazi faithful, fearing the war was lost,
Ran senseless risks. He'd seen whole units sent
To do and die, and not to count the cost—

Youthful fanatics pledge to shoot one another,
Or else themselves, before they'd ever surrender.
And dares were rife. Old rivals dared each other,
Outfacing their own fears, to kill—rape—plunder…

The *Wehrmacht's* last-ditch orders were to destroy
Revolt or armed resistance, where they unearthed it,
'With the utmost ruthless harshness'—to deploy
Round-ups, reprisals, terror to deter it:

Mercy or pity was mere Christian weakness.
Not that he'd ever held such heathen views;
But for some the faith of Jesus was a sickness
To sap the strong—hatched by (who else?) the Jews.

Others, though, blamed the Jews for killing Jesus.
Every loud weakling found some cause to hate them:
Unfairly clever, powerful, rich as Croesus…
Perverts and numbskulls strove to exterminate them…

Not being a coward, he'd had no need to prove
His manhood by inhuman, sick excesses.
Homesick and sex-starved and, worse, starved of love,
They fought, and dreamt of *Lilli Marleen's* caresses.

But you might as well waste food or ammunition
As spill your beans in war. Not soft but hard
Options meant *'Pleasure generates submission'*:
The sentimental rapist's off his guard—

And, *post coitum,* swings from sad to mad…
—I elaborate again. But, veteran or callow
Sixteen-year-old, true troopers had to be led.
Where wise or crack-brained shepherds go, herds follow…"

—"*'Goats to the left and sheep to the right.'*"
                              "*They're split*

Without much bother...' But 'our surest defence
Is something that can't be feigned—faked—imitated—
Or even shared'—and yet makes (common) sense.

Whereas the force and lures we all deploy
To get what we've been schooled—drilled—fooled to desire
Still now, with quiet legality, destroy
Our souls in the great industrial / military fire...

Like war, like work. Ambition—slogans—fads—
Or (as Bavarians say) if you drive a sow
Up the main village street, for good or bad,
Every fool tries to ride her. Then, as now,

It struck and troubled, strikes and troubles me
How nations vie like firms—how firms deploy
Their work-force like a peace-time army. We
Are briefed who to compete with, who to destroy—

Receive our orders, which we leap to obey,
Or more or less adjust to suit ourselves,
Proud of our mission, treating perks and pay
As signs of status, which all work involves...

At such a time as that, in such a place,
How many went to war in much the same
Bad faith as we to work at such as this:
Because we've learned that *'History is to blame'*?

It seems, at least, that governments, like boards,
Direct or try to choose their people's fate—"
"You chose retirement."
                              "In less retiring words,
Those killed in friendly fire left it too late!

They soldiered on. Most businessmen find peace
To their advantage. But unrestricted growth
Struggles for unrestricted means—for space
In which to grow. War is the blinding truth

Which follows as the night follows the day
When phoney friends expire. The business mind

In-forms us, pouring oil on the barbed-wire way
Down which the war-like blind then race the blind…

The paths of glory lead we all know where.
Big / bigger / biggest business names the game,
And no one can tell which future horrors war
Hauls in its wake but *More (and more) of the same.*

While 'business as usual' booms / busts / booms, though, we—
As individuals—can, we know, survive
Either by emigrating inwardly—"
"By compromising?"
                        "Or, defiantly alive—

As Rumpelstiltskin knew he wouldn't die—
By exploiting what we find. He flowed with the flow:
By raising no resistance to today
Fought on—and puts the past behind him now…

Others he'd known who, half in love with pain,
Waiting for orders, trained to hear and obey—
Too passive, with too little will of their own—
Soon died, losing themselves, or lost their way.

While many who went because they'd always done
As they were told—or (with no real idea
Of why their brothers, neighbours, friends had gone)
Because so many that they knew were there—

Soon died as well. In war you had to *fight*
Not just the enemy but senseless orders,
Lack of equipment, boots, food: every sort
Of lousy luck—foul weather—ill-mapped borders—

And, towards the end, the total madness of
(As no one dared say then) the Berlin bunker,
Whose Nordic *Götterdämmerung*—in love
With Death itself—dragging the whole world under,

Went under first. Under the circumstances,
Bigots who'd joined the *Heer* convinced they ought
To do their German duty lost their senses
As *Deutschland, Deutschland* lost all sane support…

Most genuine fascists weren't tough farmers' sons,
Or Catholics like himself, but middle-class
Embittered townees, strapped, hard-done-by since
The Kaiser's 'place in the sun' had risen and passed.

At home, before he'd left, more than a few
Had laughed at Hitler. Not that there was much
That farmers, hop-growers, fishermen could *do*
Or even say. Apart from wait and watch…

Shop-keepers, teachers, lawyers, white-collar workers
Of every kind had lost their lives or their nerve.
By avoiding heroes, burn-outs, drunks, berserkers
And cowards, he'd hoped and managed to survive…"

—"Where I grew up, the eldest son of three,
On hearing (the story went) his wounded brother
Had died in Warsaw when the Infirmary
Came under fire, had horrified his father

By angrily hanging Hitler's official portrait—
Among the other rats and bugs, he said—
Behind the pigsty, in the outside toilet.
The father, swearing they'd all end up dead,

Lugged it back in. Their youngest, home on leave,
Had tried to crush one foot with the big stone
For pressing kraut. Each time it dropped he'd move
The foot away. At last, they cracked a bone,

But only three months later he was sent
With other bumpkins less than fighting keen
On Hitler's war, to man the Russian front.
He got to Moscow—and was never seen

Again. His friend who'd helped him with the stone
Had long been badly wounded. Soon to die,
He transported his whole family from bombed Köln:
More food, no air-raids, milk, a star-filled sky…

He also had two children (one was me)
With different women. Thus his last two years
Passed quietly. He emigrated inwardly.

The village was like this one."
                              —"Though, it appears

When Rumpelstiltskin walked back out of the war
Between the woodland lakes along the track
Or *Römerweg* from Seebruck, the church looked more
Like Dresden or Berlin. Relieved to be back,

He'd swum in Hartsee, then in Kesselsee,
At his old bathing places. Nothing had changed.
Emerging from the wood to see blue sky
But no spire above the full-grown maize felt strange—

Though no one, he'd found, was hurt. He'd helped rebuild
Their bit of history. Everyone helped who could.
Already gummed and framed, his *Sterbebild*
Was left among the well and truly dead.

They wanted peace, not war, to have the last word,
He claimed, and sank that block of stone in the earth
To say it: 'GIVE US PEACE IN OUR TIME, O LORD'
It pleads with empty heaven. For what *that's* worth."

—"Perhaps such prayers aren't only a waste of breath,
If the speaker *hears* them…"
                              "Over their stone the plain
Black cross with 'IN THE MIDST OF LIFE IS DEATH'
Across its wings resembles an aeroplane

Ascending the church's blank, white Eastern wall…
His cheerful fortitude was what impressed me—
His stoical detachment. After all,
With nothing like war's crazed ordeal to test me,

I'd say I managed nothing like as well."
—"You had more choices. But did he have none?
The Nazis' words and deeds were there for all
To hear and see… What if he hadn't gone?"

—"Dachau?"
              "And yet Ernst Jandl, for example,
Called up in Vienna after leaving school,

Defected at the front. Nothing was simple,
But only Nazi thugs or rogues or fools,

Surely, kept fighting? From very early on,
Hitler made public and political use
Of violence—SA terror—such that no one
Could miss it. And so what was *his* excuse

For turning a blind eye?"
                      "He never said
A lot about it."
               "Nor about where he'd been
Either before or after he was 'dead'.
Or what he'd done and not done—must have seen…"

                      *

They paid the *Wirt,* who poured them schnapps—"On the house!"—
And wished them *Frohe Ostern,* asking after
His nephew, other colleagues, and the price
Of beer in England. With greetings and friendly laughter,

They took their leave and, alarmed to find outside
The gathering clouds of an April thunderstorm,
Cycled off quickly down the Roman road
To Gstadt—away from war's forgotten alarms.

iii   after jandl

description of a life

    (i.m. dietrich burkhard)

he has talent
the professor said to my mother.
he's very talented
my mother said to my father.
i have talent, the professor said to my mother
i said to my friend.

my father had a long life.
my father had hardly any white hair left.
my mother stopped plucking her white hair out hair by hair.
women don't want to develop a bald patch.
my father had so much time.
i won't be renewing
our acquaintance.

my name was dietrich.
at fifteen i wrote a tango.
i played the tango for my professor
and the professor said: i'll take care of
your further training and development,
and my mother said to my father
they'll take care of his training.

in 1926 i received my residence permit.
on it is written: 1926 to ....
19 in print and 26 in green ink
to the four printed dots;
the authorities were thinking of the third thousand years.
the authorities think a long time in advance.

my name was dietrich.
i had a talent for useless things.
in 1926 i received my residence permit.
i left primary school when i was nine.
at fifteen i wrote a tango.
at seventeen i passed my exams.
since 1944 i write the number 18
on official forms in the space for my age…

he has talent
the professor said to my mother.
he's very talented
my mother said to my father.
he should apply for something
my father said.
but i didn't apply for anything.

so they made me wear a grey jacket
and sat at home and wrote picture postcards
and cut their nails every day.

we'll take care of his training
the sergeant said to my mother,
and took the stalk of grass from between his teeth;
give that to his professor and tell him
it's not a question of talent, only of training.

my name was dietrich.
from 1926 to 1944.
now i don't have a name any longer.
from day to day there's less of me
and the enormous diggers of death
which for some time now
have quaked across the earth again
accelerate the process
of my further development.

(lebensbeschreibung from *Dingfest)*

what they can do to you

what they could do to you?
they could rip out your tongue.
you were never much of a speaker.
they could gouge out your eyes.
haven't you seen enough yet?
deprive you of your manhood.
you were never much use as a man.
dislocate your fingers.
you shouldn't pick your nose in any case.
hack off your feet.
at your age you ought to sit more.
torture you till you go mad.
everyone thinks you're crazy anyway.

(was sie dir tun können from *Dingfest)*

tell us about the war, dad
tell us how you signed on, dad
tell us how you shot 'em, dad
tell us how you were wounded, dad
tell us how you were killed, dad
tell us about the war, dad

    (vater komm erzähl vom krieg from *Dingfest)*

manner of speaking

i'll
break
you
yet
you
get

fatherbendmerather

    (redensart from *Sprechblasen)*

cromwell

the horizon says goodnight
and chops off heads like trees
hardly have they said amen
before they're spiked on their dreams

mrs cromwell comes and crows till they wake
grafts each head to a neck
paints cuckold blood on the stitches
soon something stirs in the commonwealth

    (cromwell from *Dingfest)*

16 years

thickthdeen years
thentral thdayshun
thickthdeen years
what'th hegoin
what'th hegoin
to do
thentral thdayshun
thickthdeen years
what'th hegoin
what'th hegoin
the lad
what'th hegoin
to do
what'th hegoin
what'th hegoin
to do
thickthdeen years
thentral thdayshun
what'th hegoin
to do
the lad
with hith
thickthdeen years

        (16 jahr from *Laut and Luise)*

she can cook

lots of dogs old women girlsheads and other needs or wishes
all get thrown into the one bucket
when she walks through the streets.
like a housewife home from market she empties on the kitchen table
kraut radishes fruit and prawns out of her shoppingbag
rolls the old women lots of dogs and the girlsheads
like raisins nuts and lemonpeel
in the pastry of her needs
or wishes—opens herself and is the oven
which does the baking. she can cook.

        (sie kann kochen from *Dingfest)*

in the deli

could you give me some maymeadow conserve, please,
fairly high up but not so steep
that you can't sit down on it.

well, then perhaps a snowy slope, deepfrozen,
containing no skiers, and a nice firtree
hung with snow, if you happen to have one.

then what about—hares, i see you've hung some hares.
two or three will do. and of course a hunter.
where do you hang your hunters?

      (*im delikatessen laden* from *Dingfest*)

surfacetranslation (1)

du bist wie eine blume
so hold und schön und rein
ich schau dich an und wehmut
schleicht mir ins herz hinein.

mir ist als ob ich die hände
aufs haupt dir legen sollt
betend dass gott dich erhalte
so rein und schön und holt.

      (heinrich heine)

do pissed v. iron a bloomer
so halt & sean & ryan
hicks how dick ann away mute
sh liked mere inns hurts he nine.

mere hissed al sob hick the end a
ow/eff sow/put deer lay gun salt
bait end ass got dicker halter
so ryan & sean & halt.

      (*oberflächenübersetzung* from *Sprechblasen*)

wht y cn d wtht vwls

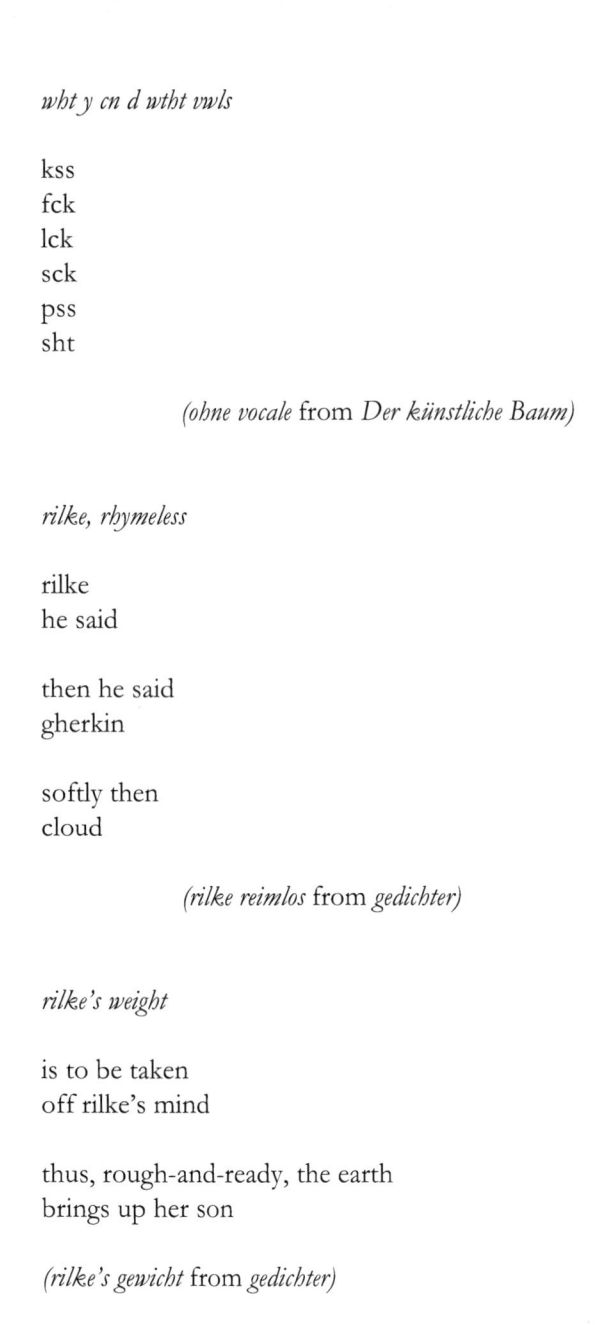

kss
fck
lck
sck
pss
sht

>*(ohne vocale* from *Der künstliche Baum)*

rilke, rhymeless

rilke
he said

then he said
gherkin

softly then
cloud

>*(rilke reimlos* from *gedichter)*

rilke's weight

is to be taken
off rilke's mind

thus, rough-and-ready, the earth
brings up her son

(rilke's gewicht from *gedichter)*

surfacetranslation (2): feel

... o	...o
sophie	sophy
so	so
solo	solo
sophie	sophy
solo	solo
so	so
o	o
so	so
solo	solo
sophie	sophy
o	o
so	so
viel	feel
vieh	fee
sophie	sophy
o	o
so	so
solo	solo
sophie	sophy
o	o
so	so
viel	feel
sophie	sophy
[etcetera]	[ate, set her hair]
o	O
sophie	sophy
so	so
viel	feel
o	o
sophie	sophy
so	so
viel	feel
o	o
sophie	sophy
so	so
viel	feel
vieh	fee
o	o

sophie   *sophy*
o   *o*
so   *so*
viel   *feel*
o   *o*
sophie   *sophy*
viel   *feel*
o   *o*
sophie   *sophy*
viel   *feel*
o   *o*
o   *o*
sophie   *sophy*

         (*viel* from *Laut und Luise*)

sonnet

an a an e an i an o a you
a you an a an e an i an o
a you an a an e an i an o
an a an e an i an o a you

an a an e an i an o a you
a you an a an e an i an o
a you an a an e an i an o
an a an e an i an o a you

an o a you an a an e an i
an i an o a you an a an e
an e an i an o a you an a

an o a you an a an e an i
an i an o a you an a an e
an e an i an o a you an a

         (*sonett* from *Der künstliche Baum*)

otto's mops

otto's mops flops
otto: on, mops, on
otto's mops hops off
otto: oho oho

otto totes coal
otto totes oats
otto stops
otto: mops mops
otto hopes

otto's mops knocks
otto: come, mops, come
otto's mops comes
otto's mops squats
otto: ogodogod

      (*ottos mops* from *Der künstliche Baum*)

owls

you owls
yes
i'm owls

yes yes
very owls

you owls too
yes
i'm owls too
very owls
yes yes

but don't want to be owls any more
been owls too long already

yes
with you here
with you here too

i'm not owls any more
i'm not owls any more either
yes yes
yes yes too

but once you've been owls
you're always owls
yes

yes yes

>   *(eulen* from *Laut und Luise)*

fifth now

> door open
> one out
> one in
> fourth now

> door open
> one out
> one in
> third now

> door open
> one out
> one in
> second now

> door open
> one out
> one in
> next now

> door open
> one out
> you in
> mornin'doctor

>   *(fünfte sein* from *Der künstliche Baum)*

judgement

the poems of this man are useless.

to start with
i rubbed them into my bald patch.
to no effect. they failed to make my hair grow.

thereupon
i dabbed them on my spots. but these
grew as big as potatoes in only a day or two.
the doctors were astounded.

thereupon
i cooked a couple.
somewhat mistrustful, i refrained from eating them,
as a result of which my dog died.

thereupon
i used them as contraceptives
and paid for an abortion.

thereupon
i wore one as a monocle
and joined a better club.
the doorman
tripped me as i entered.

thereupon
i pronounced judgement as above.

      (*urteil* from *Dingfest*)

perfection

e
ee
eei
eeio

p
pr

prf
prfc
prfct
prfctn

ep
eepr
eeiprf
eeioprfc
eeioprfct
eeioprfctn

pe
pree
prfeei
prfceeio
prfcteeio
prfctneeio

prfcteneio
prfcetneio
prfectneio
prefctneio
perfctneio

perfctenio
perfcetnio
perfectnio

perfectino
perfection

        (perfektion from *Sprechblasen)*

higher and higher

THE MAN CLIMBS ON THE CHAIR
the man stands on the chair
THE CHAIR CLIMBS ON THE TABLE
the man stands on the chair
the chair stands on the table
THE TABLE CLIMBS ON THE HOUSE

the man stands on the chair
the chair stands on the table
the table stands on the house
THE HOUSE CLIMBS ON THE MOUNTAIN
the man stands on the chair
the chair stands on the table
the table stands on the house
the house stands on the mountain
THE MOUNTAIN CLIMBS ON THE MOON
the man stands on the chair
the chair stands on the table
the table stands on the house
the house stands on the mountain
the mountain stands on the moon
THE MOON CLIMBS ON THE NIGHT
the man stands on the chair
the chair stands on the table
the table stands on the house
the house stands on the mountain
the mountain stands on the moon
the moon stands on the night

(immer höher from *Der künstliche Baum)*

time flies

fantastic!
fanfantastictic
fanfunfantastictoctic
funfanfunfantastictoctictoc
fanfunfanfunfantastictoctictoctic

(die zeit vergeht from *Sprechblasen)*

antipodes

        a sheet
and under it
        a sheet
and under that
        a sheet

and under that
> a sheet

and under that
> a table

and under that
> a floor

and under that
> a room

and under that
> a cellar

and under that
> an earth

and under that
> a cellar

and under that
> a room

and under that
> a table

and under that
> a sheet

and under that
> a sheet

and under that
> a sheet

and under that
> a sheet

(antipodes from *Der künstliche Baum)*

long load

some people think
that light and reft
can never be
contused.
> Tub bat's

a thig misfake!

(lichtung from *Laut und Luise)*

two handsigns

i cross myself
before every church
i cherry myself
before every orchard

how i do the first
all catholics know
how i do the other
i alone

        (*zweierlei handzeichen* from *Laut und Luise*)

book and nose

it was a book, and again
a book, and another, and another one
and many others; he picked one up,
leafed quickly through it, and then another,
and another one, leafing
and finding nothing, nothing at all
for him.
nothing for him now, till he remembered
dietrich's nose, his blond head
and long thin fingers, which raised
the book, some book, open till it cracked,
to his nose, which then inhaled
its bookish fragrance deeply.
dietrich whose life, before the war
ended, had ended.

        (*buch und nase* from *Der gelbe Hund*)

fallen

he fell, and now
he fell too—he,
often enough, had fallen
on his knee, and scraped
the skin, so that his mother

treated it then
with iodine. But
he fell here sounds so
heavy as if more
must have happened than
a bleeding knee, a burn, a scab
and lastly some pink
now where the scab
has fallen off.

    (gefallen from *Der gelbe Hund)*

contents

i have nothing
to make a poem

a whole language
a whole life
a whole mind
a whole memory

i have nothing
to make a poem

    (inhalt from *Der gelbe Hund)*

iv   Death and Brandner Caspar—A True Story

(after Franz von Kobell)

"But, hark! I'll tell you of a plot,
Though dinna ye be speakin' o't"
– Burns, *Death and Dr Hornbrook*

In 1871, Franz, Ritter von Kobell published a folk-tale in Bavarian dialect—now well known throughout Bavaria—called Die Gschicht von Brandner-Kasper. *In this tale, an old countryman, Brandner Caspar, is sitting alone in his cottage when Death—the* Boanlkramer *or bone-merchant—enters and tells him it's time to go. But Brandner Caspar gets him drunk and wins twenty more years by cheating at cards. Some time later St Peter discovers that Brandner Caspar is still alive and sends Death to fetch him at once. But Death has given his word: what is he to do?*

In the following adaptation, von Kobell receives a letter from Brandner Caspar's grandson. Later, he rewrites the contents of the letter to produce his own version of events:

Wiessee, 6th January, 1841

Dear Prof. von Kobell,
                Many thanks
For your inquiry *re* the *Schwank,*
Or tales told then but since re-told,
Of my notorious grandad. Old,
He took much pride in his reputation
For cunning, cards, and conversation—
And, yes, his bet with Death was the game
Of chance which really made his name…
But let me, since I've got all day
To write—my pupils are away
Visiting their own grandad!—try
To present the past more truthfully.
Locksmith, gunsmith, poacher—*Hail, fellow,*
Well met—old Caspar's fame as a teller
Of *Märchen* led the Brothers Grimm
To jot down three or four from him,
  Especially of the gruesome type,
  Recounted puffing on his pipe,
Which hid him in a cloud of smoke.
And, then, he loved to hoax or joke—
Which made it harder still to extract
The truth from untruth, fiction from fact…

One fact was, when my dad returned
From fighting Bonaparte, he learned
His dad had died the year before
(That is, in 1804),
  Aged eighty. Or had disappeared.
  It even seems foul play was feared:
The woods and hills were searched all round,
  But Caspar's corpse was never found…
  Later, when I was three years old
  Or four, my father, Toni, told
  Me *Brandner Caspar,* just as though
  He were a real-life *Märchen*-hero.
Whereas, in fact, when his wife died

And both his sons were still abroad,
Foot-slogging with their regiments,
Alone and grieving, Caspar spent
His evenings, then his afternoons
And mornings, drinking schnapps, till soon
His friends were sure he'd die as well.
My father used the same old still
For making his own *Obstler*. Even
His brothers, my great-uncles, had given
Poor Caspar up for lost. But then
One Sunday he appeared again
At nearby Gindlalm, unsteady
But hobbling unassisted, ready
To astound his *Stammtisch* pals with what
Had *knock-knock-knocked* the previous night
In Albach at his cottage door.
His two wise brothers, Melchior,
A priest in Gmund, and Balthazar,
Who poured them drinks behind the bar,
Being landlord, were among those who
First heard the tale about which you
Were asking, sir, in your good letter.
Toni would have remembered better—
But let's pretend, though he's long dead,
We know what Brandner Caspar said:

He said, "My brothers—neighbours—friends,
Last night, while musing on our ends
And means, a knock at my front-door,
Where no one ever knocks (the more
So since my dear wife Traudl died),
Amazed me. In the woods outside,
Rain crashed through wildly threshing trees:
Who's out and about on nights like these,
I wondered, *far from their own home?*
On my threshold, hunched against the storm,
As white as if he had no blood,
A sort of rag-and-bone-man stood,
A hollow-eyed and skeletal fellow,
Grasping a tattered, smashed umbrella,
In tramp's top hat and ruined suit,
But very black. And, black as soot,
His boots were too worn out and wet

To warm his bony sockless feet.
So cold he was that the streaming rain,
As if bleak March had come again,
Plastered his brolly with freezing snow.
'Either come in,' I said, 'or go
And the Devil take you.' In he jumped
And hopped on my table. My heart pumped
And pounded. Till the Bone-man said
'Caspar, now that your wife is dead,
I hoped you'd welcome me as a friend.'
But, face-to-skull with Everyman's End,
I instantly sat up straight. A cup
Of well-water helped me sober up
Before I replied, with a clearer mind,
'Well, Mr Bones, it's more than kind
Of you to think of me. I'll do
What I can to prepare myself for you…
Is that your teeth I can hear chattering?'
– 'I'm *always* cold,' he clattered: 'Stop nattering.'
'But before,' I begged, 'I meet my doom,
Allow me, at least, to tidy my room.'
He grumbled, 'Why? All right, be *quick!*'
—'Five minutes ought to do the trick.
But while you clack your heels, perhaps
You'll take, to warm you, a small schnapps?'
'I'm *never* thirsty,' Death replied.
—'Then try a titchy sip.' He tried
A largish one, and hit the ceiling.
Luckily, he can't have had much feeling
In his dead head: 'My G-d, what's that?'
He gasped—and quickly hung his hat,
With *'Christe eleison!'*, over the Cross
In *Herrgottswinkel.* 'That's my Boss,'
He whispered: 'Anyway, His Son.'
—'So, how about another one?'
I poured another, which he swallowed
In a single gulp. The leaps which followed
All round the room brought on a cough
Which might have carried the cougher off,
Had he not been himself the Grim Reaper—
Everyman's brother's undying keeper.
'That's spirits. I'm a spirit!' he
Cackled: 'That's my first joke. Tee-hee.

The bottle's half-empty, I'm half-full:
That's optimism. But why so dull,
My friend? *Prost!* One for your last road!'
—'Now, hold your horses, Bones. I've vowed
To live at least as long, if you please,
As my father, who popped off in peace
At ninety. Hence my long wry face.
Croak now at seventy?! What a disgrace.'
—'But, Caspar, you can't live forever!'
'Ninety,' I stickled: 'If you're so clever,
Let's cut the cards. Whoever draws
The Joker wins. The bottle's yours,
In any case.' Death took a slug.
Dear friends and neighbours, I'm no mug
And, dealing by far the larger heap
To pickled Bones, contrived to keep
The Joker up my sleeve. Thus his sting
Was stung by my crafty card-sharping—
Willy nilly—for twenty-odd years.
His eye-holes might have filled with tears,
Had they been able. As it was,
With a glance at his all-seeing Boss,
He groaned, 'There'll be all Hell to pay—'
'Then *keep* it under your hat! Till the day
I'm ninety. Then I promise I'll come,'
And I crossed my heart to comfort him—
Which gave him such a shock I poured
Us both a big one. 'If I get bored,
I'll let you know,' I offered, to calm
His nerves, and took him by the arm,
But dropped it like an ice-cold curse.
He snickered: 'I'll send my Messengers.
Perhaps you'll change your mind.' With that,
He hop-skip-jumped and snatched his hat
From its holy hat-rack, where it hung
Battered and black, and drunkenly swung
Or lurched, with a curse, through my closed door.
When I unlatched it, Death was no more
To be seen. The night was black as pitch.
'Mind you don't fall in Hiasl's ditch!'
I hallooed after him. But he
Was gone where living eyes can't see."

—Presuming, dear sir, that Caspar, dressed
In his best *Lederhosen,* addressed
His *Kompagnons* at Gindlalm
In some such way; with scarcely a qualm
Had faced his death full on, outstared
The Bone-man's grin, and even dared
To pit his wit against his power
By postponing for so long the hour
Of his arrival: with this tale,
Although still weak and 'unco pale',
His reputation as a sly fox
Was resurrected. When Death knocks
And enters, others leave feet first—
A fate which Caspar virtually reversed
By playing the Joker, as he came
To be known by many. Thus his fame,
Which, if not snuffed, had flickered and sunk
For the long dark months he'd spent as drunk
As Tam o'Shanter, spread as wide
As the city of Munich. When he died,
Some rhymes were found by his bed-side—
Among them this short palinode:

To My Bed

Dear bed, in which I first began
To mewl and puke like any man,
To think and act—or act and think
And, later, drown my thoughts in drink;
Where, stiff with labour, I lie down
And rest my head on eider-down;
When sick, where my poor body lies
To soothe its pain with half-closed eyes;
Where, bowed by cares, I'll even weep
Before I sink into sweet sleep;
Where, long ago, I'd often find
The joys of man- and woman-kind
When Traudl still had all her charms,
Alive and warm in her husband's arms:
Life's centre, where its joy and pain,
Disease or ease, are routed or reign;
Since, in this little kingdom's space,
So many various scenes take place,

The lessons which it has to teach
Are more than books or priests can preach—
That nothing's perfect, good or ill
Are always mingled, do what you will,
While truth and lies which look the same
Depend on what's your aim or game…

Dear bed, where I shall cease to be
When once again Death comes for me.

The question, though, remained—of where
(If not, in fact, into thin air)
The old fox vanished. Though no church-goer,
He and Great-uncle Melchior
Were thick as thieves. The parish priest,
Downing a schnapps, would bless, at least,
The trout or game his brother had poached
Before they ate it. As Death approached
Again, old Caspar soaked up more
Than he had ever soaked before,
My father claimed, who (having downed
So much himself he might have drowned
In such a vasty vatful) tried,
Before he puked his liver and died,
To blame his thirst on the family tree,
One of whose branches, though, is me,
Who have no use for potent drink.
A poor performance, sir, I think,
To decline responsibility
And blame our weakness on those we
Should thank for our existence. Poor
Toni, declining more and more,
Blamed history: "Life's a rotten bitch,"
He'd mutter: "Look in Hiasl's ditch!
You'll find me next to my dead dad.
The Brandner family's gone from bad
To worse…" Or sometimes: "But the worst
Was covered up…" Convinced he was cursed,
He died at only seventy. We
Brandners lie in the cemetery
At Gmund, where Uncle Melchior
Was parish priest. Two years before
He'd buried Balthazar as well…

What really happened? Who can tell?—
But shortly before old Caspar died,
A girl was found, the promised bride
Of, yes, my father, trampled and crushed
By stampeding cows as they kicked and pushed
Across the ditch through a gap in the hedge
Under the pine-trees, at the edge
Of the forest, where they'd stand and shelter
From the raging, blinding, deafening welter
(To which they were accustomed, though)
Of Alpine thunderstorms. I know—
I've checked the records—this poor girl
Was so de-formed from heel to skull
("Severely disarticulated",
As the *post mortem* baldly stated)
That no one at first observed the cut
Into her lower belly. But
Neither could anyone explain
What, more than lightning, wind and rain,
Had panicked thirty cows so badly
They ignored her trusted voice and, madly,
Surged like a river in full flood
For half-a-mile through the storm-tossed wood,
Lowing and lost. When they grew calm,
The *Sennerin* of Gindlalm—
For she it was—lay dead in the mud,
Her tattered *Dirndl* thick with blood,
A victim of bad luck, what else?
The mournful clank of the same cow bells
Could still be heard as Balthazar
Behind his polished brass-topped bar
Parried the awkward chat of inquirers
Or curious hikers over the years.
I heard him more than once, when young,
Explaining how the girl was wrong—
Should have known better than to try
To stop them. What a way to die!
She should have kept well out of their way:
Much more than that he couldn't say...
Though once I overheard him add:

"The storm that day was very bad:
As Melchior, my brother, can verify,

While it was raging he and I,
Visiting Caspar, were forced to stay
Until it finally died away
Later that evening. I heard the news
At Gindlalm… With nothing to lose,
Some cat then spread the vicious lie
That the girl was pregnant—though who by
Nobody cared (or dared?) to imply:
A wicked rumour, who could doubt it?
Even her mother knew nothing about it.
Her fiancé Toni was away
Fighting the French. As sweet as May,
The *Sennerin* went to church, and read
Her Bible. After she was dead,
A girl-friend catted. Whereas in the story
Everyone's heard she goes to glory—
Now would St Peter have installed
An angel who'd been mucked and mauled
To sing God's praises? As for the wound
In her belly, which was only found—
Suspiciously, it seems to me—
Before her funeral, maybe we
Should treat the facts which the tale presents
As the truest version of events…"—

The tale which everyone prefers,
The one you've heard yourself, dear sir,
Which derived, however, from Melchior—
As I discovered shortly before
He died from my schnapps-sodden father;
Though, if you think, it's clear that neither
Caspar—its (missing) hero—nor
The Pearly Gates' saint / janitor,
The sanctified *Sennerin* nor Death,
Could then (if ever) have had the breath
To tell it… After Toni died,
I swallowed my agnostic pride
And took the steamer from Wiessee
To Gmund. What Melchior had to say,
Though aged (he confided) eighty-one,
Hid more than it revealed. He spun
His pious yarn in the shuttered gloom
Of his study. In that book-lined room,

With big old leather-bound dark tomes,
Biblical commentaries, prayer-books, poems,
Lit only by large candles, I
Felt overawed. In Melchior's eye
There might have been a twinkle, while
A knowing or malicious smile—
Except that he hardly had a tooth—
Insinuated, *"What is truth?"*
Until, before I realized,
I felt as good as hypnotized
By his white face and droning voice,
Appearing, weirdly, to have no choice
But to believe his flagrant fiction
And listen without contradiction
To fibs as if they were plain facts—
Though covering which nefarious tracks?—
Also to certain details, sir,
Of which you may not be aware.
I'll try to remember who he said
Did and said what. Now Melchior's dead
Himself at last—aged eighty-nine—
As the last of our tale-telling line,
With neither wife nor child, I intend
To bring it to an honest end...
Crossing himself, and also me,
He began by sacerdotally
Intoning, "My son, how good of you
To visit me. Yes, yes, it's true
St Peter sussed out Caspar... I
At sixty was too young to die
And returned with Death to tell the tale—
Which, after all, could hardly fail
To restore his image. From the start,
I omitted or played down my part,
For reasons of humility,
In Death and Caspar's comedy
And, now, don't get a mention. But
Since, it appears, you're plagued by doubt
And fear, my son, *re* final things,
Let me assure you, pigs have wings.
At least, my brother Caspar's soul
Flew further—higher—on the whole
Than almost anyone expected.

And proven truths must be respected—
The more so if attested by
The witness of a priestly eye...
The *Sennerin,* as you know, had died
Shortly before—the promised bride
Of Toni, marching far away
Or dead himself, perhaps. I'd say—
With the death as well, some years before,
Of Georg, his firstborn, in the war—
Caspar had just about had enough
Of illness, death, and such-like stuff.
The Bone-man's Messengers, he called them.
The *Sennerin's* end confused and appalled him.
I'd gone to try and calm him down,
When in through his closed door a clown
Shocked us by hopping. Almost at once
I recognized the 'Mr Bones'
Of Caspar's tale. 'But just a mo,'
Caspar complained: 'We agreed I'd go
At ninety. That's in ten years' time.'
Bones danced a little pantomime—
Glass—bottle—*pop!*—*glug:* 'Caspar, my friend,
I know when your stint is due to end—
Unless, that is, you've changed your mind...'
—'Not yet... And yet...'
                      'I'm sure you'll find
Your last ten winters sheer delight.'
—'You look like death. Are you all right?'
—'I got the sack.'
                'Oh hell—'
                          'But then
St Peter took me on again—
After he'd wiped Heaven's floor with me—
Provided that... Well, let's say he
Agreed it would be worse than absurd
If Death were not to keep his word:
Why, then, should anybody else?'
—'But how did he latch on?'
                          'A girl's
Sweet soul came knocking at Heaven's gate
And blew the gaff. Her gruesome fate
Fluttered his hard old porter's heart...
But perhaps it wasn't *very* smart,

Caspar, to tell the whole wide world
About our bet: the Porter hurled
His hard old keys at my numb skull,
Calling me *Bonehead! Drunken fool!'*
—St Peter loved a *Dirndl,* and
A nice Bavarian brass-band:
She looked so *brav,* so innocent,
He'd enthused, that like a shot he sent
Her up to sing with wings in the Choir
Invisible, threatening Death with dire
Woe if he touched a drop again…
Whereon Bones grasped what seemed a pain
In his non-existent maw: 'But, perhaps,
Dear Caspar (you know what rhymes), a *schn- - - -*
Would really calm my nerves… And, don't worry,
No one's in any sort of hurry
About exactly when you die.
In fact, I was just passing by…
But won't you, now I'm here, at least—?'
'Melchior—Bones, Bones—Melchior the priest,'
My brother, albeit somewhat gruffly,
Obliged. Death grinned and, bowing stiffly,
Hee-hawed, 'Oho, a man of G-d!'
And kissed my hand with a wink and a nod:
'Planning, perhaps, your life after death?'—
But had to pause to get his breath
After the *Obstler* Caspar had poured him.
A cough and splutter soon restored him
To the best of spirits: 'How can I
Repay such hospitality,
Caspar, my friend?… I'll tell you what:
You can't imagine the *Gaudi* you've got
Laid up forever in Paradise—'
'Well now, I've heard it's very nice—'
'It's heaven itself! Just like Bavaria,
But bluer and whiter, lighter and airier.
Your wife and elder son will be there
To greet you, and your Ma and Pa—'
'Why didn't you tell me this before?'
—'You never asked. But at your door
My coach and horses wait for me:
We could go for a spin if you'd like to see
The treasure neither moth nor rust

Corrupts, when dust returns to dust—'
'Before I die?'
                    'Why not? I know
A spec where you can wave hello—
A ha-ha of sorts—to the Blessed inside…'
I went along for the joy-ride—
Though, passing through a black storm-cloud,
Blinded by lightning, stunned by loud
And close-up claps of thunder, squished
Between my brother and Bones, I soon wished
I'd stayed at home. Before we arrived
At the ha-ha, which (Death joked) derived
From the gap in the wall which Satan smashed
When he and his rebel angels crashed
Out of the blue, we halted by
A peep-hole: 'Since the Blessed don't die,
And the Boss forgot to give me a soul,
I'm locked out, too. But this sweet hole
(I drilled it with my sting) lets me peep
At his beautiful angels.'
                    —'*Pfui,* you creep!
Drive on, drive on!' bold Caspar cried:
'Since most of my former family have died,
We'll have a fine *Familienfest!*'—
And on we drove. You know the rest:
St Peter let Caspar walk inside,
And when he met his wife he cried;
His parents and Georg also ran
To greet him. Heavenly bells began
To ring as sweetly as they rang
In Gmund. The blessed *Sennerin* sang
On high like yodelling down the wind.
And Caspar began to change his mind—
Till, when a cherub flew to say
Death was about to wing his way
Earthwards, he murmured he'd rather stay…
And that," concluded Melchior, "was that."
But if telling history tells us what
We'd like to happen, asking *why*
Tells us about ourselves… If we die,
Like Caspar, in a ditch, or worse,
The story which the world prefers
Will be a harmless *Märchen.* And yet

> The truth is always present… But
> Here come my pupils. Please forgive
> Me if I finish now. To live,
> I work as a tutor. Which consumes
> My life. But you, sir, I presume,
> Will have more time…? Although my sort
> Prefers to test what we've been taught—
> Sift fact from fiction, *why* from *which*—
> The truth needs time. And of those not rich,
> Only the dead can neither want nor
> Work. I remain
>   Your servant,
>   C. Brandner

Postscript

In the version of Brandner Caspar *which Franz von Kobell eventually published in 1871, the Tegernseer* Schlitzohr *and poacher swindles Death by getting him drunk, etc.—as in Caspar Brandner's letter. But no mention is made of the old man's drunkenness. Von Kobell also makes no mention of Balthazar or Melchior; the circumstances relating to the death of the* Sennerin *(who is merely attacked by an angry steer); the fact that the* Sennerin *was Toni's* Verlobte; *or the disappearance of Caspar's body. Both Georg* and Toni *have died fighting for the Fatherland, so that Toni's drunkenness and maudlin suspicions are omitted from the tale as well. Above all, there is no mention of the letter from Caspar Brandner (who died in 1870) which supplied von Kobell with much of his story. What remains, as Caspar Brandner unwittingly foresaw, is, precisely, a "Schwank" or "harmless* Märchen*". As well as suppressing or glossing over the question of "What really happened? Who can tell?", von Kobell turns Heaven into a pastoral idyll where Brandner Caspar is welcomed (with all his imperfections forgotten) by Toni, Georg, Traudl, his parents, friends, the angels and presumably God… In twentieth century versions of the tale, the after-life increasingly resembles Bavaria. The first for the stage was produced in Munich in 1934 and included the heroic death in battle of Caspar's sons. In another, light operatic version Death arrives not on a pale horse but, like* Reichsmarschall Göring *himself, in a little aeroplane. Shortly after the Second World War, the film* Der Brandner Caspar Schaut ins Paradies *(Brandner Caspar in Paradise) was a hit in the south of Germany. By this time the story's idea of Heaven was Bavaria itself… Only thirty years after the war had ended with the* Boanlkramer's *triumph over literally untold millions, the Munich* Nationaltheater, *looking for a Bavarian classic, decided on* Brandner Caspar, *and a new version was written for the stage in which Heaven is a village* Bierfest *with angels in* Lederhosen *partaking of beer,* Weißwurst *and* Bretzeln. *The Devil plays a role so minor that you miss him if you blink. Thirty years later still, with the war a distant memory, a revival at the Munich* Volkstheater *ran to (almost) universal acclaim. Only the oldest Bavarians now were alive at the time of the November Putsch or remember the rise of the Nazis and the SA in Munich and the surrounding countryside. Hitler himself was of course a great lover of the Bavarian mountains and picturesque lakes such as the*

Chiemsee and Brandner Caspar's Tegernsee. And so were other prominent members of the Party—for instance, Reichsführer-SS *Himmler (a one-time chicken-farmer from Waldtrudering near Munich) and his boss, Ernst Röhm, the unruly and ambitious Chief of Staff of the SA. In fact, Röhm's ambitions came to an unruly end in the very village of Wiessee, on the Tegernsee, from which Caspar Brandner wrote his letter. Wiessee was in the meantime a spa town, and at the end of June 1934 Röhm and other SA leaders together with their hangers-on were taking a cure. In the years after Hitler himself had built it up in 1920–21, the SA had swollen to a private army of two-and-a-half million "brawling Brownshirts". Who knows whether Toni and Georg might not have joined it, had they been born in the twentieth century? As its long-standing leader, Röhm had become far too powerful and—even by Nazi standards—disreputable not only for Hitler but for the* Wehrmacht, *to say nothing of Göring and Himmler. The latter (the son of a school-teacher) was a fastidious and, if anything, even more ambitious man than Röhm himself was—a particularly ruthless in-fighter, whose SS was still no more than an arm of the SA.* Schlitzohr *as he also was, Hitler planned to get the* Wehrmacht *on the side of the Nazis by sacrificing Röhm, one of his closest friends in the movement—who had even done time with him in Stadelheim prison after the failure of the Beer Hall (November) Putsch in 1923. He had accordingly presented Röhm with an ultimatum, to rein in and purge the SA or face the consequences, at the beginning of June. But Röhm declared, "The SA is and will remain the destiny of Germany." However, he invited Hitler to confer with the SA leadership on 30 June at Wiessee in the beautiful surroundings of the* Führer's *beloved Bavaria. When not ardently active in the cause, the hard-drinking Röhm—a First World War veteran, the upper part of whose nose had been shot away—enjoyed the company of young men, and Wiessee, with its spa and gambling casino, was a fine resort for a summer holiday. But Göring and Himmler, as his main political rivals, had been feeding Hitler with rumours of plotting and an imminent SA revolt, until the* Führer *(whom no one has ever accused of cowardice) kept his appointment in a way which Röhm can hardly be blamed for failing to foresee. William L. Shirer, who was in Germany at the time and, for all I know, watched the first stage production of* Brandner Caspar *in Munich in the same year, describes events as follows:*

> *At 2 a.m. on June 30th, as Hitler, with Goebbels at his side, was taking off from Hangelar Airfield near Bonn, Captain Röhm and his SA lieutenants were peacefully slumbering in their beds at the Hanslbauer Hotel at Wiessee on the shores of the Tegernsee. Edmund Heines, the SA* Obergruppenführer *of Silesia, a convicted murderer, a notorious homosexual with a girlish face and the brawny body of a piano mover, was in bed with a young man. So far did the SA chiefs seem from staging a revolt that Röhm had left his staff guards in Munich. There appeared to be plenty of carousing among the SA leaders but no plotting.*
>
> *Shortly after dawn Hitler and his party sped out of Munich towards Wiessee in a long column of cars. They found Röhm and his friends still fast asleep in the Hanslbauer Hotel. The awakening was rude. Heines and his young male companion were dragged out of bed, taken outside of the hotel and summarily shot on the orders of Hitler. The Führer entered Röhm's room alone, gave him a dressing down and ordered him to be brought back to Munich and lodged in Stadelheim prison…*
>
> *Hitler, in a final act of what he apparently thought was grace, gave orders that a pistol be left on the table of his old comrade. Röhm refused to make use of it. "If I am to be killed, let Adolf do it," he is reported to have said. Thereupon two SS officers entered the cell and fired their revolvers at Röhm point-blank.*

At the same time in Berlin, Göring and Himmler had been busy removing their SA rivals, among others. In a Reichstag speech in July Hitler admitted to seventy-seven deaths in the purge, which he justified as necessary to stem revolt. However, in 1957, at the trial of Sepp Dietrich—who, "as one of the most brutal men in the Third Reich, commanded Hitler's SS Bodyguard in 1934 and directed the executions in Stadelheim prison" (Shirer)—the number of those who died was estimated at "more than 1,000"... If Der Brandner Caspar Schaut ins Paradies *had catered to the Bavarian idea of Heaven as Bavaria, trials such as Dietrich's showed clearly enough that the same idyllic countryside had once been—and, like any other idyllic countryside, could become again—a department of Hell.*

v   Case Studies, 1941–1945

"The most primitive man says that the horse is good and the bedbug bad, or wheat is good and the thistle bad. The human being, consequently, designates what is useful to him as good and what is harmful as bad…" – Himmler, Minsk, 31 Aug. 1942

(i)

SS-Standartenführer Rudolf Brandt, Persönlicher Referent des Reichsführers-SS

Today he wanted a batch of a hundred shot—
to observe a 'liquidation'—so as to know
what it was like. One blond-haired boy stood out,
with eyes (he told me) of piercing Aryan blue.

He stopped them: "Jewish?"—"Yes"—"Both parents?"—"Yes"—
"Non-Jewish forbears?"—"No"—"Then I can't help…"—
stepped back, and dropped his eyes… Two young Jewesses
were still alive. He yelled out, *"Shoot!* don't torment them!"

Afterwards he made a speech. This repulsive duty
must be fulfilled—though never, by Germans, with pleasure.
He hated blood. But the full responsibility,
after deep thought, was his—before God and Hitler.

He encouraged the *Einsatzgruppe* to think of Nature:
a world of combat. At the top, the Germans.
The weak go under—bedbugs, lice. The strongest nurture
what keeps them strong—exterminate vermin.

*

Rudolf Brandt, 1909–1948, was Himmler's 'Personal Administrative Officer' from 1937 until the *Reichsführer's* death in May 1945. A lawyer by profession, Brandt was described by an associate as "the eyes and ears of his master". As Himmler's omnipresent and indispensable assistant, he complained about being overworked and yet declared with pride that he produced 3,000—4,000 out-going letters per month. Among these letters were a number concerning Himmler's "many lunacies" (Shirer) with regard to medical and other experiments, the organization and co-ordination of some of which Brandt attended to on behalf of his busy chief. After the war, he was charged in the so-called 'Doctors' Trial' at Nuremberg with "performing medical experiments without the subjects' consent on prisoners of war and civilians of occupied countries". Although he had not, of course, performed experiments in person, a note appended to his affidavit includes the comment, "By virtue of his position as administrative assistant to Himmler, Rudolf Brandt played a very significant role in practically all of the crimes with which this case is concerned." He was found guilty, and hanged on 2 June 1948.

(ii)

SS-Obergruppenführer Erich von dem Bach

I did my duty. But, when Himmler ordered
the squad to carry out orders unconditionally,
and keep their conscience clear, his 'good' and 'bad'
were whose? His? Ours? His horrified cry

amazed them. *Herr Reichsführer, that was a hundred,*
I told him: *Look in their eyes. What sort of future
are we creating? Look. These men are done for
as men. Soon they'll be mad, or savage…*

But the shootings broke *me* down. I re-lived our 'work'
in lurid time-loops. As *'eisener Heinrich'*, he liked
my ruthless side, and brought his top doctor: *Get back
for both our sakes. And the Führer's…* But we lied

about the Jews. Our propaganda claimed
this race of helpless, hopeless losers was
helping the Russians, whom they feared. Word came:
Try quicker, cleaner methods. Dynamite. Gas.

*

Erich von dem Bach, 1899–1972, was Higher SS and Police Leader, Central Russia, in charge of numerous killing operations in Eastern Europe—a task which led to a breakdown which seems to have been as much mental as physical (he was operated on for serious stomach and intestinal complaints). Back in action in Poland, where he was engaged in the hopeless fight against Polish and Russian partisans, he disagreed with Himmler over the latter's recommendation that entire villages should be burned down if need be, insisting that "no country can be ruled by police and troops alone" and arguing for a less brutal and less alienating policy which would make use of the Poles' dislike of communism and encourage them to side with the Germans. Nevertheless, in Belorussia, where von dem Bach was in command during 1942 and '43, the death-rate soared. When his men were unable to trap the partisans themselves, hundreds of civilians—many of them Jews—would be shot at a time, leaving heaps of corpses in burning villages... Unusually, von dem Bach's ability to do his repulsive duty appears not always to have blinded him to how things were, and he testified with disarming honesty at Nuremberg regarding "the greatest lie of anti-Semitism", namely "that the Jews are conspiring to dominate the world and that they are so highly organized. In reality, they had no organization of their own at all, not even an information service... Never before has a people gone so unsuspectingly to its disaster. Nothing was prepared. Absolutely nothing."

(iii)

SS-Obergruppenführer Reinhard Heydrich

Am Großen Wannsee, Berlin, 20 Jan. 1942

Mental Notes for Conference re *Jewish Question*

1   Solutions so far

    1.1   Definition of Jewishness—'Law for the Protection of German Blood and Honour', 1935 (too lenient, too detailed, letting too many *Mischlinge* off the hook)

    1.2   Ghettoization: to concentrate Jewish population—sever contacts between Jews and Germans—restrict their housing—control their movement—enforce identification measures—set up and regulate Jewish administrative machinery, culminating in *Reichsvereinigung der Juden in Deutschland* (Feb. 1939)

        —Gestapo empowered to issue orders to *Reichsvereinigung* (July 1939) and all other Jewish councils: senior Jews held personally responsible for communal compliance

        —Almost all Jews in Eastern Europe now in actual ghettos or equivalent: Warsaw, Lódz, Kraków, Lublin, Lwów, Theresienstadt, etc. etc.

2   *'Endlösung der Judenfrage'*

    2.1   Estimated number of Jews (incl. England and Ireland) to be liquidated: 11 million

    2.2   Authorization for SS to proceed with 'Final Solution' across all European and former Soviet territories: drafted by Eichmann, signed by Göring, 31 July 1941 [all conference participants to bow to this *coup*]

3   *Methods to be employed*

    3.1   'SS to victims': *Einsatzgruppen*—mobile execution squads in former Soviet territory—Jews to be liquidated on the spot—launched June 1941, in conformity with 'guide-lines' from the *Führer*

    3.2   'Victims to SS': deportations to Eastern Europe in operation since Oct. 1941—Jews as forced labour (building roads, repairing railways)—many eliminated by natural causes—survivors to be subjected to 'special treatment'

    3.3   Concentration camps equipped with carbon monoxide gassing installations—tested late 1941 at Chelmno (Kulmno), using gas-vans

    3.4   Building of Brackian devices (gas-chambers) in process or planned at Belzec, Sobibór, Treblinka, using carbon monoxide (mainly)—bodies to be buried in mass graves

    3.5   Quicker, more efficient gas than carbon monoxide (experiments at Auschwitz, Sept. 1941)? Easier, more efficient disposal of bodies than mass burial or burning in the open?

*

Reinhard Heydrich, 1904–1942, was Himmler's deputy. Among many other crimes, Heydrich had been the main organizer of the infamous pre-war pogrom known as *Reichskristallnacht*, 9–10 Nov. 1938. As for the Wannsee conference, Heydrich insisted that it be kept top secret, and there was very possibly no written agenda… As ruthless a careerist as his boss, with exceptional clarity of administrative vision, Heydrich was assassinated near Prague only a few months after the conference—for which an estimated 4,500 people were killed in reprisals. But in the face of opposition from the Interior Ministry, the Foreign Ministry, the Eastern Ministry and Hans Frank's General Government, he had got what he wanted at Wannsee—namely, the agreement of all participants that Himmler, Heydrich and the SS were to be "entrusted with the official central handling of the final solution of the Jewish question without regard to borders". Heydrich achieved this by sheer force of personality plus fast thinking but also by means of Göring's letter of authorization, which was news to most of those present and which he read out in full. Although he rarely drank, Heydrich is said to have permitted himself a small cognac in celebration of this—the biggest SS power-grab since the death of Röhm.

(iv)

Heinz Auerswald, Kommisar für den Jüdischen Wohnbezirk, Warschau

The Jews lacked work, lacked food, lacked warmth, lacked strength
to help themselves. One doctor wrote to me—

not long before nine tenths of the ghetto were sent
to be 'resettled'—that energetic, busy

persons reverted to listless, sleepy
half-wits, too *schlapp* to get up to piss
or clean themselves, and drifting (though less slowly
than in old age) towards death, with breath-rate and pulse

subsiding—nothing violent, no real pain.
Those who found food could scarcely chew or digest it.
Heart, liver, kidneys, spleen all shrink. The skin
withers, awareness fades. Death in the street

was common. He needed money. We didn't have it,
and wouldn't have sent it if we had. Our view
was let the *Judenrat* put up its taxes:
Jews always relish blaming other Jews.

*

Heinz Auerswald, 1908–1970, was an SS lawyer and police officer until in 1940–41 he was transferred to the civilian administration of Warsaw and promoted to Commissar of the Warsaw Ghetto—a post he occupied until shortly before the famous Jewish armed resistance of April–May 1943. Auerswald is said to have been polite but heartless and to have insisted that 'punishment actions' against Jews be carried out by the Jewish Council, whose chairman, Adam Czerniaków, eventually killed himself. Jewish ghetto councils were also forced by the German authorities to raise funds from taxes—for example, on those who worked, those who were exempt from work, postal services, rents, rationed bread, medicines, and even cemeteries. As recorded in Claude Lanzmann's *Shoah,* the cemetery tax was one reason why there were so many corpses on the streets: their families could not afford to bury them. "When deficiencies occur," Auerswald noted with satisfaction, "the Jews direct their resentment against the Jewish administration, and not against the German supervision", as Heydrich clearly intended when setting up the administrative machinery of the Final Solution. Meanwhile, the ghettos were being emptied by deportation—again through the agency of the Jewish councils. In Warsaw, the main deportations took place in 1942. In the end, most of the ghetto's original 445,000 inhabitants perished, either through *'Aussiedlung'* (resettlement) in Treblinka and elsewhere or in the ghetto itself. Conditions in the Polish ghettos were allowed to deteriorate to so atrocious a level, and the ratio of births to deaths was so low, that no more than 5% of their original populations would still have been alive twenty-five years later. But, of course, this was hardly fast enough for the Germans. Hence the death-camps.

(v)

Hermann Friedrich Gräbe, Dipl. Ing.

We needed workers—to fulfil our contracts.
The Jews were skilled. I saved perhaps a hundred.

At Dubno, though, the SS killed 5,000—
behind our building site. Our foreman showed me

the mounds of earth—trucks—naked Jews—their clothing
and shoes in heaps—Ukrainian militia—Germans
with whips and clubs. Suddenly, machine-gun clatter.
Large families tried to comfort one another

and say goodbye—one father speaking softly
to a boy of ten—a white-haired grandmother singing
to a laughing baby. A slender girl moved past me,
pointed to herself and murmured, "Twenty-three."

Behind the mound an SS man sat smoking,
the gun across his knees. A thousand bodies
lay massed in a ditch. Some moved. Those next consoled them.
Three locals, watching, waited. One raised his camera.

*

Hermann Friedrich Gräbe, 1900–1986, was manager and chief engineer of the Sdolbunow branch (Ukraine) of the Josef Jung Construction Company, Solingen, from Sept. 1941 to June 1944. The company was building, among other things, grain warehouses for the *Wehrmacht* at the Dubno airfield. The unadorned directness, courage and compassion of Gräbe's sworn affidavit at Nuremberg made him enemies in post-war Germany, where—as W.L. Shirer noted in a related context—"most Germans, at least as far as their sentiment was represented in the West German parliament, did not approve of even the relatively mild sentences meted out to Hitler's accomplices. A number of those handed over by the Allies to German custody were never prosecuted, even when accused of mass murder, and some of them found employment in the Bonn government." As late as the 1990s, W.G. Sebald (who left Germany for England in 1966) wrote with distaste in *The Emigrants* of "the mental impoverishment and lack of memory that marked the Germans, and the efficiency with which they had cleaned everything up". In this society, which was clearly in a state of growing denial, Gräbe suffered harassment of various kinds. Unable to find work, he left Germany with his family for California, where he later died. His efforts at saving Jews included falsifying documents, inventing projects for which he needed workers, and warning them of SS operations. He was honoured by the state of Israel as 'Righteous among the Nations'.

(vi)

SS-Sturmbahnführer Konrad Morgen, Dr. jur.

Knowing the rampant power of rumours, the Gestapo
moved to eradicate this one. But too late.
The New York Times reported how the Germans
were using the fat of Jews for making soap.

This sapped morale. Worse still, it threatened to leak
our secret *Lösung*. Ordered at once by Müller
to sniff out more, my attention was soon directed
to *Sonderkommando Dirlewanger's* (alleged)

excessive cruelty. It seems young Jewish women
were rounded up and stripped. Injected with strychnine,
they writhed and choked, while 'Gandhi' and cronies watched.
The bodies, cut in pieces, were then boiled

together with horse-meat into grease or soap…
They plundered—gang-raped—tortured—whipped to death…,
but the case was never tried. The *Kommando* was posted
to Russia. Too tough a task-force. Too keen on terror.

*

Konrad Morgen, 1909–1982, was a judge and SS investigator. Morgen testified at Nuremberg that, with direct authority from Himmler, he investigated about 800 cases of SS corruption and other abuses, 200 of which were tried : "Five concentration camp commandants were arrested by me personally. Two were shot after being tried…" He claimed that Hitler's euthanasia policy and the Final Solution were beyond his jurisdiction. After the war he continued his legal career in Frankfurt. As for the soap rumour, *The New York Times* reported it on 26 Nov. 1942, quoting as its source a statement by Rabbi Dr Stephen Wise, Chairman of the World Jewish Congress. The rumour, like other reports which reached the outside world with regard to the extermination of the Jews, was treated with suspicion—at least to begin with. After the war, however, the story was widely believed… By sending Konrad Morgen to investigate, Himmler and Heinrich Müller, chief of the Gestapo, conceded that there was at least the possibility of 'experiments' by the likes of Oskar Dirlewanger (1895–1945), whose *Sonderkommando* had been created by Himmler personally—on the Romantic medieval model of Heinrich I, who employed a company of convicted poachers. Dirlewanger's men were mainly ex-convicts, released from gaol on condition that they fight. It has been estimated that Dirlewanger spent seventeen years of his working life in active service. Otherwise, he worked in business, which he had studied, and as a tax advisor. A convicted rapist and child-abuser, he was a notorious sado-masochist but also an effective task-force leader, answerable to Himmler directly. Himmler gave Dirlewanger extra-judicial power of life and death over his troops, a right which he used sparingly. He seems to have been highly respected by his regiment of criminal outsiders, who eventually numbered 6,500. His emaciated appearance earned him the nickname 'Gandhi'.

(vii)

Curzio Malaparte, War Correspondent, Corriere della Sera

I looked away. And looked. This had to be
set down: the high street, Jassy, the morning after
the pogrom, from my window—bodies piled
in gutters—lying, sitting, kneeling—twisted

grotesquely—several hundred roughly dumped
in the churchyard. A child—dead head on shoulder—leaning
against a shop-front. Jews unblocking the road
for trucks, full of their dead. And laughing gypsies

running to get their share. Some pulled off shoes,
feet jammed against dead bellies; some stripped corpses,
made off with arms piled high. A merry bustle—
a colourful Romanian fair—a German market.

Whereas, as if afraid to step on hands
or bloody faces, packs of dogs went sniffing
the bodies with tender care—in search of lost
or dying masters, moved by pity.

*

Curzio Malaparte, 1898–1957, was a prolific Italian author and journalist. Malaparte was by turns a free-thinking fascist, republican, communist, Catholic, and not infrequently in trouble with the authorities. Nevertheless, he worked as a special correspondent for *Corriere della Sera* during the war, following and reporting in daily articles on 'Operation Barbarossa' in 1941–42 and angering both the Fascists and the Nazis by saying what he saw. The novel *Kaputt* (1944), based on his experiences, is in fact a 'Self-Portrait as an Italian Officer' and amply exemplifies this genre's capacity for criticizing not only the role in question but oneself for playing it: the narrator, 'Malaparte', is a self-disgusted participant in as well as (relatively) detached observer of the decadence of fascist Europe—he does not, however, participate in its brutality. The writing is uneven in quality, but there are many unforgettable and intensely imagined scenes, including an account of the opening gambit in the *Conducator* General Antonescu's 'master-plan' to rid Romania of its Jews, the massacre at Jassy (or Iasi) in 1941. Although a work of fiction, *Kaputt* incorporates incidents which have been accepted as historically accurate. Malaparte commented in his preface to the book, "Nothing can convey better than this hard, mysterious German word, *Kaputt*—which literally means 'broken, finished, gone to pieces, gone to ruin'—the sense of what we are, what Europe is: a pile of rubble."

(viii)

SS-Obersturmbahnführer Eduard Strauch

Rough draft of letter to von dem Bach re *Generalkommissar Kube:*

And he praised my work at first: 55,000
'partisan helpers' (Jews) shot in ten weeks—
"The bestial hordes" he called them, proudly showing
his guests the church in Minsk stuffed full with their luggage…

We then shot seventy who had worked in his offices,
removing their gold teeth first in the proper way…
He called us sadists, ignorant young barbarians—
some had been German Jews, or Great War veterans,

lovers of Mendelssohn and Offenbach,
from the same cultural circles as himself…
I said they were just a few Jews. He objected violently
to our driving women, "covered with blood" (!), through the streets,

and other acts beneath a German man
and the Germany of Kant and Goethe… Kube
has clearly favoured and protected Jewry…
I beg to recommend his prompt dismissal.

*

Eduard Strauch, 1906–1955, was senior officer of *Einsatzkommando 2* within *Einsatzgruppe A*—whose commander, however, was dissatisfied with Strauch's unreliable and impulsive behaviour, frequently under the influence of alcohol. Erich von dem Bach described him as the nastiest person he had come across in his life *("dem übelsten Menschen dem ich in meinem Leben begegnet bin")*. In Nov. 1941, Strauch and twenty of his men murdered 10,600 Jews in Riga. His superior in Minsk, *Generalkommissar* Wilhelm Kube, described himself as a "hard man" and willing to deal with the Jewish problem. However, Strauch's behaviour seems to have precipitated a crisis of conscience in Kube, which grew sufficiently embarrassing in so high-ranking an official as to earn him a "serious warning" from the Ministry of the Occupied Eastern Territories in Berlin. To Himmler's relief, Kube was blown up by a bomb placed under his bed by a maidservant working for the Belorussian resistance, since as far as the *Reichsführer* was concerned his Jewish policy had "bordered on treason". Nevertheless, Belorussia had been so devastated under Kube and von dem Bach that even post-war relief workers who had seen Germany and Poland were shocked by the scale of the destruction.

(ix)

Walter Stier, Generaldirektion der Ostbahn, Sonderzüge

After the war, in Frankfurt, his career
really took off, until at last he became
the Bundesbahn's *new Head of Operations.*
During the war, he'd never left his desk,

firstly in Kraków—"*Close to Auschwitz? yes, I think*
it was"—and then in Warsaw, where the Jews
had fought for once, though Łódź and other ghettos
were still to go. Not that he or his colleagues

knew or wanted to know what sort *of passengers
filled the 'resettlement trains' for Belzec, Treblinka…
He worked on complex schedules. Some long trains—
say, fifty cattle-trucks—took hours to empty…*

*The fares were fixed per track-kilometer.
Groups of 400 travelled half-price—small children
for free—most tickets single. The SS
footed the bill—he thinks with the Jews' own money.*

*

Walter Stier, 1906–1985, was Head of 'Special Passenger Trains', Gedob—"an important railway system with major functions in the destruction of the Jews" (Hilberg)—from Jan. 1940 in Kraków, then from 1943 in Warsaw. His department was responsible for the schedules of trains transporting Jews to the death-camps of Poland. He discusses his work and post-war career with Claude Lanzmann in *Shoah*, insisting that he had never actually seen a so-called 'resettlement train', and that no one in his right mind asked unnecessary questions. He concedes that there were rumours. Eichmann pointed out, at his trial in Jerusalem, that the construction of such schedules was a science in itself, and Stier is clearly proud of his expertise. Exactly how murderous this could be in practice is recorded, for example, in *Night* by Elie Wiesel: of the hundred or so 'passengers' ("we were so skinny!") crammed into Wiesel's wagon from Auschwitz to Buchenwald, only twelve survived the journey. The railway system as a whole, without which the Final Solution would not have been possible, has been analysed by Hilberg. Lanzmann, in his note on Walter Stier, confirms one of Hilberg's principal conclusions: "What happened could not have happened without a general consensus of the German people. This business was not the doing of a few gangsters. It called for the commitment of the entire bureaucratic and managerial apparatus of a great modern state."

(x)

SS-Oberscharführer Kurt Franz, Kommandant von Treblinka

I wrote this for the Jews to keep them happy:

> "All in step we stride with our eyes straight ahead,
> Always brave and free, with a spring in our tread
> To our work! We *Kommandos* are marching.

> For us there is only Treblinka,
> Where we are destined to be.
> That's why we felt at home in Treblinka
> So quickly and easily.

> We wait on every word of our Commander,
> With duty and obedience every day!
> We want to serve and go on serving
> Until the hour our luck runs out, hurray!"

And if the dogs forgot to howl it, Barry taught them.

*

Kurt Franz, 1914–1998, was Commandant of Treblinka. Franz was one of the most sadistic and feared of concentration camp commandants. After the war, he escaped from American custody and registered himself as unemployed in his own name (a common one) in his home-town of Düsseldorf, where he then worked as a cook—his original profession—until he was finally arrested in 1959. He was tried in the 'Treblinka Case' and sentenced to life-imprisonment for multiple murder and attempted murder. The court commented on his "well-nigh satanic cruelty", his "extraordinary criminal energy" and "mercilessness towards his victims". Among many other acts of "useless violence" (Primo Levi, *The Drowned and the Saved*), it emerged that Franz would set his dog, Barry, on any prisoner he took a dislike to. Since Barry was the size of a calf, this resulted in most cases in the prisoner being no longer able to work and Franz or a medical orderly would shoot him… The song translated here is sung (twice) by the former *SS-Unterscharführer*, Franz Suchomel, in Lanzmann's *Shoah*. The words, according to Suchomel (who was a guard at Treblinka from Aug. 1942 to Oct. 1943), were written by Franz himself, while "the melody came from Buchenwald", where Franz had been a guard. All working Jews were to learn and be able to sing the song. Suchomel's comment on his rendition of it is: "That's unique. No Jew alive today can sing it" *(Das ist ein Original. Das kann keine Jude heute mehr)*. Between 12,000 and 15,000 people a day were killed at Treblinka—altogether over a million—including most of those transported from the Warsaw ghetto.

(xi)

Diplom Kaufmann Hans Biebow, Amtsleiter Ghettoverwaltung, Łódz

I took pride in my work. Our virtual expropriation
of thieving Jewry; the exemplary productivity,
under the circumstances, of eighty-six factories;
the rationalization of their surplus labour

to only the fit—no kids, or sick, or old folk—
my motto *More with less*, theirs *Work will save us*.
My finest hour, though, was my speech to the strikers
in Workshops I and II: "Workers of the ghetto,"

I began, "you know I have always done my utmost
to keep you safe here. But Russian bombs are falling,

and this one last trans-shipment of you all
is simply meant to help you. German workers

have left for the front: Krupp, Daimler-Benz, and Siemens
need you. If you fight, there'll be dead and wounded.
So, common sense. Bring forty pounds of luggage—
food's on the trains. Now Lódz, tomorrow Deutschland!"

*

Hans Biebow, 1902–1947, was Head of Ghetto Administration, Lódz. A successful grain- and coffee-merchant, Biebow got on well with Reinhard Heydrich, through whom he became head of what was the second-largest ghetto in Poland. Lódz was a highly industrialized city—once known as 'the Polish Manchester'. Under Biebow's business-like leadership the factories of the ghetto made a sizeable profit, although its living conditions—largely because of his extreme unwillingness to spend money on food, hygiene or medicine—were among the worst in Poland.

The slogan "Work will save us" *(Unserer einzige Weg ist Arbeit)* appears to have been the invention of the president of the Jewish *Ältestenrat*, Chaim Rumkowski, who was directly answerable to Biebow. No doubt Heydrich had explained the principle of *Judenrat* responsibility (see *(iii)* and *(iv)*) to Biebow when he appointed him. Rumkowski has been much blamed and derided for behaving like a little *Führer*. However, the productivity of the Lódz ghetto was such that he can perhaps be excused for imagining that working hard might save at least some of his people. Raul Hilberg has convincingly described what was probably a general, though futile, policy of *Judenräte* everywhere—to sacrifice some so as to save some. In the first five months of 1942 about 55,000 of the 205,000 inhabitants of the ghetto were 'resettled'. Most of them died in or on the way to Chelmno (see *(xii)*). In September, Biebow concentrated on making the ghetto more cost effective by closing the hospitals and transporting most of its old people and children under the age of ten. However, work saved nobody and in May 1944 Himmler gave the order for the ghetto's final dissolution. A sort of sit-down strike ensued, and Biebow made his speech on 7 Aug. The strikers were deceived, capitulated, and were transported to Chelmno, only fifty miles away, or to Auschwitz-Birkenau. In the end, no more than 5–6,000 of the ghetto's inhabitants escaped death.

(xii)

Simon Srebnik, Sonderkommando, Chelmno

In their garden in Tel Aviv, surrounded by children,
his wife asks why look back. But he decides
to return to where, in the wood, they fed the ovens
with corpses from the gas-vans. Each full load,

after a night half-starved in Chelmno church,
was gassed in transit. Some, he remembers, were burned
while still alive: "Schnell! Schnell!"—*with no time to search*
among the tangled bodies. No one returned

*in the swilled van. He laboured there six months,
inured to death from the ghetto. A boy, he survived
by singing for SS men—could run and hunt
like a dog. Though his parents died, he knew he'd live—*

*and, shot, the bullet passed straight through. He hid
in a pig-sty. Two dreams helped: one of five loaves.
Then of being left alone in the world. The loud crowd
of church-going Poles can't touch him. Alone. Alive.*

*

Simon Srebnik, 1930–2006, was a member of the Jewish forced-labour squad in the 'forest camp' at Chelmno. As one of two known survivors of the camp, Srebnik was a witness at Eichmann's trial in 1961. In 1978, Claude Lanzmann persuaded him to go back to Chelmno, where he was remembered by the Polish villagers as "the singing boy". The opening of the poem describes a scene which was edited out of *Shoah*.

Chelmno was the first German killing centre in Poland, six weeks or so before the Wannsee conference (see *(iii)*). The first phase was from 8 Dec. 1941 until March 1943. The Jews came mostly from nearby towns and villages and then from the Lódz ghetto. The forest camp was re-opened in June 1944 to facilitate what Biebow called the final *'Verlagerung'* (trans-shipment) of the ghetto. This was when Simon Srebnik arrived, as a thirteen-year-old boy, having seen his father shot by the SS in Lódz. His mother was gassed in one of the vans. The gas-vans remained in use until the camp was closed in Jan. 1945. At least 150,000 people died there. Although Lanzmann insists that *Shoah* is about death, not survival, Simon Srebnik—who was shot through the neck by the SS and found half-dead by the Russians two days later—is among the film's most extraordinary 'resurrections'.

(xiii)

Jerzy Kubicki, KZ-Außenkommando Mannheim-Sandhofen

At first we were afraid the whole of Warsaw—
its Poles, like its Jews—would be reduced to ashes.
But, after the fighting, some were spared—for work
in the Reich. At Dachau, men in dark suits

drove up and chose us. Ah, but Daimler-Benz
was worse than Buchenwald, one ex-con said:
worse hours, more beatings, colder. Such meagre rations
that three months later hundreds were sick or dead.

The front drew near, but still we starved—slaved—froze.
Poor or slow work meant 'sabotage', which meant death.

The sirens wailed—bombs fell—and our hopes rose.
But Marian Krainski's show-trial cut them off.

This harmless, worried barber, and father of four—
ill-trained—made some slight error at his machine,
for which the management and SS hanged him
in the playground of the school where some of us slept.

*

Jerzy Kubicki, 1925–1986, was a member of the Polish external forced-labour squad at Mannheim-Sandhofen concentration camp. Kubicki is unusual in having written a memoir for his family about his experiences in Germany, as recorded by P. Koppenhofer (in *Das Daimler-Benz Buch,* 1987). Himmler welcomed the ill-timed Warsaw Uprising of July-Sept. 1944 as offering an opportunity to destroy the city permanently, as Hitler wished. Unlike the Jews of the ghettos, many surviving Polish prisoners were young and fit, and around 150,000 were transported to labour camps inside Germany... By about Dec. 1944, Daimler-Benz had no further use for its concentration camp workers and many were transported elsewhere, some of them to die at the so-called '*Krankenlager* Vaihingen'. Sick prisoners were expensive and unproductive, and Mannheim was keen to be rid of them, "so that they should not be a burden on us unnecessarily" *(damit sie uns nicht unnötig belasten),* as one managerial directive expressed it. By Jan. 1945, only about 300 of the original 1,060 prisoners were still at Sandhofen, all in a precarious state of health. As elsewhere, the brutality and "useless violence" of the SS continued until the very end. The case of the Polish worker Marian Krainski later came before the American authorities. Krainski was accused by his departmental head, Karl Platzer, of 'sabotage' in Nov. 1944. All the signs point to Krainski's having dropped his template, which shifted by several hundredths of a millimetre without his noticing, so that the axles his machine was producing came out too thin. The SS demanded that the Deputy Works Manager, Robert Staffin (see *(xiv)*) report the matter in writing to Berlin, which he must (or should) have known could lead to Krainski's execution. The show-trial was conducted in front of the assembled *KZ* prisoners on 3 Jan. 1945, and Krainski was hanged next day in the presence of Staffin, Platzer and other representatives of the firm.

(xiv)

Direktor Robert Staffin, Stellvertretender Betriebsleiter, Daimler-Benz Mannheim

I blame top management. The *Wehrmacht* needed
6,000 Opel-Blitz *Dreitonner,* and quickly.
Opel was bombed in August. Daimler-Benz,
licensed to co-produce them, was short of workers.

Personell swung some deal with the Gestapo,
and a thousand fairly fit, young 'Warsaw bandits'
were picked up cheap in Dachau. But too many
were poorly trained. What's more, the war was lost:

no one expected that we'd need these workers
after, say, February 1945.
And so no money was spent to feed—clothe—house them.
Exhausted by twelve-hour shifts, they drooped and shuffled,

until some factory *Führer* shouted 'Sabotage!'
with sufficient conviction. The SS made an example
of—what was his name? insisting on total discipline,
or terror, right to the end. I carry the can.

*

Robert Staffin, 1882–1949, was Deputy Works Manager at Daimler-Benz, Mannheim—responsible, among other things, for counter-intelligence, including suspected sabotage. An alternative, in the case of Marian Krainski would have been to deal with the matter internally. But almost no thought appears to have been given in general to the well-being of the Polish labourers the company had transported from Dachau… Almost unbelievably little money was spent on them, either by Daimler-Benz or the SS. Their diet consisted of 100-120 grams of bread and two bowls of watery soup per day, amounting to no more than 500 calories—"(Let me notice in passing," Primo Levi drily observed in a similar context, "that at least 2,000 calories are needed to survive in a condition of total repose)". In Dachau they had been issued with the standard set of *KZ* clothing for summer, but at Sandhofen there was nothing extra for the winter. They were accommodated so inadequately that their health was in some cases chronically and in others fatally affected. Bronchitis, swollen limbs, swollen and wounded feet (from their wooden shoes), abscesses and vermin-related growths or tumours were all endemic. Some prisoners lost up to half of their normal weight before the last of them left in March 1945. It scarcely needs saying that racial contempt and a cold-blooded business appraisal of forced labourers as dispensable combined to produce this sort of behaviour: "Like Hitler himself, German business never saw them as a scarce or valuable resource, still less as human beings to be nurtured and preserved. Rather they were cheap commodities to be worked until they were worn out" (Mazower). At the 1946 American inquiry, three out of the four German witnesses were unable to remember Krainski's name… Staffin and Platzer were sent for trial in Poland, where Platzer was sentenced to five years imprisonment and Staffin to eight. Staffin died while in prison but Platzer returned to Germany in 1950 and was soon back at work for Daimler-Benz in Untertürkheim.

(xv)

Filip Müller (1), Sonderkommando, Auschwitz

Until the day he wanted *to die, he'd thought*
the worst was when they opened the big gas-chambers
and the dead who'd rammed the massive doors dropped out
like blocks of blood-smeared basalt. Again he remembers

the vomit, excrement, blood from ears and noses,
the menstrual blood, small children with skulls crushed

beneath their parents, struggling to escape the gas,
the strong on top. But his eyes fill

to speak again of what seemed even worse:
people from home, Czech Jews on their way,
they'd been told, to work elsewhere, now daring to curse
the SS for lying—clubbed, whipped, forced to flee

till, in the 'undressing room', they stand—sing—cry
the Hatikvah, *and their anthem. His tears swell*
at how they begged him not *to join them and die,*
gassed into silence: "Go out now, live and tell."

(xvi)

Filip Müller (2)

And so he lived—to tell of those who died.
Once, when the flues were blocked, two friends could not
go on re-burying corpses slimy with mud
washed up in the flooded pit—lay down—were shot—

while above, like diavoli neri, *the SS guards stood*
and mocked them. He passed though Hell, but wrote it down
for those who died unjustly, and some who died
of a broken conscience. Others went insane

from doing what he did, seeing what he saw.
The SS employed sheer terror. How then help
the hopeless? Inside those gates, who wanted to hear
the truth? One fellow-labourer, encountering there

a friend's wife, warned her. She panicked and, naked, ran
to the women, then the men. When no one listened,
she started screaming. They flogged her till she told them
who told her, and burned him alive. The dead don't tell.

*

Filip Müller, 1922–2013, was a member of Jewish forced-labour squads at Auschwitz. A Slovakian Jew, Müller was sent to Auschwitz in April 1942 and remained there, mainly at Birkenau, until the SS abandoned the camp in Jan. 1945. The two largest gas-chambers at Birkenau, *Gaskammer II* and *III*, were both about 250 sq. yards in size and capable of killing 2,000–3,000 people in about fifteen minutes. They were known as the *Leichenkeller*, or 'corpse-cellars'. Müller explains in *Shoah* how the victims, who had been told they were entering the shower-rooms, would rush away from the Zyklon pellets—introduced through shafts from the roof of the gas-chamber—towards the doors and how, as more and more died, the strongest would clamber on the heaps of bodies towards the ceiling, desperate for air… The Jewish *Sonderkommandos* were meant to relieve the SS of work and stress, but since their members were 'bearers of secrets' *(Geheimnisträger)* they were liquidated themselves at irregular intervals. Müller survived five such liquidations. When Auschwitz was abandoned, the last hundred members of the *Sonderkommando* were evacuated together with the other prisoners to *KZ* Mauthausen, where the SS intended to kill them, but Müller disappeared in the crowd. In 1979, he published *Eyewitness Auschwitz,* of which Raul Hilberg wrote, "I have been through this book page by page and I am hard put to find any error, any material significant error." Hilberg accordingly uses Müller as a source in *The Destruction of the European Jews*. Claude Lanzmann has written of Müller, "He is the embodiment of impossible witness."

(xvii)

Brigitte Frank, 'Königin von Polen'

    The *Führer* took my side. As if I'd let
    Hans Frank divorce me after twenty years!
    "Not now, Brigitte," he ordered: "Hans must wait
    till after the war." I don't give a toss (he knows)

    about their politics, but I could have hugged him
    when he took my hand and promised: "He'll change his mind."
    Now that's what I call a man, a *Menschenkenner*.
    As if I'd leave our castle. "Hans," I told him,

    "I've born you five pure-blooded German children.
    As if I'm going to let you marry your mistress.
    I've fought my way from rags to furs. As if
    the richest Jews in Kraków weren't my lackeys!"

    I've had, as Queen of Frank-Reich, my share of lovers.
    When *Vati* drowned himself, I swore I'd thrive.
    Gold, silver, jewels, antiques… Soon we'll go home
    to Neuhaus—lead a normal family life.

*

Brigitte Frank, 1895–1959, was known as the 'Queen of Poland'. Her father, who owned a spinning mill, had got himself into financial difficulty and committed suicide in 1908, leaving five children to be looked after by his wife and her family. Later she often said she had grown up in fear of poverty. As soon as she was old enough, she learned stenography and left home for Berlin where, as a girl with no father, she looked for other men to help her. Thus, even in the 1920s, she succeeded in finding work and in gradually bettering herself. In 1924, she met and married Hans Frank, who was at the start of his career as a lawyer and politician.

Hans Frank, 1900–1946, was five years younger than his domineering wife. From 1930 on, he was Hitler's lawyer, defending him in over forty cases. In 1939, Hitler appointed him *Generalgouverneur* of the biggest segment of occupied Poland. Frank had always suffered from delusions of grandeur (in the Academy of German Law, which he founded in 1933, his picture hung next to Hitler's in every office), and in Poland he applied the so-called *Führerprinzip* (whereby a *Führer* assumed absolute authority with respect to whatever group he was to lead, whose duty it was to obey him) with sound and fury… Frank was directly responsible for the imprisonment and slaughter of innumerable Polish civilians, as part of the Nazi repression—or attempted extermination—of Polish culture. He closed the universities and plundered the Church, museums and the Polish aristocracy for their art treasures (over which he squabbled with Hermann Göring). Although neither consulted nor informed about the SS and Hitler's Final Solution, he was fully involved in the establishment of the Polish ghettos, and then in emptying them. He and his wife would tour the ghettos and Brigitte collected an enormous number of valuable items from Jewish businesses and families who hoped that she would help them—which she never did.

(xviii)

Dr Samuel Steinberg, Häftling, Krankenhaus Block 21, Auschwitz

The doctors there made notes on their victims, I on them:

1. Sick prisoners who were no longer able to work—who had developed septic feet from their wooden shoes or swollen legs as a result of their poor diet—were examined in groups by a senior consultant and sent to Block 20. There they were told that before entering the sick bay they had to take a shower and be deloused. In fact they were conducted one by one into an examination room where they were pinioned to a chair by one medical orderly while another held his hands across their eyes. A Pole by the name of P. then administered an injection to the heart of 4cc of phenol. The patient died within seconds.

   Other injections used were an iodine substitute called Sepso, which took twenty minutes, and even benzene or paraffin.

   An estimated 25,000 prisoners died by this method.

2. In Block 21 (the surgical block) the doctors 'practised' their skills. Any Jewish prisoner with stomach pains, for example, could be diagnosed as suffering from ulcers and subjected to the standard operations, whether he in fact had ulcers or not. After the operation, such patients received no appropriate nursing, not even a diet of milk. A few days later they would be selected for the gas-chamber.

The same '*Sonderbehandlung*' (special treatment) awaited the patients of Dr K. This young doctor had qualified as a surgeon in 1943 and was keen to learn all forms of amputation. He operated on cellulitis, for instance, when a simple incision would have sufficed, by amputating the finger, or on a phlegmon of the leg by amputating the leg. All such patients were then unfit for work and certain to be gassed.

3   With the help of camp doctors, the pharmaceutical company Bayer conducted experiments with drugs and medicaments. One hundred and fifty Jewish women, whom the firm bought from the camp authorities, were removed to a building outside the main camp and used for experiments with unknown hormone preparations. During the *post mortem* operations, sections of lung and wind-pipe ganglia were removed and sent to a factory laboratory.

Prisoners with tuberculosis unlucky enough not to have been gassed were also injected with Bayer ampoules. There were further experiments in putting people down with intravenous injections of the anaesthetic Evipan. And, of course, the entirely useless sadism of the likes of Mengele.

4   No doubt for geopolitical reasons, some men were castrated and both men and women sterilized. The sterilization process was still in the development stage but was performed by X-raying the womb or testicles for up to five or six minutes. The young men would then be sent back to work but after several weeks or months recalled to Block 21. After questioning about their sexual needs, wet dreams, digestion, etc., they were compelled to masturbate and the sperm collected. Those unable to masturbate received a finger-massage of the prostate gland, which produced an erection. After a number of sessions the masseurs grew tired of this and took to using a sort of crank, which was inserted in the anus. Three or four turns were enough to produce the required effect. The sperm were then microscopically examined by a bacteriologist to see if they were dead...

I could go on. But turn *that* into four stanzas of poetry, if you will.

*

Dr Samuel Steinberg was a forced-labour medical assistant in Auschwitz from 1942 to 1945. A Parisian Jewish doctor transported to Auschwitz, Steinberg's statements in the text are based on *KZ Dokument F321* (1988)—a corrected and completed translation of *Camps de Concentration. Crimes contre la personne humaine* [Paris, 1945], which was prepared by the French authorities after the war for use by the Nuremberg International Military Tribunal. Steinberg's address is given as "3, rue de Navarre, Paris". No doubt this was one of the "forty thousand apartments" whose systematic looting by the Germans is described with characteristic precision and restraint by W.G. Sebald in *Austerlitz*—together with the uncommunicativeness of the immense new "Babylonian library" on the site of the warehousing complex where the loot was sorted, which Austerlitz feels has been specifically designed to bury what happened. Other than his statements in *KZ Dokument F321* little seems to be known of Dr Steinberg. Beginning with the so-called 'Doctors' Trial' at Nuremberg, however, much has been discovered in the meantime about some of the horrors which Steinberg mentions and about those who perpetrated them…

(xix)

Joel Brand, Jewish Rescue Committee, Budapest

After three years of going through the motions,
the foot-dragging caution, the diplomatic gestures
of bureaucrats, of politicians—while
how *many* suffered and died without help?—

here was a chance, or so it seemed,
to save some lives: "I am willing to sell you," Eichmann told me,
"a million Jews. Goods for blood—blood for goods…
We need 10,000 trucks: one truck, a hundred Jews.

"You can do this deal in Turkey. And tell the Allies
the trucks are only for the Eastern front.
100,000 Jews will wait at the border:
1,000 trucks, and they cross it."—And then? No visa

for Istanbul. No Weizmann, no Shertok—only
in British-occupied Syria. In Syria, no action—
only questions. No deals with the enemy. No
way back but on to Cairo. No help. No million.

*

Joel Brand, 1906–1964, was a founder with fellow-Zionists of the Jewish Aid and Rescue Committee, Budapest. Eichmann made his offer to Brand in Budapest in April/May 1944… The fate of the Jews was becoming clearer to the outside world as early as 1941, although many treated the reports with scepticism if not incredulity. Other than mistrust of the SS and an unwillingness to negotiate with Hitler's Germany, one of the main stumbling blocks to helping the Jews was, as the British Foreign Secretary Anthony Eden bluntly put it, "Turkey does not want any more of your people." Nor did the British or the Americans want any more of Brand's people, and impenetrable bureaucratic barriers and reasons of diplomacy were placed in the way of undertaking almost anything to stop or even limit the catastrophe.

Tempted by Eichmann's offer, the Jewish Rescue Committee telegraphed Istanbul, and received the reply, "Joel should come, Chaim will be there". They understood this to mean Chaim Weizmann, President of the World Zionist Organization. In fact, the telegraph meant Chaim

Barlasz, head of the Jewish Agency in Istanbul, who was then unable to obtain a visa for Brand. Nor could Moshe Shertok, head of the Political Department of the Jewish Agency in Palestine, obtain a visa to come and meet him, but flew to Syria instead. After fifteen wasted days in Istanbul, during which the Hungarian Jews were being transported to the Nazi killing centres at the rate of 12,000 a day, Brand went to Aleppo, where he met Shertok and the British, who flew him to Cairo for exhaustive interrogation. In Cairo, the British declined to let him go. On one occasion, at the British-Egyptian Club, Brand was addressed by a man who did not introduce himself: "But Mr Brand," said this stranger, "what can I do with your million Jews? Where can I put them?" Brand later claimed that this was Lord Moyne, the British Minister Resident in the Middle East and a close friend of Winston Churchill's. But, whoever his questioner was, the question itself was no longer relevant: most of Hungary's Jews by that time were dead.

(xx)

Henek, Kinderblockkapo, Auschwitz-Birkenau

As children's *Kapo*, I was forced to select
these for the doctors, those for the gas-chamber,
and did what I could to save a few for 'work'...
When *Ivan* came the Krauts shot all they could find.

Hurbinek is three. His little legs are crippled.
He couldn't talk, but with his furious eyes
begged me to hide him. The sick-bay was abandoned
to the dead and almost dead. But there's an oven.

Perhaps when I get home I'll become a policeman.
The SS had food. The unopened tins I've found
are under Primo's bunk, while I hunt for more.
He's good and doesn't like to steal or kill.

My father and I went out to shoot Romanians
in the woods near our farm. I've learned, and so has Hurbinek,
to use what there is: food, warmth, the Polish nurses.
He wants to learn a *word* before he dies.

*

Henek, 1929–? , was a Hungarian youth who became Children's Block *Kapo* in Auschwitz. The other members of his family had been gassed on arrival. Primo Levi's presentation (in *The Truce*, ch.2) of the symbiotic relationship of Henek and Hurbinek is one of his most memorable attempts to set down the unimaginable facts of his war-time experiences—his aim being, precisely, to resist and reverse what (in 'The Memory of the Offence' in *The Drowned and the Saved*) he called Nazism's "war against memory, falsification of reality, negation of reality". The reality was that nearly all children who arrived in Auschwitz were gassed as unfit for work together with their mothers or grandmothers. A few, such as Henek, who claimed he was eighteen and a bricklayer whereas he was fourteen and a schoolboy, survived by native wit (Elie Wiesel, who was fifteen, similarly claimed that he was eighteen and a farmer) or because some worker needed an assistant or some *Kapo* a favourite. These, and others not gassed immediately, were the inhabitants of the Children's Block to which Levi refers: when Henek was sent to Birkenau, he told the SS his actual age and became the children's *Kapo*... Some of the children in Auschwitz failed to qualify even for the gas-chamber. In Langbein's *People in Auschwitz*, Dr Lucie Adelsberger describes them dying gradually of dysentery, their starving bodies covered with scabies, their mouths full of burrowing abscesses which hollowed out their jaws and ate holes in their cheeks in the manner of a cancer. As for Hurbinek, Levi wonders if he had been born in Auschwitz. Until early 1943 pregnant women were automatically gassed; later they were allowed to bear their babies who were then drowned by female SS assistants. However, the occasional secret birth took place and possibly Hurbinek had miraculously survived after the death of his mother. If this were so, as Levi observed, he had never seen a tree. And Auschwitz was all he knew of the human project.

(xxi)

Norbert Masur, World Jewish Congress (Stockholm)

Delayed by Hitler's birthday, he drove up
at 2 a.m.. Calm and impeccably dressed,
he defended their Jewish policy as thrust upon him,
aggrieved at the outcry which greeted Bergen-Belsen.

The danger now was Russia. To show good will,
a thousand Jewish women in Ravensbrück
could be shipped to Sweden, pending further talks.
A perverse ambition shone in his eagle eye.

But Hitler brought him down with a cry of *"Traitor"*:
after the old wolf's death in his lair, no Nazi
would trust him. Nor did Churchill or Roosevelt
ever intend to march in step with Germany...

In the end, we saved seven thousand. The *Reichsführer* fled,
disguised as a private. Stopped at a British checkpoint,
he confessed his name, was searched, and swallowed cyanide.
In twelve mad minutes twelve years of power imploded.

*

Norbert Masur, 1901–1971, was a German Jewish émigré living in Stockholm, who in 1945 was chosen to negotiate on behalf of the World Jewish Congress and the Swedish Foreign Ministry at a secret meeting with Himmler. The meeting took place in the small hours of

21 April. To counter the bad publicity and "hate propaganda" which had been caused by the Allies' discovery of Bergen-Belsen and Buchenwald, Himmler agreed, after a private consultation with his adjutant, Rudolf Brandt (see *(i)*), to release at first 1,000 and then more than 7,000 Jewish women inmates of Ravensbrück concentration camp... Siemens had been one of the main employers of camp labour. But by early 1945 Ravensbrück had become almost as overcrowded and chaotic as Bergen-Belsen with arrivals from Auschwitz and other camps to the east. Under these circumstances, Himmler could easily have released more, but possibly the political embarrassment caused by Eichmann's million (see *(xix)*) held him back. Altogether about 90,000 died in Ravensbrück, many of them in the final weeks before the camp was liberated by the Red Army...

Only two days later, on 23 April, Himmler was in Lübeck to meet the head of the Swedish Red Cross, Count Bernadotte, in the Swedish Consulate. At this meeting Himmler asked Bernadotte to communicate to Eisenhower Germany's willingness to surrender to the West on condition that they continue the war together against Russia. Hitler heard of Himmler's betrayal on 28 April via a Reuter dispatch from Stockholm and ordered his arrest, expelling him from the party and all his state offices in the 'political testament' which he dictated the following day... Although Roosevelt had died on 13 April, this made no difference to the Allies' policy of unconditional surrender, and Himmler's diplomatic overtures came to nothing.

vi   Stephanskirchen (2)

"The Nazis entered this war under the rather childish delusion that they were going to bomb everyone else, and nobody was going to bomb them... They sowed the wind and now they are going to reap the whirlwind."
– Sir Arthur 'Bomber' Harris

Although he thought he'd reap what *he* deserved—
An unfulfilling, unfulfilled, dull life—
He'd found the observer too could be observed,
Unfettered, undefeated, like his wife...

*

One hot September Sunday they returned
To Stephanskirchen where, three years before,
They'd first stood in the church which, bombed and burned,
Had been restored, to mark the end of the war.

—But, leaving home, a phonecall. Her best friend
Had suddenly died. Of cancer. The previous week
They'd thought that she was finally on the mend
After her operation, though still weak.

She'd sat and cried. But then, "Let's go," she said—
"And be back in time for the funeral. She wouldn't have wanted
Us *only* to mourn for her. Although she's dead,
Her wish to be free from pain has, actually, been granted…"

– Which led to something new. He picked brown leaves
Out of her hair. After a woodland swim
She'd pulled him down on top of her. Sex grieves
With dark *élan*. And, darkly, overcame

Her old reluctance to make love outside…
A second time, when they emerged from the wood,
Some road-workers mocked them. But she flushed with pride
To do it at her age. And that it was good

To lie in last year's warm dry leaves. This year's
Were golden or, still fresh, too green to fall.
Her eyes were bright, impulsive, washed by tears
Of mingled joy and sorrow. But *Death takes all,*

Or *Life and death both come from God,* the graves
Beside the church remind them. Over the wall
Behind the graves, with branches full of leaves
And dark-blue fruit, three plum-trees rise and fall

Gravidly, while a woman wielding a pole
Relieves them of their weight. Her three-year-old daughter
Puts the ripe plums in baskets. Church-bells toll—
For whom? for what? For Sunday. The child's laughter

And high-pitched squealing pipe a brief descant as
Old Rumpelstiltskin opens the huge church-door
And grabs her—greets, though fails to recognize
The strangers—grins, and sets her down once more

Beside her mother, who addresses him
As *Opa*. Off he plods then over the fields—
First casting a curious, sidelong squint at them
In half-remembrance—to where their light-green yields

To dark-green sombre woods of close-set pines,
Between which he and his large basket vanish

In search of mushrooms, berries for thick sweet 'wines'
And home-made schnapps... Abruptly the bells finish

Their chorus. Silence fills the mellow air.
Here fat kine give rich milk, bees pine-green honey,
As now they picnic by the stone block's prayer
For peace in our time: "Just give them sufficient money

To keep them happy, Lord. Let them spin gold
From all the fresh or filthy straw they can find...
And let them keep this peace which is as old
As we are. But won't last. I've changed my mind

About how much or little one could do:
Instead of working for the enemy
And justifying our lives as going to show
How little choice we have, the mind *is* free

To choose, or not to choose—no matter what.
Like Jandl, Caspar Brandner, Norbert Masur,
And poor Joel Brand or Henek, each need not
Think herd- or swarm-thoughts—can always ask, *What for?*

'Others may join the Party. But not I,'
One teacher taught. And not even Himmler threw
Every non-Nazi in Dachau. *Let live*—not *die*—
Was what he meant. But most joined in, it's true,

While many (like me) kept making compromises.
Exile and cunning helped some few survive.
With no real knowledge of what freedom *is*,
In the fight to save it millions lost their lives...

We've had it easy: pampered, unprepared
For hardships which, then, only time resolves,
What do we *know* of those who had it hard—
Broke down—went mad—killed others—killed themselves?...

Two hundred years ago Wordsworth still thought
'The Happy Warrior'—facing blood, fear, pain—
Empowered within, transmuted as he fought
Miserable necessity to glorious gain.

Our civilization only came of age
Later—in that the gutter had not yet
Become the mainstream. In order now to wage
Our wars, we *must* deceive ourselves, forget…

As Rumpelstiltskin has forgotten us
Already. Or, perhaps, he pretended to.
Why risk another discussion? His story has
Changed with my changing mind, as stories do.

The chances are he lived by exploiting others—
Like Walter Stier or Suchomel, survived
Because they died. The youngest of three brothers
In any *Märchen* got back home and thrived…

Upright, well-trained, hard-working, smart, no doubt
His sort fought bravely back—gave rich and poor
The *Wirtschaftswunder*. But when they found out
Who Rumpelstiltskin *was*, he lost his power

And tore himself apart in a mad rage—"
"Like Hitler?"
              "And like Goebbels, Himmler, Göring,
And thousands, it seems, of others. In that age
Of *Führers* big and small—uniform-wearing

Duces and *Conductors, Póglovniks*—
Who sought to exploit both lower and upper classes,
Subordinates *and* superiors, poor and rich,
Seducing individual minds *and* masses—

What was it that was new? '*A living thing*'—
To own a living thing—'*is more to me*
Than all the gold or power to which the king
And his father-in-law, the miller, bend the knee':

Materialistic, proud, successful men,
So trodden down and so dehumanized
Their deepest pleasure was to rise again
Like gods—or wanton boys tormenting flies.

Succumbing, in the end, to the futile passion
Or *rage* to own—control or subjugate—

Other men's lives, each in his own mad fashion
Imploded with self-destructive male self-hate..."

– "Who *was* he then?"
                         "A loser. Like all who rage
To win, even *if* he'd won, he'd still have lost:
'What shall it profit a man…?' But in our age
We think the world we gain is worth the cost."

—"They also lost the war. Let's go inside
And light black candles in St Stephen's name
For those who died in the fighting—and H. who died
Last night." In the cool church, the undying flame

Hung dimly above a colourful surprise:
The altar rails and steps were decorated
For *Erntedank*. *"One generation dies,
Another is new born"*—he quietly translated

The text on a plain and simple *Sterbebild*,
Set in a bright display of fruit and flowers,
For a wife who'd died in childbirth. Again tears filled
Her swollen eyes, as they had done for hours

Already on that sadly sunny day,
And overflowed on apples, pears, grapes, hops
Twined round a bundle of sweet-smelling hay,
Dahlias, late sunflowers, roses, sweet-corn cobs.

Beside them, German radishes, huge krauts,
Potatoes, carrots, pumpkins, swedes, kohlrabi,
Sheaves of ripe grain—wheat, barley, rye and oats.
And in their midst a photo of the baby.

She crossed herself: "She'll get to know her mother
From others' memories."
                         "And that's not to say
That she won't know her, though she'll only gather
As much of the truth as she, her father, or they

Can 'resurrect'—"
                 "Like us, then."
                                 "Let's go up

To the organ loft"—whose rich and civilized view
Through the south windows pans out from the top
Of the church's low green hill, beneath the blue

And blinding white of Chiemgau's surreal sky,
Across the region's smaller lakes to the shore
Of the great lake whose busy motorway
Was built by Hitler, who planned many more

Into the heart of Poland, Ukraine, Russia:
"These windows, perhaps, were smashed five months *before*
The church was bombed: the earth here quaked and pressure
Waves burst through doors, broke glass, when the air war

Hit Munich—"
          "Over fifty miles away?"—
"It seems 131 towns and cities
Were bombed—some once, but many others day
And night—igniting fire-storms—shrivelling pity.

The plain black cross above their prayer for PEACE
IN OUR TIME is like an aeroplane, and no wonder:
The first time we were here, though, the truth is
I'd hardly heard of 'Operation Thunder-

Clap', for example. Or 'Operation Gomorrah'.
Or all their other oh-so-creative names
Encoding more than a million tons of terror
Dropped on 3.5 million German homes

And other targets. To calm my mind, I started
My own 'synoptic, artificial view'
(As W.G. Sebald says) to be read out
Here now, in memory of these things, to you

As German—by myself as English, though
Belonging nowhere, or in *Niemandsland,*
As I have come to see it. Take a pew,
And try to listen—not to understand:

Out of Niemandsland

After the worst inferno their 'block-busters'
And fire-bombs ever ignited—the Battle of Hamburg—
No battle but mass-murder—42,000
People not gassed but blown up, burnt

To ashes or, in pools of their own fat,
To shrunken brown or purple joints, some stuck
In molten asphalt (feet first, and then hands)
Which, bubbling thickly, trapped and literally roasted

Its victims when it went on fire and blazed—
As water, melting glass, heaped rubble blazed—
In Bomber Command's most hugely successful bonfire,
The likes of which had never before been seen

By human eyes, a two-mile high tornado
Created in fifteen minutes, which roared for three hours
With winds of 150 mph
Sweeping up people like dry leaves, consuming

All oxygen, uprooting trees and flinging
Great chunks of burning wood, roofs, gables, beams,
Bill-boards and dust-bins, fences and garden-gates
Up and away, while thousands died in cellars

Or air-raid shelters, baked or asphyxiated
As 250,000 dwellings, or more
Than half of those in the city, collapsed and burned
Above their heads. After the chaotic flight

Of more than a million people, dumb-struck with terror,
With shocked incomprehension—old men, old women,
Families with children, shop-girls, harbour whores,
Heading for nowhere, carrying almost nothing,

So suddenly had the Feuersturm *come upon them:*
And the Lord rained upon Sodom and upon Gomorrah
Brimstone and fire from the Lord out of heaven;
And he overthrew those cities and all the plain

And all the inhabitants of those cities… and, lo,
The smoke of the country went up as the smoke of a furnace
Of over 1,000 degrees. And its smoke went up
To 20,000 feet and formed a huge anvil.

After that worst of many such infernos—
From Aachen, Braunschweig, Brunswick, Darmstadt, Frankfurt
To Fürth and Halberstadt, Heilbronn and Kassel—
From Köln to Nürnberg, Pforzheim, Wuppertal, Würzburg—

All old and beautiful cities, all destroyed
By fire and brimstone. After that worst came worse."

—"Go on."
         "I got no further."
                  "Tell me then."
—"'The Ultimate of Talk'?…"
                    "What you remember."

—"The war was over. At Yalta Churchill offered
To ease the Russian army's rapid advance
By bombing eastern cities. Dresden suffered,
Perhaps, the most—partly, no doubt, by chance

In that the weather, as at Hamburg, favoured
An all-cremating firestorm, but mainly by
Accurate bombing. Sebald thought Harris savoured
The reek of such destruction personally,

As Hitler fought his personal *Total War*
To subjugate, control—or own—men's lives:
When heroes like Churchill lead, who asks *What for?*
(Some asked, I know.) Or when a nation strives

Against another, which of us now would see
Or say, as Joyce did: *'You die for your country, suppose.*
But I say let my country die for me'—
Or add, *'Damn death'* and *'Long live life!'*? Who knows

How he'd react? Words fail us. Who can tell
Even the things we tell ourselves we know,
Which bred word-monsters—*blitz, dehousing, fire-gel,*
Strategic bombing, fire-storm…? Catch 22

Was *LMF:* morality lacked fibre,
As madness wasn't really (was it?) mad.
Some who survived then double-bound their children
Who, later, *wrong if they didn't / wrong if they did,*

Went mad in other ways—or else grew rich.
But that's another story. Dresden was not
A threat. That 'large and splendid' *Florenz,* which
Was crammed with beautiful buildings, works of art,

Helpless civilians, refugees, was attacked
In a massive double-strike by Bomber Command
Three months before the end. If the Brits lacked
The moral fibre to tie Harris's hands,

The Americans followed suit. The result was a raid
To make one feel ashamed of being human.
The first 900 tons of bombs were dropped
On less than four square miles of city centre

At 10.15 p.m.. The fire-storm started
At once. Some choked in cellars, others burned
Outside them. The *Volkssturm* fought the fires—old men
And boys. Their hopeless task was interrupted

At 1 a.m., when thousands trying to escape
Were trapped by the next 1,800 tons
Dropped from the second wave of heavy bombers
Into and also around the raging fire-storm—

Already visible hundreds of miles away—
So as to extend it. Blow after blow, explosion
After immense explosion, until no one
Had any idea any longer what was happening.

In the cellars, panicking crowds broke through
Emergency exit walls, crashing from one
Burning, collapsing, smoke-filled hole to the next
To die in piles at the end of city blocks.

Some prayed to God in groups, who hadn't prayed
Since they were children. Others screamed, went mad.

Doors, walls blew in. A woman with three children
Slashed her wrists. One small boy barked like a dog.

Outside the fire grew higher, stronger, hotter.
Thousands were burned or buried under rubble,
Thousands fled to the Elbe. The following morning
Charred bodies lay among the ruined buildings

Like beams of charcoal. With hardly a street discernible,
The *Altstadt* was one huge mound of smouldering débris
And constantly collapsing walls. Survivors searched
For families, friends, possessions. By mid-day

The ruins were filled again with people fleeing
From where they'd lived, clutching peculiar belongings,
Some in pyjamas or nightdresses, leading
Children, grandparents, helping the sick or wounded—

When the USAAF arrived. A further
800 tons of bombs were dropped, completing
The devastation. No one could get away:
All they could do was try and control their terror.

Along the Elbe, later, suitcases, rucksacks,
And corpses: babies dead in prams, dead mothers,
Bomb-scattered limbs, heads, feet, disfigured torsos.
All of which started to rot. Workers in gas-masks

Collected what they could and burned the remains
With flame-throwers—in the *Altmarkt*, for example,
Where SS men retreating from Treblinka
Constructed enormous funeral pyres and cremated

At least 7,000. Many or most of the dead
Were neither identified nor properly counted.
Nobody knows how many died—how many
Thousands of refugees had fled to the city

From further east—how many turned to a handful
Of white-hot ash at over 1,000 degrees,
As 'fire-gel' flared and clung—a form of napalm—
And flagstones burned, glass, girders, living people…

Some of whom still survive. One was a girl
Of twenty at the time—whose mother and father,
Both blind from birth, survived in their own cellar,
After persuading her to escape with the rest.

She feels no hatred now but a wordless sorrow
Mingled with guilt and tears of grateful joy.
Expected and expecting to die of her burns,
She lived to see the baroque *Frauenkirche*,

Which stood for two whole days amid the rubble
Before collapsing, rise again, restored.
But mostly we forget—go looking for trouble—
Make war again—as if we'd never warred…"

*

Outside the sun was lower in the sky
Above the country churchyard: "Thomas Gray,
Mindful of death, began his *Elegy*
With how things end: the curfew, the ploughman's day—

Curfew being when all fires were to be out.
'Large was his bounty and his soul sincere',
His own self-portrait claimed. Far from the crowd,
Stoke Poges lacked its madding strife. As here,—

How does it go?—'beneath that yew-tree's shade,
Tee-tum tee-tum in many a mouldering heap,
Each in his narrow cell for ever laid,
The rude forefathers of the hamlet sleep…

'Let not ambition mock their useful toil,
Their homely joys and destiny obscure;
Nor grandeur hear with a disdainful smile
The short and simple annals of the poor'"…

—"Imagine *we* were dead…"
                    "Beneath two yews—
Here lie an English man and German woman.
He was a lucky poet, she his Muse:
His pen, her rose, now rest in peace where no one

Can see or hear them."
                    "Sounds idyllic."
                                        "Sounds
Ironic?"
            "'Wo wird einst des Wandermüden
Letzte Ruhestätte sein?' The sky surrounds
Our bodies here or there. The grave's a midden."

—*"How you take it'."*
                        Just then a supersonic,
Heavy, low-flying, dark-metal, delta-winged jet
Banged through the evening air like a Miltonic
'Fallen or possible' angel.
                            "Not done yet

With reaping the harvest of perpetual peace?"
He murmured, as two slower bombers toiled
Across the sky above the threatened trees
And crouching hills. The 'nature we share' felt soiled

With human sound and fury. But not for long:
The woman with large baskets full of plums
Offers them some and smiles. A familiar song
Reaches their deafened ears. Her daughter comes

Slowly along a row of older tombs
Towards them. At the foot of each she stoops
And, parting green-gold leaves or fading blooms,
Drops with a little splash in its stone stoup

Of holy water a coloured pebble she's found,
Then takes it out again, and so moves on
To the next—a fresh, impressive, flower-heaped mound.
Her words are indistinct but go to the tune

Of—what? *"A cuckoo and a donkey met,"*
He hums: *"'Twas in the merry month of May…"*—
"Maria," her mother calls. But not done yet
With taking her stone for a swim, she skips away

To the plain black family grave commemorating
Rosa and Franz's fallen sons, where she stows

Her treasure in its dried-up stoup till later—
Hidden beneath a yew-tree's dusky boughs—

And runs to where her mother waits before
Darkness surrounds the rising moon and a star:
"Tra-la-LA, la-la. Tra-la-LA, la-la.
Tra-la-LA, la-LA, la-LA. La-LA."

vii   Mary and Martha (Working for Others)

> *"…a certain woman named Martha received him into her house.*
> *And she had a sister called Mary, which also sat at Jesus' feet, and heard his word. But Martha was cumbered about much serving, and came to him, and said, Lord, dost thou not care that my sister hath left me to serve alone? bid her therefore that she help me.*
> *And Jesus answered and said unto her, Martha, Martha, thou art careful and troubled about many things.*
> *But one thing is needful: and Mary hath chosen that good part, which shall not be taken away from her."*
> *– Luke X. 38–42*

As for what really happened, "Lord, please tell
My sister to stop working now and sit
Here at your feet with me," I begged him: "She'll
Say I was slothful." I washed and oiled his feet
With my soft fingers. Martha's hands were red
From washing, cleaning, cooking, kneading bread.

"Not all work, Mary, is the sort of work
You did too long," he reproached me, "selling your body
If not your mind. Many, it's true, see work
As domination. Little Caesars. Already
Our world is work-torn, war-torn. And, worse, many
See war as work, power-greedy, drunk on blood-money.

We harm ourselves, harm nature, harm each other
Fighting to gain / regain the upper hand.
Competing to please God, Abel's big brother
First sowed bad blood. Cain tilled the guilty land.
Then he raised cities. More was always better,
Till time and money forged their double fetter.

The day that Satan chose to rise he fell—
And Rome was built. His pride, his ruthless greed—
Which he believed were virtues—made a hell
Of heaven. By other choices, others succeed
In living, converting blame or hate to praise,
In less self-punished, more enlightening ways"—

Which was, I think, when Martha interrupted,
Red in the face as well as with red hands…
He asked which part of things, though treasured, corrupted
On earth.—But then affirmed, till Death demands
His due, both parts are good. His own soul's quest
Began in Joseph's workshop, enabling the rest.

And so we went to eat the food she'd prepared:
Fish cooked with olives. He thanked her, saying right work
Dresses and tends the Tree of Life, as shared
By all things mortal. He broke the bread. Hooks lurk
In craving for and clinging to what ought
To help souls free themselves by its support.

To redeem the time, he said, we need to believe
In what we do: lies always sap resolve.
But if one had to lie so as to survive,
Then let him, later, say so. We need to absolve
Ourselves from our 'devices'. Crossed with pride,
Guilt rots or rages, drives to suicide…

And only very rarely need one die
Telling the truth—which Jew and Roman now
Were blind to. The choice was his: we should not cry
Or fast, but live in peace, observing how
He had no human enemy. As the Son
Of Man, he neither lost nor won.

Opus 3, No.3: From Outsight to Insight

Who are those who love themselves? and who do not love themselves?... All those who do evil ... do not love themselves. And although they should say thus: 'We love ourselves,' nevertheless they do not love themselves... Because whatever a man does to one whom he does not love, that he does to himself. Therefore, he does not love himself. But all who do good..., they love themselves. And although they should say thus: 'We do not love ourselves,' nevertheless they do love themselves... Because whatever a man does to one whom he loves, that he does to himself. Therefore, he loves himself.
Samyutta Nikaya III.1

*

*I want men to be free
As much from mobs as kings—from you as me.*
Byron, *Don Juan* IX.25

*

*And what there is to conquer
By strength and submission, has already been discovered
Once or several times, by men whom one cannot hope
To emulate—but there is no competition—
There is only the fight to recover what has been lost
And found and lost again and again: and now, under conditions
Which seem unpropitious.*
T.S. Eliot, *Four Quartets*

1   OT / NT

"It is choice or intention that I call karma—*mental work. For, having chosen, a man acts—by body, speech and mind."*
– *Anguttara Nikaya* III.415

i   The Death of King David

After Rilke: 'Abishag'

Now David was old and stricken in years; and they covered him with clothes, but he gat no heat. So they sought for a fair damsel throughout all the coasts of Israel, and found Abishag a Shunammite, and brought her to the king.
And the damsel was very fair, and cherished the king, and ministered to him: but the king knew her not.
– 1 Kings I.1, 3–4

I

She lay there. And her child-like arms were made
Secure by servants round the withering man—
On whom she sweetly lay while time dragged on.
He was so old she almost felt afraid.

And now and then she'd turn and push her face
Into his beard, whenever an owl hooted;
And all that Night was came, crowding the space
Which terror and desire had now transmuted.

The stars were trembling just as she was trembling.
Across the chamber wafted a curious scent.
The curtain moved by itself, like something resembling
Something in search of which her quiet look went.

But she held on tight as he grew darker, older;
And, out of reach of quintessential night,
She lay, feeling his kingly limbs grow colder,
A virgin and as light as a soul is light.

II

    He sat enthroned and thought the whole dull day
    Of things he'd done, of pleasure and frustration,
    Indulging his favourite bitch's wish to play.—
    But, in the evening now, Abishag swayed
    And arched above him. His crazy life lay
    Like a coast abandoned to its reputation
    Beneath her silent breasts' curved constellation.

    And sometimes, as the lover of many women,
    He'd recognize through brows which needed trimming
    Her unexcited, kissless mouth. He found
    Her callow feelings' green divining rod
    Was not to be tugged down to his deep ground.
    He shuddered coldly; hearkened like a hound,
    And sought himself in his last blood.

              *

Michal

And Michal Saul's daughter loved David:… and the thing pleased Saul…
And Saul said, I will give him her, that she may be a snare to him, and that the hand of the Philistines may be against him.
And Saul commanded his servants, saying, Commune with David secretly, and say, Behold the king hath delight in thee, and all his servants love thee: now therefore be the king's son in law…
And Saul said, Thus shall ye say to David, The king desireth not any dowry, but an hundred foreskins of the Philistines, to be avenged of the king's enemies.
Wherefore David arose and went, he and his men, and slew of the Philistines two hundred men; and David brought their foreskins, and gave them in full tale to the king, that he might be the king's son in law.
And Saul gave him Michal his daughter to wife.
– 1 Samuel XVIII.20–22, 25, 27

I

    And so he thought of Michal, King Saul's daughter,
      Espoused with foreskins of the Philistine—
    Torn from their humbled manhood after the slaughter
    Which Saul had hoped would leave him dead or dying.

Two hundred rings of skin for that adulteress!
She'd helped him out the window once, it's true,
When Saul was groping for his javelin. Vultures
Fed on her sister's sons, and her half-brothers too.

Oh he'd got her back all right! Had even married
Six wives meanwhile, who'd all born strapping boys.
But she, only she—that day he'd been so worried
About the ark, and made a joyful noise

Unto the Lord, leaping and dancing with gladness,
As shamelessly glorious, she'd hissed, "as one of the vain"—
Had mocked and despised him for his holy madness.
And so he'd never kissed her mouth again.

II

In Michal's mind her sons might have been kings:
Instead he'd impregnated all the others.—
How could she take revenge now for such things?
With all five nephews and her last two brothers
Hanged on a hill in Gibeah!—Who now bothers
To fulfil the withering will of a prune-faced princess?...
—His third son did his first son in for incest!

Her father told her never to trust a poet:
They always think the Lord God's on their side.
Penis or pen, they'll push, shoot, shout and show it.
Oh she'd needled his tumescent, bubbling pride!...
But his luck had held. And though she never cried,
With arms akimbo—thin hands on thin hips—
She pursed her unexcited, kissless lips.

*

Bathsheba

Then Adonijah the son of Haggith exalted himself, saying, I will be king: and he prepared him chariots and horsemen, and fifty men to run before him...
And he conferred with Joab the son of Zeruiah, and with Abiathar the priest: and they following Adonijah helped him.
But Zadok the priest,... and Nathan the prophet,... and the mighty men which belonged to David, were not with Adonijah...

Wherefore Nathan spake unto Bathsheba the mother of Solomon, saying, Hast thou not heard that Adonijah the son of Haggith doth reign, and David our Lord knoweth it not?
Now therefore come, let me, I pray thee, give thee counsel, that thou mayest save thine own life, and the life of thy son Solomon.
Go and get thee in unto king David, and say unto him, Didst not thou, my lord, O king, swear unto thine handmaid, saying, Assuredly Solomon thy son shalt reign after me, and he shall sit upon my throne? why then doth Adonijah reign?
– 1 Kings I.5, 7–8, 11–13

I

Beneath the listless breasts of Abishag,
He lay remembering now his favourite wife…
Whoever would have thought those curves could sag?
She'd been the sexiest woman in his life!

An artist, underneath or on the top,
In front, behind, between, with hand or hole.
With her he'd never failed to get it up.
Till now. And yet—he felt his old balls roll.

Repent? He'd swallowed Nathan's soppy story:
Uriah was one of his thirty mighty men!
If he'd slept with his wife, his end might have been less gory.
It served him right. Twice he'd refrained. And then

The letter to Joab… Once Uriah was dead,
He'd married her. Which put the child above board.
Till Nathan's threats had bowed his crazy head.
Regret it? No. But you don't mess about with the Lord.

II

Bathsheba thought how easy he'd been to persuade:
If you never said no, but did what he liked to do,
He'd do what *you* liked. Anyway, David made
Her feel desired—hot-blooded—a woman, who
Inspired him, drained him, straddled him anew,
Like the times he'd come while drinking Solomon's milk
From her bursting breasts… His skin still felt like silk.

Uriah, ugh! But, now, old Haggith's son—
With Joab's help—had set himself up as king,

Usurping David's throne from Solomon,
To whom he'd willed it one hot night one spring
After three crazy days of love-making...

She'd send the Shunammite out. She'd remind him why
Solomon should reign, and Adonijah die.

*

Solomon

And Bathsheba went in unto the king: and the king was very old; and Abishag the Shunammite ministered unto the king.
And Bathsheba bowed, and did obeisance unto the king. And the king said, What wouldest thou?
And she said unto him, My lord, thou swarest by the Lord thy God unto thine handmaid, saying, Assuredly Solomon thy son shall reign after me, and he shall sit upon my throne.
And now, behold, Adonijah reigneth; and now, my lord the king, thou knowest it not...
And king David said, Call me Zadok the priest, and Nathan the prophet... And they came before the king.
The king also said unto them, Take with you the servants of your lord, and cause Solomon my son to ride upon mine own mule, and bring him down to Gihon:
And ... anoint him there king over Israel: and blow ye with the trumpet, and say, God save king Solomon.
Then shall ye come up after him, that he may come and sit upon my throne; for he shall be king in my stead: and I have appointed him to be ruler over Israel and over Judah.
– 1 Kings I.15–18, 32–35

I

Somehow Bathsheba touched the very ground
Of all he was. Even when the Lord had struck
Their firstborn, seeking comfort they soon found
A motto: *'When you feel like fucking, fuck.'*

Joab, though, mocked him, having taken Rabbah—
Joab, who knew too much. And so he'd gone
To renew his grip on that old, rough power-grabber.
Also to wreak the wrath of God upon

The Ammonites. With axes—saws—a brickkiln—
And harrows of iron—he'd lopped, sawed, burned and torn
Them, sporting their king's gold crown, till, grown sick killing
That scum, he'd heard that Solomon was born.

He'd praised the Lord in an ecstatic Psalm
For thus destroying his strong enemy,
And for the son who—gilder of guile with charm—
Would thrive as king. He smiled. A king he'd see.

II

Solomon waited, contemplating the pleasure
Awaiting him. Cedar-wood, ivory, gold;
Tributes of peacocks, apes, and silver treasure.
His father's wives he'd have a hundredfold:
Doves' eyes, white teeth, roe breasts, to have and hold.
His songs, like David's, would be widely published.
But first, with God's help, peace must be established.

And so he wisely mused, while Zadok and Nathan
Prepared the people. Generals, prophets, priests
Had followed Adonijah. Soon he'd weigh them
Judiciously. After all due rites and feasts,
Their deaths, surely, like sacrificial beasts',
Would make a powerful start to a powerful reign:
Their loss, surely, would be JHVH's gain?

*

After Heine: 'King David'

Now the days of David drew nigh that he should die; and he charged Solomon his son, saying, I go the way of all the earth: be thou strong therefore, and shew thyself a man;
And keep the charge of the Lord thy God, to walk in his ways, to keep his statutes, and his commandments...:
That the Lord may continue his word which he spake concerning me, saying, If thy children take heed to their way, to walk before me in truth with all their heart and with all their soul, there shall not fail thee (said he) a man on the throne of Israel.
– 1 Kings II.1–4

Smiling despots, passing on,
Know their power is never gone:
Though they die, it changes hands.
Human bondage never ends.

Poor plebeian nags and steers—
Hauling carts for years and years!

And the stubborn neck gets broken
Which won't keep its proper yoke on.

Solomon watched as David lay
On his death-bed: "By the way,
You had better keep an eye on
General Joab, o my scion.

"That old ruthless die-hard gets
  Generally on my tits.
But he's weathered wars and purges,
  And I daren't indulge my urges.

"You, my son, are wise and strong,
  Godly and, above all, young—
And you shouldn't have much trouble
  Bursting Joab's hoary bubble.

"As for Adonijah—no
  True-bred son of mine—although
He's a wimp, don't underrate him!
  In God's name, assassinate him."

ii   Pontius Pilate's Wife, Procula, Addresses a Group of Christians, Rome, AD 39

> *"If thou let this man go, thou art not Caesar's friend."*
> *– John XIX.12*

Thank you for asking me to talk to you
About what happened while my husband (now
Deceased) was Prefect of Judaea... My recent
Letter from Gaul got lost, or so it seems—
Although Caligula has many lackeys
And Pilate's name has long been out of favour...

    I know you Christians are not liked in Rome—
    Too serious, your religion (and too bloody?)
    For well-off, self-respecting Roman pagans!—
    And understand the risk you must be taking
    By asking me to join you in your church
    Or synagogue—an honour for a Gentile
    Such as myself, in any case.

                    But where
Begin?
          I was not present at the hall
Of judgement on that Friday when the Jews
Brought Jesus to be tried by Roman law.
My husband wanted me to understand,
And so he told me what he thought had happened.
And told me, later, again. And again.
                              You see,
I'd dreamt of blood and water—warned him not
To harm that innocent man but let him go.

Instead he scourged him, had him crowned with thorns…

              *

Then came Jesus forth, wearing the crown of thorns, and the purple robe… And Pilate saith unto the Jews, Behold your King!
But they cried out, Away with him, away with him, crucify him. Pilate saith unto them, Shall I crucify your King? The chief priests answered, We have no king but Caesar.
Then delivered he him therefore unto them to be crucified. And they took Jesus and led him away.
– John XIX.5, 14–16

              *

Although his story changed each time he told it,
Let me explain—or try to. Now that he
Is where all stories end, I can no longer
Ask him. And so remain unsure of certain
Things I'd still like to know—who said what why…

I tried to save them, but…
                    When Jesus spoke,
You heard at once, if you had ears to hear,
How good—how just—he was.
                         One day these things
Should be set down in writing. Not just yet,
Perhaps. This Emperor, claiming he's a god,
And loathing Jews already, who may have
No other god but God: if he could read
That Jesus taught us—I say *us* because
I'd stand unnoticed sometimes in the crowd
And listen—"Render unto Caesar the things

     Of Caesar and unto God the things of God"—
  Well, now, if he—Caligula—could *read* such sayings,
  That might be very dangerous.

*

And when they were come to the place which is called Calvary, there they crucified him, and two malefactors, one on the right hand, and the other on the left.
Then said Jesus, Father, forgive them, for they know not what they do. And they parted his raiment and cast lots.
And it was the third hour…
– Luke XXIII.33–34, Mark XV.25

*

                         I'm afraid
    My husband also, in the end, detested
    The Jews.
                 But when Vitellius, his superior—
    Governor of Syria—sent him back to Rome
    Charged with excessive harshness, the old Emperor
    Was dead before we got here, and the young
    Caligula, as mad as he was vicious,
    Blamed him for not being harsh or cruel enough!
    Enraged by Jewish riots in other places,
    He banished him for life. As god of gods,
    He'd have a statue of himself, he ranted,
    Set in the Temple of Jerusalem,
    And force the trouble-making Jewish rabble
    To worship *him!*
                     In exile, my husband cursed
    The day Tiberius ever made him Prefect
    And, worse—the worst in all his life—the day
    Caiaphas sent Jesus to the judgement hall…

*

And one of the malefactors … railed on him, saying, If thou be Christ, save thyself and us.
But the other, answering, rebuked him, saying, Dost thou not fear God, seeing thou art in the same condemnation?
And we indeed justly; for we receive the due reward of our deeds: but this man hath done nothing amiss.
And he said unto Jesus, Lord, remember me…

And Jesus said unto him, Today shalt thou be with me in paradise.
– Luke XXIII.39–43

            *

    That night he came to bed as limp
    As if he'd lost his manhood.
                        Shattered, but
    Sleepless, by dawn he'd started talking—started
    Though with the half-truth (and half-lie) that the Jews
    Were not allowed to judge the likes of Jesus,
    Whereas they shortly after put to death
    His disciple, Stephen.
                       But my Roman husband
    Was swayed by fear…
                        Suppose he'd handed over
    Jesus—whose followers were already legion—
    To the Sanhedrin: would they really have risked
    A riot—the dark side of Palm Sunday, say—
    By stoning him? They hated what he taught,
    But feared the common people.
                            In other words,
    Jesus might not have died—at least, not then…

    —All Roman magistrates have wide discretion
    In the performance of their duties. But
    The Jews intimidated him by claiming
    Jesus had said he was their king, whereas
    "We have no king but Caesar!"
                         And so he
    Began by wanting me, you understand,
    To think he had no choice but to proceed
    As if the accused presented a real threat
    To his and Rome's authority.
                          Jesus, though,
    Told him his kingdom was not of this world.
    If it were of the Roman world, his servants—
    The sort of followers whom he did not have—
    Would fight. He might have said, *Poor Malchus' ear*
    Was healed before he knew who'd cut it off—
    Though did not.
                  —My husband was amazed at how
    Little defence he offered.

            *

Now there stood by the cross of Jesus his mother, and her sister, and Mary Magdalene.
When Jesus therefore saw his mother, and the disciple standing by, whom he loved, he saith unto his mother, Woman, behold thy son!
Then saith he to the disciple, Behold, thy mother! And from that hour that disciple took her into his own home.
– John XIX.25–27

*

      Jesus would see
At once what sort of man this Roman was:
A man of compromises, whose bad faith
Deceived itself enough to let him act
From fear and weakness, blaming others, shirking
Responsibility, evading—yes—
The truth.
    And so, when Jesus simply said
That he was of the truth, and any who
Was also of the truth would hear his voice,
He knew my husband, trying not to hear,
Would answer as he answered: "What
Is truth?"…
      And yet, I know, I heard him teach,
Let him who is without such sin—he spoke of
A woman taken in adultery
But might have meant, for instance, the worse sin
Of compromise, or siding with the enemy
Against one's better judgement—*Let him cast*
The first self-righteous stone…
       Well, now, he wanted
His wife at least to understand—and so
Excuse, I think, the things he'd done…
I understood his fears—his weakness—need
To compromise—and what he'd left *undone*.
Also, that I myself was not much stronger.
My life resembled his, and not the women's
Who followed Jesus. Nor your lives here now
Under the shadow of Caligula…

*

And when the sixth hour was come, there was darkness over the whole land until the ninth hour. And at the ninth hour Jesus cried with a loud voice, saying Eloi, Eloi, lama sabachthani? *which*

is, being interpreted, My God, my God, why hast thou forsaken me?
– Mark XV.33–34

*

After the Resurrection—even though
The watch was bribed to say that his disciples
 Had come by night to steal him while they slept—
And more so after Pentecost (I heard
Those tongues of fire proclaim the gift of tongues!),
The fame of Jesus started spreading quickly,
And other Romans asked my husband what
This Jew had done for us to crucify him.

He suffered then but was already suffering
On that black Friday.
                    He was more deeply troubled
By Jesus' death than even I'd expected—
Because, I think, his lies could not
Deceive themselves enough to let him live,
From that time on, without a gnawing sense
Of sinfulness…
              But, first, he tried again
To avoid the full responsibility
For what was his decision, and his only,
By offering to release to the Jewish crowd,
Whose leaders after all were priests and officers
Of the Sanhedrin—as was then the custom
During their Passover—a prisoner:
Either Jesus himself, in whom he tried to tell them
He found no fault, or one whom he was sure
That even the rabble would refuse to have
Among themselves again—a well-known thief
And murderer called Barabbas.
                              But I see
You know what happened.
                       Which was when my husband
 Had Jesus scourged, ordered his men to plait
A crown of thorns, robe him in purple rags
And haul him out to mock the Jews for accusing
So weak a man—*Behold the man!*—of claiming
To be their king. Also, to assert the power
Of Rome, he told me, over all things Jewish—

    King or no king. But most of all, I think,
    That shameful show, or sign, was to persuade
    Himself that he was less impressed by Jesus
    Than he was shortly forced to admit, in his heart,
    He really was.

                     *

After this, Jesus knowing that all things were now accomplished, saith, I thirst.
Now there was a vessel full of vinegar: and they filled a spunge with vinegar, and put it upon hyssop,
and put it to his mouth.
– John XIX.28–29

                     *

            Rome's power, though, far from quelling
    The howling mob, had vexed and goaded them
    Into a mindless rage which now demanded
    That he should crucify a man he knew
    To be not only innocent but noble.
    So that, when he refused, their angry leaders,
    Forgetting in their fury the sheer number
    Of Jesus' followers—contradicting also
    Their opening gambit and my husband's half-truth—
    Then roared that by their law he ought to die
    "Because he made himself the Son of God".

    At once, my superstitious husband—struck
      By fear—took Jesus back inside the hall
    To ask him, *Whence art thou?*
                            But Jesus gave him
    No answer.
             Later, he would sometimes say,
    When he had nothing left to lose by saying it,
    Jesus had made him feel at that strange moment
    By his unbowed demeanour and mere silence
    That he was more the Son of God than a son
    Of Joseph's born in some Judaean shed
    Thirty-three years before.
                       When he then told him
    The greater fault was theirs who had delivered
    An innocent man into the hands of Rome,
    This quiet assessment of his true position,

He'd also say—forgetting *What is truth?*
I think, in real astonishment at Jesus'
Unswerving, almost superhuman calm—
Had filled him with such instantaneous wonder
(With gratitude as well, no doubt, relieved
To find himself excused, at least in part,
By the very man that he and those outside
Were haggling over) that he went straight out
Again and sought to free him.

*

And when Jesus had received the vinegar, he said, Father, into thy hands I commend my spirit.
– John XIX.30, Luke XXIII.46

*

                     But now the Jews
Had also changed their mind—or come to their senses—
And cried, "Whoever makes himself a king
Speaks against Caesar. If you let him go,
You are not Caesar's friend. We have no king
But Caesar. Crucify him!"
                Deflated, he
At once took water, washed his hands—Rome's hands—
Before the crowd, declaring himself not guilty
Of Jesus' blood. And they all answered him,
"His blood be on us and be on our children!"

And so my husband gave them Jesus to lead
To Golgotha, the place of a skull.
                            He staggered
And sometimes fell, beneath the weight of the cross,
To which the soldiers nailed his hands and feet
Before they raised it.
                   Pilate wrote the *titulus*
In person: *INRI*. When they murmured,
"Write rather that he *said* he was our king,"
He answered, "What I have written, I have written."

—No half-truths this time, but *Quod scripsi, scripsi:*
What he had written was a lie. A lie
Was what he'd written—his legal justification,

An unambiguous sensible precaution
In black and white, for crucifying one
Who had (he knew) done nothing to deserve it.
Also, again, a mockery of the Jews,
Who from then on he hated more than ever
For forcing him, he'd say, to do this thing.
But most of all, perhaps, one last attempt
To tell himself he had not been impressed
By a man so foolish as to let himself
Be killed without a fight.
                       An unsuccessful
Attempt, as it turned out. He came to bed
Already then as limp as if he'd lost
His manhood—and by cock-crow had delivered
Himself of his first version of what happened.

          *

And Jesus said, It is finished: and having said thus, he cried with a loud voice, and gave up the ghost.
– John XIX.30, Mark XV.37

          *

He wanted me to say he had no choice—
Whereas in fact one never has no choice,
And he was only choosing not to choose.

He knew that then—and later knew it better…

A dreadful irony awaited him
In Rome, where *Caesar's friend* was promptly exiled
To Gaul as Caesar's enemy. He had gained
Nothing, in other words, by crucifying
A man whose aura—whose alarming peace—
He tried but was unable to forget…

In Gaul, remorse consumed him and he died.

          *

The Jews therefore, that the bodies should not remain upon the cross on the Sabbath day, besought
Pilate that their legs might be broken, and that they might be taken away.
Then came the soldiers, and brake the legs of the first, and of the other which was crucified with him.

But when they came to Jesus, and saw that he was dead already, they brake not his legs:
But one of the soldiers with a spear pierced his side, and forthwith came there out blood and water.
– John XIX.31–34

*

My husband might have lived, had he been less
Obsessed with his own fall from grace. He blamed
History—the Jews—his luck—Caligula...

—He could not see that Jesus freely *chose*,
Cost what it might (it cost him all—and nothing),
Freely to act and not be acted on—
Freely to give and freely to forgive.
Or that, to be at peace, we *must* forgive—
Surely—ourselves as well as those against us.
Poor sheep and goats who know not what we do,
We must absolve ourselves from what we know
We ought not to have done or left undone...

In Gaul, where we were left in peace at last,
He might have made his peace with life by doing that:
He might—who knows?—have laid his past to rest.
But he was weak. Too pusillanimous.

And I? who stayed with him until the end—
Guilt-stricken and embittered though he became?...
After the Emperor banished him, my parents
Suggested I should claim my dowry back
And live with them in Rome—perhaps re-marry.
My father was a powerful man, a lawyer...
But it seems I did not want another husband—
Felt safer with the one I thought I knew.

He'd say I understood him all too well.
His sins had found him out. And that was that.

Thank you for listening.
                    As I journeyed here,
(I chose to go with him, so may return),
We heard the latest news from other travellers
Of the first Gentile Christians in Judaea...

I humbly request to be the first in Rome.

2   AL VESCOVO D'ASSISI...

dal podestá di Gubbio

11 novembre, 1211

Santissima Eccellenza,
                        or
Dear Guido (if I may? as your
Old fellow-student),
                      Please excuse
A letter, but the latest news
Of Francesco Bernadone, our
Mutual acquaintance—man of the hour—
Requires (I think you will agree)
Urgent advice on WHAT ARE WE
TO DO about it, e.g. how
Are we to get Francesco—who
Is not an easy man to handle
(The way he treats his family's a scandal,
If you'll forgive me)—to persuade
The great grey hungry wolf he's made
Friends with, he claims, to go away
(I *could* put that another way),
And so relieve our streets at least
Of what they've nicknamed here 'the Beast'
Which stalks them, howling nightly.
                              We
Preferred the wolf in the wood.
                           Well he,
Francesco, goes too far. And I'm not
The first to say or think so. What,
For instance, of the 'doves' (they're *pigeons*)
Which foul our churches? The merest smidgen
Of common sense says cull them—who
Needs rats with beaks and wings? But, no,
His 'sisters' must be fed.
                      The lad
He taught to feed and release them had,
Later, a smart idea. Instead
Of snaring a handful in the wood
To barter at our fair—as he used

To do, till Francesco disabused
His mind of its error—he now breeds
Hundreds in dove-cotes, over-feeds
And crates them, live or plucked, to cooks
As far as Ancona. Dealers and crooks—
As Mayor I get to hear these things—
Are poised, like rats with bigger wings,
To 'buy' him out. Such mobsters know
How business can be made to grow;
Whereas the world Francesco inhabits
Is full of foxes which love rabbits.
He thinks all creatures should be friends—
Forgets how such old fables end.
Which was all right as long as he
Lived like a hermit; or, let's say,
Confined his preaching to the birds,
Which understand, he claims, the words
Of Jesus, *Blessed are the meek*—
Forgetting as well the crow's black beak
In the lamb's eye, the barn-owl's shriek,
The claw of the strong, the flesh of the weak,

Or that—to turn from this 'digression'—
Old wolves aren't picky *re* the flesh on
Which they subsist—that, even stranger,
A man-eating wolf means, simply, DANGER
To all but him… Well, martyrs court it—
Danger, then death. Their *Lives* report it.
And I suppose you're on his side,
The civic and religious pride
Of Assisi being the holy martyrs
He worships.
    For unholy starters,
Guido, though—it's not saying too much—an
'Accident' here could blot your scutcheon
For years to come with the blood of a child,
For example, killed or mauled by the wild
Brute which Francesco promises
Will now behave itself because
He's asked it to.
    Perhaps you can
Speak with him, as I know you've done
Before, and so avoid the worst.

—I've tried, of course. He says I'm cursed,
As his father was, by lack of faith.
But many here are afraid that death
Lurks in the empty streets, and refuse
To leave their houses.
                    The strange news
Of the wolf spread quickly. No one from
Beyond the township has—or will—come
To our weekly fair as long as he,
The wolf, remains at liberty
To slouch and feed, or sleep if he'd rather…

—Francesco's game of fighting his father
By calling God his Father was
Impeccable. And so was his
Decision to obey the Pope
(Il Papa), leaving not a hope
For his own Pa. Not that we ought
To disobey. But I was taught
To honour my parents. *And* he'll be poor,
Begging for alms from door to door,
Whose father, one of the richest men
In Umbria, hardly saw him again
Before becoming ill. He died
No doubt of Anger and hurt Pride;
And yet most men who have a son
Know put-dad-down games aren't much fun.

—Unlike yourself, dear Guido, who
Became Francesco's 'father', too.
As his spiritual mentor—more, a tower
Of wealth and strength—your worldly power,
By helping him to stake a claim
To sainthood, may earn you lasting fame.
—In fact, correct me if I'm wrong,
But I hear tell that since, not long
Ago, he came in triumph home
With Papal blessings reaped in Rome,
And then set sail for Syria where
Martyrs are ten a penny, but fair
Seas turned stormy, driving them back
To Ancona—they were nearly wrecked—
No one except (as his bishop) you,

Guido, can guide or get him to
Refrain from this or that extreme…

Real life is hard or harsh, not a dream
Or vision. Surely ecstasy
's like wine, or even women… He—
Out revelling, drinking, (whoring?) nightly—
Was not, if I remember rightly,
More temperate, either, in his youth.
You of all people know the truth
About Foligno. His day in court—
And with it your strictures that he ought
Not to have stolen Pietro's goods
To mend that chapel in the wood—
Ended abruptly when he threw
His clothes, which were his father's too,
On the floor together with the money.

His former companions found it funny
To mock (was he mad?) his shameless habit
Of running around like a skinned rabbit—
Threw mud and stones or spat in his face.

His family suffered in disgrace.

Not that, I know, you've had it easy
Yourself, as Bishop of Assisi—
He and Rufino, in ecstasy
And little else, for all to see,
Preaching (like drunkards?) in your sainted
Cathedral. His poor mother fainted
(My wife has friends in Assisi with views on
Such antics, sir, who pass the news on…).

His father sold fine cloths and clothing:
He preaches and prays in rags or nothing,
Who was the best-dressed youth in town.
And why? To put his father down,
Of course. Well, now he's down for good,
Whether he shouldn't be, or should…
Remember his first trip to Rome?
He gave his clothes away—rode home
Dressed in the beggar's rags he'd swopped

For them outside St Peter's crypt…
Then he went back to wasting time
And Pietro's money.
                    —But I digress
Again. Or do I? Let me address—
If so—the matter, sir, more briefly:
The burden of my tale is chiefly
That, though his parents tried their best,
He's *always* been a bloody pest
(Excuse my French, but they did call
Their child 'Francesco', after all)…

One cannot, perhaps, expect a mystic
To be (as we are) realistic,
But *he* does things, I swear to you,
My lord, which no sane man would do…

—This madness with the wolf began
With gutted sheep—and then a man—
And then a child: a gruesome sight,
Guido, I promise you. By night
It prowled the nearby woods and howled—
Stole geese, ducks, quail—domestic fowl
Which woodsmen nurture. Then, by day,
It mostly vanished, slipped away
Up Monte Ingino, on whose slopes
We *Eugubini* nurse our hopes—
And fears.
            The wolf is old and cunning
And knows the woods and mountains: running
Away made better sense than *after*
His silent shadow. Snarls, like laughter,
Were only heard when he attacked,
Snarling behind his victim's back…
At first not often, or too near
The town. But then, as if to sneer
At our inaction, this September,
Closer and in full view…
                        A number
Of begging brothers, passing through,
Said, *Ask Francesco what to do*.
We didn't, but they did.
                        He soon

237

Appeared... That night a gibbous moon
Lit up the fields below the town
Where the wolf hunkered. He went down
To parley with it. Well, we all
Watched from high windows or the wall:
A ragged crowd of so-called brothers
Who'd trailed along, and many others—
As, like a lunatic, he walked
Across a field and started to talk
In the white light to the wolf, whose grey
Aura resembled his habit's. They
Merged as he made the sign of the cross.
The wolf inclined its head—at a loss,
It seemed, to see why this odd person
Should preach it an unasked-for sermon,
Wagging his finger, which it might
Have thought was offered it to bite.
But, no, it listened. He stroked its head,
Shook a big forepaw, and so led
The creature quietly in through our gate.

Nobody felt like tempting fate—
Too many had already died...
Francesco, asked to step inside
The *palazzo* where the council waited,
Explained that he'd negotiated
A deal with his brother, the wolf, who'd agreed
That if the town would only feed
Him on a voluntary basis, he
Would eat his fill amicably.
The pangs of hunger drove him to treat
Us badly. An old wolf must eat...

Unsure of what to say or do
With death outside the door (would you,
 Guido, have dared refuse their offer?)
We risked a yes—and now we suffer.
The monster, overfed all day
 From house to house, is free to bay
At the moon all night. It likes to squat
Out in the Piazza Grande. What's
Ironic is that, in the arena
Of our Roman Theatre, nobody's seen a

Beast of that stripe since the beasts' heyday
Under Nero! But elsewhere its grey
Coat makes it hard to see: the stone
Our forebears used to build this town,
Its labyrinthine alleys, steep
Steps and dark passageways (in deep
Shadow for much of the day) is the same
Dull shade of grey.
     The brute's not tame,
Only not hungry.
     Either we,
To state our choices brutally,
Poison—trap—shoot—destroy it soon,
Or one dark night without a moon,
Someone will die or—worse—get mauled.

If you are (as I am) appalled
By these scenarios, the way out,
As said, is—not to beat about
The thorn-bush—tell your protégé
To get his friend to go away,
Not only from this town and wood
But Umbria. We both know he could,
So why, you may be thinking, do
I not insist but write to you?

—Because he never listens. He
Seems, when he looks, to see not me
But Gubbio's merchants' goods or land,
Their great *palazzi*'s raised doors and
Whatever else I represent
For him.
   I know no precedent
Except for his family, but I'd hate
To cross him.
     I need hardly say it
But, Guido, he thinks mayors are mayors
And bishops bishops: *Hear our prayers
And let our cry come unto thee!*...

—In short, I'm not the man to free
Our streets of this unwanted wonder.
He does not see himself as under

Civil authority. Gubbio's fair,
As far as he's concerned, is where
Young boys hawk 'doves' they've trapped. If we
Took action unilaterally
And somehow drove the wolf from our door,
We might, you understand, cause more
Trouble than has been caused—at least,
Since we've all fed it—by the beast
Itself. What might Francesco do?
What might he *not?* His followers, too,
Increase in number by the hour…
Let me just say he has great power,
Which inspires love but also fear.
Hundreds followed him up here,
And some are ruffians, begging alms
On every corner, chanting psalms
Or churning out prayers for food or money.
There are, already now, too many
'Brothers'. They say 2,000 attended
A recent General Chapter, befriended
By the pious citizens of Assisi,
Who fed them. Can't have been that easy
Either, Bishop. And just how long
Can they make do with things that belong
To others? I don't want to say
They're parasites, but surely they
Depend on the hard work and wealth
Of the likes of *me* for the spiritual health
They claim to find in Poverty?
Who pays? in plainer words. Do they
Seriously think they can found an order
On *"la sua donna"*? We can't afford her
Already! If authorized by Rome,
They'd eat us out of house and home…

Well, that's about all I wanted to say.
I will just add though, if I may,
That Frate Ginepro—once amusing—
Recently seems to me to be losing
What little nous he ever had.
—He lived in Gubbio as a lad
And 'preaches' here. Last week he chopped
A foot off a grazing pig, which hopped

Squealing back to the farmyard. He'd
Promised a brother, before he died,
A last pig's trotter. The sick brother
Recovered, but not the pig. The bother—
Pig-farmer toting blood-stained axe,
Frate Ginepro crying *"Pax
Vobiscum"*—had just settled when
He gave his clothes away again.
One sight of which we've all had enough
Is Ginepro praising God in the buff!
Laughter, contempt, mud, stones, remonstration,
Are signs, for him, that his *Imitation
Of Christ* is as it should be: He
Also bore scorn and mockery—
A view Francesco shares, whose cult
Is thus uniquely difficult
To keep in order. Prosecution
Of *any* sort is no solution...
But bishops have the spiritual clout.
So, Guido, get your finger out
Of the episcopal *culo grande*—
And *try* to make yourself more handy.

[Post scriptum:]

—Well, scribbling all that's made me feel better
At least. *Next job:* write out the letter
That he's to get. There's not a lot
Of sense in telling a bishop what
You think he's up to when your aim
Is getting him to play your game—
Still less in excommunication.
He's powerful, fond of litigation,
And very rich. So tone it down
And prune it. *NB:* the renown
Of Assisi and himself do matter
To him as bishop. Better flatter
Them more. Stress more that we *are* acquainted...
Suggest he should have their picture painted—
The trial, for example—if some Pope
(Francesco's mad enough—so there's hope)
Decides he should be canonized...
Midnight. I hadn't realized,

Dashing this off by candle-light,
How peaceful Gubbio is tonight.
The wolf still pads our alleys, though.
Write it tomorrow then.

[And so:]

Al Vescovo d'Assisi

12 novembre 1211

Eccellenza,
          Please excuse
A letter. While the latest news
Of Francesco Bernadone is
The sort of miracle we prize
Him and his followers for, we still
Require your help.
              So let me tell
Your Lordship very briefly how
Things stood before and stand here now,
Hoping that your illustrious power
Will pity Gubbio in its hour
Of need.
         The miracle concerns
A great grey hungry wolf….

3   DANTE ALIGHIERI: FROM *DOLCE STIL NUOVO* TO *RIME PETROSE*

The poetry of Dante's canzoni *and other lyrics—unlike that of the* Divina commedia*—tends to vanish almost completely if their content is separated from their form. As Dante's own detailed analyses of the* canzone *in the* Vita nuova *and elsewhere imply, he viewed the form as an inseparable aspect of the meaning in these poems. Like other Italian verse-forms, the* canzone *has had a significant influence on English poetry (for example, on that of Spenser and Milton), and I have preserved as much of Dante's stanza-forms as I could—i.e. their rhyme-schemes and approximate line-lengths—while shifting his basically syllabic verse (Italian being a 'syllable-timed' language) into the more 'stress-timed' rhythms of English. Except for the indispensable "Lady", I have done what I could as well to avoid the archaisms and inversions by which translations of this sort are sometimes weakened—also with the intention of raising more plainly the question of what do these thoughts / feelings / forms mean to us now:*

"For sweetest things turn sourest by their deeds;
 Lilies that fester smell far worse than weeds."
– Shakespeare, *Sonnet 94*

"All this the world well knows; yet none knows well
 To shun the heaven that leads men to this hell."
– *Sonnet 129*

i   *"Per una ghirlandetta" (To Fioretta)*
        (Rime LVI)

Because of a sweet garland
I've seen, all gentle flowers
  Now make me sigh.—
I saw my Lady wearing
  A garland and, above her,
I saw a little angel
  Of love devoutly fly,
While it subtly pierced my hearing
With its song: "My humble powers
Are all my Lord's. So praise him, love her."

ii *"Donne ch'avete intelletto d'amore"*
     (Rime XIV)

Ladies who live in the knowledge of love,
Let me commend my Lady now to you:
Not that my words can praise her as is due—
Yet it relieves my mind to sing her praises.
For when I think how far she is above
The rest of us, love flows in me anew
So sweetly that if all my words rang true
They'd make the world enamoured of her graces.
Though not the sort of words whose tenor raises
The tone so high that I'd lose heart from fear;
But rather let me treat love lightly here,
Out of respect for her sweet gentleness's
Feelings—with you, o Ladies and loving girls,
For my Lady is a theme for no one else.

An angel, in the fullness of God's knowledge,
Exclaims, "O Lord, among the human race
A marvel now is visible in the grace
Proceeding from a soul whose light ascends
As far as Heaven"—whose angels and great college
Of saints lack nothing but my Lady's face
And so beg God to let her grace that place.
Pity alone, speaking in God, defends
Our interests, since God's nature comprehends
My Lady: "Dearly beloved, suffer in peace:
Although your high hopes please me, let them cease
Until he loses her, whom Providence sends
To visit Hell, where he shall cry, *O lost*
And hopeless souls, I have seen the Hope of the Blessed!"

My Lady is desired in Paradise:
So make yourselves acquainted with her worth.
And if you wish to seem of gentle birth
Walk with her when she walks, for she goes by
Shielded by Love himself, who buries in ice
All wicked hearts and thoughts, like frozen earth.
But if you were to gaze on all she's worth,
You would become a noble thing, or die.
And when Love finds one worthy to set eyes
Upon her virtue, he feels the power she gives
As if it healed the very way he lives,
Or angry pride became humility.

Also, God's greatness grants that he who gladly
Speaks to her, by His grace, cannot end badly.

Love says of her: "How can a mortal creature's
Appearance be so lovely, so divine?"
He stares at her, and swears she's so refined
God must have meant to make something quite new
When He made her. Her delicate, pearl-like features
Shine softly as a woman's ought to shine.
She is as good as Nature could design—
The very paragon of Beauty, who
Will wound the eyes of any who dares view
The flame-like essences of burning love
She shoots from her bright eyes—which, when they move,
Penetrate to the heart and wound it too.
Thus in her face one sees the vital strength
Of Love portrayed where none may gaze at length.

(Congedo)

My song, when I have sent you on your way,
I know you'll speak with many women. Now
I recommend that you—in view of how
I've raised you as Love's daughter—should be plain
With everyone you meet, and merely say:
"I'm searching for the one I praise. Please show
Me where I have been told I ought to go."—
That where no love is you should not remain,
Unless you want the world to claim you're vain,
But only be quite open, if you can,
With ladies and the sort of courteous man
Who'll quickly send you on your way again.
When you find Love, you'll find my Lady too:
Remember me to him, who send them you.

iii   *"Così nel mio parlar voglio esser aspro"*
     (Rime CIII)

With words as harsh as that unfeeling block
Of loveliness, let me now carve in stone
    Her hard-faced flesh and bone,
The things she does which prove how cruel and crude
Her nature is, which, like a sparkling rock,

Is so impervious—or so far withdrawn—
    That, of Love's arrows, none
Will ever pierce or catch her in the nude.
But *her* looks kill. No man can hope to exclude
Or run from her outrageous slings and stings
    Which, as if they had wings,
Penetrate every normal sort of armour;
So that I've no idea how to disarm her.

Nor have I found a shield her shots can't shatter—
Or hiding-place from which my eyes can't see
    Her eyes. Like a flower on a tree
My love, borne up by her, sticks out a mile.
To her, my tears of bitter misery matter
No more than a ship might care about a sea
    That's calm: she forces me
Down with a weight no rasping rhyme or style
Could ever equal. Oh, heartless, fearful *file*—
Deaf and abrasive—*why* won't you refrain
    From causing me such pain
By gnawing at my heart, skin by thin skin,
As I refrain from saying whose hand you're in?

For I tremble even more when I perceive
I'm thinking of her in some crowded room—
    Where prying looks presume
The light that's in my eyes means I'm in love—
Than at encroaching death, which, with Love's teeth,
Already frays my nerves, keen to consume
    My entire life to come;
Or so I fear, till I can hardly move.—
Love's got me on the ground, and stands above
Me brandishing the sword he used to slay
    Dido. I humbly pray
For mercy.—Or, my love-tormented cries
Beg him to grant the mercy he denies!

From time to time he raises his strong hand,
Perversely challenging my helpless form
    Which lies as weak as a worm,
Too tired to put up any sort of fight.
But then again cries start to fill my mind;
A surge of blood goes rushing to my warm

    Heart which, fearing more harm,
Dilates, until I'm left as white as white…
Love wounds me under my left arm—with quite
So hard a hit that in my heart pain blazes
      Once more. And if he raises
His sword again, I swear the hand of Death
Will have me before the blow lets out my breath.

If only I might see that same sword cut
Her heart in two, whose beauty quarters mine!
      The end for which I pine
Might seem less black then… But why should *I* die,
When she's the thief, the murderess who'll do what
The night conceals, though the bright sun should shine?
      And why should she not whine
For me, who yelp for her, in Love's hot sty?
"I'll rescue you, I'll rescue you!" I'd cry
  At once to her. How gladly I'd have saved
      Her by the hair he's waved—
And gilded—to destroy me. Oh, I'd seize her
By those blonde, lovely locks. And that would please her.

Once having got my fist in her fine tresses,
Which have become a whip and scourge to me,
      I'd keep it there, and we
Would pass the hours from terce to nones, and later—
Instead of with coy noes and courteous yesses—
As if a bear had grabbed her playfully.
      Though Love whips *me* now, she
Would find that I'd avenge what's made me hate her
A thousand-fold. As if my eyes could eat her,
I'd stare at hers close up, whose sparks have burned
      My heart so long it's learned
To die alive. Nor would my vengeance cease
Till love had brought us both some sort of peace.

    (Congedo)

My song, now go away and find that woman
Who shuns my love, starving me of attention
      And other things I could mention.
Stick arrows in her heart. For I'll feel better
If you'll pursue, for my sake, this vendetta.

4 THE CARPENTER'S *COOK'S TALE. OR:* BLINDMAN'S BUFF

"Ella, rispostogli, il cominciò a guatare…"
– Decameron IX, v

"A Cook they hadde with hem for the nones
To boille the chiknes with the marybones…"
– The Canterbury Tales, 'General Prologue'

A young apprentice once lived in our town,
as clever as a weasel, handsome, brown
as Spanish leather, learning how to be
a painter—signs, mugs, portraits, pots. And he
was quick and wiry, had a shock of curls,
and was so fond of dancing, ale and girls
that he was widely known as *Pete the Reveller*—
as full of lies or tales as any traveller,
as keen on stolen kisses, love and money,
as a bees' hive is sticky-sweet with honey…

Whenever any pageant filled *Eastcheap*,
out of his master's door P.'d look and leap—
and that was that until he'd seen it all,
or sung and had a dance, or kicked a ball,
or found a gang of mates and called them brother,
who found another gang and caused some bother.

When night fell they'd arrange a time to meet
and drink or gamble in some mean back-street,
where there was no mad cap or leather jerkin
who could compete at dice with this young *Perkin*—
who'd ply his merry tool and blow the lot
in 'private' bagnios, if he won or not.

And this was bad for trade.
                            His master started
missing things—tools, wine, takings… Not hard-hearted,
he felt betrayed—then angered. Revel and theft,
it seemed, were front and back, or right and left,
of Peter and, before he'd fully served
his time, he got what he no doubt deserved:
"A rotten apple in a barrel will

rot all the others if left there, until
nothing but worms and grubs remain alive.
I'd say in your case, Peter, at least five
of the seven deadliest worms have long begun
to do their damnedest... And I'm not the one
to pluck them out, although when young I admit
I had some fun myself and went for it
where- and whenever. But you've breached my trust
by stealing from the till. Which means I must
dismiss you, I've no choice. And so—*Get out,
you thieving, greedy, lecherous, lazy lout!*—"

His indignation grew so righteous that
Peter skedaddled like an alley-cat.

But one thief always knows another thief
to help him hoodwink, fleece or bring to grief
the dupes they lend a hand to. Peter sent
one such to fetch his gear, while he himself went
to ground nearby in the small grocer's shop
this friend's wife owned.
                          She had another job
as part-time tart, or closet prostitute.

The shop itself, though, was of good repute,
having become hers when the grocer died...
In fact, her bit of income on the side
was now, since she'd re-married, not much more
than a bad habit: *Laura* was no whore
but, like the Wife of Bath, a provident
house-keeper with a *"likerous instrument"*.

Her second husband worked—as part-time pimp
and under-skinker: *Pompey* smarmed, *Why scrimp
and slave,* carissima, *to buy new dresses?
A* cortegiana *in Napoli possesses
more than great ladies.* Usura *on her back—
she lends one talent but she gets ten back...*

Tempted and hooked, the loose and lovely Laura
plied London's oldest trade, and grew no poorer,
keeping her shop as well.
                          The painter's wife

and she had known each other all their lives:
their mothers had been friends. But Laura's father
had died and left them poor. The girls would gather
berries, nuts, flowers to sell from the nearby common.
L.'s mother was a feisty market-woman
and sold herself, shooing them out to play
girls' games—tick, blindman's buff. And to that day
plump *Christiana* bought salt, sugar, flour
from Laura's shop.   Her husband, *Christopher*,
knew nothing of their grocer's sideline, which
Christiana tolerated. After such
a very old first husband, who had died
in ecstasies while somewhere up inside
his less than pleasured—widow, who could blame
poor Laura?
              She felt sorry, all the same,
when Pompey beat her: he was slightly mad,
Laura explained, but when not in a bad
temper wept maudlin rivers for the thick
lip or black eye he'd given her, or would lick
and kiss her like a dog… Felt sorry, too,
if some drunk client beat her black and blue—
which Pompey sternly treated as no joke
but, smiler with a knife beneath his cloak
or, more precisely, razor-sharp stiletto
like Sparafucile's, hired by Rigoletto,
bagged the offender and, like Buridan—
first loved, then dumped, in Paris by Queen Jeanne—
floated them down the Mincio, Thames or Seine
to ensure they'd never get a girl again.

Two things made Laura's husband feel *cornuto*—
a violent client or a love-lorn suitor…

"*Coraggio, cara!*" he then softly said,
and slid off back to work at the Boar's Head,
whose host, Ned Quickly, for a small inducement,
helped gull another Dick for L.'s seducement.

Not that she told her neighbours much of this,
and least of all a housewife like plump Chris,
even when she claimed that Chris made her feel lucky

and loved enough to get a daily fuck—he
wasn't as fit as he'd once been but still
did very nicely thank you.
                          Laura would smile
to hear it—but then deftly turn the talk
to safer subjects, such as food or work.

And so it was that Chris heard their false friend
Peter had gone to work in the West End
at a large inn, the Garter, where his uncle
was landlord.
                  Hurrying home, she broke her ankle—
a complicated fracture, which made life
painful for months. Although Chris loved his wife,
this twist of fortune got on both their nerves.
Even *if* she'd somehow got what she deserved,
Peter was gone and *Jill*, their hapless maid,
was pregnant. Chris, who for long weeks was laid
in splints across the bed, would pester Chris
to fetch and carry, fix that or buy this…

So that, one afternoon, the painter stood
in an impatient, irritable mood,
at Laura's, clutching a long list of shopping
his wife had ordered.
                          Laura had just been swapping
tit for tat with a client.
                          Her eyes shone
as, without thinking, she now turned them on
this man with paint and egg-white on his shirt.

Before he knew it, Chris began to flirt
and, though for twenty years he had had eyes—
well, almost—for Chris alone, stared in surprise
as a sunbeam lit up Laura's auburn hair
and long bare milk-white neck. Gasping for air,
he felt her brush against him with her breasts.

She soon forgot him. He could hardly rest
until he'd found a reason to come back.
He bought a bag of nuts. "Mind you don't crack
your eyeballs," Laura laughed, who'd heard meanwhile
of Christiana's fall.

                    Her loose-lipped smile,
which looked (she couldn't help it) more than naughty,
now made the painter feel, though long turned forty,
like a young tyro with a loaded brush,
unsure if he should jab, dab, pull or push—
which made him (nor could he) look such a fool
that Laura very softly flicked his tool,
explaining hers was not a knocking shop,
and if he thought it was, he'd better stop
before she flicked him harder.
                            The next time
that Chris went shopping, the whole pantomime
was viewed by Peter through the window—who
had got his eye on loose-lipped Laura, too,
but was afraid of Pompey, who distinguished
clients from lovers/rivals, and extinguished
the flames of love (P. knew), if they appeared,
with mezzogiorno ruthlessness.
                            He leered,
You fancy her as well, old man, I see,
but frowned and bit his thumb-nail enviously
as Laura, making bedroom-eyes, now led
Chris down into her cellar, where a bed
lurked in a curtained niche (P. also knew)—
scented by apples—spices—*Oh no you
don't, you old lecher! Or not yet,* he thought,
and clattered in—just as his master brought
a solid sack of walnuts up the ladder.

Pete smirked to see Chris look, abruptly, sadder—
but passed the matter off with "Where's Pompey?
—I was supposed to meet him here today...
And no hard feelings, *maestro*. Why not let
bygones be bygones?" And so on.
                            To cut
etc., P. contrived a clever plan
to get his master kicked out too *(Like man,
like master)*—first of all, ingratiating
himself with Chris, and then negotiating
a deal for him to paint and re-design
his prosperous uncle's crudely daubed inn-sign,
as well as to replace in sets of ten
his mugs, bowls, plates, which P. collected when

each batch was ready.
                         All of which dispelled
their troubled past.
                         Even Chris (still laid up) quelled
the qualms of vague mistrust she'd always had
regarding Peter, who had something bad
(she feared) about him—not that she could prove
anything now—whereas Chris, being in love,
trusted him more, and life in general, too,
gaily re-painting London town sky-blue
with rose-pink borders and a golden frame.

Middle-aged men, L. mused, are all the same,
including artists, who are even blinder
than most—until some hard-and-fast reminder
of who's who, what's what, rips the blindfold off.
And then they realize *Enough's enough*...
This artist, though—she guessed—was narcissistic
and easily flattered (Laura was realistic
about her friends): a well-heeled master, too—
wealthier than most with whom she had to do,
and more polite... And yet she didn't want
too much attention to her famous *queynte*—
which, like the Wife of Bath's, was highly praised
by all and sundry—such that she'd lose face,
or start perhaps (a chastening thought) to seem
a *Mistress Overdone*. She'd always creamed
the biggest spenders off, while too much screwing
was also dicy if it stopped her doing
her duty to her husband's satisfaction—
which easily caused a 'slightly mad' reaction—
and could, as she well knew, be just as dull
as not enough, like feeling over-full
of fish on Friday...
                         What with thoughts like these,
all L. did next was flirt a bit and tease
her new admirers, master more than man—
whose 'love', though, far from hampering his smart plan,
propelled it forward with the acrid power
of jealousy, whereas Chris felt by now
confused and slightly vexed by L.'s reaction
on top of Chris's agonized inaction.

At Peter's reckless age, he'd run as wild
a riot, or wilder. As an only child,
he'd blown his father's money even faster
than Peter had blown his, and riled his master
with similar *"litel japes"*... In fact, they soon
found things to laugh about.
                              One afternoon,
when Peter came to fetch a batch of plates
which hadn't yet been fired, and had to wait,
the painter (who had no idea at all
that he was fooling with a jealous rival
for Laura's favours) started cracking jokes
about the sort of Judy bloke-ish blokes
crack jokes about, and passed a rude remark
about their friend—one bird who, for a lark,
he'd love to get his hands on...
                              Now P. had
a clear enough idea how sad or mad
Laura might make a man and, seizing this chance
to call the tune and lead old Chris a dance,
confided how he'd known her for some time—
a merry widow, and still in her prime,
though Pompey's foreign or half-mad distinctions
had led (he'd heard) to more than one extinction
not just of hope but of the very hoper.
They should have been content to pay and grope her!
But why not try a gift? As long as he
was—or, at any rate, appeared to be—
only a punter (wasn't that the word?),
Pompey would turn a half-blind eye. Absurd,
but there it was.
                              Chris stared. Nonplussed at first
by this unwelcome news, he inwardly cursed
Italian migrants and, above all, Pompey
for wiving, thriving, getting in the way,
corrupting English girls, above all Laura,
who had no need, with so much going for her,
to play that sort of game. And surely wouldn't,
unless she had to. Pompey probably couldn't
earn anything like enough to make ends meet:
a *little* gift, perhaps—sweets to the sweet—
offered discreetly, then, could not do much
real harm—and might well help...

                        Amazed that such
a lovely woman should have stooped so low
and married a mere tapster/gigolo,
he even quizzed his wife (who'd know) on how
she'd lost her standing.
                        "Well, since when have *you*
troubled your head, my dear, with Eastcheap's wives?"
she smiled—but winced with pain: "We get the lives
we earn. And even the luck. Anyway, Laura
and her old mother kept on getting poorer—
until she married, well, an older man…
After her mother died, she carried on
with other men behind his creaking back.
One night it creaked so much she heard it crack,
and that was that. She inherited the shop
and all that he possessed. But why, then, stop
playing the games she'd started? Times were hard…
Pompey, as tapster and as part-time bawd,
was not, you see, so very far below her…"

But Chris saw Laura as the topmost *flower*
of female beauty. As his wife suspected.
—Trouble, in fact, was almost to be expected
under the circumstances. Still in pain,
she tried to move her legs—but failed again
to part them without wincing.
                        And quite soon
her husband swinked elsewhere all afternoon.

Now L. had always thought the mouse which had
only one hole was soft or thick in the head—
You're cat-food once the cat discovers it!—
and made full use of every hole or slit.
—The little gifts Chris brought, like magic charms,
were all it took to have her in his arms.

To inflate his self-respect, she then requested
some work of Chris's own—a tried and tested
method with even the average artisan,
and Chris was an artistic, cocksure man—
to go with his more mundane contributions,
which helped her pay their bills.
                        Two loud intrusions

by neighbours shouting *Shop!* and the constant threat
of Pompey blundering in on them, soon led
to Peter's slyly offering to keep nix,
while Laura taught her ageing dog new tricks.
But, standing like a lemon in the shop,
P. fancied he could hear them on the job;
and, once, when Pompey banged in with a fellow-
Italian for some *vino* from their cellar,
felt sourly tempted to tear down the sign
which told him Laura had a paying client.
Pompey was an Italian, after all—
and, surely, this might serve as Chris's fall?
But, gambling on an even worse disgrace,
he cut off his nose again to spite his face,
and Pompey stamped off with an angry frown…

When Laura smirked, "Don't let it get you down,"
P. threw her such a furious glance that she
suddenly felt afraid.
                Before long he
was also allowed to leave her little *donnés*,
consisting largely of ill-gotten moneys.
And Laura assured him, as he grasped her hips
and kissed her hot and slightly puffy lips,
that he was so much stiffer than his master—
who once or twice had had a slight disaster
and was much less attractive than he dreamed.

Peter mistrusted Laura, but she seemed
in fact to find him sexier than old Chris,
whom once she stood up in his favour.
                              This
pleased and excited Peter rather more
than he admitted—L. was only a whore,
when all was said and done—and drove him on
to visualize the details of his plan,
which might, he now perceived, also deter
Laura from screwing Chris—or him from her—
depending on which ways their bit of fun
turned nasty.
              Very soon the deed was done.
When Chris's leg was healed enough for her
to hobble round on, Peter showed her where

a basement window in the grocer's yard
revealed her husband and the grocer, hard
at work on a large bed in a dark corner.

Pete whispered that he'd felt he had to warn her—
although he'd hesitated, as their friend—
and yet it would have come out in the end,
as these things do...
      Now Chris was badly shocked
to see her husband's straining body locked
below her in a passionate embrace
with someone else's. Hiding her white face,
she stared between cramped fingers—till a cry
of angry pain caused cock and hen to fly
apart as quickly as if the bed had burst.

They glimpsed poor Chris and—cowering as if cursed—
shielding their nakedness, like Adam and Eve
shut out of Eden—saw her quickly leave
the little window vacant, like the eye
of heaven.
    Then silence.
        A whole week went by
while Peter waited for a bigger bang—
and then two weeks...
      But they could all go hang,
for all he cared.
    L. said there'd been a fuss,
which ought to leave "more time", she smiled, "for us"—
but had less time than ever.
      Then, one day,
when L. had let him have—for once—his way,
fearing his temper and the angry glow
which filled his face whenever she said no,
he bounced off Chris while sidling idly out.

The look she shot him left him in no doubt—
*("My sone, keep wel thy tonge, and keep thy freend:
a wikked tonge is worse than a feend")*—
of where he stood.
     He eavesdropped at the door—
could hear excited voices, not much more,
until the cellar trap-door banged. Was this

some sort of scrap at last?
                        So as not to miss
the teeth and claws, he scuttled round to the yard
and squatted by the window, breathing hard,
craning his neck to sneak a better look,
and saw them—*laughing.*
                  Then Laura, smiling, took
a black silk blindfold from her box of tricks—
which Chris admired—plus several hand-carved pricks,
seeming to offer them. But Chris declined
shyly. She was about to change her mind
when Laura spotted Peter.
                      Off he scurried ,
though not before Chris too had glimpsed his worried
and puzzled face.
                Laura so far had not
tumbled to Peter's sly Boccaccian plot,
but Chris, in tears, now told her how she'd come
to get a bird's-eye-view of Chris's bum
between her parted knees. And straight away
Laura decided that the only way
to rid themselves of Peter was to lie
to Pompey—how he'd sworn to God he'd die
if Laura didn't give him love, refusing
to accept the simple deal (beyond her choosing)
whereby the only 'love' she had for him
was if he coughed up coins to grease her quim…

She knew exactly what to do and say
to egg her husband on. The following day
was his young rival's last. So much for Peter.

As for nice Chris, whose husband never beat her,
who craved no other, nor a better man
(even if he'd fallen for Pompey's courtesan)—
or so she claimed—who was an honest woman,
L. had been moved not only by their common
memories, however much they'd grown apart
in matters of the body and the heart,
but how she'd come to ask her if she'd *help*
and not to tear the hair from off her scalp,
or scratch her cheeks, or slit her pretty nose,
screaming it from the roof-tops to expose

her guilt—as peeping Peter still expected
while crouching at the key-hole undetected…

All Chris had said was Chris had sworn / would swear
not to return to Laura's. But hot air,
she sighed, cost nothing, and she was afraid
of what L. knew, that most men's fifth decade
made them less faithful, not to say more foolish,
while mid-life hard-ons can be downright mulish.
And so, though pained, she'd swallowed her hurt pride,
begging her childhood friend to take her side
if and when Chris went back and broke his word:
she loved him, which was utterly absurd,
perhaps—but there it was. L. didn't need
the money, surely? Or would soon succeed
in finding someone more to her real taste—

At this point Laura, clasping her plump waist,
had kissed her mouth to close it: "To my mind,
it's lust," she blinked, "not love at all that's blind"—
and placed a sticky piece of candied ginger
between her friend's hot lips, and licked her finger…
"Like lots of men, he's half-blind anyway.—
Do you remember how we used to play,
as adolescent girls, at blindman's buff
with some dumb boy-o, who'd get biffs enough
before he snatched a blouse or groped a skirt?
Sometimes we'd kick him where it really hurt,
or spin him round so quick it made him dizzy,
or strap one boot to a chair to keep him busy.
And what was his reward for all of this?
To give the girl he caught a blindman's kiss.
We were too shy to let him see whose mouth
he had his tongue in. Well, goodbye to youth,
but let me show you something—"
                                                 And they went,
banging the trap-door, down into the scent
of Laura's spicy cellar.
                       Laura knew
that men like Chris imagine if they screw
another woman in another bed
the wife they have at home must be half-dead.
And nothing either she or Chris could *say*

would make much difference.
                              "But why don't we play
a game of blindman's buff—"
                              She was about
to explain when Peter left them in no doubt
of his ill will by showing his real face
in the same frame he'd used to try and disgrace
his former chief…
                    Well, let him bite his thumb.
Hard-faced, hard-bitten as she had become,
Laura still felt his plan should be frustrated
and Chris returned to Chris—and concentrated
her mind on that…
                    Later, she sent Chris home
with two fine dildos, carved by hand in Rome,
a gift of Pompey's—to be left around
where the old goat her husband would be bound
to spy them.
               Which he did. One in the hand
of Jill their maid, who didn't understand
the look he gave her, having found it on
their unmade bed.
                    He found the other one
being used by Chris, who felt a pang of shame
but kept her eyes tight shut and sighed and came
as if he wasn't there.
                        She then felt shifty.—
But *how* could he have lived to almost fifty
and not know women get frustrated, too?

Jill railed that you could *talk* till you were blue
between the legs. Look at her new-born child,
whose father hadn't listened to her mild
entreaties to be careful…
                              Jill turned red:
"And then he said he'd fallen in love," she said,
"with someone else."
                        Chris, who'd been fairly sure
P. was the father, wasn't any more—
and felt another pang, but overcame
her stinging tears and, since their little game
of blindman's buff required one other 'girl'
at least for Chris to chase, suggested Jill

might like to play a part in Laura's plan
to help her show her dick-head of a man
how wrong he was.
                         To judge from the fierce light
that flared in Jill's dark eyes, Chris had been right
on several counts—and Jill said, "Count on me!"
nursing her baby, *Jack*, self-righteously…

A fortnight passed.
                        After the interlude
with Laura's dildo, Chris had shown renewed
interest in Chris. But such is the blind power
of what we imagine or expect on our
immediate feelings that, like a cold sword
between them lay the thought that he was bored
compared with when at Laura's.
                                  Till at last,
he imagined the main danger was now past—
and, having put L. wise the previous day,
laid the white lies on thick to get away.
Pete had by then gone AWOL for some time—
questions were being asked—some feared a crime.
And so, as his ex-master, now his friend,
Chris was invited up to the West End
for jaw-jaw at his well-off uncle's inn,
the Garter, where he'd actually never been—
not even to inspect his own inn-sign
in situ, though he'd heard that it looked fine…

—All this though Chris herself looked fine as ever,
whereas he hummed, *"To one thing constant never"*
as, sure enough, the old temptation grew:
if he could swing it, why not swive with two
lovers, one here, one there? Why should they be
so difficult to cope with separately?—
And various schemes soon filled his swelling head.

Later, when Chris and Laura were both dead,
and Chris and Jill were looking after Jack,
a poet-courtier, dressed in sombre black
and nondescript dark-grey, with goatee beard
and vulnerable eyes, one day appeared
in Eastcheap and commissioned Master Chris

to paint his 'final' portrait.
                              Vis-à-vis
Chaucer—for he it was—who sat so still
that words at once welled up to break or fill
the utter silence, Chris began to tell
his story, starting with that ne'er-do-well
'Peter' *et al*—a cast so nearly the same
as Chaucer's *Cook's Tale* that the one changed name
permitted me to use it as the start,
roughly, of my own story.
                          Easing his heart,
'Chris' (as I've called him) blurted a whole version
of whatever really happened—some distortion
is only human—and, in a single session
less of self-portrait than ersatz Confession,
arrived at Laura's ploy of blindman's buff.

And some of this raw yarn was novel stuff
(an unsubmissive and yet loving wife—
a lily flowering in low London life)
for Chaucer *re* male/female interactions;
but he'd already written his *Retractions*,
preceded by *The Parson's Tale*…
                                  He told
most of the story, though, to me—his old
acquaintance—well, I think we can say 'friend',
though he of course was at the upper end
of the overcrowded ladder of the court,
from which he duly toppled, knowing he ought
never to have wasted so much life and time
on the hand- and foot-holds of that slippery climb…

It just so happens he and I would meet
for dinner at the Garter, where young Pete
flourished as ex-apprentice and head-skinker.

Pompey was an occasional fellow-drinker,
a former smuggler and Boar's Head rampallion,
spicing his English with ribald Italian.
After he'd married Laura—*"come Petrarca"*—
his dark, louche face at times looked even darker:
Chaucer would watch *("he was a good felawe:*
ful many a draughte of wyn had he ydrawe

from Bordeux-ward, whil that the chapman sleep.
Of nyce conscience took he no keep.
If that he faught, and hadde the hyer hond,
by water he sente hem hoom to every lond")—
and sometimes write a few quick phrases, tapping
the ale-house table, sometimes seem to be napping,
but *"Rivo!"* he'd smile—and never miss a thing.

Before his exile, once, our present King
and his tall, skinny ten-year-old son, Hal,
with Sir John Falstaff—now his humorous pal—
rode by as we stepped out.
                       And Bolingbroke
whispered to Falstaff, who flashed back a joke—
at our expence? Well, Chaucer already knew,
or so he claimed, what Henry was up to…

I'd met him on the pilgrimage.
                       For years
I'd worked on Chester quire. Great hopes, great fears…
When Richard came of age, he was promoted
to Clerk of the King's Works. Though he devoted
far too much energy (I thought) to what
others did better, I helped him on a lot
of buildings—some begun by Richard, who
was wasteful, arrogant, but brilliant too,
and open-minded. But at last he fell
a victim to Archbishop Arundel,
a man whom he'd offended many times,
not least by knocking clerics in his rhymes
as scroungers, thieves or wealthy hypocrites,
which got on this rich, worldly cleric's tits.
He had him robbed and badly beaten up—
twice—like a helpless lackey or young cub.
After the *coup*, he was convinced his days
were numbered, though he rented a new place—
I built his library—in the Abbey garden
at Westminster.
                    But nothing now could pardon
his *Tales*, he feared, in the eyes of Arundel.
Still insecure—one month a mere exile,
the next in power—King Bolingbroke and he
demanded hymns of praise, not irony,

or disrespectful fabliaux with fat friars,
summoners, pardoners, monks—all rogues and liars.
The new regime's diktat was *Church and state
dispense the truth.*
                    Laws meant to intimidate
rebellion or revenge were quickly passed.
Free-thinking speech became a thing of the past.
Richard was soon to die, his name disgraced.
Chronicles were censored, manuscripts defaced.

Chaucer, who'd long observed high politics,
remarked, "Next they'll be burning heretics."
Revenge and violence, though, he'd always said,
would heap more dead on those already dead—
and feared the rabid dogs of Civil War
would harry the Dance of Death from shore to shore.

And yet his pale and deeply worried face,
protected briefly from His worrying Grace,
still lit up with delight and, yes, surprise
when telling Chris's story.
                              His tired eyes
closed with exquisite joy—when Chris requested
a further tryst—at what L. had suggested.
She felt so shagged, she coolly shammed, that the best
thing *she* could do was take a well-earned rest.
Pompey suspected everyone. Young Pete,
she'd bet her boobs, had been dispatched to meet
his fellow-revellers in the halls of Hell—

Chris looked her up and down: *What, him as well?*
he didn't say but, slightly less in love,
felt peeved.
              When she suggested blindman's buff
with local wives and 'colleagues', he had mixed
though potent feelings. So a time was fixed
for two days later. Chris could have the one
he caught. Of course, they'd all have nothing on,
including him. The only little rule—
which wouldn't make him feel, she hoped, a fool—
was that he mustn't take his blindfold off,
no matter what, until he'd had enough
of what she guaranteed he'd get more than

could be enjoyed by almost any man,
and left her house. Her friends were part-time, too,
and weren't quite sure yet if he should know who
he'd have his dick in.
                        Laura's way with words
(no metaphoric honey-bees, no birds—
no poetry) had always shocked and charmed him.
Her offer now excited and disarmed him,
reminding him of certain wild week-ends
as a reckless youth—with loose, like-minded friends
at a small private brothel in another
part of the town—arranged by the girls' mother.

—Would L. play too, he'd asked.
                                       She hadn't planned
to do so, she replied. But, since demand
stimulates growth, "Well, then, if you insist…"
she yielded coyly, though would not have missed
for all the world—nor Jill—the chance to get
her own back for what life and luck had let
men do to them.
                     This almost went too far
when Chris got biffed and battered on a par
with his misdeeds, but stopped at last when they
let him catch Chris: *"Ther is namore to seye,*
but al that nyght this peyntour wol embrace
his wyf al newe, and kiste hir on hir face,
and up he gooth and maketh it ful tough.
'Namoore,' quod she, 'by God ye have ynough!'
And wantownly agayn with hym she pleyde,
til atte laste thus the peyntour seyde:
'I knowe thy voys!' 'Tehee,' quod she. Anon
she caughte his coillons and they were atoon
agayn. On his owen wyf he leith on soore.
So myrie a fit ne hadde he nat ful yoore;
he priketh hard and depe as he were mad.
This joly lyf han these two loveres lad
til they waxe wery in the dawenynge."

They heard the birds outside begin to sing.
The third cock crew.
                        She crooned, "My love, my life,
had you not better go home to your wife?"

Chris laughed out loud: "I *know* your voice! Let's see
your face now," laughing louder still as she
grabbed his soft tool and pulled his blindfold off...

Chaucer concluded with a modest cough,
commenting (when I asked) on how, at last,
making such love can flood and drown the past—
also the future, to which all men come
(but what on earth's the point of looking glum?)—
and is another blindfold, although they,
as lovers, *chose* to wear it from that day,
which made it seem a harmless, happy one...
Death's our last blindfold in that it stays on.
Chris died in childbirth. A late pregnancy
blessed and then blighted unexpectedly
their game of love.
                    If turds like Arundel
and Perkin Reveller, who belong in Hell,
stuck up the Devil's arse, don't always get
their sour revenge, the lives and luck we let
accumulate around us still conspire
to show the *more* our hearts and minds desire
the more they suffer. And the more we plan
to win against or screw another man
or men, the more we lose.
                            After Chris died,
Laura screwed more and more. She lost her pride,
and then her caution.
                        Someone cut her throat.

Pompey was picked up in a rowing boat
beside a tall ship bound for Italy:
"È morta, è morta!" he wailed unhappily,
then wept so much he couldn't say a word.

The judge decided he was too absurd
or mad to hang, if guilty, which was not
proved beyond doubt, and gaoled him.
                                        Pompey's lot
was as odd as Pompey. Chris heard he'd become
a hangman and was known as Pompey Bum...

I went to see Chris later. He remembered
Chaucer's conviction that his days were numbered,
the greyness of his aura, like a veil,
his pleasure, even so, in their 'Cook's Tale'
(which made him think of something in *Boccacce*—
a funny / heartless tale he couldn't place)
and Jill attending to her baby's needs.
He'd sat and smiled—and told his black prayer-beads…
The painter felt oppressed by a sense of sin.
He died soon after and is buried in
St Luke's, of course, the patron saint of all
who leave their mark, like snails, on wood or wall.

5   THE DANCE OF DEATH

(after *Totentanz der Stadt Basel*)

"Dance, dance, dance till you drop"
– W.H. Auden, *Death's Echo*

i   The Pope

Come, Holy Father, show them how
You do the dance and make your bow.
Though triple-crowned and double-crossed,
Your powers to bind and loose are lost.

*

Alive, they called me 'Your Holiness'.
Selling indulgences made me wealthy.
I was God's mouth on earth, no less—
But now my breath couldn't smell less healthy.

ii   The Emperor

Imperial Highness, grim and grey,
It's too late now for looking sorry:
I'll pipe you down death's dusty way.
So off you dance—I'm in a hurry.

*

Able not only to defend
My empire but to make it bigger,
Here I cut a sorry figure:
Death's dominion has no end.

iii   The Empress

Empress, for you I'll demonstrate
The dance—just trip along behind.
The court has left you to your fate.
Dance, dance while I rob you blind.

                *

A lusty life I thought I led
As a rich kaiser's fubsy *Frau*.
I've danced my last dance, anyhow,
And lack all pride and joy, being dead—

iv   The King

O King, relax. Don't waste your breath
On giving orders. My thin hand
Makes all men weak and powerless, and
Crowns their bowed heads with a dry wreath.

                *

Living, I loved to wield my power,
Raised to the highest ranks of honour.
And now? I'm nothing but a goner:
Shackled and gagged, I await my hour.

v   The Queen

Queenie, your fun and games are over,
So down you flop into your grave.
Your beauty, health and wealth can't save
Your face—from pushing up the clover.

                *

Oh help, where are my maids to cheer
And grace my chamber? Someone please
Come here and set my mind at ease!
Or is my end so near?…

vi   The Cardinal

Off you waltz in your crimson hat,
Monseigneur, mind you don't fall flat!
You've blessed or cursed the dead with a text,
But I'm afraid it's your turn next.

*

I was a well-known Cardinal,
An apple of the papal eye:
The whole world honoured me—must I
Keep dancing till I fall?

vii   The Bishop

Learned defender of the Faith,
Bishop, you've often turned aside
Into the primrose way of pride.
But you can't run away from death.

*

Flattered by sacristan and flunkey
As long as I lived as a Reverend Sir,
Breathing death's deconstructed air
I dance and chatter like a monkey.

viii   The Duke

With ladies you have danced, proud Duke,
And had them come and had them go.
The dead may make you want to puke,
But take their hands and say hello.

*

Dammit, must I be off so quickly
And leave land, friends, wife, children, fame
Behind, until I look the same
As these—as thin and sickly?

ix   The Duchess

My gracious lady, be of good cheer!
Although you come of a noble line,
Loved and respected by all up here,
Down there, my love, you're mine all mine.

                    *

My lute is cracked. And no dissembling
Affects this bony dancing horror.
Duchess today but not tomorrow,
I dance in fear and trembling.

x   The Earl

Although my news has brought no joy,
My lord, feed me in your French cuisine,
Before you hop it… Or are you itching
To join the hoi polloi?

                    *

A noble earl I was. My name
Was known and feared in all the world,
But death has danced me off and hurled
Me down, and felled my fame.

xi   The Abbot

Abbot, come here and let me knock
Your mitre off and break your staff.
Good shepherds always put their flock
First. You're good for a laugh.

                    *

I rose to be abbot, biggest of brothers,
And lived empowered and honoured, until
Nobody dared oppose my will.
But death has culled me like the others.

xii   The Knight

Sir Knight, your name is on my list.
Your sword-hand had the power to kill,
But the thrust of my armour-piercing fist
Cannot be parried by strength or skill.

*

A conscientious, valiant knight,
I served the world with derring-do.
Breaking my order's rules, I now
Must dance a last good-night.

xiii   The Lawyer

No dodge or obsequious flattery
Can get you off; there's no appeal.
My prison cells set no one free,
Cleric or lay. I over-rule.

*

Man's law derives from God on high,
As all may read in learned books.
Lawyers should not behave like crooks,
But love the truth and hate to lie.

xiv   The Alderman

Although a gent of this great city,
One who's done business here, and sat
On board and council and committee,
Please bow your head while I eat your hat.

*

I worked my fingers to the bone
To see the common good protected.
Both rich and poor should be respected,
Not live or die as if on their own.

xv   The Canon

O Canon, chanting loud and clear,
Leading your nice cathedral choir,
Listen: my scrannel pipe shrieks higher.
—Life's old sweet song croaks here.

*

I loved to swank in cope and frock,
And warble sacred melodies:
Death's clashing discords cut through these
And gave me a nasty shock.

xvi   The Doctor

Doctor, please check my anatomy,
That all is as it ought to be.
You used to treat, for a fat fee,
Patients who shortly looked like me!

*

An expert in urology,
I hoped to help both man and wife.
Who'll check *my* water, now that my life
Is pissing away so rapidly?

xvii   The Nobleman

Come, noble warrior, sheathe your sword,
And screw, if you want to save your face,
Your courage to the sticking place.
Death is the hero's last reward.

*

I terrified my enemies,
Though armed and in harness cap-à-pie—
As death has seized and rattled *me*,
Grimly forcing me to my knees.

xviii   The Lady

Milady, all this beauty-care
Is nothing but a purblind error.
Your body—skin—face—hair—
Are grey as ashes. Look in your mirror.

     *

My eyes were blue, my hair was gold,
But all I can see in my mirror's a skull.
What a horrible shock! And, then, how dull
To feel my blood run cold.

xix   The Merchant

Business as usual, sir? Well, not
Much longer. Though a proper toff,
Nothing you've got can buy me off.
Come dance till you rot.

     *

My time was money, and I learned
To get rich quick by ruthless thrift.
But death, devaluing my gift,
Robs me of everything I earned.

xx   The Abbess

My lady Abbess, full of grace,
How flat your little tummy's grown.
Not that I'd ever cast a stone!
The grave's a peaceful place.

     *

I've read my Bible, sung from the Psalter—
No hymn or prayer can help me now
To put off when or impede how
Death leads me to the altar.

xxi   The Cripple

Hobbledehoy on your ancient crutch,
I'll help you limp, I'll help you hop.
You may not count for very much,
But come and dance with me till you drop.

				*

Dragging along as if in fetters,
I'm neither use nor ornament.
With Death as my friend I'm more than content
To dance and hobnob with my betters.

xxii   The Hermit

Brother, stop cowering in your cell.
Come out, stand still, while I douse your light.
With your long white beard, you know full well
You've a journey to undertake tonight.

				*

Sackcloth and ashes I have worn,
Which hasn't done my health much good.
No longer safe in my cell in the wood,
Was it for this that I was born?

xxiii   The Youth

Where are you off to now, my lad?
I'll show you a path which leads elsewhere,
To a private place. Though I'm afraid
Lots of laddish lovers lie there.

				*

Wining and dining and having it off in
 Bordellos run by fat madames,
 My life was nothing but fun and games…
 I never dreamt I'd fill a coffin…

xxiv   The Usurer

Your money's of no use to me,
You crooked, god-forsaken Croesus.
Your tables were overturned by Jesus.
Now I'm your private company.

     *

I set no store by Jesus Christ:
Business pre-occupied my mind.
But all my savings stay behind—
Where life is prized, not priced.

xxv   The Young Woman

My dear, your lovely rose-red mouth
Will soon be pale. No boring wife,
With boys you've danced away your youth:
With me you'll dance away your life.

     *

Help, help! Though I don't want to die,
Life's somehow not much fun any more.
Even the Dance of Death's a bore,
Forget it. And so, *Goodbye, goodbye…*

xxvi   The Piper

What reel will you play on your bagpipes now?
'The Beggar Boy' or 'Black Man's Jig'?
No fair was fun without you. How
Can you not join my whirligig?

     *

That's it then. Before I ran out of luck,
No fair was too far—I loved to travel…
My piper's motley sleeves unravel.
I lost my pipes while drunk.

xxvii   The Herald

Herald! your red official hat
No longer serves to distinguish you.
Nor does your mace, or drum's rat-a-tat.
Shut up while I extinguish you!

                        *

Emperor and princes knew my worth:
My purse was heavy, stables stocked.
Many who heard my voice were shocked,
But death has filled my mouth with earth.

xxviii   The Mayor

Now, Mr Mayor, you know it's time
For body and soul to call it a day.
Playing my lute, I sing and rhyme:
Come dance while I rhyme and sing and play.

                        *

I tried in my judicial role
To see that fair was fair, not fudged.
On the day that rich and poor are judged,
May God have mercy on my soul.

xxix   The Executioner

Disposer of other people's lives,
In your red jerkin and fur hat,
You don't look happy. But so what?
After I've sentenced them, no one survives.

                        *

As all who dared to look could see,
I treated everyone alike:
A faithful servant of the Reich,
I discharged my duties peacefully.

xxx   The Fool

Hey-diddle-diddle, come dance to my fiddle,
And jump with me over the moon.
Poor fool, leave your bauble, don't dally or dawdle.
Are you cold? You'll be colder soon.

*

I'd sooner be beaten black and yellow
Four times a day by my lord and his thugs—
Lug logs home—live off bugs or slugs—
Than fight with this bony fellow!

xxxi   The Pedlar

You, penny-pinching pedlar, come—
You petty swindler and crier-up-allies—
And let some shameless factotum
Flog your knicknacks to bimboes and wallies.

*

I've travelled far by river and road,
Exchanging foreign currencies:
Dollars, crowns, guilders, gold guineas.—
Who'll pay me now what I'm owed?

xxxii   The Blindman

Ragged old blindman, no one can save
Your bacon. In your hour of need,
Allow me to cut your guide-dog's lead
And guide you to your grave.

*

I can't earn my keep or my daily bread.
As blind as a lemon or a log,
I can't go a step without my dog.
Thank God I'll soon be dead.

xxxiii   The Cook

*John Cook, roll over here. You've got
So fat that you can hardly trot.
You love sweet puddings. But the hour
Has struck which turns all stomachs sour.*

*

I've basted capons, roasted geese,
Steamed fish for king and nobleman.
Venison, pâté, marzipan—
My belly aches to leave all these.

xxxiv   The Peasant

*You've laboured long in the sweat of your brow,
From dawn to dusk, each day without fail.
I'll free you from your burdens now:
Hand me your basket—dagger—and flail.*

*

Hey, give me back my old felt hat!
I don't mind working any more,
As I've always worked. I'm old and poor
And weary. But what's wrong with that?

xxxv   The Poet

*Poet, put down your raging pen:
Your artful words won't help you when
I come for you like other men
(Death's 'now' has neither 'then' nor 'then').*

You've given me shocking / mocking lines …
Are you (or your family) better prepared
Than the Pope et al., to whom you've dared
Assign such cries and groans?

*

…

279

xxxvi   The Poet's Wife

Mother and wife, you needn't grieve
For them much longer. Depend upon it,
The time is ripe for you to leave.
Let me relieve you of your bonnet.

*

I've always been resigned to death,
Always believed in eternal life;
But this hard double-grief, as wife
And mother, sorely tests my faith.

Coda

Adam and Eve

> "... *how you take it!*" – The Tempest

If she and I had ever been
At home in Eden, original sin
Entered our minds when we questioned why
We of all creatures had to die.

Made in God's image, or so we thought,
Our SELF-IMPORTANCE filled the air,
Oceans and all the earth…, till nowhere
Was safe from the fire with which we fought…

Stealer of fire, and then fire's slave,
Afraid of what we'll lose or find
Today—tomorrow—or in the grave—
The what-if / what-if-nots of the mind—

Our self-assertive song and dance
Contrives to shift the blame
To God or Life-and-Death or Chance.—
Victims in all but name,

Our world is, still, the way we make it:
Death's a blank fact like other facts
Of life. And life is—how you take it.
I *think*, therefore I *act*.

For man alone, of all that dies
Passively under the passive sun,
Is blessed with active words and eyes
To do / undo what's done / undone.

6   BENVENUTO *E GLI ALTRI*

"Questa mia vita travagliata io scrivo" – Cellini

I wrote *my troubled* Life *so as to give*
Praises *and thanks to God, the Lord of Nature.*
He *made my soul, then cared for me, His creature,*
So *that, through my achievements, I might live.*

God *helped me to defy my destiny,*
And *made my life successful beyond measure.*
In *gold and bronze, none can compare with me*
For virtù… *And yet, have I, in laying up treasure*

On *earth, not also erred? How right was I*
To *wreak such vengeance—slaughter many more*
In *battle? Old as I am, and though the Pope*
Himself *absolved me of my sins, what hope*
Remains *of peace or pardon? Disheartened, less sure*
Of *myself than then, what would—might—others say?*

*

Giovanni Cellini

"My father put a legend in Latin round a looking-glass he had made for himself: Rota sum:
semper quoquo me verto stat Virtus."
– *La vita* I. v

I want to write some lines in praise of my son
Before I die. In Firenze, the plague is worse
Than any time since *The Decameron*
Taught us to rise above its raging curse

And seize the day… I feared the Sack of Rome
Would be his end. But, no, he overcame
The worst—fought bravely—worked in gold—came home
Wealthy. Relieved that he's safe elsewhere, I blame

Myself though still. His stubborn violence grew,
God knows, from hating me. I forced him to learn
Music—to play in consort. But he can

Only excel alone. Renaissance man
Must win against the world—(but why?)—must earn
Riches, respect, renown—must make, must do—

              *

Pope Paul III

"'That devil Benvenuto will not tolerate rebuke. It is not right to behave so arrogantly with a Pope.'"
– La vita I. lvi

I make no claim to be a saint—but he
Would try the patience of our Lord in person!
Not ill-disposed at first, I got him free
Of a murder charge. But now—the Church's curse on

His head! He'd served Pope Clement, too—as a brave
Gunner—a brilliant jeweller, goldsmith, musician—
Until he got above himself and gave
Nothing but trouble with one major commission

After another, insisting he be *paid*
Before he'd go on working. And so with me—
Who mind St Peter's pence. He can't expect
To raid Rome's coffers. I bind, I loose. More respect
Is due to Popes. Thief or no thief, may he
Rot in Sant'Angelo until he's dead.

              *

Giorgio Ugolini, Castellan of Sant'Angelo

"The Castellan, after giving the most cruel orders for my death, suddenly countermanded them, and said: Is not this Benvenuto the man whom I know to be innocent and who has been so greatly wronged? Oh, how shall God have mercy on me and my sins if I do not pardon him?..."
– La vita I. cxx

Now that the time has come for me to die,
Let me admit I hate but also love him.
He does what he likes! On parole, he was left free
To work, meet others. The Angel stood guard above him.

But then, like some ill-omened bat or bird,
He escaped. Re-caught, defied me to my face—
Showed no regret. While breaking his solemn word,
He also broke a leg. In pain and disgrace,

Sunk in my foulest dungeon, he *praised* it!... His faith
Moved heaven and earth to help him. My sins appal
Even myself. May God have mercy on
Our souls. Despite his pride and self-assertion,
Such faith—hope—love—instruct and inspire us all.
Nor will I now despair in the face of death.

*

Pagolo Micceri, Goldsmith

"*Now Pagolo Micceri, having learned to keep my accounts, went on doing this work for me in return for a liberal salary. He appeared to be a very honest lad, for I noticed him to be devout, and when I heard him muttering psalms and telling his beads, I reckoned much upon his feigned virtue.*"
– *La vita* II. xxviii

I kept his books—he kept my Caterina
To serve him as his model. He abused
Her body also, ramming his tool between her
Prostitute's thighs or buttocks. She was used

To men like him. But, once she knew I loved her,
Wanted to stop it. Her mother said *Take him to court*.
But he bullied even the judge. And so I moved her
To a house of her own. He crashed through the door and caught

Us *in flagrante*. I thought he'd kill me. But
He got cold feet, and forced us to marry instead.
An odd 'revenge'. Though was it—was *I*—too late?
Indulging his sick need to dominate,
He beckoned, she came. He paid, then beat her. Half-dead
With cuts and bruises, she went back for more, the slut.

*

Ascanio di Giovanni de' Mari, Goldsmith

"*I made Ascanio and Pagolo Romano guardians of my castle and all my property in Paris… I bade Ascanio remember what great benefits I had bestowed upon him… He replied with the tears of a thief and hypocrite: 'I have never known a father better than you are, and all the things which a good son is bound to perform for a good father will I ever do for you.' So I took my leave.*"
– La vita II. xlix

In Paris we were nothing once he'd gone.
Nothing but goldsmiths. At last I came back home
To Tagliacozzo. Pagolo stayed on.
I wanted to see his *Perseus*. But he'd become—

Or so we heard—convinced we'd betrayed him. Why?
I'd risked my life for him. In affrays in France,
Siena, Rome. As a thirteen-year-old boy,
I helped him cross the Alps. Entirely by chance

We survived, and met the King. Then back again—
Sadly—unwell—to quarrelling with the Pope.
I worked in his shop. After his great escape
I left again to serve him… Things change shape,
But stay the same: mistrustful, we grasp—fight—grope
In the dark… He's ill. I'll wait. See Perseus then.

*

Agnolo Bronzino (1)

"*I said to myself: 'If God but grant me to finish my Perseus, I hope by its means to annihilate all my scoundrelly enemies; and thus I shall perform far greater and more glorious revenges than if I had vented my rage upon one single foe.'*"
– La vita II. lxvi

Our art will live, we die. I painted the Duke
(No poet, or artist) as *Orfeo*, the faithful lover,
Sinewed like *Ercole*, poised to seize and choke
Cerberus (more his way). All dukes discover

That flesh is grass. Perseus, for Cosimo, stood
For law and order. For Benvenuto, though,
He was born of gold—an avenging son of god
Raising a headful of dead snakes? "*Un sol*

Giovin ch' all' ali"? But poisonous women, sour men,
Have stopped him working... Thought, even so, is free.
I too am underpaid—which matters less,
I find, than that the work gets done. A curse
On penny-pinching patrons! As for me,
I serve my art. Would choose to serve it again.

*

Mona Fiore

"*Through the last decade of his life Cellini was self-employed... He cared for his family, employing an organist to give cembalo lessons to his daughter Liperata. Like other Florentines, moreover, he was interested in betting, especially on the sex of unborn children...*"
– John Pope-Hennessy, *Cellini*, p.282

He's bet this baby's a boy. One thing's for sure:
It's my last chance and his. Three others have died—
One mine. He loves the girls, but wants to ensure
A future for his name and masculine pride.

Dealing in gold, jewels, land, he's grown to detest
Our aging ruler—but fears him. What he wanted
Was honour more than money. The Duke's tight fist
Always gave less than promised—grudged what it granted.

I kept his house—then him. I saved, he says,
His life—his work—his all. With him I learned
Not to say no. My widowed heart's warm ache
Welcomed his fullness. Compelled always to *take*
Beauty—male, female—body and soul—he burned
Hotter than Perseus' now cold, broken furnace.

*

Agnolo Bronzino (2)

"*In August 1570, six months before his death, Cellini made his final claim for his Crucefix on the Gran Principe: 'I have made it at my own expense and to my own satisfaction, solely to prove that through the force of my own art I could surpass all those sculptors greater than myself who had never undertaken such a task.'*"
– Pope-Hennessy, *op cit*, p.260

Another self-portrait? His first Christian work,
Unless I'm much mistaken. Also his last
Of any value. Staring into the dark
Ahead makes most old men review their past.

And yet he and the Duke have—what? in common:
Self-interest—self-importance—prowess—greed?…
The Duke is nothing, though, but a money man,
Whereas his art makes gold, bronze, marble bleed.

Since I don't share his constant need to defeat
His rivals, we stay friendly. A terrified madness
Burns deep in his eyes, when thwarted—a forge which makes
Fine art and, quietly, quells the Gorgon's snakes
Into metal, or stone: no colour. This white Christ's sadness
Has lost which battles? Are we *condemned* to compete?

*

"When I asked the Duke for leave of absence, he refused to grant it, and at the same time he gave me no more commissions, so that I could serve neither him nor any other man. Nor was I able to find out the reason for the evil plight I was in…"
– Cellini, *Trattato dell' Oreficeria* xii

The Duke, I sometimes think, can hardly tell
The difference. Why *stand Bandinelli's sack*
Of melons next to David?!… *And so I fell*
Victim to Baccio's slurs—Giorgetto's talk—

Eleonora's vanity—Cosimo's power…
Where art was not much more than a (lasting) façade
To mask the machinations of the hour,
What might I have done better? Was I mad

In fact when in Sant'Angelo I saw
The sun give birth to my white Crucefix?
Surely Christ's loss was our gain? I lost, too. But
Father, he prayed, *forgive them… I know what*
I did: *I hated. Kicked against the pricks,*
When I might have lived, let live—let be—worked more.

7   VITZLIPUTZLI

(after Heine)

"This is Amerigo's land!
This is yesterday's New World!"

i

On his brow a wreath of laurel;
On his boots a golden spur
Glinted. Neither knight nor hero
Helping victims in despair,

But a sort of robber-chieftain:
Cortez was his brazen name,
Scribbled with his brazen fist
In the Book of Lasting Fame,

Under *Christopher Columbus*,
Where the 'New World' entries start;
And the school-boy at his school-desk
Has to learn their names by heart.

By such quirks of fate a hero's
Name may end up coupled with
Some ignoble malefactor's—
As their history turns to myth…

Might it not be better if
One could fade away unknown,
Than to drag some rascal's name
Down the ages with one's own?

Master Christopher Columbus
Was a hero. And his spirit
Was as generous as the sun—
And as pure. His greatest merit

Was, while others came—saw—conquered,
He alone presented our

Old World with a wholly new one:
And it's called America.

Though, of course, he could not free us
From the dreary toil and pain
Which make earth a prison, he
Managed to expand our chain.

And we really should be grateful,
Who are bored to euthanasia—
Now—not only with old Europe
But with Africa and Asia.

One alone, another hero,
Gave us more and took us further
Than Columbus: he alone who
Gave us God. His loving father,

Less well known, was Amram; his
Mother Jochebeth by name:
He himself is Moses—holiest
Hero in my Book of Fame...

But, my Pegasus, you dawdle
Far too long with C. Columbus—
Don't you know we fly today
Re that lesser man, H. Cortez?

Spread your brightly coloured pinions,
Winged steed, and off we go
Once again to that enticing
New World land of Mexico.

Carry me to that great palace
Which King Montezuma placed
At his Spanish guests' disposal,
So that no one should lose face.

Not just more fresh food and shelter
Than they needed—but the King
Gave these foreign vagabonds
Golden arm-bands, golden rings,

Also fine, elaborate jewels
Set in solid gold. Thus he
Showed his royal grace and favour
And his generosity.

Montezuma condescended,
Then, to join a celebration
In his honour—to be held
By the Spaniards in their fashion.

As a blind, uncivilized,
Superstitious heathen, he
Valued honour and the sacred
Right to hospitality.

So the king with all his courtiers
Came to where the Spanish waited,
And they paid polite attention
Till the fanfares had abated.

What the name of this charade was,
I don't know. Perhaps its author
Called it *Spanish Promises*—
Made and broken now by Cortez,

As he gave the cue to kidnap
Montezuma, and to hold
Him as hostage, till his subjects
Brought the Spaniards *all* their gold.

But King Montezuma died.
And the dam which had held back
His offended people's fury
From the bold adventurers cracked.

And a storm began to rage,
Like a wind-tormented sea—
Rising, roaring, raging closer,
Waves of mad humanity.

Oh, the Spanish fought back bravely!
But each day the storm came bursting

Once more round the palace walls;
And the battle was exhausting.

After Montezuma's death,
No provisions were provided:
As united in their gloom
As their rations were divided,

Spain's tough sons soon sat and sighed,
Pulling long, dejected faces,
Thinking of their homes—and other
Nice familiar Christian places:

Of their precious fatherland,
Where the church-bells welcome you—
Where, in every kitchen, there's a
Gently simmering pot of stew,

Thickened with the best *garbanzos*,
In among which, you might guess
From the roguish smell, are lurking
Mother's garlic sausages…

So their top brass held a pow-wow
And decided to retreat
Early in the morning. Latin
Armies hate the mid-day heat.

But to come turned out to be
Easier than it was to go:
Only bridges, rafts and fords
Led away from Mexico.

Trying to steal a march, before
Dawn, they left the island-city,
Minus drum or trumpet, since
The strategic nitty-gritty

Was—a hundred thousand Indians
Bivouacking there each night.
So the guests got up and left
While their hosts were sleeping tight;

But their moonlight flit was foiled—
For, in fact, the hosts had risen
Even earlier. To the Spanish,
Mexico became a prison

On whose bridges, rafts and fords—
With a bloody farewell treat—
Sentries waited. Soon blood ran
Down their boots and round their feet.

As they wrestled man to man,
Spanish armour's arabesques
Boldly printed their design
Onto naked Indian chests.

Some were choked, and others strangled,
While the whole slow massacre
Rolled on slowly over bridges,
Rafts and fords, in blood and horror.

And the Indians sang and howled,
But the Spanish fought in silence,
Forcing inch by inch a pathway
Through the Indians' frenzied violence.

Trapped in bottle-necks, the Old World's
Style was cramped, as all their stuff—
Armour, cannon, guns, war-horses—
Hardly left them with enough

Room to swing a sword. What's more,
Many bore great packs of gold,
Plundered or extorted, which—
Having tempted their poor souls—

Now weighed down their bodies and
Hampered them while fighting. Thus
Can that sinful yellow metal
Be the double death of us.

Meanwhile that great lake was covered
With canoes and little boats;

Archers sat in them and shot
At the bridges, fords and floats,

And they hit, in all that turmoil,
Many of their own brave brothers.
But they also killed or wounded
Some *hidalgos*, among others.

On the third bridge, for example,
Gaston fell—amid the surging
Mob—who bore the Spaniards' banner,
With its portrait of the Virgin.

Six bright Indian arrows had
Pierced this portrait and remained
Stuck in Mary's heart, where they
Symbolized the sacred pain

She, as *Mater dolorosa*,
Suffers each Good Friday when—
In procession—golden arrows
Pierce her sacred heart again.

As he died, Don Gaston passed
That torn banner to Gonzalvo,
Who in turn was greeted by
Death's sharp sting within a salvo

Not of guns but arrows. Cortez
Now took up the precious banner—
Bore it on as darkness fell,
Leading in his manliest manner

Till the battle was concluded.
Twice as many Spaniards died
As the eighty which the Indians
Caught and charged with regicide.

Many who'd been badly wounded
Died within the next few days.
And they'd lost a dozen horses,
Killed or captured. The last rays

Of the blood-red sun were fading
As they reached at last the shallows
Of a safe, deserted shore-line
Planted sparsely with green willows.

ii

After that day's fearful battle
Came a ghostly night of triumph,
And a hundred thousand lights
Burn and flare across the island.

Lights of victory and rejoicing,
Resin torches, fires of pitch,
Throw a garish sort of daylight
Onto forts and guild-halls which

Stand with palaces beneath
Vitzliputzli's massive temple,
Whose red brick reminds one of
Ancient Egypt, for example,

Or Assyrian—Babylonian—
Monstrous piles, which play a part in
Paintings of colossi by
That great Briton, Henry Martin.

Yes, here are the same vast flights of
Sloping steps—so long and wide
Several thousand Indians flow
Up and down them like a tide,

While the warriors drink their palm-wine
On the steps in drunken groups:
Then as now, such boozing usually
Over-intoxicates the troops…

At the top the flights ascend
In a zigzag to a platform,
Where the temple roof consists of
One immense, imposing flat form

With a balustrade. And here,
On his throne and/or his altar
Sits the war-god Vitzliputzli—
Mexico's blood-thirsty monster—

Whose peculiar curlicues
Look so childish, though—so silly—
That his inner horror scarcely
Stops you laughing willy-nilly.

On his left side stands the priesthood,
Laymen stand towards the right.
Priests in feathers—highly coloured
Vestments—strut their stuff tonight.

On the altar's marble steps
Squats a hundred-year-old soul,
Bald and beardless, in a sort of
Little scarlet camisole.

As the sacrificial priest, he
Strops his sacrificial knife—
Smiles—and squints up at the god
Whom he's honoured all his life.

Vitzliputzli seems to welcome
His devotee far beneath—
Seems to wink or move an eyelash—
Seems to smile—or show his teeth.

Also on the steps, musicians
Blow their horns for calling cattle—
Crouch behind the temple drums—
Beat and blow and toot and rattle—

Rattle, beat and blow and toot!
And the temple choir starts bawling
Forth a Mexican *Te Deum*,
Like a fearful caterwauling—

Or the wild, nocturnal chorus
Of some larger sort of cat,

Such as tigers, which, instead of
Mice, eat men up—just like that!

And the night-wind bears this racket
Off to that depressing shore
Where the Spaniards are encamped—
Which depresses them the more.

Sadly under weeping willows,
Looking out towards the city
Over that dark stretch of water
Where, without a spark of pity,

All its burning joy is mirrored,
Mocking them, the Spaniards stand
As if in the cheaper stalls
Of a National Theatre, and

Vitzliputzli's temple's platform
Is the brightly lighted stage,
Where a solemn Mystery Play
Feeds the god's victorious rage.

Human Sacrifice it's known as—
And the story's very old.
If the well-known Christian version
Fails to make your blood run cold,

With its blood turned into wine,
And the body rendered safer
By being transubstantiated
Into thin and harmless wafer,

Aztec ritual was more savage
And the fun direct and crude:
What they ate was actual flesh,
And the blood was human blood.

This time it was undiluted
Early Christian vintage—nor
Had it ever been polluted
By the blood of Jew or Moor.

Vitzliputzli, aren't you lucky
To be doing quite so well?
Spanish blood to please your nostrils—
Feed your greed with its warm smell!

Eighty Spaniards, duly slaughtered,
Should provide enough roast flesh
For your priesthood's groaning tables—
Who prefer their victuals fresh.

Even priests are only human,
And the human being—poor sod—
Has to eat and cannot simply
Live from smelling, like a god…

Now the drums of death start booming
And the shrieking cattle-horn
Greets the climbing file of men, who
Soon will wish they'd not been born.

Eighty Spaniards—humbled, naked—
Hands behind them—tied with ropes—
Now are drummed and hauled or harried
Up the temple stairway's slopes;

Reaching Vitzliputzli's idol,
Are compelled to bend the knee,
And to dance the victims' dance.
Then they're tortured cruelly.

And so dreadful are these tortures
That their screaming and their bawling—
Pain and fear—out-howl the priesthood's
Cannibalistic caterwauling.

On the shore beneath the willows
Cortez and his soldiers hear—
And can recognize—the voices
Of their friends in pain and fear.

On the stage in lurid firelight
They can see the priest's raised knife,

See their comrades' forms and faces
And the stroke which ends their life,

Till they kneel and take their warriors'
Helmets from their humbled heads,
Start to sing the *De Profundis*,
Praying for mercy on the dead.

Of the fallen, young Raimondo
De Mendoza was but one—
Yet he was the lovely abbess,
Cortez' first love's only son.

When he glimpsed the gold medallion
With the image of his mother
Round the young man's bleeding throat,
Cortez wept like any other

Member of that band which, sighing,
Sang to God for mercy. Whether
Heard or not, he dried his eyes
With a rough glove of hard leather.

iii

Now the stars are shimmering palely
And the morning mists—like fleeting,
Silent phantoms—hide the water,
As if dragging lengths of sheeting.

All the ritual fires are out
At the temple of the deity:
On its bloodied platform, priests
Snore in consort with the laity.

In his blood-soaked vest, the eldest
Priest still watches, still invoking—
By the last fire's light—his god,
Sweetly grinning, darkly joking:

"Vitzliputzli, Putzlivitzli,
 Little god-head, have you felt

Honoured—and had fun—tonight,
When the best of smells was smelt?

Did you like the Spaniards' blood?
O it smelt almost attractive—
Sweetly steaming! Your excited,
Gleaming nose was hyperactive.

In the morning there are horses—
Noble, neighing monsters—beasts
Which the wind-god and the sea-cow
Sired and bore to grace our feast.

If you're good, I'll even slaughter
My grand-daughter's little boys.
Sweetest blood! And just the kind of
Kiddies my old age enjoys.

But you must be good and help us,
Vitzliputzli, Putzlivitzli:
Help us, little god of blood,
To another bloody victory.

Oh, destroy these crazed marauders,
Who have come across the ocean
Out of distant, undiscovered
Lands of which we have no notion.

Why should they have left their homeland?
Are they driven by guilt or hunger?
*Live at home and ply an honest
Trade*, we say—*and you'll live longer!*

What's the point of stealing gold
When they claim it's only later
In their Heaven that men are happy?
First we thought they were a greater

Race of men—or from the sun—
Waging war immortally,
Armed with lightning, smoke and thunder.
Now we know that they can die,

Know that knives and arrows kill them
Just like any other men—
And tonight my gleaming knife has
Proved it eighty times again.

No more beautiful than we are!
Come to that, it's almost scary
How some look like ugly monkeys,
With their faces just as hairy

And, they say, with monkey's tails
Hidden in their baggy trousers.
For if some of them aren't monkeys,
Why on earth do they need trousers?

Morally obscene they are—
Impious, sacrilegious lot!
Why, I've heard they even eat—
So must defecate—their god.

Oh, destroy this wicked race,
Vitzliputzli, Putzlivitzli—
These malicious god-consumers!
Help us gain the final victory."

Thus the priest addressed his god.
And the god's voice—like a sighing
Night-wind through the rushes—or a
Dry death-rattle—hissed, replying:

"Red Vest, Red Vest, blood-red butcher,
Manifold man-slaughterer, may you
Stick your sacrificial knife
Now where it will quickly slay you!

May your soul then leave your body
Through the wound your flint has slit:
Over roots and pebbles, down to
Where the frogs spawn, let it flit.

Squatting in that pond, my auntie,
Queen of all the rats, will say:

'Well, good morning, naked soul.
How's my nephew-god today?

Is my Vitzliputzli happy—
Bathed in honey-sweet, gold light?
Does his luck still put his worries—
And the flies—to rapid flight?

Or do wicked Katzlagara's
Nasty bugs pursue and catch him?
Or her paws of rusty iron,
Dipped in adders' poison, scratch him?'

Naked soul, may you reply:
'Vitzliputzli sends his greetings,
And he hopes your cursed rat-gut
Gets the gut-rot after eating!

Your advice was go to war.
But the age-old prophecy
Now begins to plague us. All your
Brinkmanship will fail, you see.

For it's said the realm's destroyers
Shall be men like bearded beasts—
Furious men on wooden birds,
Flying hither from the East.

And another saying is
Woman's will is God's will—but
God's will's doubled when the woman
Is the Mother of the God!

Proud she is, and Queen of Heaven.
Aah, for us her reign is tragic!—
An immaculate young girl,
Working wonders, versed in magic!

I could scream, it's so unfair
How she helps them! Soon we'll go
Under, I—a poor old god—
And my poor new Mexico.'

Red Vest, when your naked spirit
Ceases squeaking, go and creep
Down a sand-hole. Armageddon
Needn't pain you if you sleep.

When these temple walls collapse,
I myself shall simply sink
In the fug—the smoke and rubble.
I'll have had my lot, they'll think.

But we gods don't die: like parrots,
We just moult and grow new feathers.
Old but young, we keep on changing
Like the seasons or the weather.

Their Old World's called Europe—where
I shall shortly reappear
On the run. My long-term aim is
To begin a new career—

As a devil. By persuading
Them I AM—a God-be-with-us—
I, the god of raging warfare,
Shall possess these unbelievers

Till some vast catastrophe
Strikes them! War in Europe, say?
Or in *all* their sphere of influence?
Given the mad, insatiable way

That their anxious, ruthless minds
See and treat their world, they're sure,
In the end, to lay it waste—
Sure to wage the first 'World War'!

Anyway, I shall torment them,
Shock them with the clash of nations—
And, like Hell, with burning sulphur,
Stifle their benumbed sensations.

Yes, I shall become a devil,
And I greet the exclusive club—

Satan, Ashtaroth and Belial—
Even foul Beelzebub.

But above all I greet Lilith:
Sin's great mother, temptress, snake—
Teach me cruelty, teach me how to
Lie for all my people's sake.

For though my beloved priesthood—
Temple—bridges—all must go,
I'll revenge them cruelly, sweetly,
And remember Mexico."

8 SHAKESPEAREAN SONNETS

"What do you read, my lord?"—"Words, words, words."
– *Hamlet*, II.ii.191–192

i *"The Concord of this Discord"*
         (*A Midsummer Night's Dream*, V.i.60)

The Taming of the Shrew—Hortensio

   "… And the moon changes even as your mind."
   – IV.v.20

As mad Petruchio's friend and Bianca's lover
Disguised as music-teacher, I felt free
To change my role. No play goes on for ever.
The widow and I agree to disagree.

She lives her life, I mine. We meet in bed.
Sometimes we chat. As for love, I'm not so sure.
When Lucentio lost the wager, Bianca said
The more fool you! more shrewdly than bargained for.

In Petruchio's headstrong house, there'll be no lack
Of blunt "unhappy words", and time to kill.
A loud-mouthed ruffian and a surly Jack
He is. And she a long-tongued brawling Jill

Who'll see him hanged! My widow cooks. Well, she
Likes bed, loves board… But is that enough for me?

                    *

The Comedy of Errors—The Abbess Emilia

   *"I to the world am like a drop of water
   That in the ocean seeks another drop…"*
   – I.ii.35–36

I never thought I'd see them all again—
Or any one of them. But now all three

Are here in Ephesus. Life ended in
A shipwreck. Lost, I—they—saw only sea…

For years my griefs flowed—ebbed—in unspeakable
Grey waves. Our rule of silence helped me—to find
Myself, then words again. My heart was full
Of storms or mist. I saw, but I was blind.

My twin—and Dromio—came here next. It seems
My husband gave his pair the names of those
He thought he'd lost. They met as if in dreams:
Two men, two masters—different eyes, same nose.

It's what we think that sees. I might have found
My two here. Now we learn to live, who drowned.

*

Two Gentlemen of Verona—Silvia

> *"Is she kind as she is fair?*
>   *For beauty lives with kindness.*
> *Love doth to her eyes repair*
>   *To help him of his blindness…"*
> – IV.ii.43–46

They ask me who or what I am. So what
Am I? My father's gift to one man or
Another? Even *if* one loved, that one could not
See me. Love feeds, chameleon-like, on air.

More talked about than talking, how am I
To be myself? I look, see others looking—
Metamorphosed by this or that man's eye
In the wood of the world, see beasts and lovers lurking.

Poor Launce is truer to his wretched cur—
Taking the blame for Crab's ill-bred misdeeds—
Than any of them to me. If he loved her,
A man might hazard *all* for his woman's needs!…

One raped my mind with unreal words. Real life
Now takes me for his faithful friend's true wife.

*

Love's Labour's Lost—Berowne

> *"When shall you see me write a thing in rhyme?*
> *Or groan for Joan?"*
> – IV.iii.178–179

We gave our word—a college of young *fools*
To swear we'd only study for three years!
Obey a senseless list of monkish rules,
Make war against our own and the world's desires.

We play with words as if they were mere foam
Blown here and there by stormy nights or days—
In court, town, tavern, or in bed at home,
Desiring this man's hurt, that woman's praise.

Honey-tongued when it suits us, imprecise
And usually in disguise, let us here vow
To mean what our words say—straight no, plain yes—
And keep the things we promise... Except that, now,

Why should these French girls trust us? Or why we
Our shallow oaths' impure integrity?

*

A Midsummer Night's Dream—Hippolyta

> *"Merry and tragical? Tedious and brief?...*
> *How shall we find the concord of this discord?"*
> – V.i.58,60

—Or *make* the concord which we cannot find?
The story shall be changed—and changed again...
Till fantasy and reason, heart and mind,
Re-dream *themselves*... Poor women, poor moon-mad men,

Can see no further. But of all creation
We see the best. Theseus, as duke, thinks words
Can comprehend the truth! imagination,
Brief as forked lightning, hot as squabbling birds,

306

Disperse and leave cool, clear reality
To dawn! And yet what joy apt words can bring:
Though "laurel" is no laurel—"Daphne" no tree—
When beauty blinds us, words flash—fly—bloom—sing…

And all our minds', could they be heard together,
Might *be* the story of the night told over.

*

The Merchant of Venice—Jessica

> *"But though I am a daughter to his blood,*
> *I am not to his manners."*
> – II.iii.18–19

Wise, fair and true he says I am. I hope
 His hopes are more than love—or 'harmony'…
– A thief, a puny liar, how will I cope
With old laws, new laws? What does it *mean* to be free?

Starting from nowhere, I must choose my world:
Between the Christians' and my father's hate—
Their vengeful envy—live and learn to wield
Forgiveness like a candle. In any night

Venice treats Jews like dogs. How can I bear
What I've done? Our house was hell. Love's unthrift thrives—
But loses what it buys with too much care.
The Christians broke their oaths *and* keep their wives.

I'll give and hazard all I have. But, rather
Than sell it, keep my mother's ring for my father.

ii   *"The Swelling Scene"*
            (*Henry V,* Prologue l.4)

The Life and Death of King John—Philip the Bastard

> *"Since kings break faith upon Commodity,*
> *Gain be my Lord, for I will worship thee."*
> – II.i.597–598

Richard the Lion-heart was my father. And,
Being dubbed 'Sir Richard' by my Uncle John,
I'm rich in honour now. But, poor in land,
I lack as much as a mole-hill to mount on.

Since mountains come to no one, I must go
Where bell, book, candle shall not drive me back
If gold or silver beckon. A bastard must grow
By fair play, foul play. Black is white, white black,

When my all-changing, faithless lord and master
Tempts me to rise by means of smooth-faced reason
And tickling rhyme—by (playing looser / faster)
Sweet poison for the age's tooth, hot poison

For weak king or strong claimant: I am I
Most truly when I play. Or cheat. Or lie…

*

King Richard II—Queen Isabel

> *"Thus play I in one person many people,*
> *And none contented."*
> – V.v.31–32

Though I loved him blindly, even I could see
How he, confusing thought with thing, used words
To fend off fear, miscall necessity
Virtue. As if a prisoner, imagining birds

Piping sad songs, believed real live musicians
Had come to play for him—twenty false shadows,
Cast by his grief, to dance. Life's lean conditions
Drive us to hope death's dust makes heavenly meadows.

Others just lied. Richard, my fair rose, dreamed
He *was* a king, the earth of England his
By God's command. When mustering angels seemed
To guard his throne the East, how *could* he lose?

Taking his role for real, he lost his sense
Of right and wrong. Gained death in recompense.

*

1 Henry IV—Edward Poins

"*I have vizards for you all.*"
– I.ii.123

I was always a thief. My fortunes ebb and flow
By moonlight. Labouring hard in my vocation,
I walk invisible. Pilgrims come and go—
Bring gifts for my Mercurial delectation.

A sister and three bastards also depend
On my works and worship in the all-masking dark.
My father swore I'd come to a crack-hemp's end.
As second brother turned St Nicholas' clerk,

I steal—eat, drink—hoax—whore—from dusk to dawn,
With the Prince as my atoning elder brother.
His father stole poor Dikkon's rightful crown:
He spends pure gold. Men butcher one another

In civil wars. Though fighting's all the fashion,
I'll risk my neck in my preferred profession.

*

The Merry Wives of Windsor—Master Fenton

"*—thou must be thyself.*"
– III.iv.3

If I can't persuade Anne's father to approve
Of me before we wed, he'll have to embrace
Our lawful plot. To get her rich sweet love
I've cut the Prince and Poins—changed my wild ways—

Avoid fat Falstaff's riotous gang of revellers—
Eschew the pleasures of the road by night.
I can't knit knots or heal my state with travellers'
Robbed baggage and shared purses, try as I might…

Am I in love with this well-kempt good girl?
Is *she* my harvest-home? My golden gain?

How many oysters bear a precious pearl?
I hope she's somewhere more than in my brain!

She's sixteen years of age. I've spent my last
Money to woo a future, dump a past.

*

2 Henry IV—The Lord Chief Justice

> *"If the young dace be a bait for the old pike, I see no reason in
> the law of nature but I may snap at him."*
> – III.ii.325–326

Nobody names me, though I have a name
As well as office. But my reputation
For truth is false. The eyes and tongues of Fame
Misunderstand, divide our fearful nation.

"A hundred thousand rebels" are to die
At the hands of the biggest rebel of the lot,
The Regicide who seeks to justify
His past in word and deed—the fool who thought

That nothing could seem foul to those that win
And now seems foul to himself. Half-truths, half-lies,
Are all. Ashamed to serve this king, whose sin
Corrupts, I cannot flee, but compromise

While hope persists, contriving to train and nurture
New growth, resisting Falstaff's law of nature.

*

Henry V—The Chorus

> *"O God, thy arm was here."*
> – IV.viii.108

The Bishops made an offer to the King
To raise a mighty sum, which helped him claim
The throne of France, leaving their choirs to sing
God's praises for thus helping *them* at home:

The Commons wanted half the Church's land,
The war distracted them. The unruly minds
Of earls and barons, fighting in God's hand,
Were also 'busied'. Once aroused, blood blinds—

Of course, I couldn't say as much on stage.
As for Hal's former friends, fat Falstaff babbled
And died. Poins vanished. Bardolf thought he could wage
A godless war. Pistol shogged off. Untroubled,

Hal's offer was French blood should flow, towns burn—
Till France (and Kate) were offered in return.

*

1–3 *Henry VI*—The Earl of Warwick

"What plain proceeding is more plain than this?"
– 2 Henry VI, II.ii.52

At Towton even I lost heart—until,
Trampled by hooves, my dying brother cried
To me to take revenge. I swore I'd kill
My horse before I'd fly… Thousands more died—

Blood stiffening in the snow—before white won.
I, setter up and puller down of kings,
Saw red—saw son kill father—father son—
Saw twenty thousand left as lifeless things

Grinning like gargoyles… Was it a waste of time?
Does pride—does honour—matter? Was I a fool
To weep for England—let my high hopes climb
From king to king, when none was fit to rule?

Measure for measure *must* be paid. If not,
Mere vice or folly reigns—all roses rot.

*

Richard III—The Duke of Buckingham

> *"When holy and devout religious men*
> *Are at their beads, 'tis much to draw them hence…"*
> – II.vii.91–92

Half of my great-grandfather's lands were lost
When his younger daughter married Bolingbroke—
That sly usurper… The lands and I have crossed
From red king to white king. I want them back.

Knowing how sweet is zealous contemplation,
I let myself be drawn from that good life…
We know each other's faces. Greed, ambition,
Have plotted, lied and killed with sword—axe—knife.

And now, it seems, two innocent princes are
To die. Their fresh young growth may damage his
Foul play. He takes, he gives. We're in too far
To stop for breath… The King averts his eyes.

I had enough. But, now, cannot go back.
And if not on, York's sun turns brutish—black.

iii   *"For Man is a Giddy Thing, and this is my Conclusion"*
       (*Much Ado About Nothing,* V.iv.107)

Much Ado About Nothing—Benedick

> *"Come, lady, die to live; this wedding day*
> *Perhaps is but prolong'd…"*
> – IV.i.253–254

Because our custom has not been to speak
The simple truth, how can we easily now?
Claudio is Hero's husband. Fashionable, weak,
What's 'love' to him but a word? What's in a vow?

Pedro's a prince, but neither strong nor wise—
A self-regarding wit, a shallow youth.
I play the merry fool in their blind eyes:
Show me the man who'll tell a prince the truth!

We hide and seek to hear what others say
About us. See ourselves in how they see us.
A change of heart—or mind—changes the way
We see things, say things. The Friar plotted to free us

From biting error. Can souls so giddy survive?
How much of all our *nothing* is really alive?

*

As You Like It—Rosalind

> "*…the truest poetry is the most feigning.*"
> – III.iii.16

To pass the time in Arden, I, a boy,
  Pretended to be a girl pretending to be
A boy who took a lover's pride and joy
  In playing the part of Rosalind, who he—

More so than *I*—both was and will be. Thus
  We choose our many roles on Jacques' stage,
And play them as we like them… None of us
  Lives on—except as words. No act, no age

Of man is golden. Winter's biting wind
  Howls through the wood—persuades us what we are.
Wrestling with Fortune, we must learn to find
  Sermons in stones, music in storm and star.

Ages ago in Arden, I, a boy,
Once played a master's mistress' living joy.

*

Twelfth Night. Or: *What You Will*—Viola

> "*When that I was and a little tiny boy,*
>   *With hey, ho, the wind and the rain,*
> *A foolish thing was but a toy,*
>   *For the rain it raineth every day.*"
> – V.i.388–391

Who was in love with whom? Orsino thought
He loved Olivia. So did I. But men
Indeed say more, swear more. Their words distort
Their masculine world, our words a world of women.

Self-love is not the only love which tastes
Its fancy food with a sick appetite.
Virtuous or drunk, love feeds—fools—drowns us, wastes
Our time, fills wilful lives: love's wrong is right.

Sebastian thought the people were all mad.
When we named ourselves, 'Cesario' disappeared.
One face, one voice, one manner. And both dead.
Or so the other thought. Olivia feared

The Duke might kill me. Now that she's his sister
And I'm his wife, I wonder has he missed her?

*

All's Well That Ends Well—Helena

> "*Our remedies oft in ourselves do lie*
> *Which we ascribe to heaven; the fated sky*
> *Gives us free scope…*"
> – I.i.212–214

Boccaccio was content to make me clever
And brave enough to get my husband's ring
And bear his child—two hopeless 'ifs' he'd never
Imagined I'd fulfil. The play's the thing

Which tests my love. Bertram's a boy, it's true,
Too young to marry, too wild to go to war.
I caused him to do both. I think I knew
My 'cure' was too ambitious. Wanted more

Than I could have. He paid me back with less
Than nothing. Now he says he'll love me dearly.
But he'll say yes, think no—say no, think yes—
Then do what he likes. He'll please *himself* sincerely…

His love may grow—in time, may learn to live
As if to give were take, to take were give.

*

Measure for Measure—Vincentio, Duke of Vienna

> *"If you think well to carry this, as you may,*
>   *the doubleness of the benefit defends the deceit…"*
> – III.i.257–258

Taking my cue from Helena, my role
Was playing roles. She went too far. Did I?
I told myself I cared for Isabel's soul—
Exhorted her: "All must, like Claudio, die…"

To stand aside because afraid I'd turned
The law into a scarecrow where the birds
Had learned to perch seemed right. Or had I learned
To dress my thoughts up too in empty words?

I left the work to others. At least my lines
Scared them, as actors in *my* plot or play!…
I might have told her Claudio lived. The signs
May mean I seldom mean the things I say…

Implying I *could* by saying I *will not* hurt you
Gave me a sense of power, as much as virtue.

iv   *"The Tragicall Historie of …"*
            (*Hamlet,* title page (Q1))

Romeo and Juliet—Friar Laurence

> *"The earth that's nature's mother is her tomb."*
> – II.iii.5

Why did I lie? why help their violent love?
Its childish greed, its hot romantic blindness
Would soon have soured or blunted—quietly relieved
To slacken into mid-life loving-kindness.

I hoped they'd live. She adored him like a god,
He called her *Jewel*—his saint-seducing idol.
Was *life* to flower here—bad blood nurture good?
Would love, not rancour, rock an empty cradle?...

It *all* went wrong. An even earlier grave,
A womb of death, swallowed their thing of nothing.
They took Queen Mab for real: her stars would save
Not cross them. Till that hag in glitzy clothing

Ditched them. And yet their grace still lights more joy
In all our hearts and minds than vaults destroy.

*

Hamlet—Horatio

> "*The spirit that I have seen
> May be a devil, and the devil hath power
> T' assume a pleasing shape...*"
> – II.ii.594–596

His father's ghost, if sunk indeed in fire
With all his imperfections still unpurged,
Would cry for blood. But, unfulfilled, desire
Hears what it wants to hear—unasked, unurged.

Damned if he did and if he didn't, how
Else save his immortal soul but by denying
Our right to take revenge—there then, here now,
Leave Priam—King, Queen—"so many princes"—dying?

Laertes, daring damnation, would have cut
Prince Hamlet's throat in the church. Was Hamlet wrong
To spare the King while praying? If he was not,
His ghost's a devil. Let be. Angelic song

Lives and lets live But, deaf and blind, we're led—
Drunk on hot blood—to feast on our own dead.

*

Othello—Cassio

> "Oh beware, my Lord, of jealousy;
> It is the green-ey'd monster, which doth mock
> The meat it feeds on."
> – III.iii.169–171

As Governor now, Iago's punishment
For his strange crime, still unexplained, of killing
Four innocent victims *(five if—as he meant—*
He'd run me through) is mine to enforce. Unwilling

To have him tortured, I—still maimed—get drunk.
Sometimes the way we see things is so far
From true that we might just as well be drunk.
What blindness—blackness—made the Moor blame *her?*...

Too sure that he could do no wrong—that all
He felt and thought was 'noble'—meant that he,
As *one that loved not wisely but too well,*
Could weep big tears, then kill self-righteously...

Unsure of how he stood in others' eyes,
He looked big, talked big—saw with big green eyes.

*

King Lear—Edmund

> "An admirable evasion of whoremaster man, to lay
> his goatish disposition to the charge of a star!"
> – I.ii.133–134

I didn't die. I hired another sworder
And got to France. My virtuous brother rules
In Britain—hopes to set the world in order
Which I let slip. Of all that crowd of fools,

The King, his daughters, Albany, Cornwall, Gloucester—
All self-deceived and most deceived by me—
Only hot France, who loved his wife and lost her,
And Edgar still ride high. But thought is free.

I don't deceive myself, nor blame the star
That made them / marred me—choose instead to defy
Misfortune—see myself and them as we are.
I've made mistakes… But this French king and I

Have common hatreds—wishes to be fulfilled.
He cannot know I had Cordelia killed.

*

Macbeth—Macduff

> *"I cannot but remember such things were,*
> *That were most precious to me."*
> – IV.iii.222–223

All that was many years ago—my wife,
My children. How could any man forgive
The furious shadow which cut down his life
To less than nothing? How forget? How *live?*…

Blood required blood, murder more murder, to make him
Safe from the likes of me, who found the king—
Who'd knocked, but knocked too late. Nothing could wake him…
Leaving my children with only their mother's wing

To shelter under, I fled. From England, we
Avenged ourselves for all who'd stayed and died.
His death brought peace—and no peace. Minds which free
Themselves of guilt—of blame—must quell their pride.

Unless I can forgive myself—as well
As him—the air's still foul, this place still hell.

v   *In "the High Roman Fashion"*
        (*Antony and Cleopatra,* IV. xv. 87)

Julius Caesar—The Poet Phaonius

> *"Love and be friends, as two such men should be;*
> *For I have seen more years, I'm sure, than ye."*
> – IV.iii.130–131

He found it fitting to give *me* bad verses
And Caesar—Cassius—Brutus—mighty lines
To justify themselves. Mockery and curses
Are all poets get, he knew, in war-torn times.

The powerful wield plain words to hide or twist
The truth—deceive themselves as well as others.
The man who knows he's lying 's less dishonest
Than noble-minded souls who stab their brothers.

The crowd took Cinna for the conspirator Cinna,
And then presumed his poetry must be bad.
They couldn't read, but killed him. Sleepless, thinner
Than Cassius, who "thinks too much", I might go mad

Writing how envy—greed—ambition—rule
The tongue-tied world. Safer to play the fool.

*

Troilus and Cressida—Priam

> "What's aught but as 'tis valued?—It was thought meet
> Paris should do some vengeance on the Greeks…"
> – II.ii.53, 73–74

I died in *Hamlet*. The hellish Pyrrhus killed me…
When Hector died, I turned to broken stone.
Paris's rape of Helen at first filled me
With pride in Troy. But Fortune's wheel whirls on.

The winner loses and the loser wins—
Revenge brings in revenge, blood spills more blood.
Patroclus dead, Achilles' Myrmidons
Butchered my gallant son. What gain, what good

Can come of this lust-dominated, hate-
And rage-engendering, brutal slaughter now?
Troilus has lost his Cressida. Too late,
I realized it was she who'd taught him how

To sigh and day-dream. Since she's gone, he wreaks
Nightmares of vengeance on any and all Greeks.

*

Antony and Cleopatra—Octavius Caesar

> "*Is Caesar with Antonius priz'd so slight?*"
> – I.i.56

They made me—*me!*—look small. Now both are smaller.
The others—Pompey, Lepidus—were fools.
But he—outstared our stares, spoke loud, strode taller.
—We could not stall together in the whole

Wide Roman world… My plan was to bring *her* here,
And show her like a puppet. She mocked me, I know—
With *"He words me, girls…"*. At least their bastards fear
My greatness now: 'Augustus' *means* to grow!

As for his children by my sister—well…
As *Princeps Civitatis*, too much terror
Would set a bad example—though Machiavel,
Later, would judge it, too, a grievous error

To have let Caesarion live… Great Julius ploughed
Her and she cropped. *I'm* 'Julius Caesar' now.

*

Coriolanus—Menenius Agrippa

> "*It is held
> That valour is the chiefest virtue and
> Most dignifies the haver…*"
> – II.ii.83–85

I used to be the sane, the cunning one.
It must sound odd, then, even slightly mad,
To say I loved and miss him like the son
I always thought I wanted—never had.

It's hard now still to think of him as wrong.
He fought to please himself and, more, his mother.
She saved all Rome: Martius did not belong
To Rome, he thought, but Rome to Martius. Another

Would condescend. Too proud, too vengeful, too
Boyish—too falsely modest to regret
His heartless anger with the rabble, who
Opposed him… Rome—and we—could have burned. And yet

All Romans play to win. Some fight to live—
And so cannot let live, let go, forgive.

vi   *"The Rarer Action"*
          (*The Tempest,* V.i.27)

Pericles, Prince of Tyre—Pericles

             "O, come hither,
Thou that beget'st him that did thee beget;
Thou that wast born at sea, buried at Tarsus,
And found at sea again."
– V.i.194–197

Old now, I ask myself what did I do
To earn Marina. Nothing. My closed heart,
After we'd lost her mother, only grew
Softer because of *her*, a baby. To part

Was wrong. I should have brought her home—not left
Others to nurse, then envy, her sweet grace.
When she too seemed to have died, black guilt bereft
My mind of thoughts, my mouth of words, my face

Of loving kindness… Alive and well, she found me.
And the stars helped us find her mother, living
Withdrawn, a priestess. Storm-free, her children surround me.
Soon my Queen died. Receiving is not giving.

I have not loved much. Tired, do *my* eyes shine
To see her baby daughter's smiles meet mine?

                *

Cymbeline—Iachimo

> "The heaviness and guilt within my bosom
> Takes off my manhood."
> – V.ii.1–2

My hero was Iago. No one remembers
My name, though some the thing I did. If only
I could forget! Unspied-on, Imogen slumbers
Peacefully now... Once I was smeared with honey—

Tied naked to a stake—and stung to death
In the burning sun of Egypt, a heartless example
To other heartless deceivers... In good or bad faith,
Pardon's the word to all—but no more simple

Or pure a *thing* than is repentance. The man
I wronged the most's forgiveness irks me. Ashamed
To be so weak, unable to withstand
My conscience, let me—if 'guilty'—be blamed!

The strong defy compassion. Manhood regrets
Nothing—asserts itself—deserves what it gets.

*

The Winter's Tale—Hermione

> "I see the play so lies
> That I must bear a part."
> – IV.iv.655–656

Say Imogen had died. What sort of play
Would that have been? Hardly a tragedy...
A winter's tale, perhaps, like mine. Today
The dead and gone came back. Not all. And we

Who did are almost strangers... How could I let
Paulina bury me for sixteen years?
The Oracle, it's true, gave hope. And yet
I hated him. Both children gone, my tears

Burst bleeding from my heart... Time tries us. Must
Forgiveness, though—must penitence—be as long
As a child is in ripening? Might the lost
Not sooner find their way? right what went wrong?...

*"The rarer action is / in virtue than
In vengeance,"* affirmed an active, vengeful man.

                                         *

The Tempest—Miranda

> "Miranda: *O, wonder!*
>   *How many goodly creatures are there here!*
>   *How beauteous mankind is! O brave new world,*
>   *Which has such people in it!*
> Prospero: 'Tis new to thee."
> – V.i.181–184

The only men I'd ever seen were old
Or ugly. And my father told of others
Who'd taken all we had. Of men who'd sold
Or fought their fellow-men, or killed their brothers.

Caliban found me bathing once. He swore
He'd take his island back—take all—take me.
My father's Art prevents him—makes him roar
With pain and anger all night long. But he—

Ferdinand—wants to *give* me all he has:
His very life, he says. His father's King
Of Naples; I'll be Queen. My father was
Their enemy, but not now. No loveless thing

Lives long. Love heals the past, outlives the future.
O brave new world, to bring me such a creature!

                                         *

Epilogue—Shakespeare

> *"… the rest is silence"*
> *– Hamlet* V.ii.363

After such words—words—words, what was there more
To say? Since words are never things, they can
Do nothing—sometimes may lead *to action… Before*
The world—all things—all actions—as much as began,

The Word was with God, was *God—or so the Word*
Of God says: "And God said, *Let there be light"…*
—Wordless, we're in the dark… Strange then—absurd—
How seldom poets see or say things right.

Mine are all fools. Or liars on the make.
Kit Marlowe—Chaucer—all too few—perhaps
Were not. We poets are only people. Take
Us all in all, dogs squabbling over scraps.

Enough's enough. I'll stop while fighting fit,
Bury my book. Who knows what may root in it?

9 THE GIFT

Oliver Cromwell lay buried and dead,
Until the new king's men
Declared he should pay for the old king's blood,
And dug him up again.

They dragged him publicly through the streets
From Westminster Abbey, and hung
His carcass up like a common thief;
The common people flung

Brickbats and mud at his winding sheet.
As though he were still not dead,
The hangman cut him down again
And chopped off his stubborn head.

The Tyburn hangman hacked off his head
With eight cloth-muffled blows.
And so the new king had his way
With the Old One's 'Lancaster rose'.

They chopped off his fingers, his nose and and ear
And threw his trunk in a pit.
But they kept his shaven head—to do penance
As the king and his men saw fit…

From a spike high up on Westminster Hall
King Oliver's head looked down—
On the time-serving merchants and bankers
Of a richer and safer town,

Where prudence, self-interest, piety and thrift
Loved *More* and hated *Less*—
Whipped beggars, seeking Justification
In Industry and Success.

Reviewing thus his lifetime's work,
Oliver groaned and wept
In self-disgust and disenchantment;
And when at last he slept

He dreamt he was hunting wolves—in the dark—
Across the Irish Sea;
His favourite daughter, returned from the dead,
Rode with him fierily.

They raced through the stormy air till they heard
The songs of a twangling isle,
Where they stopped. An old man welcomed them
Who had a young man's smile.

His songs turned slowly into a dirge,
And, slowly, he grew as young
As Oliver's daughter. His smile became
As old and strange as the spring.

The daughter thought, "If this young man
Will only sing for me,
I'll love him forever with all my heart."
But he sang on carelessly.

She sighed and thought, "If this young man
Will only lie with me,
I'll do whatever he likes best."
But he turned and looked away.

She thought at last, "If this young man
Will only marry me,
He shall be richer than the sun."
But his eyes flashed dangerously.

She said, "Your eyes are green as the grass
On my father's richest land—"
But her clothes turned into beggars' rags,
As he placed his green eyes in her hand.

The eyes turned into emeralds
As bright as a soldier's sword.
But she buried them next to the broken bones
Of their dead without a word.

From the eyes two trees sprang up through the bones,
Whose branches grew into each other.

Now Oliver saw the man as his son—
His daughter, as her brother.

Oliver gave him his daughter as wife.
She died giving birth. A girl's sight
Soon blest her father's homeward path
Into the vanishing light.

*

Oliver Cromwell lay buried and dead,
    Heigho! buried and dead!
There grew a green apple-tree over his head,
    Heigho! over his head!
The apples were ripe and all ready to drop!
    Heigho! ready to drop!
There came an old woman to gather the crop,
    Heigho! gather the crop!

10 THREE FABLES ANCIENT AND MODERN

i Baucis and Philemon—A Pastoral Dialogue
   (after Ovid, *Metamorphoses* Bk VIII)

"Don Pedro: *My visor is Philemon's roof;*
             Within the house is Jove.
 Hero: *Why then your visor should be thatch'd.*
 Don Pedro: *Speak low if you speak of love.*"
– *Much Ado About Nothing*, II.i. 88–91

One of the inspirations for Shakespeare's romantic comedies, it seems reasonable to imagine, may well have been the wish—or even need—*to resolve the tensions and double-binds which find expression in what one might think of as the Borgesian labyrinth of the* Sonnets *(cp. section 3, 'From* Dolce stil nuovo *to* Rime petrose'*) but which are scarcely overcome there. The above exchange from* Much Ado About Nothing, *during the festivities at which Don Pedro has undertaken to woo Hero for Claudio, is a good-humoured reference to Ovid's tale of Baucis and Philemon, in which an elderly couple—seemingly endowed with loving-kindness and good will towards others by nature—is described as living in the sort of harmony with themselves, the gods and Nature which Shakespeare would presumably have seen as a consummation devoutly to be wished, however rare in real life… In the following version of their story, their equilibrium is presented as hard won, their longevity as a counterbalance (as in Ovid himself) to the early and unhappy deaths of Orpheus, Eurydice, and others in* Then and Now… *The old couple's story has always been popular. Shakespeare would have expected his allusion to be recognized, and he even imitates the fourteeners of the best-known translation of it in his time—Arthur Golding's. Another fine translation is to be found in Dryden's* Fables Ancient and Modern. *As Golding begins it,*

>   The mightie Jove and Mercurie
>   his sonne, in shape of men,

were once looking for somewhere in Phrygia where they could spend the night:

>   A thousand houses when
>   For roome to lodge in they had sought,
>   a thousand houses bard
>   Theyr doors against them.

Baucis and Philemon, however—who are poor but contented with their lot—make the strangers heartily welcome, cook them a meal and invite them to stay. Two uncanny events surprise them. In Dryden's version,

Mean time the Beechen Bowls went round, and still
Though often empty'd, were observ'd to fill:
Fill'd without Hands…

Moreover, the couple's only goose, which they decide to roast for their guests, runs for her life—

… she flies,
And close between the Legs of Jove she lies:
He with a gracious Ear the Suppliant heard,
And sav'd her Life.

Whereupon Jove tells the couple who their visitors really are:

For wee bee Gods (quoth he) and all
   this wicked towneship shall
Abye their gylt. On you alone
   this mischeef shall not fall.
No more but give you up your house,
   and follow up this hill
Togither, and upon the top
   therof abyde our will.

They haste, and when their legs grow tired and slow,
Each helps the other on. Still a stone's throw
Away from the steep hillside's rugged top,
But safe already, they decide to stop
And, lying down together, fall asleep.
A watery desert rises, cold and dark and deep…

(i)

Baucis:

Philemon, wake up. Look! the gods are gone—
   And, look, down there the flood
Has filled the village—left it silent—deserted.
Our house—has become a temple of white stone!
   The flocks are all departed—
The neighbours' houses roofless—full of mud…

Philemon:

Come lie down, Baucis. What on earth's the good
Of getting up before it's even light?—
The gods may still be watching somewhere near.
   We're safe and dry up here:
When morning comes, we'll see what happened last night.
Come lie here on my shoulder. Give me your arm.
The summer grass and last year's leaves are warm.

(ii)

Baucis:

It's almost light already. Look, the sky's red.
   They must have all been caught
Asleep, or eating supper, when the weight
Of Jove's almighty anger struck them dead.
   But why? Was it too late
For them to learn? or do whatever they ought?

Philemon:

Learn what?—to buy and sell? be sold, be bought?
Whatever we ought, in Nature as in love,
It seems we all "receive but what we give".
   And if that's how lives live—
Or how they die—the same is true of Jove:
If you can't see the trees for cutting down the wood,
Soon you won't see the river for the flood.

(iii)

Baucis:

You mean life's *always* 'give' as well as 'take'?…

Philemon:

   And, really, people know it—
Until our fears, greeds, envies make us forget
And want too much. As if drinking wasn't to slake
   Your thirst but only to get

Drunk—and then drunker—like some Bacchic poet.
We don't know much (our poets more than show it!),
But if all the stuff and status which we fight
To have and hold is what we hope to shore
    Against the ramshackle door
On which the Unknown comes knocking in the night,
We'd better forget the future / forgive the past,
And be content with what there *is* at last.

(iv)

Baucis:

I know: forget and give / forgive and get.
    But *"Those to whom evil is done*
Do evil in return", though no excuse,
Is one of the simplest explanations yet
    Of why, if we win, we lose—
Or how, before it's over, the whole game's gone.

Philemon:

There needn't be a game. Whoever won
Or lost only believed so. Change your mind
And all things change... *We've* wanted more than enough
    Not just of status and stuff—
But Cupid must be stupid more than blind!
I played with fire—got worse than burned...
Yet why regret how we lived if we think we learned?

(v)

Baucis:

But was it you—or I—who played with fire...?
    Forgiving *is* forgetting!

Philemon:

Let's say, if you try to douse its flames with *No*
Too coldly, fear or greed will turn desire
    To anger or machismo,
As rapacious pride resents a nasty wetting,

Till only hate can grow. Giving *is* getting—
And hoping for too much can only lose,
As Hell is born of Heaven. A mundane law
   Of human life is the more
You hate the more you're hated. Whereas, if you choose
To love / let love—as we did—strangely, the less
You crave to have, the more *No* turns to *Yes*.

(vi)

Baucis:

And so it seems we *can* learn after all.
   For though I could only take—
Beg, buy or steal—and neither receive nor give,
I really thought that I would never fall,
   But fell. No wonder if
You looked elsewhere for love that wasn't fake.

Philemon:

To learn we need to bend or even break—
Mistrust/observe heart, mind, tongue, ears and eyes
In and beyond pain/pleasure. Oh, being very
   Ignorant and ordinary,
In self-contempt/self-love, we try to rise
Too far and fall. And then crawl on—as if
We really knew the way we ought to live…

(vii)

(Coda)

Philemon ceas'd. Forthwith the gods appear'd,
And bade their former Hosts be nothing fear'd.
Then thus almighty Jove, with Look serene,
Speak thy Desire, thou only Just of Men,
And thou, O Woman, only worthy found
To be with such a Man in Marriage bound.

A while they whisper. And to Jove address'd,
Philemon then prefers their joint Request—

Your Chapleynes for to bee, to keepe
  your Temple. And bycause
Long yeeres in concord wee have spent
  I pray when death neere drawes,
Let bothe of us togither leave
  our lives: that neyther I
Behold my wyves deceace, nor shee
  see myne when I doo dye.

    And so they kept the church. And when
        (Among young women and young men)
At last their hour was come, while they relate
Their past adventures at the temple-gate,
Philemon saw old Baucis suddenly
Sprout fresh green leaves. Part woman and part tree,
Baucis then saw where old Philemon stood,
His withered arms becoming branch-like wood.
Next, roots begin to fasten down their feet.
Their bodies stiffen in the mid-day heat
As bark replaces skin. They smile goodbye
Before their mouths and eyes are closed—then die
As human beings. In Ovid's ancient tale
They live as trees there still—and always shall.

ii   The Chest

   "Apri questa cassa"—*Decameron* VIII, viii

The chest or trunk Boccaccio had in mind
Would either be the heavy bedroom kind—
Painted on both sides—an expensive wedding
Present for stowing curtains, sheets or bedding—
Or else the sort of coffer where the man
Concealed himself who spied on Imogen
In *Cymbeline*—as, in another tale
(II, ix), one lurked and listened. On the whole,
The former seems more likely. But the latter
Puts a more tragi-comic mask on the matter…

       *

Shortly before their tale was told—let's say—
Outside the gates of Florence, on the way
To Fiesole, two well-known painters, who
'd been friends since early childhood, lived in two
Cottages where they shared a workshop and
Some goats—pigs—poultry on a patch of land,
Which they'd imagined would be all they needed
To work and play. Moreover, they'd succeeded,
By painting in the same style as each other,
In getting much of their main work together,
Frescoing villas—had, in fact, been doing
At Camerata one well worth the viewing
(As humorously recorded in a fine
If heartless story—*No.5, Day 9*),
Surrounded by tall Tuscan cypresses,
Vineyards and olive-groves—as it still is…
Bruno and Buffalmacco were their names,
Famous as well for zany fun and games,
Hoaxes and jokes, though only played on others:
As youths, they'd sworn to live and die as brothers.
They went to church to paint and not to pray,
But married in one on the same feast-day
Two girl-friends whom they'd known since they were little,
Playing at 'doctors' in their own 'hospital'.
And so they'd lived as neighbours for some time.
Until, one Easter, Bruno went to Rome,
Fulfilling every up-and-comer's dream
Of plying his brush in Giotto's top-notch team—
Although why *he* was chosen, not the other,
Was a hard question for his envious brother
Who, sourly, stayed to finish Camerata.
Each April evening his *Innamorata*
Welcomed him home, though. Bruno's wife would eat
Her supper with them, after the Spring heat
Had cooled, beneath the great magnolia tree
Which scented their whole courtyard. Until she,
After a lonely fortnight, feeling itchy,
Told her best friend she needn't be so bitchy
Just because she forgot to milk the goats!
Next day they jumped down one another's throats
About who should have fed the geese and ducks…
—*She's also far too noisy when she fucks,*
She thought, alone in bed: *Why don't they keep*

Their window closed? Some people need their sleep!—
But when she said so, felt herself go red,
Till Buffalmacco laughed: "It's hot in bed!"
A few days later, helping her to mend
A broken shutter, he watched her slowly bend
So far towards him that a breast flopped out
Of her loose bodice. With a pretty pout,
She pushed it back. He grinned: "I haven't seen
The other one for years! Perhaps fifteen?"
Vexed and confused at first—then thinking *Men!*—
She blushed, and smiled: "It's grown a bit since then…"
And, blushing deeper, lowered her bright eyes…
What happened next will come as no surprise
To readers of Boccaccio (whose narration
Seldom permits a pudibund translation,
While even an adaptation such as this is
Can hardly stop at unrequited kisses…),
Till Buffalmacco, being a young, well-fed,
Successful artist, loped from bed to bed,
Less discontented now to be at home
Instead of working wifelessly in Rome—
Contriving, too, that his own trusting wife
Saw nothing much. He led this lone wolf's life,
Keeping both women happy with no bother,
Till Giotto's pack, including his blood-brother,
Returned. *This can't go on,* both lovers thought.
The last time that they risked it they were caught,
If not exactly in the act, in doing
The sort of thing which quickly leads to screwing,
By Bruno's yellow eye, from where he sat
Drawing a sheep a field away: *Ha! What
In hell's name*—? Open-mouthed, he saw them move
Towards the bedroom: *Hey, they're making*—!
Deprived of words and movement, he sat on,
Plotting revenge, until the summer sun
Distracted him by setting with such beauty
That he forgot for several minutes his duty
As an offended male. When he came to,
The evening star was shining in dark blue.
And so he strode off home, and shocked his wife
By brandishing a pointed boning knife,
Commanding her, on peril of her life,
To tell his faithless, good-for-nothing 'friend'

That he'd been called to Florence to attend
A funeral—would return the following day—
Which meant another chance for them, hurray.
"But once you've got him into bed, undressed,
You'll hear me hurrying back. The bedroom chest
Is big enough to hide him. Open that,
And lock him in it. Then we'll see what's what!"
And slammed the knife into the chest he meant,
Where it stood quivering. This great ornament
Had once belonged to Bruno's father, who
Had bought it cheap from somebody he knew
In Leghorn, where an English pirate had
Sold it, who claimed he'd got it from his dad,
The English then being not as they are now—
Less decent and plain-dealing, anyhow…
But where the chest had come from no one knew.
The side that Bruno liked was mostly blue—
The sea, the sky, and Venus on a shell,
Her curves emerging from the waves' soft swell,
Crowned by red roses, looking sweetly scented,
While all around white flickering doves ascended.
Next to her you could see her blind son, Cupid,
Shooting the arrows which make people stupid,
And round the margins love-lorn knights—kings—queens,
And allegorical figures set in scenes
Of pleasure, hope, lust, falsehood, flattery,
Wasteful intrigue, with jaundiced Jealousy
Wearing a twisted wreath of marigolds and
Carrying a cuckoo, chained to her left hand…
The chest's original owner had preferred
Not to show Venus nude, or this mad bird,
But turned them to the wall—as Bruno turned
The other side, where Troy, for instance, burned
Under the auspices of blood-red Mars.
William of Raby, knighted in the wars
Against the French, had brought the chest from Paris
Together with a matching bed and arras,
Admiring their stern heroism, or
Stoic depiction of the world at war,
As he had known it—the fury and the clamour
Created by King Edward, as the hammer
Of Scotland, Wales and France… Thus Mars's temple
Of burnished steel and iron, for example,

Seemed built to last forever, while the god—
Armipotent, colossal—grimly stood
With a great red-eyed wolf at his bronze feet,
Which had been given a dying man to eat,
No doubt a Trojan soldier. William found
Homer's description of Troy's fate profound,
And all of Homer, come to that, sublime,
As true for William's as for any time
Before or after Ilium's loss of hope—
Including that of Alexander Pope,
Or even Dryden/Virgil's flattering slant
On empire-building heroes. Decadent,
Rapacious, proud, good enemy / bad friend,
Old Troy got its come-uppance in the end:
The fatal day, the appointed hour was come
When wrathful Jove's irrevocable doom
Transfers the Trojan state to Grecian hands.
The fire consumes the town, the foe commands;
And armed hosts, an unexpected force,
Break from the bowels of the fatal horse…
What tongue can tell the slaughter of that night?
What eyes can weep the sorrows and affright?
An ancient and imperial city falls;
The streets are filled with frequent funerals,
Houses and holy temples float in blood,
And hostile nations make a common flood.
All parts resound with tumults, plaints, and fears,
And grisly death in sundry shapes appears…
Thus William, with war-warped imagination,
Saw painted on the chest fair retribution
For what lewd Paris and his mates had done—
Helen avenged, Troy gutted in the sun—
But failed to notice, not being very observant,
The master murdered by his treacherous servant,
The stables burning with thick banks of smoke,
The smiler with the knife beneath his cloak,
The sow which ate a baby in its cradle,
The cook's hand scalded, *malgré* his long ladle,
A man who'd killed himself in utter despair—
His life-blood clotted in his yellow hair—
Or how a conquering hero on a throne
Sat in a tall dark tower all alone,
With a sword hanging right above his head,

Suspended by a thin and subtle thread…
All this was in the margins round the glory
Of Mars's temple and half-eaten, gory
Trojan. Which deeply suited William's mood
As he rode home. Though something of a prude,
He'd married, eighteen months or so before
He'd gone to screw the French in Edward's war,
The youngest daughter, *née* Elizabeth
Poole, of a local priest, whose sudden death
Had left her on her own. No one quite knew
What wealthy William thought he was up to
In taking this wild-eyed, red-lipped, black-haired
Wench as his wife—who'd never greatly cared
For girls before, whose tall and strait-laced mother
Thought boys should play with boys, not with the other
More frivolous sex… And yet Liz soon adjusted
To being a lady. Olive-skinned, big-busted
Yet slender, she had once been famous among
The village-children for her cat-like tongue,
Which easily touched the tip of her sweet nose,
For picking nuts up with her long brown toes,
And for her pointed teeth. As a young miss,
She'd shown her girl-friends how the Frenchies kiss,
And licked them where it tickled. By the time
Her husband went to war, she'd had the time
To learn her Ps and Qs—and start to feel
Bored and frustrated, though each ample meal
She ate recalled how often she'd gone hungry.
William had dimly sensed that she was angry,
But rode to archery contests—jousted—hunted—
And shrugged it off as not knowing what she wanted,
Or eating too much meat. But, though a tall,
Good-looking husband, he was rather small
For her capacious, all too frequent wishes.
Once as a youth, when shooting bolts at fishes
Together with his friend, William de Ley,
At Raby Mere on a hot, sultry day,
They'd slid in from the boat and tried to swim.
He'd seen there was a difference between him
And his much slighter but well-hung companion,
But fended off the pang. In his opinion,
That sort of thing was not important. Willy,
As he was called—or, since some found this silly,

Will—was a youngest son, who hadn't married,
Nor would, he said, before his brothers buried
Themselves and he could more than swing a cat
(Liz stretched and smiled whenever she heard that)
Around the farm where he and they'd been born.
The friends were cousins and blood-brothers, sworn
To help each other—though all's fair in love
And war—especially in times of war and love,
For better or worse, in sickness and in health,
Regardless of their poverty or wealth...
Or so they'd vowed in the innocence of youth.
Also, of course, to tell each other the truth.
And apart from various milkmaids, shepherdesses,
And village virgins (one with coal-black tresses
And cat-like teeth), whom Willy didn't bother
To mention, they'd kept faith with one another—
Until their first real conflict *re* the war.
Willy's three brothers went. As No.4,
His business was to tend the family farm,
The three decided. Willy's weedy arm
Was not a warrior's (though at archery
No one could match the sharpness of his eye
Except, occasionally, William): i.e. they
Could better help the Hammer win the day.
Rich William had a steward (whose real name
Was not Malvolio but, since cast in the same
Sour and efficient role, let's call him that),
Who'd run the estate and see to Liz the cat
While William rode in search of martial glory.
Fearing a nasty twist to their straight story,
Willy demanded William stay as well.
But William laughed out loud. *Then go to hell,
My friend,* thought Willy, also miffed to know
He'd lost the chance of shining with his bow,
As William would, he knew, and might get knighted,
While he, at home, remained ignored and slighted—
It wasn't fair. Liz listened to his case
With half-closed eyes. She found it a disgrace...
And yet was grateful for Will's company—
Too much alone since William was away...
What happened next soon made the sting of staying
Feel easier—and reminded him of laying
Her deep in Storeton Woods with nothing on

For half the day until the summer sun
Went down that whole hot June before she married…
Not that they saw their oaths as dead and buried,
But in abeyance for as long as (they
Agreed) his friend / her husband stayed away:
Later all oaths were to be reinstated.
Or so they reasoned. But, so long frustrated,
Lizzy, *née* Poole, began to fall in love—
At least, could hardly ever have enough
Of Will before she wanted him again.
And he performed like half-a-dozen men.
Her eighteen months of boredom, put to flight,
Had left her with a ravening appetite,
Also for meat and drink. And many a feast
Of roasted loin or heart of hunted beast
And strong red wine concluded their long sessions,
Or opened them again. To hide their passions
Was not that easy. William had a page,
Whose job it was to tend his equipage
At jousts and archery contests. Cherubino—
Let's call him that—became their go-between. O
Heartless disloyalty of adolescence,
Obsessed with hair-do's, pimples and tumescence!
The more Liz teased this boy's sweet dick the faster
He zipped between them and forgot his master—
Too young for France but not to hide and peep,
Which Liz allowed for helping them to keep
Their trysts a secret from Malvolio, who
Was not a fool, though, and already knew
What was afoot, but chose to bide his time
Rather than face two lovers in their prime…
After twelve months (and how were they to end
Such loving then?) her husband / his best friend
Returned from France, where he had had to quell an
Unpleasant feeling she might be a Helen,
Not a Penelope—although, in dreams,
The niggle burrowed on, like hidden streams
He did his best to ignore. Thus this straight man,
Who always finished what he had begun,
And had entirely trusted his straight mother,
Tried hard—one woman being much like another—
To trust his wife. And brought the bed, plus chest
And arras home. But, then, his steward confessed

He'd smelt a rat—though, fearing for his life,
He'd not yet dared confront Sir William's wife
With *who* exactly slithered to and fro
When they presumed he wasn't there. And so
The matter hung. After so much spilt blood,
Sir William was in grim, Homeric mood.
Though his heart sank, he quietly swore he'd kill
Anyone who betrayed him, even Will.
Not that his friend would ever let him down,
But from the lowest beggar to the crown,
Fear of retaliation was what kept
The world in order. Even while you slept,
The greater fear of what might happen when
The deed was done deterred nine out of ten
Murderers, adulterers, thieves, and other rabble,
And helped to keep most people out of trouble.
Without such fear most soldiers would desert.
Punishments must be seen, and seen to hurt.
"Yes, yes," Malvolio slobbered. "But the best
Place to find out who's who is madam's chest.
And should not you, sir, be the first to know
Whoever is your good wife's gigolo?
When Cherubino slinks across the fields…"
Another blow. But which good steward shields
His master from the truth? Malvolio blurted
It all out now—how often C.'d deserted
His post to pimp for Liz, how often she'd
Been busy, morning, noon and night, when he'd
Had business to discuss—"And, by the way,
That little dog has more than had his day
At playing Peeping Tom!…" A few days later
William was back in France, the perpetrator
Of three bad ends. Crammed in the chest, he'd knelt
Or lain, and heard and seen, until he felt
Like a Greek waiting in the Trojan horse,
Or spare prick at a wedding. Or, of course,
A foetus huddling in its mother's womb,
And, lastly, like a corpse shut in a tomb,
Or dead heart in his own unfeeling chest.
Speechless and stunned, he felt as though the best
Of life was over. But what should he do?
Hours passed. Then he recalled they'd planned to go
To Chester on the following day to shoot

In an archery contest. In the woods *en route*—
Down in dark Dibbensdale, where William knew
No one would see the thing he planned to do—
The traitor Cherubino suffered the fate
Of false Melanthius, barred inside the gates
Of Ithaca, who'd turned his coat to please
The suitors, and abandoned Ulysses
To his ill luck: *His zealous men fulfil*
At every point their master's rigid will:
First bind his hands and feet behind his back
And hoist him by the rope, till his joints crack,
Into a tree, where his own writhing weight
Causes the splintering bones to dislocate.
The howling felon swung from side to side—
Until they gagged him. Then they left him tied
And tortured in mid-air, awaiting Will,
Who soon came cantering down the wooded hill.
He stopped in horror when he saw the page,
Two hooded men, and William white with rage—
Till, frowning grimly, with a dreadful look
That withered Willy's heart, his best friend spoke:
"Dog, you have had your day! To England's shore
You hoped her husband would return no more."
William had fetched his father's great long-bow,
Which only he could draw. He drew it now—
Almost as if, before his friend lay dead,
The immortal lines went shooting through his head:
And now the famous bow Ulysses bore,
Turned on all sides, inspecting it before
He strung it lest time's worms had done it wrong,
Its owner absent, and unused so long…
Then, as a minstrel strings anew his lyre
Or fits the dumb lute with a singing wire,
Relaxing, straining, drawing to and fro,
So the great master drew the mighty bow,
And drew with ease—until the string, let fly,
Twanged short and sharp, like the shrill swallow's cry.
Swift as a word, the parting arrow sings,
Bearing the sting of death on its black wings:
Full through the throat Ulysses' weapon passed—
And pierced Will's neck. He fell and breathed his last,
With streams of dark blood gushing from his head
And severed veins. A puddle quickly spread

Around him on the ground. But, not content,
William attacked the corpse, as if he meant
To kill it twice—cut open Willy's chest—
Tore out his treacherous heart—and flung the rest
As carrion to the crows now circling round.
Next they dropped Cherubino to the ground,
Who'd seen all this, cut off his nose and ears
And voyeur's genitals with shepherd's shears
And fed them to the dogs, which wolfed them down
Before the boy had ceased to cry and groan:
His hands and feet last felt the cruel steel,
He roared, and torments gave his soul to hell…
Returning home at once, Sir William took
The heart, wrapped up in leaves, to his French cook,
As if it were the heart of a wild boar,
Requesting him to mince it and prepare
The finest and most succulent dish he knew.
The cook produced a bowl of rich *ragoût*.
That evening Liz and William dined alone.
William felt sick. Liz ate the stew on her own.
She'd always had an excellent appetite.
Her husband watched her, turning deathly white:
The heart, he hoped, had pleased her as much dead
As when it was alive. "What's that you said?"
She almost spat, afraid of his strange look.

*

What happened next depends which poem or book
You're reading. Or: how high, how low, you think
This Mars or Venus might ascend or sink—
Whether, like Tosca from Sant' Angelo,
Liz would defy her fate and nobly throw
Herself from the high window of the tower
They found her mangled body under—or,
Backing away from him in horror and fear,
She didn't think the window was so near,
And simply tripped—or whether he intended
Only to slap or beat her up but ended
By losing all control until he pushed
Her hissing and spitting out. The sheer drop crushed
Her head and limbs so badly no one could tell
What happened in the tower before she fell.

Except that, just before she toppled from it,
She left behind a cat-like pool of vomit…
Afraid of Will's two brothers (one was dead)
And Cherubino's family, William fled
By ship the following morning from Parkgate
To Plymouth and then France. Filled with self-hate
After a night of contemplating what
He'd done—but they deserved all that they got,
Surely?—he cursed his friend, but never told
Anyone how Liz fell. Malvolio sold
The arras, chest, and desecrated bed…
—Before the year was out, William was dead.

*

The bed was separated from the chest—
And, later, itemized "my second-best"
By another well-known William in his will.
The arras hung around in Stratford, till
Its worn remains were carted to the Globe
Where it served to carpet throne-rooms, make a robe
Or a furred gown, and be the actual arras
Which helped another vengeful blade embarrass
His relatives (and lug his victim's guts
From then to now) with all the ifs and buts
Which he or Will could think of… But the chest,
More than two hundred years before, sailed west,
Stolen by pirates, down the ebbing Dee
And south to Leghorn in hot Tuscany,
Then on to Florence, where our tale began—
And where, meanwhile, another unhappy man
Was hiding in it. Buffalmacco knelt
Or lay stretched out, like William, till he felt
The chest begin to jerk, and even creak,
With the unaccustomed weight, for an antique,
Of his wife and Bruno tupping on its top.
Poor Buffalmacco thought they'd never stop.
Bruno's own wife was now outside the door,
Weeping. He'd sent her, as a punishment for
Deceiving him, to undeceive her friend—
Who, he'd suggested, might keep up her end
By doing as she'd been done by. To save face,
He hoped to implicate her, and disgrace

All three—thus keep things private... *What a cow!*
Thought Buffalmacco's wife. Then showed them how
To keep your end up for an hour or more.
Bruno lost count of *her* orgasms, but four—
Or was it five?—was his own personal best
At breakfast-time. They did it on the chest
(She thought) because her neighbours' marriage-bed—
The idea of which kept running through her head—
By then had been sufficiently defiled,
Which made her blood run quite so hot and wild
That, when they stopped, she started off again
Sighing and grunting as if in sweet pain,
Just minutes later. Bruno's unhappy wife
Eavesdropped. This bout of intermarital strife
Ended, as Bruno flagged, with her friend on top—
Though, when he limply signalled her to stop,
She twisted round to *soixante-neuf* instead
And came again while sitting on his head.
Her very last was a DIY job,
Concluding with deep groans and then a sob,
Which Bruno found unnerving. Such excessive
Female excitement made him feel quite passive—
But, leaping from the chest, he lugged his wife
Into the room and, grasping the long knife
With which he'd frightened her, and which had lain
Unseen beside them, frightened her again
By pointing at the chest without a word.
As if (while her friend sobbed) she hadn't heard
The whole performance, sighs and sobs and all,
And ground her teeth and cursed them through the wall,
She laughed and passed it off with "Well, my dears,
You've paid me back in kind all right. But here's"—
Unlocking and then lifting up the lid—
"Another who's been done by as he did."
If Buffalmacco had not felt so harassed,
He might have laughed to see his wife embarrassed
So cleverly by Bruno's practical joke,
Who'd laid her as if lying on her bloke.
But that was *him!* And, more undressed than dressed,
He virtually vaulted out of William's chest.
All four then stood there wondering what to do,
Bruno in dubious triumph, and the two
Women not knowing what to hope or fear,

Till Buffalmacco had a bright idea:
"My friends, we've known each other for so long,
And shared so much, I think it would be wrong
To be tight-fisted when it comes to love.
So why not share our spouses? Why not have
Two each, in other words? Each man two wives,
Each woman two men, living out our lives
In harmony and friendship till the end?"…
And so wife shared with wife and friend with friend,
Nor did this new arrangement ever lead—
They say—to strife or jealousy. Indeed,
Since jealous thoughts can turn a heaven to hell,
This was—they might have added—just as well,
And of imaginable endings seems the best
Way to wrap up these stories of the chest.
As for the plainer versions to be found
Planted in *The Decameron's* fertile ground,
Who now can tell if, then, Boccaccio knew
Or cared if either one of them were true?

iii   Tancred's Daughter

*"Tancred, Prince of Salerno, kills his daughter's lover, Guiscard, and
sends her his heart in a golden cup…"*
– Decameron IV, i

*

Ghismonda Bewails the Death of her Lover

"I wish I were where Guiscard lies!—
I'd kiss his stone-cold lips and eyes.
Before my raging father dies,
    I'll make him grieve for me.

I'll make him howl. The only one
I loved and who loved me is gone.
And I am weary of the sun
    For his sake who died for me.

Our secret! We thought no one knew it.
To think he must have watched us do it.

Tancred, you sick *roué*, you'll rue it
    Until the day you die!

My heart is like an open sore
To think he'll hold me close no more!
Father, you'll shortly see I care
    So much that I could die!

And yet Prince Tancred's long been noted
As gay Salerno's most devoted
Parent. *Ha!* it's clear he doted
    More than paternally.

I was the first to plight my troth.
Although we're parted now by death,
I know that he and I will love
    Till the stars fall out of the sky.

And nothing Tancred does will ever
Stop us from loving on or sever
What binds our hearts to one another,
    If I live or if I die.

Guiscard, you dared your life: I'd dare
Death for a lock of your black hair,
And give you one of mine to wear
    As a ring eternally.

I wish that I were in my grave,
And lying in your arms, my love:
The grave's the only peace we'll have
    From Tancred's tyranny.

My curses, father, on your head!
You shed his lovely blood: now shed
Your blood-red tears. And till you're dead,
    May you remember me!

Soon I shall be where Guiscard lies,
And lie with him and close my eyes…
For I am weary of the skies
    Since he died because of me."

*

Why Tancred Swore to Punish the Lovers

Her father swore a solemn oath
    To punish their deadly sin.
He cut out Guiscard's heart and chose
    An urn to put it in.

He chose the golden cup in which
    Guiscard had served his wine:
"It serves him right, the common lout,
    For bedding that girl of mine.

A prince's daughter and, what's worse,
    Neither engaged nor married!
I'll feed his flesh to dogs and crows:
    By Christ, he'll go unburied!

I'll grind his bones to powder, I'll—"
    And, seething with indignation,
He sank his teeth into Guiscard's heart—
    For mounting above his station.

Prince Tancred sent his daughter the cup
    To punish her sinful lust:
"A fish-wife! She can bait her hook
    With his heart. The rest is dust."

With it he scrawled a blood-stained note:
    Your father sends you this
To comfort you for losing what
    Caused you (he saw) such bliss!

For what he'd seen and heard them do
Tormented Tancred's brain.
How could he ever now forget
Such pleasure mixed with such pain?

So let her lustful eyes look on
His lustful heart. Instead
Of lust, a lesson. Let
His heart disgust her, dead.

        *

From Boccaccio to Dryden

"*Tancredi, prencipe di Salerno, fu signore assai umano
e di benigno ingegno…*"

> Till, turn'd a Tyrant in his latter Days,
> He lost the Lustre of his former Praise;
> And from the bright Meridian where he stood,
> Descending, dipp'd his Hands in Lovers Blood…

"*il quale in tutto lo spazio della sua vita non ebbe che una
figliuola…*"

> And bless'd he might have been with her alone;
> But oh! how much more happy, had he none!

"*Costei fu dal padre tanto teneramente amata, quanto alcuna
altra figliuola da padre fosse già mai…*".

> She was his Care, his Hope, and his Delight,
> Most in his Thought, and ever in his Sight:
> Next, nay beyond his Life, he held her dear;
> She liv'd by him, and now he liv'd in her.
> For this, when ripe for Marriage, he delay'd
> Her Nuptial Bands, and kept her long a Maid,
> As envying any else should share a Part
> Of what was his, and claiming all her Heart…

*

"… Ghismonda, having poured poison over the heart, drinks
the liquid and so dies."
– *Decameron* IV, i

*

Ghismonda Comforts her Father

> "Father, don't waste those tears of yours:
> Lovers all know that love has claws;
> When lovers' red blood rains, it pours
>   As it's pouring now from me.

Father, stop sobbing. Wipe your eyes,
And lay my corpse where Guiscard's lies.
Carve there—so that, for centuries
   After our dying, we

May prove that star-crossed lovers have
No peace until they're in the grave—
   Who can resist the power of love?
   Death alone set us free."

11   PETER BELL THE FOURTH

"Peter Bells, one, two, and three,
O'er the wide world wandering be…"
– Shelley, Peter Bell the Third

"It will be the wish of the Poet to bring his feelings near to those of the persons whose feelings he describes, nay, for short spaces of time, perhaps, to let himself slip into an entire delusion, and even confound and identify his own feelings with theirs…"
– Wordsworth, Preface to 'Lyrical Ballads'

There was a time when humankind
Listened with faith—or hope—or love
To myths and mysteries in verse:
Then, Poets fearlessly rehearsed
Tales of the gods—or God—above.

But, now, I love the things I see—
The night that calms—the day that cheers;
The common growth of air and earth
Suffices me—our tears, our mirth,
Our common hopes and fears.

These given, what more need I desire
To stir—to soothe—to elevate?
What nobler marvels than the mind,
In any place, may find—
At any time, create?

*

This Peter Bell, for many years,
Had been a woodland pedlar;
But, more and more, when he appeared,
He was mistrusted—sometimes feared—
As a thief or sullen meddler.

He roved along the banks of streams,
In the green wood and hollow dell;
They were his dwelling night and day,—
But Nature could not find a way
Into the heart of Peter Bell.

In vain, through each evolving year,
The seasons flourished. As before,
Primroses by a river's brim
Were yellow primroses to him—
And nothing more.

Though some have looked on trees and sky
And felt (so I've heard say)
As if the moving time had been
A thing as steadfast as the scene
On which they gazed themselves away,

Within the breast of Peter Bell
Was no such saving grace;
He was a churl as rough and rude
As any hue-and-cry pursued—
Or won that wretched race.

There was a hardness in his mien,
A savage cunning in his eye,
As if he'd fixed his stubborn face,
In many a solitary place,
Against the wind and sky.

*

One night, along the moonlit banks
Of the Swale, he strode alone—
Whether to buy or sell, or led
By mischief running in his head,
Will never now be known.

Chancing to notice a short cut
Through a thick wood, he pushes
Into the darkness, undeterred
And whistling—buried like a bird
Among the trees and bushes.

But quickly Peter's mood is changed,
As on he shoves with cheeks that burn
And eyes now flashing black:
There's little sign the track
Will serve his turn.

The way grows dim and dimmer, while
Now here—now there—it weaves and wends.
Until, abruptly, his legs carry
Him into a deserted quarry.
And there it ends.

He paused—as shadows, strangely shaped,
Massive and black, arose or lay;
But, onward through the dark and cold
And yawning fissures, Peter—bold
And angry—forced his way.

Across the deep and quiet space
Beyond, he pushes through the grass
Towards the skirting trees,
When, turning suddenly, he sees
A solitary ass.

He glances round. There's nothing but
The moonlit sky, woods, rocks which gleam—
And this one beast, that hangs his head
From the green meadow's silent bed
Over the muttering stream.

"Gotcha!" cries Peter—with a jerk
Which would have pulled from a dungeon-floor
A solid iron ring;
But still the heavy-headed thing
Stood as before.

And Peter peered about again,
But all is silent. Far and near
There's not a house in sight:
No woodman's hut, no cottage light—
No one to see or hear…

Suspicions ripen into dread;
Yet, raising his staff with slow
Deliberate aim, he gauged its length
And, summoning all his strength,
Delivered a savage blow.

The creature staggered with the shock;
And then, as if to take his ease
In a quiet uncomplaining mood
Where up to now he'd stood,
Dropped gently to his knees;

And gently fell down on his side,
Lying as one who mourned might lie
Beside the river's brink, where he
Turned on Peter—patiently—
A shining hazel eye.

But the staff came down on the beast's head;
His lank sides heaved and his limbs stirred;
He gave a groan, and then another—
But his tormentor's heart heard neither—
And then a third.

Weakened, the ass lay still as death;
The furious man's lips quiver:
"You little mulish dog!
I'll fling your carcass like a log
Head-foremost in the river!"

But now among the rocks and crags,
Into the mountains far away,
The half-starved ass let out
A rueful, deep-drawn shout—
The hard dry see-saw of his horrible bray.

This outcry gladdened Peter's heart;
Blindly his staff lashed out again.
But the ass repeated that strange sound—
Till the rocks staggered all around,
Moonlit and blenched, as if with pain.

The echoes died away. In the rocks
Was something Peter didn't like.
His arms and raised staff sink:
"If anyone should see, they'll think
I'm helping this poor tyke."

His scorn returns—his hate revives;
He stoops maliciously to seize
The ass—but gets a sudden fright
As, in the pool, a grisly sight
Meets him, among the inverted trees.

Is it the moon's distorted face?
Or ghost-like image of a cloud?
Or stubborn spirit doomed to yell
In solitary ward or cell?
Is it a coffin—or a shroud?

Is Peter frightened of *himself?*
He sees a motion—hears a groan;
His eye-balls bulge—his heart will break—
And with a strangled sort of shriek,
He falls to the ground like a stone.

*

At length the moonlight on his eyes
Wakes him. Still perplexed,
He sees his staff—the rocks—the wood—
Then looks into the sullen flood,
Where, staring, his eyes stay fixed.

A face, enduring its last sleep
Beneath the surface, swims in view.
He looks—he cannot choose but look—
Like someone reading in a book,
Undecided what to do.

Suddenly, close by Peter's side,
The ass gets up and quietly stands,
While Peter, probing here and there,
Twines his staff in the floating hair.
The little ass licks his hard hands.

He pulls—and looks—and pulls again;
And he whom the ass had lost,
The man who had been four days dead,
Head-foremost from the river's bed
Rose like a ghost.

Thick eels protrude from eyes and mouth;
His nose and ears are almost gone;
The crinkled skin is blue or grey,
And the fingers nibbled away
Down to the very bone.

But Peter draws him to dry land,
While poignant twitches pass
Through his brain—fast and faster:
"He must be the dead master
Of this miserable ass!"

The meagre beast looks on,
Then kneels—to tell (as best he can)
Peter to mount: "Come weal or woe,
I'll do what the ass would have me do,
For the sake of this poor drowned man."

With unfamiliar feelings, he
Thus mounts the grateful ass,
As, firmly and without delay,
The earnest creature turns away
And leaves the body on the grass.

But soon a burst of doleful sound
Reaches the ears of man and beast.
Is it a lynx—or barking fox—
Or night-bird hidden in the rocks,
Clawing a bloody feast?

This unintelligible cry
Convinces Peter on the spot
Some vengeance worse than all
That ever fell would fall
On him that night. But what?

And while the ass pursues his way,
He sits in expectation—
Certain that he, a reprobate,
This very night will meet his fate
In some unholy visitation.

Now, though, the animal has climbed
To a green path, which wends
Where, shining like the smoothest sea
In undisturbed immensity,
A level plain extends.

And yet a faintly rustling sound
Makes Peter feel he's being chased.
—A withered leaf was close behind,
A plaything for the moaning wind
Crossing that lonely waste.

When Peter saw the moving thing,
It only doubled his distress:
"The very leaves are after me,
Though here there's neither bush nor tree—
So great is my wickedness!"

And so they come to a narrow lane,
Where, as before, the patient ass
Shows neither need nor wish to stop—
Nor even turn his head to crop
A bramble leaf or blade of grass.

Between the hedges as they go,
The white dust sleeps on the lane;
And Peter, every now and then,
Looking behind him, sees—on a stone
Or in the dust—a stain.

It was as if the moonlight made
A trail of blood look wan.
But how did a trail of blood get there?
And why these sinkings of despair
In the heart of this hardened man?

At length he perceives a bleeding wound
Where he had struck the ass's head;
He sees the blood, knows what it is—
And a glimpse of sudden joy was his,
Which quickly fled

As he thought of him whom sudden death
Had seized, and of the faithful ass.
And once again those ghastly pains
Shoot from his heart to the ass's reins—
And through his brain—and pass.

*

The moon blazed on. Soon Peter began
To try, in his troubled heart,
To ease his conscience of its pain:
"Blood drops—leaves rustle—but it's plain
Worse is afoot," he thought.

"How did the dead man meet his end?
Tempted to steal his ass in the wood,
I resisted. If it weren't for me,
He'd never be buried properly.
I've done the best I could."

Or so he told himself, until
They reached a sheltered place
In which a chapel, overgrown
With greenest ivy, stood alone,
As if in a state of grace.

Dying insensibly away
From human thoughts and purposes,
It seemed—wall, window, roof and tower—
To bow to some transforming power,
And blend with the surrounding trees.

A ruined chapel. Peter thought
Of another such in his life—
Which served his turn when, following still
The dictates of his ruthless will,
He'd married his youngest wife…

The innocent creature bore him on,
Till they passed a bright and crowded inn;
But a stifling power oppressed his frame
And a swimming darkness came
Over that drunken din

As, turned adrift in his past,
He found no comfort in its course
But, moonstruck as before,
He trembled, shaken to the core
By compunction and remorse.

And, above all, his heart is stung
To think of her, almost a child,
That sweet and playful Highland girl
As light and lovely as a squirrel,
As lovely and as wild.

Her dwelling was a lonely house,
A cottage in a furze-filled dell;
And she dressed herself in green,
And left her mother at sixteen,
And followed Peter Bell.

And she had good and pious thoughts
And went to the kirk to pray—
Even as a child, content to go
Two long cold miles through rain or snow
Twice every Sabbath-day.

But when she learned how Peter lived
She drooped and very soon was worn
To the bone. Her future fell apart,
And she died of shame and a broken heart
Before her child was born.

—Beside a brake of flowering furze
Above which shivering aspens play,
Peter now sees a ghost-like creature,
Himself in form and feature,
Close to the broad highway.

And stretched beneath the furze he sees
The Scottish girl—no other;
And hears her crying as she cried
The very moment that she died,
"My mother! oh, my mother!"

The sweat pours down his stricken face:
So grievous is his heart's contrition,
The agony makes his eyeballs ache
In the white moonlight by that brake,
As they behold that vision.

"Repent—Forgive—Forget!" The ass
 Passed calmly by a church-door, where
These words reached Peter's ears—
"And save your souls!" The joy, the tears,
Were as much as he could bear:

Hot tears of hope and tenderness,
Which fell like a bursting shower.
 His nerves and sinews seemed to melt
As, through his iron frame, he felt
A gentle, a relaxing, power.

Meanwhile, the persevering ass
 Bore Peter half a mile or more
Along a dark and stony lane
Until, inaudibly, he came
To a lonely house whose silent door

Was shut. Was this the poor man's home?
They waited. All that could be heard
 Was the trickling household rill.
 But then, across the cottage-sill,
A little girl appeared.

As if she were blinded by the moon,
She screamed, "It's him!" Her mother,
Hearing the cry with joy and fright,
Rushed past her out into the night—
And saw it was another

Man on her husband's ass. She fell
Beside the creature's hooves and lay
Senseless, while Peter's confused mind
Looked sadly on, unused
To helping his own kind. This way

And that he turned. But then dismounted
And, propping her against his knee,
Began—when she came round—to tell
His tale—in a trembling voice—as well
As he was able. She

Cried out, "Oh God be praised! My heart's
At ease! But—dead, forever dead!
And, oh, there was no warning pain—
And now he'll never come home again.
– If only he'd died in his bed!"

Peter supports the woman. And
Feels his heart opening more and more.
A holy sense pervades his mind,
As he feels what he—for his own kind—
Has never felt before.

At length, she sends her child
To bid the neighbours come:
"Ask them to lend their horse tonight—
And this good man, whom Heaven requite,
Will help to bring the body home."

Away goes Rachel, weeping. Now
A baby, waking in distress
Inside the house, begins to cry;
And Peter hears the mother sigh,
"Seven children—fatherless!"

So step by step he learns to feel
Man's heart is a holy thing,
Receiving from a world of death
The life it gives—a second breath
More searching than the breath of spring.

The widow sits on a moonlit stone
In agony of silent grief;
His thoughts make Peter start—
He longs to take her to his heart
From love which cannot find relief.

She goes to still her child. He turns
Aside among the welcoming trees,
Where he sits down—not knowing how—
With his hands pressed against his brow,
His elbows on his trembling knees.

There, self-involved, he sits—as if
He were a tree himself, or dead,
Or his mind were sinking deep
Through years that have been long asleep.
The trance is passed: he lifts his head—

And sees the ass. And then a man
Leading the neighbours' horse.
They rode off straight away;
And, with due care, by break of day,
The ass brought back the corpse.

12   FAIR'S FAIR
(after Grimms' *Märchen*, No.15)

Hansel and Gretel—like Jack and Jill—
were not the kind you'd think would kill.
But, later, they claimed their childhoods were lacking
in normal parental love and backing,
and so felt not unjustified
when someone in their story died…
One morning, after an all-night coven,
the Witch had Gretel heat up the oven
to bake her brother. Now was it a sin
for Gretel to shove the old hag in?
The Witch was the Jew-in-the-Bush's wife:
he'd stolen their money; she'd threatened their life—
until they came up with their final solution
to rid the woods of sub-human pollution.
Such scum has only itself to blame:
an eye for an eye. Fair's fair! In the name
of *Freedom* they took this desperate measure,
and hiked off home with the Witch's treasure.
In the meantime, Gretel's mother had died,
and Hansel's father falsely cried—
or so they thought—to have them back.
This Gretel or Jill and Hansel or Jack—
ill-treated, as step-sister and -brother,
by father/step-father, mother/step-mother—
resisting multiple temptations
to flee from home's obscene vibrations,
ignored the sad old bastard's tears
and, compensating for their fears,
consolidated their position.
Jack handled his father with suspicion
(his tactics made old fogeys squirm)—
and muscled in on the family firm.
But who that you and I now know—
X/Y—Jane/Tarzan—Mary/Joe—
with childhood memories like the hell
of fetching water from a well,
peeling bananas, humping wood—
and damned if they were bad *or* good—

would treat that kind of oldster better?
Honour thy father's a very dead letter…
Although they say Jack's weak-willed dad,
compared with Jack, was not that bad:
people were grist to J.'s machine
for printing bank-notes. Lean and mean,
his motto was worry 'em—bully 'em—shirk—
and get rich quick on others' work.
But—ruthlessly streetwise, cool and witty,
and up-and-coming in the City—
at home he was moody, anxious, bored.
So most of their time was spent abroad
in exotic and expensive places.
J. and J. gave themselves airs and graces,
since "We were the poorest of the poor:
what else is life worth living for?"
Until Jack's father kicked the bucket.
"Oh no, Jill," Jack exclaimed. "Oh, fuck it,
I didn't mean that dad should *die!*
Why has this happened? Why, oh why?"
Jilly was older now, of course:
both of them suffered pangs of remorse.
They tried to forget, they tried to forgive,
they'd only wanted to live and let live!
And so they married. But married life
soon became blissless, non-stop strife.
Who—what—was to blame? As sister and brother,
they'd only wanted to comfort each other.

13   A BRIEF PRELUDE (3)

"When old age shall this generation waste,
    Thou shalt remain, in midst of other woe
Than ours, a friend to man…"
– Keats, *Ode on a Grecian Urn*

He / I once thought that *nothing* came of how
and where they lived until he was, what, twelve
years old, but guilt and fear. And yet (if I
remember rightly) was there not his mother's
smile before switching off the light and leaving
three brothers safer in their beds? the pre-
pubescent thrill of her ample bottom, just
our height? his laughing father—salt, bread, coal
in hand—gone out the backdoor, in the front,
on New Year's Eve? And fireworks? Pancakes? Bob-apple night?

*

I've read some stuff of his about us all,
but there was more—much more—to it than that.
I hated where we lived even more than he *did—*
meithered and nagged until we left. The Mersey
stank, actually stank—so foul, so dead it was.
His father didn't care. He liked the pub,
his cronies, even the neighbours. I did what I could,
all mothers do. I told them Do your utty*—*
the worst of times can turn into the best.
Five children, then a sixth. I've left my mark.

*

"We are such stuff
As dreams are made on…"
– *The Tempest*

Two very early memories resemble dreams…
One winter night on someone's arm—his father's?—
looking across the black but shimmering Mersey:
a little crowd of people's *Oohs* and *Aahs*

at distant fireworks, brilliant in the darkness...
And out for a walk one Sunday afternoon
in summer, he and his brother holding on
to the baby's pram, his mother pushing, his father
leading the way to statues with no clothes on
in the Lady Lever Gallery, Port Sunlight...

*

*We took them out. Five children on the bus
to Meols or Hoylake. Old photos show them playing
together on the beach, their father (hanky
on head and trousers rolled) asleep in a deckchair;
one of him in the water, puffing and blowing—
he couldn't really swim: quiet, sunny days,
my sister and her children sometimes with us...
She died. I miss her—she was always there.
Two of the five have died as well. I told them
Never give up, though. And I don't give up.*

*

After their back-to-back, the semi's garden
had flower-beds, apple-trees, old roses needing
compost and pruning, lawns to be mowed, tall hedges—
scutch-grass and weeds... In the end, even the weeding
(at first a chore) became a peaceful way
to fill a Sunday afternoon. Plants like
to know they're liked—and cared for—he decided.
A callow thought—and laughed at. Whereas the yearly
miracle of Christmas roses, tulips, pinks,
irises, broom, was not so soon derided.

*

*Though useless with machines, he seemed to like
hard labour—cutting, loading slabs of silage,
milking all forty cows. He rode his bike
up Storeton Hill to get here too—through wind
and rain that summer... Only a few months later
he started at Oxford. The pay was nothing. Why
bother? We need them, they need us, he murmured,
but hated the fledgeling chickens' pecking order,*

*the cat in a flurry of feathers, old cows—their strength
once gone—cold-shouldered by the heartless herd...*

*

Mountains—lakes—woods—brought unexpected peace.
They minded their own business, didn't care
about his past or future, or their own.
Their beauty seemed mysterious. Mountain-air,
after home's dangerous, overcrowded life,
felt free and easy. The chaplain's greedy eyes
could be ignored / took photos of boys and views
as if he owned them... Later, I and my wife
made love by woodland lakes. *We* care—about
Nature, and for each other. Takers lose.

*

*Shy of the new, he'd say he didn't know
about that sort of thing. I said, "Well, if
you refuse to look or listen, how will you
discover more?" Too buttoned-up, a stiff
school-uniformed headboy, at last I gave him
a ticket for the Phil—Dvorak's New World...
'The Globe' came next: King Richard swinging his chains
in Pomfret's dungeon...*
                          —Words alone would save him...
*My Film Club, too, turned classrooms into Rome—
the Antarctic—Casablanca...*
                        —Art remains.

*

*I rowed for Cambridge. Power was essential, but
what won was skill—the cox, the stroke. The way
words pull their weight in a poem—its style—and not
its creed—still less the fashion of the day—
in the course of time makes / mars it. So I taught
close reading: metre / syntax— imagery / sound—
stanza-forms, rhyme—which lines were living, which dead...
He acquiesced—worked hard—one class, though, said
the poetry mattered but, since words have meaning,
it also mattered what its maker thought...*

*

> "... *you are the music*
> *While the music lasts*"
> – T.S. Eliot

Music, food of the Muses, moulds its feelings
Into pure sound. Its forms address themselves
To body—heart—and more. Invisibly revealing
All times, all places, music evolves; *in*volves
Timelessness, placelessness; and yet takes place
At times, in places: then in Oxford, here
In Munich now, Bach's world is a concert hall
Where vast sub-/superstructures praise/embrace
All life, all death—Mozart casts out all fear—
Stravinsky fills his old/new forms brim-full…

*

> *"They passed, like figures on a marble urn,*
> *When shifted round to see the other side"*
> – Keats, *Ode on Indolence*

The old stone spires of Oxford framed the scene.
His landlord was a Christ Church gardener. He
Helped out. Dons and gowned students crossed the lawn
In April's *yonge sonne*. Italy
Beckoned… What were the Italian words for *grass*—
For *rose-beds*—early *tulips?* For *"a host*
Of golden daffodils"?… Pruning old trees,
They worked, then rested. Soon that time would pass…
That these few things should not be wholly lost,
I set them down here in a verbal frieze.

*

> "*Guido, i' vorrei che tu e Lapo ed io*"—Dante

Guido, I wish that Lapo, you and I
Were in a ship, and that the winds would blow
Us and your Vanna, Lagia, also my [...]
Across the waves, wherever we chose to go
With them—so that we all might talk
Only of love and of each other, till
The women, praised and loved, at last would be

*As quiet and bright as if in some fine work
Of Giotto's. Then we'd kiss. And they'd be still
Brighter, and quieter. So, I think, would we.*

*

(for M-N. D)

Crossing the meaningless black plunging sea,
The ferry trailed its sparkling wake through the night.
On deck, a girl—alone. Through wind-borne spray
He approached, and stood beside her. Looking out
On nothing—total darkness—soon they fill
Its vacancy with words, looks, smiles. Then kisses.
And find a quieter place where, warm and dry,
They spend the night—in love, until
At cold grey dawn their time together passes...
Waving, he cycled off. Goodbye. Goodbye.

*

His first magnolia bloomed in the heat of May
At Villa Camerata, Florence—which
Here now reminds me of Massetto's way
With nuns, of Chaucer's May without a stitch
On underneath her smock, of Calendrino
And his infatuated 'innocence'...
And yet my wife (in red bikini) and I
Also sat looking there at Botticelli's
Vision of *Spring* as natural forces tense
With violence: Chloris, raped, became Flora, while
Venus presided... Shot by her son from above,
A Grace transformed his bolt to married love.

*

*"Which Grace?" I asked him. Pictures leave us free,
He'd smile, to interpret what (for us) they mean.
The world, our very lives, mean nothing—we
Give them their only meanings. What he'd seen
In Florence meant so much to him because
Of where he'd come from: "Where I came from," he
Stressed. "—And still come from, yes. I was*

Another person, though. I say and see
Another world, another life. But they
Are threatened still—at times still fouled—by past
Nightmares from hidden swamps, which have to be
Awoken from, cleaned up, re-dreamed each day
I go on living."
                Others taught him. The last
I heard was he'd gone back to Italy.

*

Why write? —He knew he'd never go again
To "Oxford and his friends". They'd soon forget
To miss him. He too forgot—and forgave—when
She opened her door in Riva. Their eyes met,
Reminding him of Florence—Botticelli—
The garden where they'd met three years before.
From Chloris' breasts to Flora's flowering body,
Venus ruled Riva, while the god *Amor*
Shot bolts into the following forty years
With arbitrary blindness. Zephyrus blew,
Wild Chloris bloomed. But who were the three Graces?
Body / heart / mind—or 'soul'—shall we say? His fears
And guilts died down as, rapt, their twined souls grew
Into a thorny climber, bearing roses.

14 FROM OUTSIGHT TO INSIGHT

"The world is led by mind."—*Samyutta Nikaya* I. 39

i Nine Poems After Rilke—The Turn

Archaic Torso of Apollo

We never saw or heard the numinous head
Whose eyeballs blazed like apples ripely growing.
But still his torso's somewhat softer glowing,
As of a branching street-lamp, holds instead

The brilliance of his look. Or how could the prow
Of his breast blind you? Or the subtle turning
Of his loins light a smile and send it burning
Into the procreative centre? How

Could he not seem disfigured, not seem short
Beneath the shoulders' fallen nought?
Or shimmer like a predator's bright fur?

Or break forth, like a star which seems to strive
Beyond its bounds? For there's no place from where
He cannot see you. You must change your life.

*

Saint Sebastian

Standing up like someone lying down,
Force of will alone can have supported
This… As nursing mothers are transported—
Self-involved—he wreathes himself a crown.

Arrows come—here—now—as if
Springing from his loins. But, unastounded,
Darkly smiling still, he seems unwounded
As their quivering shafts grow stiff.

Only once his sorrows grow,
And his eyes expose his suffering, though
Soon reject again as merely petty—
And contemptuously let go—
Such destroyers of a thing of beauty.

*

Corrida
(In memoriam Montez, 1830)

Since he lightly burst from the *toril*,
Almost small, with startled eyes and ears,
Taking on the stubborn picadors
And the banderillas—look, the bull

Like a storm-cloud has increased
To a massive, black, accumulated
Hatred, as of all he's hated—
Clenched his head into a fist,

Taking nothing now from any man
Lightly: now, with bloody banners showing
Over lowered horns, obscurely knowing—
Having *always* been against the one

Who, in his embroidered, pink silk-suit
Quickly turns and, like a black bee-swarm,
Lets the deeply consternated brute
Pass beneath his mauve and golden arm—

Raising easily misdirected, hot
Eyes again towards his still ungored
Rival who, performing on the spot
Chiaroscuro circles without thinking,
Till the bull stands blindly blinking,

Now prepares—serene, unhurried, calm,
Cool, and leaning forward on his arm
Over that on-coming, great
Wave with all its thrust of wasted hate—
Almost gently to insert his sword.

*

The Last Graf von Brederode Escapes from Turkish Imprisonment

They followed, shooting multicoloured death
From far behind him. Lost and terrified, he
Fled on, aware of nothing but the threat
He fled from, while his far-off ancestry

Appeared as nothing now: hunted by men,
Even a beast will flee. Until, at the side
Of a flashing, roaring river, the will to decide
Raised him above distress, turned him again—

As if among fine ladies, smiling sweetly—
Into a princely son of royal blood:
They smiled upon his radiant face, completely

Fulfilled—so young. Great-hearted, on he rode
Aglow with blood. And his horse bore him greatly—
As into his own castle—into the flood.

*

The Gazelle
(Gazella Dorcas)

Enchanted one, how can the sound of two
Selected words ever achieve the rhyme
Which comes and goes in you, like beating time?
Your lyre-like horns ascend as if leaves grew

On them—and all about you has so often
Figured in songs of love, which soothe and soften
Like roses' petals on the closed eye-lids
Of a reader who no longer reads

In order to see *you*, borne there as though
Each run were fully loaded with long leaps
Which wait to shoot away just so

Long as your neck's alert, like one who keeps
On breaking off her woodland swim to take
A look who else is swimming in her lake.

*

The Death of the Poet

He lay there, his uplifted countenance
Pale with denial in its pile of cushions,
Now that the world, torn from his sense impressions,
With all his knowledge of its forms and fashions,
Had lapsed into the year's indifference.

No one who saw him there could guess
How much he'd been at one with all existence;
For *this*—these depths, these meadows, this persistence
Of water—this in fact *was* his real face.

And, oh, his face was all that—far and wide—
Approaches now as if to court him here;
Whereas his mask, which passes on in fear,
Is soft and open as the inner side
Of fruit, which decomposes in the air.

*

L'Ange du Méridien
(Chartres)

With all the force of nihilistic thought,
A tempest tests this huge cathedral's strength;
And so it's with a sense of something sought
That we're attracted by your smile at length,

O feeling angel, by your gentle smile
Whose mouth is sculpted from a hundred mouths…
But are you aware—or not—of how life's hours
Slip from the fullness of your dial,

Whose figures show the whole day's total, which,
Equally real, are balanced there as fully
As if all hours were ripe and rich.—

What do you, stone one, know of our Being's plight,
Turning, perhaps, with deeply, even wholly
Ecstatic looks, your sun-dial towards the night?

*

The Turn

*The way from intense awareness to greatness is
through sacrifice.* – Kassner

Long had he triumphed by looking.
Stars would drop to their knees,
Wrestled there by his gazing.
Or, if he knelt to look,
Even the gods grew weary
Breathing his powerful incense;
Smiled at him in their sleep.

Towers he would look at until—
Frightened—they shook;
Building them up again, quickly, in one!
Yet how often the landscape,
Heavy laden with day,
Rested at last in his peaceful awareness, evenings.

Animals, trustful, moved
Into his open gaze,
Grazing. The captive lions
Stared, as at inconceivable freedom.
Birds went flying through him—
Straight through his soul; and flowers
Looked again in his eyes, as
Large as in children.

And rumours that someone was *looking*
Moved all the less, the
Questionably visible,
Moved the women.

How long looking?
How long inwardly lacking—
Pleading from deep in his eyes?

While he sat waiting, away from home; a hotel's
Distracted, averted bed-room
Sullen around him, and in the evaded mirror
Again the hotel-room
And, later, from the miserable bed

Again:
Consultations held in air,
Incomprehensible consultations—
Over his feeling heart,
Over his heart which in spite of his pain-racked
Body still made itself felt—
Were taking place and deciding:
That it had no love.

(And denied him greater glory.)

For there's a limit, you see, to looking.
And the well-looked-at world
Wishes to flourish in love.

Work of the face is done,
Now do heart-work
On the images captured within you; for you
Overpowered them: but, now, you don't know them.
Look, inner Man, at your young inner Woman,
At the one you have won from
A thousand natures, at
The creature you've still only won, the
Never yet loved one.

*

From *Sonnets to Orpheus (1.1)*

A tree ascends! O unimpaired transcendence!
O Orpheus sings! O high tree in the ear!
And all grew silent. Yet in that deep silence
New bearings, and new clues, and change were there.

Drawn by such stillness, creatures thronged from the clear
Relaxing wood—from nest and hiding place;
Until it seemed their inner quiet, their grace
Of movement came from neither greed nor fear

But from their listening. There in that bright clearing,
Their heartfelt howls, shrieks, roaring were no more.
And so, with hardly shelter to receive it—

A burrow or den, as dark desires conceive it,
Or hut with quivering door-posts and one door—
Your song created temples in their hearing.

ii   Siddhartha and Others

> *"All that we are is the result of what we have thought; it is
> founded upon our thoughts, it is made by our thoughts."*
> – Dhammapada 1

Rilke: Buddha ("Als ob er horchte")

As if he were listening. Stillness: as if from afar…
We go our way, and can no longer hear.
He, though, is star. And other massive stars
We cannot see now stand around him here.

O he is all. We wait till he at least
Notices us. But does he, really, need to?
And if we knelt to him, whom all things kneel to,
He'd stay inert, as deep as stone or beast.

For that which here now at his feet compels us
To fall evolved in him light-years ago.
And he forgets the only things we know,
And what he thinks and knows expels us.

                *

I, Channa

All right, I'll tell you why I left the *sangha*.
But only if you'll promise not to gossip
to all and sundry, friends and relatives
about what really happened. Don't forget,
I *am* your husband now. Your reputation
is one with mine. You promise? Good. Well, then,
one reason was what we've just done, my dear.
My Middle Way includes your middle way—
I'm not the first ex-monk to have thought that.
Celibacy causes trouble, to put it mildly—
I won't go into detail…—Which makes now

A more appropriate time to talk than most.
Besides, I need a break before…—Yes, yes,
you're right—I could, of course, have told you
earlier, before we married. But, you see,
I was to blame as well for what went wrong—
and, at my age, was loath to spoil my image
in your young eyes, or tarnish my name and fame
in your rich parents'. Siddhartha was my friend:
before his death he helped me; after his death
those who had never liked me, who were envious
of my repute, his fondness, as good as forced me
to surrender my position as an *arhat*
and leave…

           But where to begin? I don't suppose
you know a lot about what happened—say,
some thirty years before your birth? Then I'll
go back to how Siddhartha—who was born
a prince—became the future Buddha. His father,
King Suddhodana, naturally hoped his son
would follow him as king. But then Asita,
a wise ascetic—also a gifted seer—
predicted at his birth-day celebrations
that if Siddhartha later renounced the world
he would become a great and famous *sadhu.*
"But why renounce the world?" the King inquired.
Asita answered: "If he sees four signs—
an old, decrepit man—a very sick man—
a corpse—and an ascetic beggar or 'monk'—
the Prince will not become a king but lead
a holy life."

           And so King Suddhodana
sent guards to man the gates of his great palace
and to patrol its parks and pleasure gardens
in order to prevent his son from glimpsing
any such painful, ugly 'signs' as Asita
had listed. And for years this worked. There were,
of course, small problems. A favourite cat which liked
to bring him half-dead birds or mice; a dancer
who slipped and broke her ankle; his wife in labour
before their son was born. This last, I'd say,
impressed him most. The King was furious; but
her labour pains had started far too soon—
before the planned diversions…

                              After the birth,
I'd sometimes find him brooding. He'd begun
to notice things. One evening, a young woman—
one of a troupe of travelling entertainers
(and there was always entertainment)—sitting
after their show alone, began to sing,
as night came on, a sad and beautiful song
about the home she'd left, about her friends
and family far away. I stood and listened
beside him. As his charioteer and servant,
I often stood beside and slightly behind him
to do his bidding. When the song had ended,
"Channa," he asked, "why does she *suffer* so?...
And where is 'far away'?"
                          By birth a Warrior,
I had, as a matter of fact, already fought
in battles far beyond our tribal borders.
"The world goes on and on," I dared to tell him.
"I want to see it," he said: "I haven't seen
even the city which I know is there
outside the palace gates." He begged his father
to let me show it him. Instead the King
arranged a grand procession along the main
thoroughfares of the city.
                          But his son
was looking now and, up an alley, saw
a very old, decrepit man with a crutch
about to be removed by a palace guard.
Dismounting straight away, he ordered no one
apart from myself to follow him, and hurried
after the wretched beggar, along the alley,
into a poor and run-down quarter where
the sick lay unattended—where diseases
spread like slow fire—where real fire burned the dead
beside the river which received their ashes.

A skull exploded as Siddhartha watched;
a widow screamed, on fire beside her husband;
another tried to flee, her clothes on fire.
Beyond the funeral pyres ascetics stood
or sat cross-legged or squatted. "Who are they?"
Siddhartha wondered. "Seekers," I replied,
though I knew little of them. "After what?"

—"Freedom," I said: "They mortify the flesh,
striving to rise—as if on fire within—
to bliss, perhaps omniscience"…
                          Deeply troubled
by all four 'signs' at once, Siddhartha (as
Asita knew he would) renounced the world—
his kingdom, wealth, security, comfort, family.
He wanted from the start to find a cure
for people's suffering. One moonlit night he woke me
and ordered me to fetch his horse, Kanthaka—
a powerful stallion, white and swift. Before
we reached the great main gates, he visited
his wife and son. He stood and watched them sleeping
for a long time. Then left them. Tears ran down
his cheeks. He whispered, "Channa, first I'll become
a Buddha—then return to see my son."
If the gates had failed to open, I believe
Kanthaka would have leapt them. But it was
as if a powerful god had opened them—
muffling Kanthaka's neighs and placing the palms
of his hands beneath his hooves.
                          Without a sound
we left. A full moon lit our way. When we reached
the river Anoma, far beyond the city,
he stopped to let me sleep…—But *I* won't stop
to let *you* sleep, my love. Come here and let me
wake you by slapping this or that sweet cheek.
Aha, you're wide awake—were merely resting
your eyes and eyelids? Listen!—I *need* a listener
before I die… Yes, then you'll be a widow.
You needn't look so shocked, love. Yes, I promise
to see to it that you don't burn when *I* do.
—Just listen. And perhaps you'll understand
why superstitions of that sort have nothing
to do with how Siddhartha lived and died…

Where were we? While I slept, he'd cut his hair.
Down by the river, four or five ascetics
were meditating. So would he, he'd decided.
He gave me his fine clothes, his ornaments
and horse. Then told me to go home. I begged him
to let me stay there. But, he explained, he needed
to find his way alone. Three times I begged him,

to no avail. I was to tell his parents
and wife that he was well. Also to fetch him
three simple robes, a bowl for alms, a razor
to shave his head, a water-strainer, needle
and belt. The rest I took.
                        From that day on
he led the life of an extreme ascetic
who hoped to reach enlightenment by burning
the foulness of his former lives away
and mortifying the flesh, as said, in *this* one.
Not my idea of fun—nor yours, I think,
my fleshly love... Like everything he did,
he did this then with concentrated commitment—
for six long years. And "long" they seemed! I knew
his whereabouts and often spied on him.
I left him food he often left untouched.
He grew so weak and so emaciated
his spine stood out like corded rope, his skin
turned black, his ribs projected like the roofless
rafters of an old cowshed, his shining eyes
were sunk so far into their sockets that
their light was like the distant gleam of water
in a deep well.
               One day I saw him fall
and hurried to help him. When at last he recovered
he smiled to see me: "Channa, you disobeyed
my orders to go home. But now I'm glad
you did so. Give me food and drink. These six
hard years of starving now seem all at once
like trying to tie the air in knots, instead
of simply breathing. In all this strenuous time
I have not gone a step beyond the self
whose life, as I now know, is nothing other
than suffering: greater or lesser suffering. Since
the way beyond cannot be more extreme,
it must be less—more ordinary, perhaps.
The striving soul, in the end, has only striven.
So give me the food and drink I know you've brought
for me. I might have died without your help.
But now let me breathe in, breathe out..."
                                        A sound
of music reached us while he ate and drank
—a travelling band of dancers and musicians

was passing by. One player tuned his *veena*.
Siddhartha watched. Then said: "If you stretch the strings
too loose they cannot play. But if too tight
they break." And so he took the Middle Way,
begged ordinary food in villages, and slept
in barns. For his ascetic followers—who
had viewed him as their *guru*—this amounted
to weak and culpable luxury, and they left him.

Soon after that I found him seated quietly
beneath a bodhi-tree. The following day
he had not moved. And so for five more days.
His eyes were closed. An almost visible aura
of peacefulness surrounded his still form.
At last he smiled—looked—ate and drank—and told me
it was a matter of Awareness—bodily,
mental, and spiritual observation. Since
the observer must be more than the observed:
more, for example, than the air he breathes,
his bodily sensations—than his mind's
chimeras and red herrings, hopes and fears,
his craving, clinging, unfulfilled desires,
his anger and his hatred—lust and love—
or even (he thought) real pain, the pain of death;
and since the observer too could be observed
on planes of undelimited time and space,
of undelimited consciousness of nothing,
of neither perception nor of non-perception:
self-observation, or Awareness, was
the way—available to each and all—
Brahmans and Warriors, Husbandmen and Servants—
to free one's heart and mind, to free one's spirit
from suffering, from rebirth, from life itself,
unfettered to the point of real extinction.

He'd almost reached this point when he turned back
in order to tell others. That was the sort
of man he was. A teacher, a great *sadhu*,
who cared for others almost more than himself...
I know he said these things because he asked me
to learn them off by heart, repeating—and
repeating—what I'd forgotten. In other words,
I was his first disciple... I remember

once, while I watched, a terrifying storm.
Big trees blew over. Tremendous wind—forked lightning—
torrents of rain… Unmoved, he sat right through it,
as if the sun or moon were shining quietly.
Later there was a story—absurd, of course—
that a king cobra had emerged from the jungle
and spread its hood to shield him… Not long after,
when there were more and more of us, I joined
the *sangha* as his servant, his assistant,
at his request.   He kept on trying to teach me.
I'm no great meditator, but I've learned
enough to understand his Eightfold Path…
I'm no great teacher either—I don't care
what others can or can't do. But if you
would like to try, I'll show you: "Go and look
for yourself," he always answered… —I'm too lazy
to want to spend all day cross-legged, observing
my expirations / inspirations. Either
too lazy or too active. Probably both.
And you? Not lazy, eh? Well then, we'll see
if I can teach you. I'm too sensuous also—
in case you hadn't noticed. There are ten
'fetters' which have to be cast off before
enlightenment can occur. Of these, I am—
Siddhartha assured me—weighted down by five.
—What *are* they? Well, I'll tell you. First of all,
my Warrior's pride. Then animosity
towards those I ought to tolerate, even love.
Self-righteousness and ignorance (made worse
by idleness). That's four. And fifthly—I'm
not sorry to add—my sensuousness. Well, you're
a sensuous person too. I thought as much
before we'd even married… But I'd loved
and served Siddhartha—brought him food (he knew
I had, you see). He smiled his enlightened smile
and made me a sort of honorary *arhat*.

This irritated some—for instance, Ananda—
his other close companion—and his two
leading disciples (so they called themselves),
Sariputta and Moggellana. Now these men
had all been Brahmans. I think you know, my dear,

that in real life—or 'unreal' life, perhaps—
the Brahmans, though superior to us Warriors,
do not wield power. We Warriors fight—but also
rule and administer, pay for them as priests,
as intellectual parasites or teachers,
and for their temples' upkeep. But in the *sangha*,
where social classes are—at least in theory—
no longer valid, Brahmans, like it or not,
have power and use it. So many meaningless rules
to be obeyed / transgressed, remembered / forgotten!
Now I am not, by nature or by birth,
obedient. But neither was Siddhartha, who
not only understood but tolerated,
up to a point, my (shall we say?) eccentric
behaviour. Ananda and the others griped
that I'd abused them. What I'd done, in fact,
was tell them what I thought of them—that's all.
On more than one occasion, I admit…

Siddhartha asked me to control my tongue.
And I did try—for *his* sake, more than theirs
or mine. He died not long ago—unbowed
in spirit—at almost eighty. But his body
had grown as sick and tired, perhaps, as any
old man's—less fit than some, from so much sitting.
After his death, they held a synod—mainly
to jaw about how, Brahman-like, his teaching
should be preserved. I left them to it. They also
announced the *brahmadanda* punishment
of me—yes, me—for insubordination.

The brethren asked Ananda what this meant,
since I was the first to be thus punished by—
the Brahmans claimed—the Buddha. So Ananda
explained: *Let Channa say or do what he likes,
the* bhikkhus *may not warn—exhort—or speak
to him, unless he begs for pardon*. Well,
I may not be enlightened but Siddhartha
had never thought such thoughts or uttered such words.
In fact, he told me: "Channa, you will not
be punished *for* your angry words and deeds
but *by* them."—You're quite right, my love: that's *karma*.
You needn't blush, or drop your eyes. I see

that you know more, perhaps, than I'd imagined.
If so, you'll know as well he meant not only
my words, *my* deeds, but words and deeds as such:
meant hatred brings more hatred, love more love,
and that the hater suffers in himself,
whereas the lover lets things go—lets live…

The synod knew I was a Warrior—fierce
and easily angered—and sent a hundred *bhikkhus*
with old Ananda to deliver judgement.
They found me with—what can I say?—a 'friend',
a favourite courtesan, who ran a famous
house in Benares, where I sometimes stayed
incognito, I thought… Well, I did tell you
celibacy causes trouble. My friend was nothing
compared with—but I won't divulge their secrets…
Flagrant infringement of celibacy, though,
is one of four Brahmanic grounds for expulsion—
along with murder, if you'd like to know,
and theft and shamanism. So, you see,
I would have been expelled, in any case,
had I not left the *sangha* there and then
of my own free will. But, first, I took the risk
of boxing Ananda's ears: their *brahmadanda*
was nothing but a lie, I yelled, concocted
by envious Brahmans, whose authority—
or so they feared—was under threat from me.
The brethren bridled, but enough of them
were Warriors—friends of mine—to save my skin…

—And that's my story. Famous, but disgraced,
disrobed, as good as dispossessed, I needed
somewhere to live. After so many years
I was unsure of where to turn. Your father
invited me to stay. And here I am…
And here *we* are, as man and wife, together.
—But don't misunderstand me. Siddhartha's truth
was more than I could see or say. And yet
I, Channa, don't regret a thing. I praise
his words and deeds—his Noble Eightfold Path
I'll never reach the end of. And I praise
our other path, our life of fettered freedoms—
our joys, our pains, of mind and heart and body—

your perfect eyes, your more than perfect mouth,
your climbing legs, your perfect breasts, my love,
and the low moan that snares me every time,
a willing victim. Let my old hands hold
your flowering youth. Look at me. Let me look
at you! We're born—and die—alone. Between,
a man might be so lucky as to have
and hold a girl like you. The end, we know,
comes soon enough. So what? Let's seize the day.

*

Rilke: Buddha in Glory

Centre of all centres, core of cores,
Almond, self-enclosing and self-sweetening,
All we see beneath the circling stars
Is your fruit-flesh: hear our prayer—our greeting—

You who feel now nothing clinging to you,
And whose shell is in the Infinite,
Whence strong saps arise and, pulsing through you
Here, are helped by radiance from without.

For, above you, all your suns,
Full and glowing, turn: you turn them—
While, within, what now begins
Will outlive, outburn them.

iii   Epilogue

Rilke: "O, sage, Dichter, was du tust"

Say, poet, what it is you do?—*I praise.*
But Death and nightmare mar our days:
How can you stand, how stomach them?—*I praise.*
But all that lacks a name, the Anonymous,
How, poet, can you summon it?—*I praise.*
Masked and disguised in ever-changing ways,
What right have you to claim the truth?—*I praise.*
And why should star and storm both recognize
In you their peace and strife?—*Because I praise.*

Acknowledgements and Notes

ACKNOWLEDGEMENTS AND NOTES

Some of the poems in *Opus 3* first appeared in the following magazines: *Acumen, Agenda, The Amsterdam Review, Areté, Babel, The Dark Horse, HQ Magazine, The Interpreter's House, Leviathan, Long Poem Magazine, Metre, Modern Poetry in Translation, New Walk, Orbis, Oxford Poetry, Pennine Platform, Poetry Nottingham, Poetry Review, Poetry Salzburg Review, Poetry Wales, Scintilla, The Shop, Stand, The Warwick Review.* Five of the childrens' rhymes in *No.1,* section 5, were included in Anthony Rudolf's privately printed *Paula* in 2014. Two selections from the book—*Boccaccio in Florence and Other Poems* (Shearsman, 2009) and *Afterwords* (Shoestring Press, 2014)—were published while it was still in progress, and *A Giotto Triptych* appeared as a pamphlet from Shoestring in 2014. The translations (and, in some cases, imitations) of poems by Ernst Jandl in *No.2*, section 2, are published by kind permission of Luchterhand Literaturverlag.

As in Books I and II of *Then and Now,* the 'Acknowledgements and Notes' in *Opus 3* are intended to complement and in some cases to act as a form of counterpoint to its main text. For this reason I have done what I could to avoid the sort of academic references found, for example, in the concluding pages of *The Waste Land;* nor have I commented on everything on which a comment might have have been written: *Then and Now*—like life—is nothing if not eclectic. The notes are, of course, subsidiary to the poems and prose they refer to. Some of them consist of essay-like commentary as much as if not more than background information. The book has been written, even so, to be read like any other annotated text: i.e. the main sections or subsections first, since these can for the most part be understood without the notes, which then add to them.

OPUS 3, NO.1: THE DEATH OF INNOCENCE

p.3, ***A Giotto Triptych:*** Most of the poems in this section are adapted from Giorgio Vasari's chapter on Giotto in *Lives of the Artists* (1568). Part iii is a version of Boccaccio's *Decameron* VI, v, and vi of Grimms' *Märchen* No.87, although the motif of travellers in need of shelter who turn out to be gods or angels is an old one: as well as the stories of Abraham in *Genesis* and Baucis and Philemon in Ovid—adapted in *No.3,* 'Three Fables Ancient and Modern'—there is, of course, the Nativity itself... The concluding poem (viii) is a straight translation of St Francis' famous *Cantico.*

p.3, ***"Credette Cimabue ecc.":*** These lines from Dante's account of the proud in Purgatory could approximately be translated:

> In painting Cimabue held the field,
> > Or so he thought. Now Giotto's all the rage.
> > One star burns bright—another's light must yield...

According to Vasari, Dante (1265–1321) and Giotto (1266–1337) were on friendly terms. St Francis (1181–1224) was a source of inspiration to both of them and—again according to

Vasari—Dante may well have provided ideas for Giotto's early frescoes on the life of St Francis at Assisi as well as for his work in Naples (see v). Giotto continued to paint St Francis throughout his life. The epigraph of vii—"… a sun was born on earth"—comes at the beginning of a long passage in the *Paradiso* in celebration of St Francis and in particular of his love for *"la sua donna"*, Poverty—who, Dante explains, had lost her first husband more than one thousand one hundred years before…

p.8, **The rounded sails of Giotto's** *Navicella:* Giotto's great mosaic "above the three doors of the portico in the courtyard of St Peter's" is praised at length by Vasari, who mentions, among other details, the wind filling a sail "which seems to be in such high relief that it looks real". Vasari's point seems to be that Giotto could have produced more such mosaics if he had chosen to. Giotto's point was, perhaps, to broaden the *then* of his frescoes' *now* and demonstrate in the process that the old medium could be used in a new way. As Vasari says, "It must have been extremely difficult to achieve with pieces of glass the harmonious composition shown in the lights and shadows of that great sail; even a painter working deftly with the brush would have found the task challenging." Unfortunately, the mosaic was remodelled in the seventeenth century.

p.8, **St Francis called himself God's fool**—/ *Un tondo*—**no one:** Although he does not go into the many further implications of his anecdote, Vasari says that it gave rise to an expression still used in his time for calling someone stupid: "You're more simple than Giotto's O"—the Tuscan word *tondo* meaning both a circle and a fool. Vasari seems to think that Giotto was calling the Pope's messenger a fool, which he may well have been. On the other hand, the Biblical tradition of "fools for Christ" began with St Paul *(1 Corinthians IV.10,* etc.) and St Francis was its most famous medieval exemplar. Others were his followers, Frate Ginepro (Brother Juniper), who gave his clothes away to any beggar who asked him (although the order tried to restrain him, Francis himself is said to have remarked, "Would to God, my brothers, that I had a forest of such junipers") and St Anthony of Padua. The sermon which St Anthony preached to the fishes in Rimini—at any rate, in the version in the *Fioretti di san Francesco* ch. XL—is in fact a little masterpiece: the fishes should praise God for giving them more blessings than any other creature—allowing all of them, for example, to survive the Flood. Whatever the saint said, though, has not always been taken quite so seriously:

St Anthony of Padua's
Sermon to the Fishes

From *Des Knaben Wunderhorn*

St Anthony's sermon
(I translate from the German
As set by G. Mahler)
Described with due ardour
Hell-fire and damnation
To no congregation

Of stiff-necked, hard-hearted
Fat kine, who'd deserted
The church of our Saviour,
But down by the river
Where carp full of roe
Swam stately and slow,
Mouths gaping, scales glistening,
Apparently listening,
While pike with sharp snouts
For fighting it out—
Grown piously curious—
Arrived fast and furious,
And even that odd-
bod ersatz, dried cod,
Which constantly fasts
For as long as it lasts,
Turned up for the homily;
Fine eels for a family
Of gourmets, large sturgeon
To blunt hunger's edge on—
These too condescended
To be still and attended,
With turtles and crabs
Up for grabbing and grabs
From the stream's muddy bed,
To what the saint said
Of 'ought not' and 'ought to'—
Which to fish out of water
Never sounded profounder:
No dogma was sounder.

Thus big fish and small fish
And some which weren't all fish,
Obeying the word
Of Christ, their fish-god,
In Italian (not German)
Sat out the saint's sermon
Till, when it was over,
They all dived for cover...

The pike are still frantic,
The eels still romantic,
The crabs aren't straightforward,

> The carp eat still more food,
> The cod are spoiled rotten:
> The sermon's forgotten
> On the stream's muddy bed—
> Where, despite what it said,
> The fish all prefer
> To stay as they were.

St Anthony was no doubt imitating St Francis himself, who, according to *Fioretti,* ch.s XXI–XXII, not only preached to the birds but held a memorable conversation with the great wolf of Gubbio (cp. *No.3, 'Al Vescovo d' Assisi').* In the church of *'il santo',* which with its eight domes is the most imposing in Padua, St Anthony's tongue, voice-box and Franciscan robe can still be venerated. Also in Padua is Giotto's greatest extant work, the Scrovegni Chapel, which he seems to have frescoed almost entirely without assistance. In March 1944 this small and irreplaceable building narrowly escaped destruction by an Allied bomb. Andrea Mantegna's equally irreplaceable frescoes in the *Chiesa degli Eremitani* less than a hundred yards away received a direct hit… If the collective state of mind—or 'culture'—which led to the great wars of the twentieth century was essentially a post-Renaissance development (cp. section 3, *Jove's New World),* how are we to understand *now* what came before our present belief in acquisitiveness if not greed and in the technology which empowers it? At the time of St Francis, Reginaldo Scrovegni, the father of Enrico, who built the chapel, had become fabulously rich by practising usury—for which he was consigned to the seventh circle of Hell by Dante. It was later said that Enrico defended himself from a triplet by Alighieri with a church by Giotto. Even so, he built his chapel with two entrances—a public one at the west end, and a private one up at the front for himself and his family:

> The fish all prefer
> To stay as they were.

p.11, **Boccaccio in Florence:** Although he was almost certainly born in Florence—in 1313—Boccaccio spent most of his youth in Naples, where, as a son of the general manager of one of the biggest Italian banking concerns, the Compagnia dei Bardi, he had access to the enlightened, early-Renaissance court of King Robert of Anjou (cp. *A Giotto Triptych,* v)… In 1348, according to the famous introduction to the First Day of *The Decameron,* he witnessed the Great Plague of Florence, in which between a third and half of the population died, including his father and step-mother. Some of the details of Boccaccio's account of the *'magna mortalitas'* or Black Death, as it came to be known, are included at the beginning of *The Dream*—an adaptation of *Decameron* II,v in which my idea was to show how *The Decameron* might have started but presumably didn't. Nevertheless, the book was certainly written between about 1348 and 1350.

p.12, **I'm illegitimate too:** In spite of a stubborn tradition that Boccaccio's mother was a Frenchwoman, even a king's daughter—and that his birthplace was Paris—nothing in fact is known of her. He himself, however, according to Vittore Branca, *Boccaccio—The Man and His Works* (1976), had at least five illegitimate children, and never married.

p.12, **My sweet, she whispered, etc.:** Cp. Shakespeare, *Venus and Adonis*, ll.229–234. Although Shakespeare, in his principal adaptation from Boccaccio, *All's Well That Ends Well*, infuses the typical moral concern of his mature writings into the rather loose amorality of *The Decameron* (somewhat as Lessing turned Melchizedek's shrewd escape in I, iii into Nathan's moral and spiritual conundrum in *Nathan the Wise*—see *From Now to Then*, pp.136–150), it is tempting to imagine that Boccaccio's primarily sensuous and for the most part virtually 'innocent' world-view at this stage exercised an influence over at least *Venus and Adonis* and possibly other early work such as *The Rape of Lucrece,* whether through Tudor translations or even the original Italian, and at any rate by way of Chaucer. Be this as it may, I have used the *Venus and Adonis* stanza for *The Dream,* as appropriate to these aspects of its subject-matter.

p.16, **The Convent Garden:** This poem is an adaptation of *Decameron* III, i, as though it were the story which Boccaccio heard *Filostrato*—whose name means 'vanquished by love'—narrate in the cathedral. Apart from the two young nuns seeming somewhat brazen as they plan to wake up the gardener, there is not the slightest indication in Boccaccio's version of events that anyone is doing anything they shouldn't. Similarly, in his version of *The Dream,* there is no indication that the hero does anything more reprehensible than allow himself to be tricked… Although Boccaccio seems to have suffered some sort of conversion around the age of fifty, and in later life came increasingly under the influence of the rather strait-laced Petrarch, who encouraged him in the writing of humanistic treatises in Latin, his earlier work in the vernacular thus took a very different view of social or Christian mores from that of either Petrarch himself (whose reputation as a moralist as well as a poet was already flourishing) or Dante, their common master. As Dante idealized Beatrice, Petrarch later idealized Laura. In *The Decameron,* on the other hand, while there is certainly an official morality, which is all right in its way, anyone with any sense doesn't pay it much attention. And so almost anything goes: adultery is implicitly recommended to anyone bored with their spouse, clerics would be fools if they didn't make the most of any opportunity which the Good Lord places in their path, and all kinds of sexual excess, oddity and perversion (as it used to be called) are taken for granted and illicit love enjoyed. Nor is there the slightest hint of irony when Boccaccio ends such stories, as he often does, with the likes of "May God grant that we enjoy ours also."

As well as personal inclination, one reason for such evident differences between Dante (1265–1321) and Boccaccio (1313–75) may well have been the appearance of the Black Death in Italy in 1347. Of the plague at this time and later, it has been said that only the most obstinately devout could have seen its unprecedented horror as part of some Dantesque or medieval divine plan. Philip Ziegler, in a long and complex chapter on 'The Effects on the Church and Man's Mind' in *The Black Death* (1969), considers the ways in which—although the plague did not directly *cause* the Peasants' Revolt or the Reformation—a state of mind had been brought into being by virtue of which doctrinal truth and the *status quo* could more easily be called in question… Of course, Boccaccio was at the very beginning of this process but the actual arrival of the plague in Europe must have seemed to many as cataclysmic as the Fall of Man. While he does not go so far as directly to question the social or religious fabric of medieval society, Boccaccio sometimes comes remarkably close to doing so—and an unmistakable atmosphere of *carpe diem* permeates *The Decameron* as a whole.

p.17, **God knows I've wept, etc.:** Adapted from Chaucer, *The Merchant's Tale* (ll.1544–1553), in which there is a more obviously post-lapsarian garden than in *Decameron* III, i. Chaucer was much influenced in his poetry by Boccaccio—but also outgrew him. In his later tales, his great gift lay in showing how people are and what they do, condemning no one and yet making his moral viewpoint perfectly clear. In this respect, Chaucer's so-called *Retractions* at the end of *The Canterbury Tales* are more puzzling than Boccaccio's conversion, since he had condoned nothing 'sinful'. In fact, the *Retractions* have been suspected of having been written under duress—of which more in *No.3*, 'The Carpenter's *Cook's Tale*'…

p.23, **Lucrece came first, etc.:** Cp. *The Rape of Lucrece,* ll.974–994. Shakespeare's other long poem is only superficially more morally aware than *Venus and Adonis.* Innocent victim though its heroine is, her confused and confusing idea of innocence in general leads her (though not in her own or Shakespeare's view) disastrously astray and she kills herself out of shame or physical shock, wounded pride and a desire to avenge herself, however self-destructively, on her attacker. The behaviour of the (otherwise unnamed) Traversari girl in *Decameron* V, viii—the source of this subsection—is similarly self-destructive, and the *Lucrece* stanza seemed a natural choice for my adaptation. Moreover, Shakespeare almost certainly borrowed it from its inventor, Chaucer, whose most famous poems in the form are *Troilus and Criseyde* and *The Clerk's Tale* of patient Griselda—both of whose sources, again, were stories by Boccaccio… Troilus himself is hardly more morally aware in Chaucer's poem than is Lucrece (cp. *Troilus and Criseyde* Bk.V, ll.1219–1246, with **The next was Troilus, etc.** here). For Shakespeare, perhaps, Tarquin and Lucrece stood between Troilus and Criseyde to the one side and Griselda and her husband Walter to the other, each of them illustrating different aspects of the idea of innocence and therefore guilt. The Necromancer (developed from *The Franklin's Tale,* itself a refinement of *Decameron* X, v) can thus be considered as holding the mirror of art up to Nastagio's life by inviting him to consider these three archetypal relationships… In some respects, the "magicien" or "subtil clerk" of *The Franklin's Tale* resembles Prospero, as Shakespeare seems to have noticed:

> And whan this maister that this magyk wroughte,
> Saugh it was tyme, he clapte his handes two,
> And farewel! al oure revel was ago.
> And yet remoeved they nevere out of the hous,
> Whil they saugh al this sighte merveillous,
> But in his studie, ther as his bookes be,
> They seten stille…
> *The Franklin's Tale*, ll.1202–1208.

And so such stories continue to grow and, as it were, to annihilate time. Not, however, that it is necessary to know their sources so as to read them. And yet one or another sort of re-creation, or necromancy, is clearly an age-old function of the poet's art. "For storytelling is always the art of repeating stories", as Walter Benjamin wrote, and "the more self-forgetful the listener is, the more deeply is what he listens to impressed on his memory…" *(The Story-teller,* 1936).

p.27, **The Clouds dispell'd, etc.:** An adaptation of the end of Dryden's adaptation—entitled 'Theodore and Honoria'—of Boccaccio's story, in *Fables Ancient and Modern* (1699)... Among the translations and adaptations in *Fables Ancient and Modern* are a number of paraphrases from Chaucer. In his 'Preface' Dryden wrote: "So from *Chaucer* I was led to think on *Boccacce*,... the Genius of our Countrymen being rather to improve an Invention, than to invent themselves;... yet it appears that the Tales of *Boccacce* were not generally of his own making, but taken from Authors of former Ages, and by him only modell'd..." Dryden was perhaps unhappy in love (the London of his time was in any case plagued by venereal disease), and his main addition to *Decameron* V, viii is an element of revenge in the behaviour of the black knight. However, in his versification and story-telling he is at the height of his powers...

As for the anachronisms here and elsewhere in *Boccaccio in Florence,* they are, I suppose, the now of Boccaccio's then, or the then of his now, or both. And a time-honoured now and then at that.

p.28, **Sousa had, at least, a / Catholic church:** Sousa is situated on the Tunisian coast, two hundred miles or so across the Mediterranean from Sicily. The early African church had flourished from about the fourth to the eighth centuries, producing famous saints and theologians such as St Anthony (d. 356) and St Augustine (354–430). The Christian and Muslim cohabitation of Sousa is described in *Decameron* V, ii. Otherwise *Alibech and Rustico* combines and adapts two unrelated stories, III, x and V, v.

p.29, **Her brow was overhung with coins of gold:** This is the first of several borrowings from Byron's *Don Juan* (II.116), the poem as a whole being in Byronic *ottava rima* or 'octaves', as he called them. Byron's discovery of this originally Italian verse-form in 1817–18 seems to have released or brought to maturity an aspect of his genius scarcely evident in his Romantic tales and dramas—namely, his own mock-heroic sense of humour, combining satire on the one hand with good-natured tolerance of human folly and foibles on the other. If *The Decameron* can be said to be not so much immoral as amoral (or "virtually innocent") in its overall tenor and yet to *approach* a sort of ethics as well in places, Byron in his ironic mode—transforming and transcending his own Romantic mode—goes several steps further and attains to an ethical view of things, however insecurely. There are certainly lapses in *Don Juan,* for example—the Haidée episode, or the Daniel Boone stanzas, or that humourless Byronic Heroine, Aurora Raby. Nevertheless, in a couple of lines relating to his detestation of despotism of all sorts,

> I wish men to be free
> As much from mobs as kings—from you as me
> (IX.25)—

lines which can easily be extended to issues of personal domination—Byron summarizes wittily and clearly what his poems in *ottava rima,* of which *Beppo* is perhaps the most faultless, express for the most part with new-found energy and discrimination. In *Alibech and Rustico,* Alibech may be said to be 'amoral' and Giacomino 'Byronic' in this sense—while Rustico by the end of the poem has got somewhat further... One sign of the insecurity of Byron's ethics is the occasional sloppiness of his writing (i.e. he sometimes wrote—as in everyday life he frequently *did*—what he felt like, with scant interest in improvement or correction), and I have taken the liberty of tinkering, where this seemed possible, with any repetitiveness, excessive inversion, etc. in the various stanzas I have borrowed from *Don Juan*, which I have also altered to suit my purpose (for the interested reader, these are: II.116–117, I.47, I.63–64, I.35, VIII.82–84, in that order)… As Yeats above all has shown, *ottava rima* is capable as well of a seriousness beyond irony. Hence, I hope, the change in tone in 'Rustico's Ottave Rime' at the end of *Alibech and Rustico*—a change which is at any rate pointing elsewhere.

p.29, **He believed the Fall / … caused Adam's fleshly lusting:** Cp. Article IX of the Anglican *Articles of Religion,* "yet the Apostle doth confess that concupiscence and lust hath of itself the nature of sin"—as, for example, in Milton:

> O Eve, in evil hour thou didst give ear
> To that false worm…
> Bad fruit of knowledge, if this be to know;
> Which leaves us naked thus, of honour void,
> Of innocence, of faith, of purity,
> Our wonted ornaments now soiled and stained,
> And in our faces evident the signs
> Of foul concupiscence…
> *(Paradise Lost,* Bk IX, 1067 *et seq)*

By the twenty-first century one might have hoped it would go without saying that ideas of sin and lost or unattainable innocence and 'purity' such as these, when exalted to a credo, are in dangerous denial of life itself. And yet they remain a principal cause not only of endless suffering in individuals but, directly and indirectly—since unfulfilled desire fuels monstrous behaviour—of far-reaching damage to the development of, especially, Middle Eastern and Western civilization, including (among other things) the subordination of women to men and of the individual in general to the power of family, village, church or state. Societies, needless to say, among their rules and regulations, need *thou-shalt-nots* of one sort or another. But to view these as absolute is to slide, however imperceptibly, into tyranny or social coercion. In other words, the rules must be meaningful and free to change. In the case of "foul concupiscence", they had—and have—neither characteristic to any clear degree. Milton (who, perhaps more than any other great poet, confuses dogma and reason—or, worse, reasoning— with the religious state of mind) unwittingly exposes the obstinate blindness, even stupidity, of (his version of) the myth of Eden and the Tree of Knowledge by insisting that God's prohibition plus His threat of punishment is, like the prohibitions of tyranny, not to be obeyed because it is meaningful in itself but *because* it is God's prohibition plus threat. Adam and Eve, of course, feel guilty. In fact, the idea of innocence in this sense seems more of an unhealthy excrescence or side-effect of our dominant obsession with evil and guilt than a guide to any realizable mode of conduct in itself. Dostoyevsky's horrendously dysfunctional nineteenth century Russians, for example—locked as regards their family- and sex-relations generally in their futile struggles for power, in their love-hate clinches, their diabolism and (above all) their guilt—make the innocence of Prince Myshkin (in *The Idiot*) seem almost desirable, almost real... But what if one were to relativize such guilt, in preference to seeing it as a function of absolute Evil? Considering the human misery it has generated, the idea that sin or guilt—a question of more or less ephemeral social values—should be of such overriding concern to the mind of God that it should need to be eternally punished or atoned for and the innocent rewarded in heaven may come at last to be viewed as one of the most damaging mistakes of the Abramic religions, effective as it no doubt was at keeping primitive or disorderly nomadic tribes more or less in line... The Buddha's *karma*, whereby one's deeds have consequences—i.e. 'good' or 'bad' deeds will reward or punish themselves—seems, in comparison, sophisticated, humane and, above all, true: "The world is not perfect; the Golden Age never was or will be," the Russian dissident Joseph Brodsky warned his American students... From these points of view, the sooner the Christian *idea* of innocence dies, i.e. is relegated, like alchemy or human sacrifice, to our collective past the better. And if this sounds unlikely, there is no reason to abandon the technical possibility, at least, that more individuals if not the species might learn to accept (or make a more serious effort to understand) the nature of the world and how human nature relates to it. The fact that every individual is (potentially) free to do this is in itself a source of hope...

p.30, **Like St Augustine in his fine *Confessions*:** The source for this stanza as a whole is *Don Juan* I.47. Byron's own note on this line is: "By the representation St. Augustine gives of himself in his youth it is easy to see that he was what we should call *a rake*. He avoided the school like the plague; he loved gaming and public shows; he robbed his father... Etc." Byron makes effective use of notes such as this in what one might term the *de-Romanticization* of the subject-matter of his *ottava rima* poems.

p.38, **"The love of self extending to contempt / For God":** The second half of Augustine's aphorism on the unbelief of the damned and the faith of the elect in his late work, *The City of God,* is "... and the love of God extending to contempt of self". Other references to St Augustine in *Alibech and Rustico* are to *The Confessions* Bk II.1–2, 10 and Bk III.1, in which he describes the turbulence of what was probably a more normal adolescence than he imagined and his arrival as a nineteen-year-old student in Carthage. Like Rustico in his youth, St Augustine—although he was devoted to his Christian mother and she to him—seems not to have got on with his father, who was (at least in his son's view) a licentious and choleric pagan whom he refers to as "her husband" and then only briefly. One of his mother's chief virtues was Continence, the female personification of which emphasizes his need for the help of his Father in heaven: "Thou standest upon thyself, and therefore it is thou standest not. Cast thyself upon him and fear not, he will not withdraw himself and let thee fall." Here and elsewhere in *The Confessions* one finds more or less explicit statements of what Jean-Paul Sartre would have called the 'bad faith' inherent in Christianity whereby the individual avoids responsibility for his actions by means of the all-seeing omnipotence and authority of God, which in Augustine led at last to a doctrine of predestination so severe that the Roman church has never accepted it.

p.40, ***Two Extracts from 'The Testament'***: Villon's *Le Testament (ca.* 1461) is in the medieval form of a mock testament. Although the poem (of which ll. 329–356 and ll. 413–532 are translated here) includes the usual jocular and satirical elements, it is also a deeply serious work, notably in its opening section of 832 lines, in which Villon writes on death and 'death's messengers', among other things, as very few poets have written before or since—with a rare (though also Chaucerian) combination of tough-minded realism and compassion. Although he pays lip-service to the Virgin, the idea of innocence in Villon, one might say, is as much "last year's snow" as the women of his famous *Ballade*… One reason for this in so young a poet (Villon was born in 1431) may be that he had been closer to death at an early age than most of us are now until we at last begin to disintegrate as 'senior citizens'… Be that as it may, little in fact is known about Villon's life—other than that he was frequently in trouble. Having spent some years as a student in Paris, he got into a fight with a priest—killed him—was pardoned for the murder—was one of a gang of student-thieves who stole 500 *écus* from the College of Navarre—was imprisoned—pardoned again, but (very possibly because as a known murderer he was more or less unemployable) was soon in trouble again (like the old woman in the *Ballade* which follows the second extract in Villon's original, he might have complained, "I can't get into circulation / Any more than worthless currency"!) until at last, as the result of a street-fight, he was arrested and sentenced to be hanged. At some point amid these vicissitudes, he wrote the famous quatrain:

> My name is François, that's my curse,
> Born in Paris, near Pontoise,
> And from a six-foot cord in a noose
> My neck will feel the weight of my arse.

However, as far as is known, it never came to this. His sentence was commuted, but—"because of the bad way of life of the said Villon"—he was banished from Paris. The year was 1463 and Villon was thirty-two. He seems to have left the city and, except for his poems, disappeared from history.

p.40, **And where's the queen who ordered her guard / To tie up Buridan etc.:** Queen Jeanne of Navarre was a fourteenth century French queen who was reputed to have had her lovers, after three days of merry-making, tied up in a sack and thrown out of her window into the Seine. The story may or may not be apocryphal according to which the philosopher Buridan was subjected to this treatment while a student but survived by arranging to have a barge full of hay float past the window at the critical moment…

p.45, ***by flooding the world and drowning everyone except Deucalion and his wife:*** Jove justifies this to the other gods by promising

> for to frame a newe,
>   an other kinde of men
> By wondrous meanes, unlike the first,
>   to fill the world agen.

In fact, Deucalion and Pyrrha, who survive "in a little Barke", multiply, to begin with, by throwing over their shoulders the bones of their Grandmother Earth—i.e. rocks and stones—which turn into people. And so the mischief is reincarnate:

> Of these we are the crooked ympes,
>   and stonie race in deede,
> Bewraying by our toyling life
>   from whence we doe proceede.

Jove later drowned everyone again, except for Baucis and Philemon, the poor peasants who were the only people willing to invite himself and Mercury, disguised as travellers, to stay with them for the night (see *No.3*, section 10, 'Three Fables Ancient and Modern'). But humanity makes its gods in its own image, and Jove's new world—as Ovid clearly realized it would—turned out again to be all too human.

p.46, **Acrisius, Danae's father, etc.:** When Acrisius, king of Argos, consulted an oracle on how to get a son, he was told he would have no sons but that his grandson would kill him. He therefore imprisoned his daughter Danae—who had already been seduced by his twin brother, Proetus—in an impregnable tower. When Danae gave birth to Perseus, Acrisius would not believe that Jove was the father but, suspecting his brother again, set his daughter and her child adrift at sea. However, after many heroic and bloody adventures, Perseus was attending a games in honour of a neighbouring king's dead father when his discus was guided by Jove and Acrisius was killed as the oracle foretold.

p.47, **Neptune's lightly trod / The waves:** After claiming the throne of Crete in defiance of his brothers, Minos boasted that the gods would show their approval by answering his first prayer. And sure enough, when he prayed to Neptune for a bull to sacrifice, a beautiful and dazzlingly white specimen emerged from the waves. But Minos was so impressed by this creature that he kept it, and sacrificed another. Neptune was, of course, enraged and, to punish him, made Pasiphae, Minos's wife, fall in love with the bull.

p.47, **Sly Daedalus helped:** Daedalus, the famous Athenian craftsman, was living in exile in Crete after murdering a rival. He helped Pasiphae by constructing a hollow wooden cow in which she could conceal herself. After she had borne the Minotaur, Daedalus also constructed the Labyrinth—in which King Minos imprisoned the Minotaur. In fact, as Joseph Brodsky wrote in *Watermark* (1989), "The whole business is, in a manner of speaking, Daedalus' brainchild, the labyrinth especially, as it resembles a brain."

p.48, **Tyndareus:** King of Sparta and Leda's husband. Of the belligerent twins, Castor and Pollux, the latter was an Olympic prize-fighter and could be told from the former by his broken nose, missing teeth, etc. Whether Jove fathered all four children or not, this less than immaculate conception led in the fullness of time not only to the Trojan War but to the Dioscuri's bloody rivalry—as a result of which Castor was killed—with the twin sons of Tyndareus' brother,

Aphareus, and to all the horrors of the House of Atreus. Or, as W.B. Yeats, two millennia later, more memorably put it:

> A shudder in the loins engenders there
> The broken wall, the burning roof and tower
> And Agamemnon dead.
>   Being so caught up,
> So mastered by the brute blood of the air,
> Did she put on his knowledge with his power
> Before the indifferent beak could let her drop?

p.49, **The Childhood and Song-Book etc.:** German versions of most of the songs in this section are to be found in H.M. Enzensberger's excellent anthology of children's rhymes, *Allerleihrauh* (1961). As Enzensberger points out, many of the rhymes—which are all anonymous—in his book are found in other forms, and rewriting them to some extent in translation seemed a valid procedure in this case... *Allerleirauh* (literally, 'All-sorts-of-furs') is also the title of Grimms' *Märchen* No.65, on which the poem as a whole is based. I have avoided the English word *fairy-tale* in the title as, nowadays, more or less belittling and encumbered with twee and/or commercial associations. The German *Märchen* are not only highly imaginative and often instructive but, in some cases (such as *Allerleirauh*), have the power of myth—as recognized by writers from Goethe to Günter Grass in their so-called *Kunstmärchen* and novels (for example, Grass's *Der Butt* and *Die Rättin*), which are intended exclusively for adults.

p.51, **I made up songs to amuse the cook:** One way of reading *The Childhood and Song-Book* is as a condensed form of Freudian 'Case History', the main differences being that Allerleirauh's songs and *Märchen* have been substituted for the genre's dreams and childhood memories respectively. Moreover, the 'evidence' or 'facts' of the case are presented *creatively*—and the 'analysis', as it were, conducted—by the protagonist herself. This approach to her own history (or so, again, one might read it) leads her in a direction which emerges as freer or less deterministic—more independent and less passive, as well as more *fluid*—than Freud's, replacing as it does his insistence on unconscious repression with a deliberate attempt to accept and transcend what happens to have happened to her in her innocence or ignorance, allowing and even encouraging this to die (there is a hollow tree—perhaps a Tree of Ignorance—in her story) and then 'resurrecting' it in the growing awareness and activity of her life and songs.

p.57, **I slipped away to hide in my coat:** As well as more 'adult' myths, *Märchen* (or 'fairy-tales', as—like it or not—the word is translated) and occasionally children's rhymes are dealt with in Freud's writings—for example, in *From the History of an Infantile Neurosis (the 'Wolf Man')* (1918), where *Little Red Riding Hood* and *The Wolf and the Seven Little Kids* play a prominent role. In his introduction to another well-known Case History, *Analysis of a Phobia in a Five-Year-Old Boy ('Little Hans')* (1909)—the first instance of child analysis as such—Freud observes with regard to his patient's obsession with horses and other animals, "Animals owe a good deal of their importance in myths and fairy-tales to the openness with which they display their genitals and their sexual functions to the inquisitive human child." While one would hesitate to go so far as to claim that the father of psychoanalysis had a one-track mind, animals rather clearly fascinate children (see Allerleirauh's songs) for other reasons as well, including perhaps (as in the case of her coat) the very opposite of what Freud suggests. In fact, Jean-Paul Sartre (who happens also to have been one of Freud's harshest critics) says in *Being and Nothingness*, "To put on clothes"—let alone to conceal one's skin with a coat of furs cut from every animal in one's father's kingdom—"is to *hide* one's object-state; it is to claim *to see without being seen*; that is, to be pure subject" (my italics)... The *Märchenerzählerin* might well have felt, had she be able to read them, that both great thinkers overstate their cases. And as the girl in her coat of furs progresses from starlight to moonlight to sunshine, the 'fairy-tale' succeeds in getting it both ways—a characteristic which fairy-tales not infrequently share with poems.

p.60, *"... innocence is the last thing etc."*: Brodsky is in the process of pointing out, in his second essay on Auden in *Less Than One*, why one ought to read the complete poems of at least one great poet or, for that matter, of any poet one finds appealing. "The real story behind our species clinging to immaturity," he writes, "has to do not with man's reluctance to hear about death but with his not wanting to hear about life." And yet "Innocence fades. It cannot last, / Nor should it...", as 'Heine' says in 'In Lieu of a Manifesto: Heine's Grave' in *Words in the Dark*. Or as Brodsky continues, "The beginning makes sense only in so far as there is an end... Poets tell us the whole story..." Elsewhere, however, he remarks that "Death is always a song of 'innocence', never of experience."

p.60, **The night and the streets are still:** A translation of *"Still ist die Nacht, es ruhen die Gassen"*. Both this poem and *"Der Tod ist die kühle Nacht"* are to be found in *Die Heimkehr* (The Homecoming), which forms the third part of *Buch der Lieder* (1827)... In spite of earlier Romantic tendencies *("Du bist wie eine Blume, / So hold und schön und rein"*, etc.), Heine—like Byron—transformed and transcended these and became, in the course of time, as tough-minded a realist as his fellow-Parisian Villon, for example, whose writings he may well have known.

p.60, **Three Poems on the History of Religion:** A descriptive title of my own. Although the six poems in this sequence are straight translations, the sequence as a whole includes some elements of adaptation, of which the overall title, the quotation from Joseph Brodsky, the arrangement and this title are four.

p.67, **And their gods cry out and quail:** The plural in Heine's original *("Christengötter"*—literally, Christian gods) presumably refers to the Father, the Son, the Holy Ghost and the (in Spain) ubiquitous Virgin Mary—who would constitute more than one god in the eyes of Almansor.

p.68, **Heine... might have experienced the third, which was annihilation:** Some manifestations of the anti-Jewish policies described by Hilberg are considered further in *No.1* in 'Gretl Braun Remembers Her Sister, Eva' and also (in greater detail) in *No.2*, section 2...

p.69, **On the almemor's balustrade:** The almemor is "the pulpit in the centre of the synagogue" (Branscombe). The word is absent from *The Oxford English Dictionary*.

p.70, **Don Jehuda ben Halevy:** With typical license, Heine changes the name of the great medieval Sephardic poet Judah ha-Levi (1075–1141) to fit his metre. The beautiful but ambivalent poem, *Jehuda ben Halevy*—a masterpiece of digression and (as "Sometimes in Arabian folk-tales") of digressions within digressions—follows *Prinzessin Sabbath* in *Hebräische Melodien,* throughout which (as J.L. Sammons expresses it) "the complex, antithetical facets of Heine's revived Jewish feeling find expression."

p.71, ***Schalet, schöner Götterfunken, etc.:*** Heine is, of course, adapting and making fun of Schiller's *Ode to Joy,* schalet (which made it into the *OED Supplement* in 1986) being a delicious Jewish dish of meat and vegetables, traditionally prepared on a Friday for the Sabbath. The stanzas from Schiller's undeservedly famous piece of Romantic / Germanic enthusiasm (published in 1786) which were selected by Beethoven for his Ninth Symphony can be translated as follows:

Ode to Joy

Heavenly Joy, Elysium's daughter,
Brightest flame of love divine,
Drunk with drinking your fire-water,
We approach your holy shrine!
Re-united with each other,
Parted souls draw near and marry;
Each shall be the other's brother
Where your soft wings waft and tarry.

All who've won a friend for life,
Or for every situation
Gained a faithful loving wife,
Join with us in jubilation!
Even if only one loved heart
Has been placed in his safe-keeping!
Otherwise, let him depart
From our magic circle, weeping.

All things bright and beautiful
Drink of Joy at Nature's breast;
All things good, bad, great and small
Follow her rose-scent. The best
Kisses are from her, and wine,
Or a friend true unto death.
Worms rejoice to drill and mine,
Cherubs to inhale God's breath.

> Brothers, run your conquering course
> Like a hero on his horse—
> Lighting up His splendid sky,
> As His fixed stars gladly fly.
>
> Millions, I embrace you all!
> World, I kiss you as a whole!
> Brothers, o'er the stars above us,
> There must dwell a God who loves us.
> Millions, do you bend the knee?
> Can you, World, your Maker see?
> Seek Him o'er the stars above us:
> There a God must dwell who loves us!

It ought, perhaps, to be emphasized that this is a translation, not a parody… Heine's joke is good-humoured enough and one hesitates to overload it. Nevertheless, in the context of *Prinz Israel's* exclusion, as though he were a dog, from the brotherhood of man, the lines *"Otherwise, let him depart / From our magic circle, weeping"* take on—however fleetingly—a more ominous shade of meaning. Who or what is to decide, after all, who is to join in the general rejoicing and who not? Who, in other words, is to be designated—and by whom—*persona non grata?* Beethoven's symphonies, of which the Ninth is perhaps the greatest, were popular among Nazi audiences, who did not (as W.G. Sebald says in *Air War and Literature*) "go deeply into the complex question of the relationship between ethics and aesthetics…" The *Führer's* other favourites were Wagner, Brahms and Bruckner. Thus, "Whenever it seemed advisable to invoke the gravity of the hour a full orchestra was conscripted, and the regime identified itself with the affirmative statement of the symphonic finale"… Hitler's word was, in other respects, literally law and later in Schiller's poem there are four lines which were, fortunately, not included by Beethoven but which any SS man—*"Meine Ehre ist Treue"* (my Honour is Loyalty)—could, unfortunately, have subscribed to:

> Weave our sacred circle tightly,
> Swear upon this golden wine;
> Swear to keep our oath divine
> To the One who judges rightly.

The fact that *"Rettung von Tyrannenketten"* (salvation from the chains of tyranny)—Schiller's very next line—can all too easily take on tyrannical aspects of its own is (or should be) clearer now than it was perhaps then. Two hundred years of European history later, Joseph Brodsky—himself a Jewish *émigré*—wrote of the inherent danger in the modern world of large-scale political, social or religious groups (all of which have their own literatures, music and other art-forms) and thus of the importance of thinking and acting as an individual rather than thinking and doing what one's neighbours think and do because one is afraid not to think and do it: "Regardless of whether one is a writer or a reader, one's task consists first of all in mastering a life which is one's own, not imposed or prescribed from without…" Any such prescription will lead to cliché or catastrophe or both—"no matter how noble its appearance may be", Brodsky added *(On Grief and Reason,* p.47).

p.72, **Where it sputters and goes out:** Heine's ending is no doubt intentionally provocative in its hopelessness. The following, more hopeful if less obviously realistic adaptation of the last eight stanzas of Heine's original, in which Israel thinks about *how* "to break the spell" (p.68), may turn out to be less 'innocent' or naïve in the long run than perhaps appears at first glance. As a matter of fact, some members of the pioneering *Verein für Cultur und Wissenschaft der Juden,* including Heine, discussed ideas of a similarly agnostic sort at the time:

> Usually, when he eats his schalet,
> Israel's princely eyes start gleaming,
> But, today, his thoughts are elsewhere,
> And he sits as if day-dreaming:
>
> "Schalet's fine, but not this sabbath.
> Customs matter *and* don't matter.
> Even as a poor dog's-body,
> I've been getting lazier, fatter,
>
> Grown too used to spending time
> Seeing myself as others see me,
> Looking forward to the rituals
> Of the day which seems to free me…
>
> And although I've heard the Jordan
> Streaming and the rumbling springs
> Of the palmy vale at Bethel,
> Camels, distant ting-a-lings
>
> Rung by herdsmen's fat bell-wethers
> As they lead their lambs and sheep
> Evenings down Mount Gileath's slopes to
> Fields where they can safely sleep,
>
> Heard and loved them—love them still,
> Eating schalet—now it seems
> Memories matter but don't matter:
> Why indulge the same old dreams?
>
> Or the same old gruesome nightmares:
> How am I to *break* the spell?…

Not by fighting / biting back!...
Princess, only time will tell

Whether we can free ourselves
In another, more humane,
Human, more compassionate way...
First, though, either I'm insane

Or I've never *been* a dog!
True, there have been times so bad
That I almost feared I must be—
Times when I was almost mad—

But, for all I barked or whimpered,
In my deepest mind or heart
I was conscious I was human.
Which is where our freedoms start—

Not as princes or princesses.
No such role is what we *are:*
Princes matter and don't matter—
Self-importance fouls the air...

And each human being, each essence,
Is a real, not abstract thing—
Lives, lets live, is one with others,
Joyful, still, not suffering,

Always active—timeless, spaceless—
Neither in nor out of fashion,
Healing—because wholly common—
Rifts of hatred through compassion,

Which (we know) might save the world
From destruction or pollution
By our internecine greeds...
It's not that there's *no* solution...

But, although we know all this,
Pride and terror thrive on schism.
Christian, Hindu, Moslem, Jew,
Welcome fundamentalism."

Soon the sabbath will be over
And, as if on shadow-legs,
Like a dog the hour comes running.
Israel's courage sighs and sags,

As he feels its mocking, ice-cold
Eyes transfix his heart of hearts.
And a shudder runs right through him
Now, in case the dog-change starts,

Till the kindly princess hands him
Her nard-box of solid gold.
Slowly he inhales it, hoping
That its airy charm will hold…

Quickly the sad princess pours him
One last goblet. Once again,
He as quickly drains it. Only
A few drops of wine remain.

These he sprinkles on the table
In the flickering candle-light.
Dips the candle in the puddle,
Where it sputters and goes out.

Pascal long ago observed that "Man is so made that if he is told often enough that he is a fool he believes it" *(Pensées* 99 / 536). Pascal's brief comment in the same fragment on how difficult it is to prefer one's own judgement to that of many others (resembling Joseph Brodsky's remarks in the preceding note) is vastly expanded by Sartre in *Being and Nothingness,* who sees the tactic of "Seeing myself as others see me" as a form of 'bad faith'—our main means of avoiding the anguish inherent in facing up to and accepting the fact (or, more accurately, 'facticity') that man is "condemned to be free", that is, to take responsibility and judge for himself. All fundamentalist religious teaching is deeply hostile to such individualism. "Fundamentalism" may be a recent word but it is an old phenomenon—peculiarly intensified, however, by modern cultural conflicts, exacerbated as these are by so-called communications technology plus increased mobility and by humanity's lamentable failure in general to live and let live… Under certain circumstances, of course, one has no alternative but to 'bite back' if one wishes to survive—a reality courageously faced by Primo Levi, for example, in his novel, *If Not Now, When?* The difficulty of deciding under *which* circumstances is clearly an ethical one and is considered in greater detail in *No.2* and *No.3*.

p.76, **How Jack Got On in the World:** This section of the sequence is loosely based on Grimms' *Märchen* No.81, an example of the Eulenspiegel-wins-all variety of German peasant humour and wiseacre worldliness, which shows signs of having originally been more meaningful. The Grimms' tale is here rewritten as more of a *Kunstmärchen* than a *Märchen* proper and, as such, is closer to, say, Goethe's famously cryptic one-off tale, *Das Märchen,* than to its own source. One might even claim for the sake of argument that in the *Kunstmärchen* of Goethe, Brentano and others the *Märchen* lost its innocence as a genre. Whereas the characters of traditional *Volksmärchen* or 'fairy tales' are more straightforward, or more simply good or bad, Jack—who in *The House That Jack Built* was still one of them—now finds himself trying to understand not only his own life but life in general: his apparent innocence, that is, was either foolishness or inexperience and in any case unsustainable... As regards the level of Jack's development up until the end of this poem, Geoffrey Hill's deservedly famous line from 'Genesis' in *For the Unfallen,* **"There is no bloodless myth will hold",** still applies to it. Jack's sister, however, is already more or less free of this relatively primitive or 'innocent' world-view, in which physical drives and/or the emotions may be said to dominate. Lacking the restraint or guidance of some more consciously purposeful system of ethics, in other words, the innocent or ignorant do more or less what they feel like. Until there are more such 'sisters' in the world, as Hill says in *Doctor Faustus,*

> The Innocents have not flown;
> Too legendary, they laugh;
> The lewd uproarious wolf
> Brings their house down.
>
> A beast is slain, a beast thrives.
> Fat blood squeaks on the sand.
> A blinded god believes
> That he is not blind.

Even under circumstances such as these, however, the individual is always free—to think and do otherwise, if he chooses.

p.85, I'm in! he whooped. A softer voice denied it: The dream which began in the first stanza of subsection v with Necessity's daughter generating a fog of wish- (or, better, hope-) fulfilment comes to an end here. In *Existential Thought and Therapeutic Practice* (1997), Hans W. Cohn—a poet, among other things—considers the kind of 'bad faith' described in the concluding paragraph of the above note on p.72, "Where it sputters and goes out", and also Jack's kind: "Sartre's concept of 'bad faith' is often seen as a characteristic of living inauthentically. It is the denial of our freedom to respond to what we meet, and thus of our responsibility. This denial expresses itself in phrases like 'I can't help it, this is the way I am' or 'circumstances don't leave me any choice'." Of course, man is also "condemned to be free", in Sartre's famous phrase—and when he claims to have no choice is really choosing not to choose, while evading the anguish he would experience if he admitted this. But Cohn finds another—one might almost say *the* other—aspect of bad faith no less important, namely that it "is also—and this is rarely sufficiently stressed—the denial of our 'facticity', the 'given' aspects of the world in which we find ourselves": for example, being-with-others, the body, sexuality, the emotions, our own and others' history or what happens to have happened or could happen at any moment. He goes on to quote a colleague on "this double aspect of freedom": "I fall into bad faith if I take one or both of the two dishonest positions about reality: If I pretend either to be free in a world without facts or to be a fact in a world without freedom" (Betty Cannon, *Sartre and Psychoanalysis,* 1991). Over-simplifying to stress his point, Cohn strikingly comments, "The first of these positions could be called manic—'there is nothing I can't do'—and the other depressive—'there is nothing I can do'." The first is considered in *How Jack Got On in the World* and the second in *Princess Sabbath.*

p.87, **a Celtic king:** The first section of *Orpheus and Others* is a re-make or 're-write' (cp. *Boccaccio in Florence and Other Poems,* p.133) of the Middle English verse romance known as *Sir Orfeo* which, apart from Chaucer's *Wife of Bath's Tale* and *Franklin's Tale,* is usually thought of as the most successful among English poems classed as Breton or Celtic *lais.* As well as adapting Ovid's story, which was well known in medieval Europe, the anonymous author of *Sir Orfeo* introduces assorted Celtic folklore motifs and, by a sophisticated sleight of hand, metamorphoses Orpheus's Thrace into Orfeo's Winchester, and *vice versa.* The *Song of Innocence* takes over some of these motifs and omits and adds some. It also takes over its source's basic verse-form. Of course, one's choice of verse-forms was more limited in *ca.* 1375 than it is in the twenty-first century. However, the octosyllabic couplet is as well suited now as it was then to this sort of subject-matter—and relates, in any case, to the un-rhymed verse-form of the *Song of Experience* which follows it.

p.87, **by some rare device:** Cp. *Kubla Khan,* "'It was a miracle of rare device, / A sunny pleasure-dome with caves of ice!"… Like *Sir Orfeo,* Coleridge's poetry incorporates folklore motifs. The re-make alludes to *Kubla Khan* at other points and also in general.

p.93, **Orpheus. Eurydice. Hermes:** A straight translation of Rilke's poem, which he included in *Neue Gedichter* (1907–8). In his essay on Rilke in *On Grief and Reason,* Joseph Brodsky seriously over-rates J.B. Leishman's poor to middling translation of *OEH,* praising it in particular for reproducing the original's verse-form. In his later theory and practice, Brodsky seems to have lost sight of the entirely valid principle expressed in three famous pages of his 1977 essay on Mandelstam in *Less Than One*—namely, that the translator's task is to search for an equivalent of his original's form and not for a substitute. One would have thought that it was self-evident—as Dryden's great translations from the classics alone are enough to show—that such an equivalent is not always a mimesis or reproduction. But, later, Brodsky seems to have imagined it was just that—and he pays no attention to the adding, padding and thinness of texture which characterize Leishman's imitation of Rilke's iambic pentameter… As to *why* so fine a mind as Joseph Brodsky's should have committed so basic an error—evident above all in his own translations—as to imagine that equivalence *is* mimesis, this remains a matter of speculation. The standard view (which he seems not to have disputed) that attempting to imitate Russian verse-forms in English is contrary to the genius of both languages may in a perverse sort of way have egged him on—the more so when critical voices (as was to be expected) were raised in protest. Brodskyan assertions such as "Basically, talent doesn't need history" ('Nadezhda Mandelstam*:* An Obituary' in *Less Than One*) are at first exhilarating, then problematic. It is one thing to say, as in his essay on Mandelstam himself, that "Art is not an attempt to escape reality but the attempt to animate it", but quite another to idealize (for example) Tsvetaeva's "denial of reality" in general and declare her "the most interesting thinker of her time". In his determination not to play the role of victim (a role, however, which he does not always avoid), one might say that Brodsky took a step—or several steps—too far in the right direction. As *The Death of Innocence* is designed to show, among other things, we ignore or "deny" reality—or history—at our peril. When such a denial of reality includes, for example, the nature of Russian and English, and the fact of one's inability to master the latter, the result may be not much worse than cumbersome or non-standard or 'Russianized' writing. When it includes the state of one's health, though, it may result in premature death… But none of this, it goes without saying, should lead us to deny the reality of Brodsky's unique and valuable contribution to English letters. Nor is this his final appearance in *Opus 3*.

p.96, *"Ich bin nicht schuld":* "It's not my fault" or "I'm not to blame"—typical expressions, that is, of Sartrean 'bad faith'. At this point in her diary Eva Braun is telling herself that her behaviour has had nothing to do with the fact that Hitler (by this time her lover, or "he only needs me for certain purposes", as she wrote on 11 March)—has hardly been in touch for three months. A further diary entry for the same day declares her intention of swallowing thirty-five sleeping pills—"to make dead sure this time". This was to be her second attempted suicide (cp. iii). It seems that one of her sisters found the diary beside the unconscious Braun and tore out its last twenty pages, perhaps with the intention of hushing the matter up. These twenty pages (printed in full together with a facsimile in 1974 by Werner Maser in *Adolf Hitler: Legende, Mythos, Wirklichkeit*) were the only part of Eva Braun's diary to survive the war. They are accepted as genuine by most historians, including Heike B. Görtemaker in *Eva Braun: Leben mit Hitler* (2010, trans. 2011), to which the poem and these notes are indebted for many of their historical details.

p.97, **The Grandfather's Tale (1):** The sisters' grandfather is presented as telling them a version of Grimms' *Märchen* No.161—a brilliantly imaginative tale. Unfortunately, there is nothing holy about the imagination, however, and by no means all of the *Kinder- und Hausmärchen* collected by the brothers Grimm—including this one—are as edifying as *Allerleihrauh,* for example. *Schneeweißchen und Rosenrot,* in addition, has been over-sweetened—almost as if to conceal its nasty centre. The Grandfather—*ca.* 1920—turns out to be made of sterner stuff…

p.98, **across the Inn from *Braunau*:** Hitler was born in Braunau am Inn in Austria, although he always regarded Linz (where he grew up) as his hometown. The NSDAP headquarters in Munich was called the *"Braune Haus"* and the Nazis were known, of course, as *"die Braunen"* (Brownshirts)… The **Photohaus** where Eva Braun started work in 1929 belonged to Heinrich Hoffmann, who was Hitler's and the Nazis' official photographer and grew rich on the proceeds. The meeting with **Herr Wolf** took place in October 1929, only a few weeks after Braun had landed her job. Hitler sometimes travelled under the name of Wolf, and may have introduced himself as such on entering the premises. His Prussian headquarters during the war was known as the *Wolfsschanze*—the Wolf's Lair… Gretl Braun refers to Hoffmann as **the boss** because from 1932 she also worked at the *Photohaus.*

p.98, **Then tried to kill herself:** In spite of her diary entries for 28 May 1935, Eva Braun's motives for her early suicide attempts (she was twenty years old when she tried to shoot herself) remain obscure. Heike Görtemaker supposes that she hoped to influence Hitler by drawing attention to her plight. But both the diary and the facts of Braun's life allow of the opposite interpretation as well—that is, of the *hopelessness* of trying to influence him. Hitler demanded absolute loyalty and obedience from those around him on a personal as well as a political level. Anyone who refused beyond a certain point to sacrifice their individuality to his increasingly psychopathic leadership was more or less drastically attacked, not infrequently with fatal consequences. In the case of Eva Braun, who survived in Hitler's immediate vicinity for sixteen years, an unwillingness to accept responsibility for her actions together with a tendency to look the other way or deceive herself as well as others, amounting to a belief in her own 'innocence' *("Ich bin nicht schuld")*, is everywhere apparent in her words and deeds. She was a girl of seventeen when she met him. But as Sartre wrote in *Being and Nothingness*, "There is no such thing as an 'innocent' child." And others of Braun's circle excused themselves in similar ways—at the time and later. In spite of Eva Braun's hopelessness, if such it was, in early 1935, however, Hitler at last fulfilled the intention he had (apparently) expressed to Hoffmann, after her first attempted suicide in 1932, of taking better care of "the poor child". As always with Hitler, the personal and the political were inextricable and Görtemaker is no doubt right to suggest that he was (also) intent on avoiding the scandal which would certainly have resulted if his lover had succeeded in killing herself.

p.100, **or like old Fritz:** Gretl Braun is referring here to one of the Nazis' and in particular Hitler's various Romantic role-models, Kaiser Friedrich II of Hohenstaufen (1194–1250), a Holy Roman Emperor as famous for his ruthless cruelty and efficiency as for his artistic ability. Friedrich's expansion and consolidation of his power in both Italy and Germany was exalted by the Nazis into a 'First Reich', which had never in fact existed… The retirement residence Hitler dreamed of at Linz (cp. ix) was to some extent inspired by the building projects—above all the Castel del Monte in South-east Italy—with which Friedrich seems to have occupied himself as a sort of hobby between military campaigns. Eva Braun, whom Hitler consistently involved in his project at Linz, no doubt imagined, as Görtemaker suggests, "a glittering fairy-tale future at Hitler's side". As far as Hitler was concerned, there is perhaps some truth as well in the suggestion that she was part of a private and irrational fantasy or pseudo-paradise in his mind which may have helped him to pursue his monstrous policies all the more persistently.

p.100, **like Brandner Caspar:** The Bavarian folk-tale of Brandner Caspar, a huntsman and poacher—a 'sly fox' *(Schlitzohr)*—who outwits Death, is adapted at length in *No.2,* section 2.

p.100, **Look at Eisner:** Kurt Eisner (1867–1919) was a Jewish journalist and radical socialist. Shortly before the end of the First World War, he led a rally in Munich which ended in the flight of King Ludwig III and the establishment of the Democratic Social Republic of Bavaria, of which Eisner was made Prime Minister. This sequence of events was later transformed into the so-called *Dolchstoß Legende,* whereby the Nazis claimed that Jews and Communists had stabbed Germany in the back and caused it to lose the war. Only three months later Eisner was assassinated, resulting in two (very) short-lived but violent and chaotic Soviet-type republics, the second supported by the Soviet Union. Needless to say, these events were likewise transformed by the Nazis into propaganda against 'Jewish Bolshevism'.

p.100, **Karl Brandt once mentioned Kaspar Hauser:** The reverse side of fantasy is, as often as not, nightmare, as the reverse side of Paradise is Hell. Karl Brandt was a young and ambitious doctor who, having succeeded in gaining Hitler's personal confidence, was put in charge of the latter's 'euthanasia' programme, otherwise known as *Aktion T4,* after its headquarters at Tiergartenstr. 4 in Berlin. Brandt was a member of Hitler's inner circle and frequently at the Berghof, where he and Eva Braun seem to have got on well... Kaspar Hauser was and to some extent remains an enigma. He had spent his childhood—or so he claimed, once he had learned to talk—chained to a wall in a low-ceilinged room where he could not stand up. He was fed but never saw his gaoler or anyone else until he was taken to Nuremberg in 1828, when he was fifteen, and abandoned there. By turns well- and ill-treated by the authorities and his carers, he was at first severely retarded, but so sweet-tempered that for some he became an embodiment of the Noble Savage. He was also willing to learn, which he did until he was mysteriously murdered in 1833. Whoever he was (he may have been a pawn in some South German dynastic intrigue), it is impossible not to regard him as an innocent victim.

p.102, **Morell, of all / people:** Dr Theodore Morell was the most important of Hitler's personal physicians, in constant attendance on the *Führer* and regarded by some who were also close to 'Patient A'—Karl Brandt among them—as a swindler and a quack. In the last four years of his life Hitler took as many as eighty-eight medical substances on Morell's recommendation. When Brandt eventually accused Morell of practically poisoning the *Führer,* Hitler saw this as a conspiracy against a man he trusted and it was Brandt who was expelled from his inner circle... The official 'euthanasia' programme, which was mainly targeted at physically and mentally handicapped Germans, was ended by Hitler himself—largely because of increasing public unrest—in August 1941. Over 70,000 people had by then been gassed or poisoned. However, the programme continued under the guise of medical treatment, mainly in psychiatric institutions, and it is now estimated that about 90,000 people, many of them children, were poisoned or starved to death in the following three years of 'decentralized euthanasia'. The starvation diet approved by the Ministry of the Interior Health Department in Munich was completely fat-free, as a result of which patients died of famine edema within three months. The diet was introduced (and doctors' cooperation checked) in all psychiatric institutions, although there seems to have been no written order. By 1943 Brandt was being informed that many psychiatrists were leaving their positions ("It has come to an exodus of capable doctors from psychiatry", as one professor wrote to him). Nevertheless, the programme continued until the war was over.

p.102, **close friends, like Röhm. Or Hermann, my husband:** Ernst Röhm was Chief of Staff of the SA and one of Hitler's oldest comrades-in-arms. When the SA grew too powerful, Hitler had him and others more or less associated with him shot in June 1934. The story of this notorious purge—in which about 1,000 people died—is told in *No.2,* section 2... Gretl Braun was married to Hermann Fegelein, a senior SS-officer, in June 1944. He was summarily shot on Hitler's orders on the very day (28 April 1945) that Hitler heard of Himmler's secret talks offering to surrender to America and England.

p.107, (**if I remember rightly**): In the hospital episode of *Ulysses,* in which Leopold Bloom awaits with compassion the birth of Mrs Purefoy's ninth living child (some have died), Joyce half-humorously observes, "And as no man knows the ubicity of his tumulus nor to what processes we shall thereby be ushered, nor whether to Tophet or Edenville, in the like way is all hidden when we would backward see from what region of remoteness the whatness of our whoness hath fetched his whenceness." The suggestion that no man knows *now* very much about the *then* of his past as well as of his future is, in the context of Joyce's writings, a calculated paradox. Wordsworth's *Prelude*—to which *A Brief Prelude* obviously alludes—is more straightforwardly past-oriented, but at the beginning of Bk II (1805) he similarly notes:

> A tranquillizing spirit presses now
> On my corporeal frame, so wide appears
> The vacancy between me and those days,
> Which yet have such self-presence in my mind
> That sometimes when I think of them I seem
> Two consciousnesses—conscious of myself
> And of some other being.

Nevertheless, Wordsworth continued to refer to that other being as "I". In places this leads to what may be uniquely Wordsworthian levels of Romantic self-inflation, as when—to compensate for the uncomfortable memory, perhaps, of having done less than well at Cambridge (Bk III)—he trumpets

> Of genius, power,
> Creation, and divinity itself,
> I have been speaking, for my theme has been
> What passed within me. Not of outward things
> Done visibly for other minds—words, signs,
> Symbols or actions—but of my own heart
> Have I been speaking, and my youthful mind…
> This is in truth heroic argument,
> And genuine prowess.

Though no doubt intended as a new theme for epic poetry, superceding the war-like epics of Homer and Virgil and the Christian epics of Milton, this rings untrue. "A tale / Of matters which *not falsely* I may call / The glory of my youth", he asserts *(my italics)*. But the truest poetry may be in fact the most feigning, and Joyce's decision, in *A Portrait of the Artist as a Young Man* and *Ulysses,* to speak of himself as "he" and under the name of Stephen Dedalus, permits him as author to translate and adapt his own past into a work of art which is quite clearly from the very beginning no more (and no less) than analogous to his actual life and not to be confused with it.

Autobiography is, for the most part, a relatively recent and Romantic genre. It may also be a flawed one, raising expectations of accuracy and/or honesty virtually impossible for any writer to fulfil—such is "The vacancy", as Wordsworth called it, "between me and those days." That Wordsworth, in any case, saw his autobiographical poetry as (among other things) an opportunity to adjust or modify his past self in order to cut a better and, as time went on, a more respectable figure is clearly reflected in his revisions of *The Prelude*. Once one has accepted its limitations, one can enjoy his poetry for what it is, of course—profoundly perceptive about certain subjects and, at its best, also deeply humane. Of which more later…

p.107, **Which may be why he later thought of the arts / … as what offered / his squalid past a future:** It may be that the most effective as well as rewarding way of living with the fact or (more exactly) unavoidable facticity of human consciousness is creatively—or *actively*, as opposed to passively. For the sake of argument, we may speak of active or passive *doing* and *being*, whereby what is traditionally known as the 'active' life can be passive and the 'contemplative' life active. Perhaps very little of what we do / are is either purely active or purely passive, and even highly creative writers such as Wordsworth or Matthew Arnold may have a surprisingly deep streak of passivity. If only life were as innocent as it once was, or if the ideal were only real, they imply, all would be well in the world, forgetting that 'historical' facts, as Sartre said, are nothing in themselves but that every individual is always responsible for how he takes or *makes* reality (cp. *No.1*, title page)—which, however, we need to meet or shake hands with halfway in the sense that facticity or contingency or 'history' remains what it is. Although we are "condemned to be free", in Sartre's phrase (cp. note on p.85, "I'm in! he whooped…"), some are more conscious—or, rather, *choose* to be more conscious—of the fact than others: he also wrote, "I am responsible for everything" (including choosing *not* to choose) "except for my very responsibility." The more any person or group or institution seeks power over others—whether for personal, social, economic or political reasons—the less they will be in favour of individual activity or conscious 'freedom' of this sort. Neither will those be in favour of it who, for whatever reason, *prefer* passivity, miserable though it frequently is. Again, these two groups are rarely pure, but they form the vast majority, like it or not (the more so since they are, as it were, in each other's interest). With both in the back of his mind, Stephen Dedalus reminds himself, "You will not be master of others or their slave… I want his life still to be his, mine to be mine." And Byron at his most enlightened has already been quoted in these notes: "I wish men to be free / As much from mobs as kings—from you as me." For the moment and for the foreseeable future, though, anyone who believes and acts on this is choosing, in effect, to live as an outsider. Arnold was sufficiently aware of the fact for it to worry him increasingly as time went on. In *The Scholar-Gipsy (ca.* 1852–53), the scholar is seen as not entirely wrong to leave Oxford in search of truths of which Oxford may know little or nothing. But by the time he wrote *Thyrsis* (1864–65), the death of his friend, the poet and academic Arthur Hugh Clough, is presented by implication as a *result* of his leaving. Arnold had by then been Professor of Poetry at Oxford for seven or eight years and felt he belonged there. The biassed and misleading account of Clough's life and poetry which is what *Thyrsis* amounts to, well-written though it is, is clearly related to Arnold's idealization in later life of Oxford itself, as in his famous 'Preface' to the second edition of *Essays in Criticism* (1869)—"Beautiful city! so venerable, so lovely, so unravaged by the fierce intellectual life of our century, so serene!… Adorable dreamer, who hast given thyself to sides and heroes not mine, only never to the Philistines!" Idealism believes, of course, in types of beauty and truth which are nowhere to be found—ideas of pre- and post-lapsarian innocence being primary examples. It therefore dislikes the real world and either 'purifies' in order to praise or blackens in order to condemn it—one way or the other subjectively distorting things as they are. Arnold quotes Goethe's praise of Schiller as having surpassed "the bondage of *'was uns alle bändigt, DAS GEMEINE!'*" as if the same were true of Oxford. If it was true of her in the 1860s (which one may doubt), it can scarcely be said to be so any longer. Business Studies and applied sciences plus 'technology' are what count in the twenty-first century. A fund-raising body labouring under the misnomer 'Oxford Thinking' appears not to think about the humanities at all. And which of Oxford's *alumni* now hears from her other than when she wants *das Gemeinste von allem*—money?

p.109, **Milton … viewed Christian dogma / as a form of 'science':** Milton's sometimes convoluted efforts to treat dogma and Judeo-Christian cosmology 'scientifically' tended (unlike those of Pascal, for example) to stifle the spirit of the very religion he was attempting to 'prove' (cp. note on p.29, "He believed the Fall / … caused Adam's fleshly lusting"). Arnold in his later prose books was still worrying that if proof was not forthcoming with regard to the truth of Christianity, the religion was doomed. He famously remarked that "… men cannot do without it", but "they cannot do with it as it is" *(God and the Bible,* 1875). His solution was to argue that, although the miracles and prophecies and dogmas of Christianity were in fact not subject to scientific proof, the effect of the religion on the righteousness of people's conduct was self-evident—a highly questionable point of view when one considers Christian conduct as exemplified by the Crusades, the wars of the Reformation, the Inquisition, European colonialism, the slave-trade, sectarianism, the soul-destroying tendencies of Puritanism, and so on. Arnold, like many if not most Christian apologists, including his father Dr Thomas Arnold, the celebrated headmaster of Rugby, believed that conduct was the aim of religion and that "Conduct is three fourths of life" *(Literature and Dogma,* 1873)—whereas if the religious state of mind were taken to be the aim of conduct (as in Theravada Buddhism, for example), the world might be not only a less materialistic but a better-behaved place.

p.109, **God gave despotic power / to men (according to Samson) over their females:** It seems that the only commentator ever to call Samson's sainthood into question was Rupert of St Heribert, who suggested that he performed his wonders by black magic—an accusation specifically denied by Samson in his slanging match with Harapha of Gath *(Samson Agonistes,* l. 1139 *et seq)*. In Milton's 'tragedy', though, the supposed saintliness of Samson consists of little more than belligerent machismo in the service of religious fundamentalism (as it has come to be called) along the lines of whose god is strongest ("Thou shalt then see, or rather to thy sorrow / Soon feel, whose god is strongest, thine or mine", ll. 1154–5)—together with a deep and in places ludicrous streak of puritanical misogyny:

> Therefore god's universal law
> Gave to the man despotic power
> Over his female in due awe,

> Nor from that right to part an hour,
> Smile she or lour:
> So shall he least confusion draw
> On his whole life, not swayed
> By female usurpation, nor dismayed…

In the end Samson avenges himself on the sons of Gaza by pulling a great building down on top of them. Nor is there the slightest indication in the text (in spite of special pleading on the part of some modern critics) that this might be in any way disagreeable to God.

p.110, He found he cared / and didn't care about do's/don'ts: At the beginning of *Ulysses*, Stephen Dedalus is troubled in the night by the "oxy chap" Haines's bad dreams. When Stephen's friend Buck Mulligan dismisses their English visitor with "He's stinking with money and thinks you're not a gentleman" and offers to give him "a ragging worse than they gave Clive Kempthorpe", Stephen recalls what might happen to you at Oxford not long ago if you didn't care *enough* "about do's/don'ts":

> Young shouts of moneyed voices in Clive Kempthorpe's rooms. Palefaces: they hold their ribs with laughter, one clasping another, O, I shall expire! Break the news to her gently, Aubrey! I shall die! With slit ribbons of his shirt whipping the air he hops and hobbles round the table, with trousers down at heels, chased by Ades of Magdalen with the tailor's shears. A scared calf's face gilded with marmalade. I don't want to be debagged! Don't you play the giddy ox with me!

Joyce tellingly concludes his account of the ragging of Clive Kempthorpe as follows:

> Shouts from the open window startling evening in the quadrangle. A deaf gardener, aproned, masked with Matthew Arnold's face, pushes his mower on the sombre lawn watching narrowly the dancing motes of grasshalms.

In the Nighttown episode, "*The Siamese twins, Philip Drunk and Philip Sober, two Oxford dons with lawnmowers*" unexpectedly appear. Philip Drunk impatiently defends himself against Philip Sober's warnings to take care not to waste his money with the words, "Ah, bosh man…! I paid my way." Their lawnmowers begin to purr, relating them to Joyce's no doubt intentionally un-funny references elsewhere to "Lawn Tennyson" (see also xxi)… For Arnold and his influence see also 'Heine's Grave' in *Words in the Dark*. Heine's stance as a voluntary outsider in exile seems to have worried Arnold as much as if not more than Clough's turning his back on Oxford, and he made something of a fool of himself by attacking Heine "for want of moral balance" *(Words in the Dark*, p.137). Arnold's twentieth century equivalent, T.S. Eliot, comments strongly, in *The Use of Poetry and the Use of Criticism* and in his essay *Arnold and Pater* (1930), on what Arnold imagined to be his morals, remarking of *Culture and Anarchy* in the latter that "what Culture and Conduct are I feel I know less well on every reading"—though "As an invective against the crudities of the industrialism of his time, the book is perfect of its kind." In *The Use of Poetry…*, however, he oddly says, "I am not sure that he was highly sensitive to the musical qualities of verse." Beginning with Wordsworth and Coleridge, and continuing with Arnold, Eliot, Pound, Larkin, Donald Davie and others, Anglo-American poet-critics have exhibited sufficient crudity of their own in commending directly or indirectly by means of their reviews or critical writings their own sort of poetry, as if it were an inherently better product or brand. As a matter of fact, one of the principal attractions of Arnold's poetic opus is the consistently high quality of its verse, which, at its best *(Dover Beach, Sohrab and Rustum, Rugby Chapel, The Scholar-Gipsy, Thyrsis)* is unmistakably the work of a stylist of both traditional and innovative genius.

p.112, **Italian / landscape appeared to *be* a work of art:** In the growth of any poet's mind from childhood to youth to age, the relative significance attached to appearance and reality no doubt shifts from the first to the second as time goes on. And yet we *always* experience the second through the first. The idea that we experience reality, or 'nature', through minds whose expectations may be better nourished by art of one sort or another than by the lives we happen to lead in the environments into which we have been arbitrarily 'thrown' is not entirely absent from Wordsworth. In the incident of the drowned man in *The Prelude* Bk V, for example, his nine-year-old self is less shocked than he might otherwise have been when

> the dead man, 'mid that beauteous scene
> Of trees and hills and water, bolt upright
> Rose, with his ghastly face

for the entirely credible reason that his "inner eye had seen / Such sights before" in his childhood reading. And yet he remained, by his own admission, relatively indifferent to the arts:

> Not that I slighted books—that were to lack
> All sense—but other passions had been mine,
> More fervent...

Wordsworth's occasionally almost infantile passivity—his orphan's longing for caring parents (his mother died when he was seven and his father, to whom he was never close, when he was thirteen)—emerges fully at this point in the 1805 version of *The Prelude* Bk III:

> ... soothed and lulled
> As I had been, trained up in Paradise
> Among sweet garlands and delightful sounds

—a memory of prelapsarian childhood 'innocence' in the bosom of Mother Nature removed by 1850 but obviously reverberating throughout his poetry. In *The Prelude* Bk IV he describes his soul, while walking by Esthwaite, as "naked as in the presence of her God" (l.142)—where else but in the Garden of Eden? In Bk V he writes of "Nature's self, which is the breath of God" (l.222). In Bk VIII, 144 and 818 the Lake District is again compared to Paradise... It is, as a matter of fact, as good as impossible to read demanding literature passively (one reason why poetry is no longer popular being that we live in an increasingly passive society) and it is concomitant with his own passive tendencies that Wordworth generally takes the view that Life or 'Nature' is the better teacher, forgetting that life frequently, even predominantly, vulgarizes if not brutalizes whereas art refines. This is, of course, one of the meanings of Yeats's Byzantium poems, Yeats having been exposed to twentieth century brutality ("The fury and the mire of human veins") of a sort which Wordsworth would presumably have evaded if he possibly could. Arnold himself observed, "But Wordsworth's eyes avert their ken / From half of human fate" *(In Memory of the Author of 'Obermann')*—and, again, in his essay on Heine in *Essays in Criticism*, "The gravest of [the English Romantics], Wordsworth, retired (in Middle-Age phase) into a monastery. I mean he plunged himself in the inward life, he voluntarily cut himself off from the modern spirit"… The Art versus Nature discussion is, as one might expect, an old one. Joyce's epigraph to *A Portrait of the Artist*—from Ovid on Daedalus contemplating flight—is translated by Arthur Golding as

> This sayde, to uncoth Arts he bent
>   the force of all his wits
> To alter Nature's course by craft…
>   *(Metamorphoses,* Bk VIII)

Ovid's (and Golding's) admirer, Shakespeare, is constantly aware of the complexity of the relationship of art to life—also of their oneness, as in Polixenes' and Perdita's celebrated discussion in *The Winter's Tale* IV.iv… Ten years before Arnold's essay, in *Men and Women* (1855), Browning had had Fra Lippo Lippi comment that we first see certain things after they are painted—"Art was given for that"—and Picasso similarly observed that art influences how we see nature, revealing much that would otherwise be invisible or which we might see in a different way. That is, since the artist re-creates reality most persuasively (and we always re-create reality) our ideas of nature derive to a large extent from how artists represent it.

p.115, *"Enough! or Too much":* The Curse virtually reverses the meaning of Blake's dictum in *The Marriage of Heaven and Hell,* where it implies that "The road of excess leads to the palace of wisdom"—a superficially exciting but half-baked idea, of the sort for which T.S. Eliot, in his 1920 essay on Blake, rightly took him to task. The point of view of the poem—whose "ecstatic garden" is related, of course, to the various ideas of innocence represented in *No.1* (including those of Rilke's which follow)—is more that of ecologists such as Gregory Bateson, who wrote in *Mind and Nature* (1979):

> Desired substances, things, patterns, or sequences of experience that are in some sense 'good' for the organism—items of diet, conditions of life, temperature, entertainment, sex, and so forth—are never such that more of the something is always better than less of the something… More calcium is not always better than less calcium. There is an optimum quantity of calcium that a given organism may need in its diet. Beyond this, calcium becomes toxic. Similarly, for the oxygen that we breathe or foods or components of diet and probably all components of relationship, enough is better than

a feast. We can even have too much psychotherapy [!] A relationship with no combat in it is dull, and a relationship with too much combat in it is toxic.

And so on. To deny that there are or ever have been heavenly or ideal states of innocence together with analogous equivalents in day-to-day existence is not, of course, to exclude the possibility that things in general and/or in the life of any individual may get worse—or better. Bateson observes of "the philosophy of money": "This characteristic of biological value does not hold for money… More money is supposedly always better than less money." However, "…when we consider money, not by itself, but as acting on human beings who own it, we may find that money, too, becomes toxic beyond a certain point. In any case, the set of presuppositions by which money is supposedly better and better the more you have of it, is totally antibiological." Not to mention power—fame—technological prowess—and other idols of modern man. Eliot's response to the modern world was famously conservative:

> We have the same respect for Blake's philosophy… that we have for an ingenious piece of home-made furniture: we admire the man who has put it together out of the odds and ends about the house. England has produced a fair number of these resourceful Robinson Crusoes; but we are not really so remote from the Continent, or from our own past, as to be deprived of the advantages of culture if we wish them.

And yet "the divorce from Rome", which Eliot goes on eloquently to regret, was as inevitable as the collapse, in the meantime, of Protestantism (I exclude all forms of fundamentalism as irreligious). If not Robinson Crusoes, we are all Prodigal Sons and Daughters now, with no home to return to—as Eliot, in fact, was sufficiently aware: "The fault is perhaps not with Blake himself, but with the environment which failed to provide what such a poet"—and not just such a poet—"needed; perhaps the circumstances compelled him to fabricate…" What seems not to have occurred very clearly to either Eliot or Bateson is that a person or group of persons might free themselves sufficiently from "the circumstances" so as to be able to *choose*, not to "fabricate" (with its nuances of falsity), but to transform or re-create what they think and therefore do.

p.115, **Early Apollo:** Rilke's poetry is for the most part stronger on the physical/emotional and spiritual aspects of human life than on the ethical. The translations from *Neue Gedichte* in this section have been selected as appropriate in particular to the physical/emotional bias of *The Death of Innocence*. Rilke's short 'Self-Portrait from the Year 1906' implies that he expected to go further. Others in *Neue Gedichte* go as far as he ever went (see *No.3*, section 14):

> *Self-Portrait from the Year 1906*
>
> An ancient, aristocratic ancestry,
> Whose eyebrows' arches brook no compromise.
> The fears of childhood still in his blue eyes,
> And here and there a deep humility.—
> A servant's. Or a woman's. No stable-boy's.

> The mouth formed as a mouth, large and precise—
> Not to persuade but state what's just, what's free.
> The forehead without guile, contentedly
> Shadowed and bowed in spiritual exercise.
>
> These scattered features time will make or mar,
> Which have not yet been fully concentrated
> By suffering or success, or penetrated
> To lasting goals. Yet a real face seems fated
> To come together here, as if from far.

p.119, whereas its gaze, which no / Object restricts, cast visions on the gloom / Weaving a saga cycle in deep blue: The unicorn, we should not forget, is no more than a vision—is itself "no object"... Rilke is clearly aware in this poem, as in other poems from his great *Neue Gedichter* volumes of 1907 and 1908, that the individual mind's ability to transform reality is capable as well of falsifying in order to escape from it. No doubt it is in the nature of how we perceive things that the difference between creative transformation and the mind's habitual tendency to avoid or ignore reality is—to say the least—not always obvious. In late 1915, for example, while living in the Keferstrasse near the *Englischer Garten* in Munich, where his landlady was (as he expressed it in a letter) "a blonde and very beautiful and quite special woman who has rented me the 2nd floor while her husband is away", Rilke wrote the following short series of 'Seven Poems'. The poems may have been inspired either by Rilke's landlady, or by the twenty-three-year-old painter Lulu Albert-Lasard, with whom he was having an affair at the time, or by neither or (possibly) both of them. At approximately the same time as he was writing the poems, heavy fighting was reported in France, the Balkans, Italy and elsewhere, so that he also found himself (as he also wrote) "a witness to the world's disgrace". The question therefore arises (as analogous questions arise in our lives) of whether the series is a form of withdrawal or of spiritual progress:

> *Seven Poems (1915)*
>
> i
>
> The girl who gathers roses suddenly
> Grasps the full bud of his life-giving limb
> And, shocked by the difference of him/her, her/him,
> Her [fragrant] gardens shrink, or try to flee
>
> ii
>
> The summer which, for me, you suddenly are
> Has drawn the seed up into my tall tree.
> (Spacious within, o feel there the arching sky
> Of Night, in which it stands mature!)

And now it rises into your firmament,
A growing image of real trees.
O fell him, so that (upside down) he sees,
Deep in your lap, the anti-Heaven meant
To make him really soar, really confront
Its dangerous landscape, such as prophetesses
Scan in their globes: that inner space
In which vast star-filled outer spaces hunt.

iii

Our glances close the circle, till a vision
Fuses the random tensions white in both
Of us—while your unknowing, blind decision
Raises a column in my undergrowth.

Stirred up by you, the god's tall image stands
At the silent crossroads, covered by my clothing;
My entire body invokes him. We are nothing
But spell-bound creatures on his spell-bound land.

And yet you must decide, if you're to be
Both grave and Heaven for the Herma. You
Can set the god amid his bee-swarms free
Of shrugged-off broken stone by letting go.

iv

Shy one, who know nothing yet of towers,
All of that's about to change
In the rich and strange
Space within you. Close your eyes, whose powers
Have, along with your sweet face
And your innocent body, raised
One tower, rigid and complete. Amazed,
I inhabit towering space,
Into which I'm forced to cram
While you praise my progress—to the dome
Where across your soft night-sky I ram,
Like resplendent rockets shooting home,
Greater verve and feeling than I am.

v

How too much space dilutes us! till we're thin
As air, remembering superfluities.
And now our silent kisses sieve the lees,
Trickling with bitter wormwood or absinth.

How *much* we are! Out of my torso juts
A whole new tree, whose overflowing crown
Rises towards you. What would it be but
For the summer in your lap? Now fully grown,
Am I, are you, the one we satisfy?
Who is to say, as we both disappear?
A joyous column holds up the curved sky
Of our room, perhaps, now lingering longer here.

vi

To what are we closer? Death or the day
Of lives not lived yet? What would clay on clay
Be if the god were *not* to form the figure
Whose limbs now bud between us? But think bigger:
This is my body, which is resurrected.
Help him now quietly out of his hot grave
Into the Heaven which you and then I have,
Until our bold survival is projected
Through him—and you, young grove of deep Ascension.
You air of summer, dark and pollen-filled.
When all its thousand dancing spirits are spilled,
My stiff corpse gently sheds again its tension.

vii

How did I call you? With mute calls,
Which have become as sweet as they were wild.
As I push on inside you step by step,
My seed climbs on up like a happy child:
Ur-Mount of Venus, you, to whom we come, it
Breathlessly springs as I ascend your col.
Give in now—feel us coming—for you fall
The moment that we beckon from your summit.

p.122, *At Rilke's Grave:* Rilke's gravestone (in Raron, high above the Rhone valley) bears only his name and epitaph. The epitaph (quoted and translated in the poem) was written and included by Rilke in his will in October 1925, when he was already seriously ill. Rilke's last poem, *"Komm du, du letzter"*, was found in his notebook after his death on 29 December 1926. This poem constitutes a possibly unique first-person attempt to represent without falsification the reality of terminal illness (cp. the preceding note). Rilke in fact insisted, once he knew that his condition was incurable, on dying his own death as he had lived his own life, refusing to allow himself to be drugged with heavy painkillers. Asking a close friend (Gudi Nölke) to help him ensure that his death would be his own, he wrote, "I don't want the doctors' death—I want to have my freedom."

p.124, *The Blessing (after Chuang Tzu):* As in 'Lazarus (after Heine)' in *From Now to Then,* some of the ideas—and also certain phrases—in this poem derive from Burton Watson's translation of the Chinese Taoist philosopher, Chuang Tzu, especially ch.6. Chuang Tzu (369?–286? BC) is unusual among philosophers in the irony and wit with which he approaches even the knottiest of problems. He and Heine would have appreciated each other's realism and sense of humour. He is also a mystic and from this point of view would have understood the spiritual tendencies of Rilke's writing... The first part of the poem is based as well on a traditional Buddhist/Taoist parable, known to me orally (and adapted, as I discovered recently, by Hermann Hesse in his appropriately titled *Mit der Reife wird man immer jünger*—The Older You Get the Younger You Get).

OPUS 3, NO.2: AFTERWORDS

p.127, *All that we are, etc.:* The opening words of the *Dhammapada*—a poetic and ethical work in 423 stanzas—have been variously translated. This version is that of Christmas Humphreys in *Buddhism* (1964). The *Dhammapada* has been called the Sermon on the Mount of Buddhism.

p.129, *A Brief Prelude (2):* Bearing in mind the limitations of autobiography as a genre outlined above—in note on p.107, "(if I remember rightly)"—this section of the book covers a similar period of 'autobiographical' time to *A Brief Prelude (1)* and also *(3)*. The difference in each case is related to the physical/emotional and ethical/spiritual emphases of *No.1* and *No.s 2 & 3* respectively. All such categories overlap, of course, and may frequently be indistinguishable from one another. On the other hand, each of us chooses, more or less consciously (which in practice means more or less freely) to emphasize this or that aspect of our lives in preference to others... As well as fulfilling their own functions, the physical/emotional and ethical aspects may serve to enable or increasingly 'liberate' the life of the spirit—or they may hinder it... Matthew Arnold having disqualified himself from being taken with seriousness on the subject of ethics by his position on Christian 'conduct'—absurdly exemplified, in *Then and Now,* by his remarks on Heine (cp. 'Heine's Grave' and notes—especially p.137—in *Words in the Dark)*—and by his woolly-minded and/or time-serving adulation of Oxford's "ineffable charm" (cp. notes to *A Brief Prelude (1))*, has thereby disqualified himself as well from this part of the sequence.

p.129, ***all this may be transmuted by ... poetry:*** The epigraph is taken from a late essay by Borges entitled *Immortality* (1978). In another late essay, *Blindness*, Borges describes how the "slow nightfall" caused by his degenerative eye-disease finally led in 1955 to "the pathetic moment ... when I knew I had lost my sight". Paradoxically this resulted not in despair but in his revoking what Sartre would have called his "original choice", i.e. in his abandoning the characteristic fatalism which expresses itself in many places throughout his writings and replacing it with the transformative power of the individual mind, particularly in art: "Everything that happens, including humiliations, embarrassments, misfortunes, all has been given like clay, like material for one's art. One must accept it. For this reason I speak in a poem of the ancient food of heroes: humiliation, unhappiness, discord. Those things are given to us to transform, so that we may make from the miserable circumstances of our lives things that are eternal, or aspire to be so"... 'The Story from Rosendo Juárez' (in *Brodie's Report,* 1970) rewrites his own earlier story 'Streetcorner Man' (1933) in such a way as to illustrate with particular clarity this development not only in art but in a person's life.

p.129, ***Apron-Strings:*** The theory of the double-bind as a cause of mental unbalance ('schizophrenia') and/or creativity was first developed by Gregory Bateson and taken up by R.D. Laing and others. Laing was referring to double-binds in the title of his book *Knots* (1970). Bateson's theory is complex and takes up a hundred pages or so of his collected papers, *Steps Towards an Ecology of Mind* (1971). Bateson's earlier work was in anthropology and his knowledge of other cultures than our own was unusually wide, as the following passage illustrating the effects of double-binds goes to show:

> In the Eastern religion, Zen Buddhism, the goal is to achieve enlightenment. The Zen master attempts to bring about enlightenment in various ways. One of the things he might do is hold a stick over the pupil's head and say fiercely, "If you say this stick is real I will strike you with it. If you say this stick is not real I will strike you with it. If you don't say anything I will strike you with it." We feel that the schizophrenic finds himself continually in the same situation as the pupil, but he achieves something like disorientation rather than enlightenment. The Zen pupil might reach up and take the stick away from the master—who might accept this response, but the schizophrenic has no such choice since with him there is no not caring about the relationship, and his mother's aims and awareness are not like the master's.

p.130, ***"dared / to be a Daniel":*** The chorus of a popular nineteenth century hymn by Philip P. Bliss could only have been written by a Protestant individualist:

> Dare to be a Daniel,
> Dare to stand alone!
> Dare to have a purpose firm!
> Dare to make it known.

p.130, ***Better not burn:*** For historical and, presumably, personal reasons, St Paul found celibacy more commendable than the normal processes which lead to the bearing of children: "I say therefore to the unmarried and widows, It is good for them if they abide even as I. But if they cannot contain, let them marry: for it is better to marry than to burn" *(1 Corinthians VII. 8–9)*—a text which may well qualify as having caused more trouble in everyday Christian lives than any other in the Bible… In *Exodus III,* God spoke to Moses in the **burning bush** to encourage him to liberate His people Israel from Egyptian slavery.

p.131, **weighed / in the balance:** The prophet Daniel interpreted the writing which the finger of God wrote on the wall during a feast in the palace of the Babylonian king, Belshazzar, as meaning, "Thou hast been weighed in the balance and found wanting" *(Daniel V)*… The Oxford (and Cambridge) Christian apologist C.S.Lewis meant by ***The Problem of Pain*** the theological problem, given the existence of an omnipotent God. Like sex and death, pain only becomes a 'problem' in the context of Christianity and similar religions. Rilke's great poem on pain and death, *"Komm du, du letzter"* (p.122) treats neither as a 'problem'.

p.131, ***"The mountain snob is a Wordsworthian fruit":*** Auden continues in his *Letter to Lord Byron* (who, appropriately, made fun himself of "all the Lakers", including Wordsworth, in the 'Dedication' to *Don Juan):*

> He tears his clothes and doesn't shave his chin.
> He wears a very pretty little boot,
>   He chooses the least comfortable inn;
>   A mountain railway is a deadly sin;
> His strength, of course, is as the strength of ten men,
> He calls all those who live in cities wen-men.

Etc.

p.132, **poor Oscar's trial:** For a note on what was in effect the formidable double-bind from which Oscar Wilde escaped only temporarily in his comedies and social repartee, see *From Now to Then,* pp.285–286.

p.132, **how to get by boat from Padua / to Venice:** In Act 1.i of *The Taming of the Shrew,* Lucentio, who has arrived in Padua to study at the university, is waiting for one of his servants to "come ashore". Commentators imagined this meant that Shakespeare mistakenly took Padua for a port, until it was pointed out that North Italy, even in the sixteenth century, was intersected by a network of canals and waterways, which were used for precisely the sort of travel and transport which Shakespeare had in mind. While there is no proof that Shakespeare had been to Italy, there is a substantial amount of circumstantial evidence of the sort mentioned in the poem. He also appears to have been able to read Italian… Titian painted a number of versions of Venus and Adonis and at least four of Lucrece. *The Flaying of Marsyas,* which was painted in the 1580s (cp. note on p.137, *Self-Portrait as a White-Collar Worker (4)—Afterwords),* shows the satyr Marsyas being flayed by Apollo for daring to think he could rival the god on the flute… The famous story of the woman who fell in love with Richard Burbage while he was playing Richard III and invited him to her bed only to find that Burbage's rival 'Shagspere' (as he once spelled his name) arrived first was recorded by John Manningham in his diary (1602–3).

p.134, ***And so we all of us in some degree / Are led to knowledge:*** Wordsworth is in the process, in *The Prelude* Bk VIII, of comparing the advantages of his upbringing in the innocence of the countryside over that of most of us, belaboured as we are by:

> the weight of meanness, selfish cares,
> Coarse manners, vulgar passions, that beat in
> On all sides from the ordinary world
> In which we traffic.

He has above all the subject of Bk VII, London, in mind, and "the deformities of crowded life", but is so rash as to mock as well the *active* creativity of others as opposed to his own *passive* education in the bosom of Nature (cp. note on p.107, "Which may be why he later thought of the arts"):

> Call ye these appearances
> Which I beheld of shepherds in my youth,
> This sanctity of Nature given to man,
> A shadow, a delusion?—ye who are fed
> By the dead letter, not the spirit of things,
> Whose truth is not a motion or a shape
> Instinct with vital functions, but a block
> Or waxen image which yourselves have made
> And ye adore.

As one might expect, that universal symptom of Sartrean bad faith—God—is introduced at this point, as if to clinch the argument:

> But blessed be the God
> Of Nature and of man that this was so,
> That men did at the first present themselves
> Before my untaught eyes thus purified,
> Removed, and at a distance that was fit.
> And so we all of us in some degree
> Are led to knowledge, whencesoever led,
> And howsoever—were it otherwise
> And we found evil fast as we find good
> In our first years, or think that it is found,
> How could the innocent heart beat up and live?

While no one would wish to question that young children need as much love and help as we can give them, city-dwellers in general or those who were less well-treated than they might have been—and in particular the lower or uneducated classes—are not to be dismissed as Wordsworth dismisses them on the basis of the opinion that shepherds in general are pure and innocent and the countryside Paradise (cp. note on p.112, "Italian / landscape appeared to *be* a work of art")… In *Self-Portrait as a White-Collar Worker (4)* and its notes attention is drawn as well to to the fact that the Bavarian and Austrian countryside is some of the most beautiful in Europe—and to what, among other things, came out of it: *viz.* Nazism on the one hand and sentimental and/or questionable folklore on the other (cp. note on p.97, *The Grandfather's Tale (1)).* To give Wordsworth his due, however, he admitted elsewhere that exposure to Nature may have little or no effect on a hardened heart: cp. *No.3,* 'Peter Bell the Fourth', in which "Nature could not find a way / Into the heart of Peter Bell" (p.351).

p.135, **He's been to visit… / But this isn't for Oxford cissies:** Cp. *From Now to Then,* 'Mementos' and 'Liverpool Revisited—A Winter's Tale' (especially pp.184–185). For related 'autobiographical' material in *From Now to Then,* see 'Four Sections of a Prologue' in 'Self-Portrait as a White-Collar Worker (3)'. These parts of *Then and Now*—like 'A Brief Prelude'—are obviously fictionalized up to a point, as are other seemingly autobiographical sections of the work as a whole.

p.137, **Self-Portrait as a White-Collar Worker (4):** While the 'afterwords' of which *A Brief Prelude* and Pt (4) of this sequence-within-the-sequence consist are in both cases autobiographical and/or historical, those of the latter can also be read as an extended postscript to the 'Epilogue: Report from Munich', which concludes Pt (3) in *From Now to Then.* For Pts (1) & (2), see *Words in the Dark.*

As common in painting as it is in literature, the 'self-portrait as …' is, potentially, a more fanciful and also, from an ethical viewpoint, more complex genre than the straight self-portrait; and many artists and writers from Botticelli to Picasso and from Chaucer to James Joyce have exploited its double-edged capacity for criticizing a) the role in question and b) themselves for playing it. Thus Botticelli paints himself as an arrogant hanger-on in *The Adoration of the Magi (ca.* 1475); Titian as King Midas in *The Flaying of Marsyas* (1570); and Rembrandt as a drunken Prodigal Son toasting the viewer (1638). In his first preparatory drawing for his famous etching, *The Sleep* (or *Dream) of Reason Begets Monsters* (1787), Goya incorporates no less than three portraits of himself—not only as the dreamer but as two disembodied heads among howling gargoyles, bats, dogs, a donkey and a lynx… In other examples of the genre the artist may or may not have played the role in question in actual life. Chaucer may in fact have been a Canterbury pilgrim—though scarcely one so incapable of telling an interesting tale in decent verse that the Host has to cut him off (see 'Chaucers Tale of Thopas' in *The Canterbury Tales).* Although Joyce was himself an *Artist* and once *a Young Man,* many aspects of his *(Self-)Portrait as…*—which continues into *Ulysses*—are obviously fictional. A peculiarity of all four parts of *Self-Portrait as a White-Collar Worker* is that the poems and translations of which the sequence consists are presented throughout as *by* the persona as well as about him, whose identity is thus built up—in fact, develops—as time goes on (in Pt (4) *ca.* 4–5 years). "The other one"—the one who contrives his literature—Borges wrote, in the hall of mirrors which is *Borges and I,* "is the one things happen to." But whether or not *I* was once a white-collar worker ("I am quite aware of his perverse custom of falsifying and magnifying things," Borges continued), the background of Pt (4) of the sequence, or the landscape in which it is set, is again Bavaria and the city of Munich—where I confess to really having lived since 1973.

p.137, *"The poetry doesn't matter":* Of course, the opposite is also true—and Eliot's unpoetic assertion in *East Coker* is followed by an increasingly beautiful passage on the self-deceptive "wisdom of age" and the limited value of "knowledge derived from experience":

> The knowledge imposes a pattern, and falsifies,
> For the pattern is new in every moment
> And every moment is a new and shocking
> Valuation of all we have been. We are only undeceived
> Of that which, deceiving, can no longer harm.

What Eliot meant by "The poetry doesn't matter" was the same as what Brodsky meant in *Watermarks,* his little book on Venice (where he is now buried):

> *The Cantos* left me cold; the main error was an old one: questing after beauty. For someone with such a long record of residence in Italy, it was odd that Pound hadn't realized that beauty can't be targeted, that it is always a by-product of other, often very ordinary pursuits. A fair thing to do, I thought, would be to publish his poems and his speeches in one volume, without any learned introduction, and see what happens.

The *Self-Portrait as…* has also been influenced by the extraordinary, genre-crossing—in effect, genre-*querying*—semi-autobiographical prose-works of W.G. Sebald (Wertach in Allgäu, 1944–2001, Norwich). One result of this has been that, where verse or poetry seemed inappropriate, I have used the (generally) more straightforward medium of prose—in the main text as well as in the notes—rather than not say what needed saying. Even so, the section as a whole has been written to be read like any other in the book: i.e. the main text first, since this can be understood without the notes, which then add to it.

p.139, **the German landscape Primo Levi / Found "rich and civilized":** At the end of Levi's novel, *If Not Now, When?,* there is a briefly startling moment when its narrator—one of a group of Russian Jewish partisans passing through South Germany in 1945 with the aim of reaching Palestine—observes from their train, after all the German-induced horror and devastation he has witnessed, "the fertile fields, the lakes, the farms and towns of the Upper Palatinate, then of Bavaria. Neither he nor any of his companions had ever inhabited a land so rich and civilized." These observations are the more striking because one knows that Primo Levi himself passed through Bavaria by train on his journey home to Turin from Auschwitz. And the richness and civilization of the German equivalent of the English Lake District—one of the most picturesque *and* sublime landscapes of Europe, surely—remain a mystery when one contemplates what emerged from and in some sense returned to it only a lifetime ago. Rational analysis helps, of course, but something was set loose for which we have no words (in *A Vision* Yeats spoke of "the new era … bringing its stream of irrational force"), killing upwards of fifty million people in six years, and perpetrating in the process atrocities which no mind can imagine. Or even, perhaps, remember—given, that is, the practically universal (and therefore 'banal') human tendency, following "the devices and desires of our own hearts", not only to justify or excuse but to falsify or simply erase what we have left undone and what we have done. *The Book of Common Prayer* continues, "Spare thou them, O God, who confess their faults." But how confess the unspeakable? When the prophet Jeremiah lamented, "Cursed is the man that trusteth in man… For the heart is deceitful above all things, and desperately wicked," he added: *"Who can know it?" (XIX.9)*

p.139, **an outing with the firm / The previous summer:** In Pts (1)–(3) of the sequence, the—obviously English—persona is imagined as having worked for "an electronics communications multinational" first of all in England and then in Munich. His wife (as she herself later mentions) was born in a Bavarian village in the last months of the war.

p.140, **Thirty-three *Sterbebilder,* in a frame:** In South Germany, as in other Catholic parts of the world, a photograph of the deceased—a *Sterbebild*—is sometimes found on gravestones. It is also common practice to include such a picture with the dates of birth and death and a quotation or short text in a leaflet to be distributed to friends and relatives or displayed in the church itself as a memento. Of the sorts of men from Hemhof (Chiemgau) who died in the war, the boys and those without uniform may well have been called up into the *Volkssturm* in the last few months of it—a last-ditch Dad's Army, as it has been called, given minimum training, black arm bands and a rifle before being sent to defend the Reich… One might expect more than **A Nazi or two.** However, fascist movements had trouble almost everywhere in appealing to the genuinely traditional elements in rural society (Eric Hobsbawm, *Age of Extremes,* ch.4). For all his initial policy of attempting to co-opt the churches, Hitler's ideology was, of course, profoundly un- and anti-Christian. Moreover, although the Catholic church, which has flourished in Bavaria since the first millennium, dithered between supporting and opposing Hitler's regime—they had the same enemies but not the same goals—it was never fascist.

p.141, ***Stammtisch:*** In a society in which much value is placed on togetherness and belonging, who sits where and with whom are matters of some importance. Thus every Bavarian *Wirtshaus* has a table—the *Stammtisch*—where only regulars and their guests are allowed to sit or where others may only sit with the landlord or *Wirt's* permission. Other meanings of *Stamm* are: tribe, stock or lineage, permanent team or workforce, tree-trunk.

p.141, **He'd volunteered before / Being press-ganged by the *Waffen-SS,* etc.:** As *Reichsführer-SS,* Himmler was constantly trying to expand the mandate and thus the size of the SS. In the occupied territories, particularly in the East, there was no great problem in finding ethnic Germans (and others) who were willing to sign up. However, in the Reich itself many young men were anti-*Waffen-SS* and SS-recruiters were sometimes reduced to scouring the Hitler Youth and obligatory *Arbeitsdienst* (Labour Service) where they virtually press-ganged 'volunteers'. One way of escaping the clutches of the SS was to volunteer first for service in the *Wehrmacht,* whose reputation was less unsavoury, before one was called up. Whether there was in fact much danger of being conscripted into the *Waffen-SS* against one's will in so remote a village as Stephanskirchen is hard to tell. However, the historian Joachim Fest admitted to having joined the *Wehrmacht* for this reason as a young man. His father Johannes was a Catholic school-teacher who lost his position because he refused to join the Party: "Everybody else may join," he said, *"aber ich nicht"*—"but not me"—when his wife pleaded with him to say the right thing for the sake of the family. Johannes also took the view that "one does not volunteer for Hitler's criminal war", although he later told his son: "You weren't wrong—but I was the one who was right." His view was perhaps righter than either of them knew at the time. Fest himself was taken prisoner in France, where the war was conducted, for the most part, with comparative restraint and in accordance with international law. Elsewhere, especially in eastern Europe and the Balkans, this was not the case and, though some notorious atrocities (for example, towards the end of the war in Italy) were 'explained' as military tactics, the post-war myth of the relative decency of the *Wehrmacht* has been gradually dispelled by later historians.

p.142, **The Jews were *different,* etc.:** The series of rather commonplace explanations in this section of the poem offered by the old man, as reported and elaborated on by his interlocutor, for the unprecedented flood of anti-Semitism which culminated in the massacres and calculated genocide of the Second World War have the usual effect, it will be noticed, of softening or reducing the things which really happened. If this is sometimes the result of prevarication and/or ignorance, it was also in fact the case that so much of what happened was indescribable:

> Mere anarchy is loosed upon the world,
> The blood-dimmed tide is loosed, and everywhere
> The ceremony of innocence is drowned…
> (W.B. Yeats, *The Second Coming*)

What really happened—"A gaze blank and pitiless as the sun"—could scarcely be grasped or clearly retained by anyone's memory:

> The darkness drops again; but now I know
> That twenty centuries of stony sleep
> Were vexed to nightmare by a rocking cradle,
> And what rough beast, its hour come round at last,
> Slouches towards Bethlehem to be born?

Hence the very great importance, as is everywhere recognized, of books of witness such as Elie Wiesel's *Night* or—written within a few months of the event—Primo Levi's *If This is a Man,* whose literary strategies have been described (by Anthony Rudolf in *At an Uncertain Hour*) as enabling, paradoxically, "the saying of the unsayable, the bearing witness to the unbearable". Levi himself was (of course) aware of the dangers of his "war on behalf of memory" (Rudolf): "Perhaps one cannot, what is more one must not, understand what happened," he wrote in his

'Afterword' to *If This Is a Man* and *The Truce,* "because to understand is almost to justify." Similarly, to explain is almost to excuse. **Macht mit,** for example, is the virtual equivalent of "Come and join us" or "All for one and one for all!" And **"The socialism of idiots"** was used by the German working-class socialist leader, August Bebel, to dismiss the rise of political anti-Semitism in the late nineteenth century… In *Stephanskirchen (1),* the persona's relative ignorance of the terrible excesses and sheer scale of man's inhumanity in the Second World War is not untypical of his generation—as he acknowledges later. The more aware one becomes of what happened, though, the less sense it makes. The virulence of Hitler's own blind and fanatical anti-Semitism was presumably psychopathic in origin. The superficially 'political' uses to which he and other top Nazis deliberately put their openly racist ideology, on the other hand, and the reactions to it of ordinary sane individuals all over Europe are in some ways more disturbing. Levi epitomizes Auschwitz in a famous few lines: "Driven by thirst, I eyed a fine icicle outside the window, within arm's reach. I opened the window and broke off the icicle but at once a large, heavy guard prowling outside brutally snatched it away from me. *'Warum?'* I asked him in my poor German. *'Hier ist kein warum'* (there is no why here) he replied, pushing me back inside…" And yet if Auschwitz, by common consent, was humanity's nadir, the inexplicable happened everywhere. How *could* anyone 'explain' the spontaneous orgy of anti-Semitic violence and looting which erupted in Vienna, of all places, on the eve of the *Anschluß,* before the German army had as much as arrived, when the Jewish community was so terrified and disoriented that an estimated five hundred people committed suicide? Or even the merciless enthusiasm—taking the SS itself by surprise—with which the local inhabitants of less sophisticated areas in the Ukraine and the Baltic states, for example, participated in public massacres in the market-places of villages and towns, or in municipal gardens and recreation spots, until Himmler's deputy, Reinhard Heydrich, sensing an opportunity, ordered his men to encourage townsfolk and peasantry to begin "attempts at self-cleansing on the part of anti-communist or anti-Semitic elements", permitting a further spate of atrocities?

Elsewhere, it was the political élite which was ready to take advantage of Hitler's lethal brew of intense racism and equally intense nationalism. For example, in Romania—Germany's ally from 1940/41 onward—where much of the country's administration, under the leadership of General Ion Antonescu (or the *Conducator,* as he was known), was already anti-Semitic: "Romanian anti-Semitism had been a matter of international concern as far back as the nineteenth century; now, under the aegis of National Socialist Germany, the country's rulers saw the chance for radical measures of the kind the democracies had always prevented them from undertaking" (M. Mazower, *Hitler's Empire).* The result, in Romania as elsewhere, was previously unimaginable violence directed against civilians, and especially the Jews. In less than twenty-four hours, on 28/29 June 1941, for example, between 13,000 and 15,000 people died during the enforced 'evacuation' of the border town of Jassy. The doors of Christian houses in the town were marked with a cross to distinguish them, and soldiers, gendarmes, policemen, and hundreds of civilians rampaged through the streets, broke into houses and brought their occupants back under arrest to police headquarters, where more than 1,000 were gunned down in the grounds when the Germans opened fire at random. Many Jews were killed or attacked wherever they were found. Thousands of others died of dehydration in the overcrowded trains transporting them in the summer heat out of Romania into German-occupied Ukraine. When Romanian and German troops finally took Odessa (in October 1941), a delayed-action Soviet mine blew up the Romanian commander and sixty soldiers. By this time, the identification of the Jews with Bolshevism and with partisans and saboteurs in general was virtually routine (although it had almost no basis in fact) and thousands were immediately hanged or shot throughout the night in a spontaneous 'punishment action'. The next day, Antonescu—one of the *Führer's* favourite strongmen—ordered that a further 18,000 'Communists' should be killed: i.e. reprisals of about 300 to one. In fact, an estimated 25–30,000 Jews were rounded up with the help of Ukrainian auxiliaries and shot or burned alive in warehouses at Dalnic, ten miles west of the city. By the end of the occupation, more than 300,000 Romanian and Ukrainian Jews are estimated to have perished.

In the end, the only 'explanation' for such appallingly inhuman—and all *too* human—behaviour which is not also an excuse for it (and these, of course, are only a few of countless possible examples from the Second World War, not to mention what came after it in Stalinist Russia, Communist China, Cambodia, Rwanda, Iraq, and elsewhere) may be that offered by Joseph Brodsky in his magisterial yet disarming open letter to the President of Czechoslovakia, Vaclav Havel, *Letter to a President* (1993), in which he frankly mocks "the premise, however qualified, of man's goodness, of his notion of himself as either a fallen or a possible angel". Having lived the first thirty-two years of his life under Russian Communist totalitarianism—which he saw less as a political problem than "a breakdown of humanity, a human problem, a problem of our species"—Brodsky tended to the view instead that much of the twentieth century might serve as a reminder of Original Sin: "not such a heady concept", he explains—"translated into common parlance, it means that man is dangerous…" Brodsky saw the commonest source of this danger in what one might call "unenlightened self-interest", and comments that, at the very least, "it seems more prudent to build society on the premise that man is evil than the premise of his goodness… Maybe the real civility, Mr President, is not to create illusions."

The reason why this explanation is not an excuse is that, although always a danger to himself and his fellow creatures, man is also and at all times, no matter what the conditions, endowed with free will. As Brodsky's letter implies throughout, each one of us can always *choose*—between barbarism and mutual tolerance, between the rule of the strongest or the most ruthlessly ambitious and 'live and let live'. Johannes Fest could not have put this more clearly: "Everybody else may join—*aber ich nicht.*" The human ability to categorize, to decide on *which* devices and desires we mean to follow, to sort reality into mental boxes such as 'us' and 'them', if it helps to preserve our sanity, is capable as well of permitting us to view as 'normal' acts of individual cruelty, mass-murder or mass-destruction. The springs of pity, it plainly seems, can be turned off at will—individually or, more often, collectively. In other words—to anticipate 'The Dance of Death' *(No.3,* section 5)—"I *think,* therefore I *act".* As Hitler and Goebbels clearly understood: hence the enormous pains they took not only with what Hitler in *Mein Kampf* called "spiritual and physical terror" but with propaganda, rhetoric and stage-management, each of which is a form of art—debased and perverted in this case but practised nevertheless by men who regarded themselves as, among other things, artists and connoisseurs whose duty and mission it was to defend German "richness and civilization" against the machinations of international Jewry and the hordes of Asia. Individual and collective feelings of every sort—from pity to heartlessness or sadism, from euphoria to loathing, from ecstasy to real or apparent madness—occur or run to excess within certain frameworks. The more we allow these frameworks, or our 'devices', to be manipulated and perverted, the more manipulable and perverse will be our desires. The demonstrable fact, in other words, that human thinking permits or forbids—facilitates or hinders—clarifies or confuses human action matters immensely: "The world is *led* by mind."

p.143, **Mercy or pity was mere Christian weakness:** Orders and directives such as that of Hans Frank, the Nazi governor of much of Poland, to his staff with regard to the *Judenfrage* (Jewish question)—"Gentlemen, I must ask you to rid yourselves of all feelings of pity"—became commonplace during the Third Reich, many of them deriving directly or ultimately from Hitler himself. As a connoisseur of German culture, Borges was at first as distressed and puzzled by this as anyone. However, his excellent story, *Deutsches Requiem,* is a powerful study of how a highly educated and civilized concentration camp commander, Otto Dietrich zur Linde, became convinced that "Essentially, Nazism is an act of morality, a purging of corrupted humanity… The world was dying of Judaism and from that sickness of Judaism, the faith of Jesus: we taught it violence and the faith of the sword." Thus not only **Perverts and numbskulls** strove to exterminate the Jews but cultivated intellectuals such as Borges' hero (he sees himself as heroic) and anyone else to whom, for whatever reason, the Nazis' ideology and propaganda appealed. These ranged from young Romantic adventurers *(So why not go,* he'd thought, *and* make *things change!)* such as Odilo Globocnik in Poland, who became the driving power behind Operation Reinhard, which killed 1,200,000 Polish Jews in 1941–42 alone, to cold-blooded SS bureaucrats such as Eichmann—proud to the last of his organizational efficiency—or the highly intelligent lawyer, Werner Best, who was one of the first to contemplate racial extermination openly. Ambitious men such as these relished the career opportunity which the administrative challenges of the *Judenfrage* offered them, and were out to impress their bosses (above all, Himmler). Beneath them, there was the whole bureaucracy of *Ja*-sayers who, as Raul Hilberg showed in *The Destruction of the European Jews*, were knowingly involved in the genocide. Hilberg's pages on 'The Perpetrators' (ch.7) include a convincing account of how ordinary white-collar workers persuaded themselves that what they were doing was at least not bad—or not *as* bad as what others were doing—and in any case no more than part of a large-scale, justifiable and *necessary* operation… Even those who did the killing were to draw a sharp line "between killings pursuant to orders and killings induced by desire. In the former case a man was thought to have overcome the 'weaknesses' of 'Christian morality'; in the latter case he was overcome by his own baseness".

p.143, *'Pleasure generates submission':* This begins a series of quotations from *Words in the Dark* ('Paradise Island', 'Heine's Grave', 'The Park on Sunday') and *From Now to Then* ('Lazarus')—on themes relating to this part of the poem.

p.144, **How nations vie like firms—how firms deploy / Their workforce like a peace-time army:** Hitler himself had little knowledge of or interest in economics, and tended to prioritize short-term policies which amounted, especially in the East, to not much more than plundering occupied territories. Otherwise, the ease with which the belligerent mentality can mesh with the business mentality and the latter feed into the former so as to cooperate in an actual war-effort was everywhere apparent during the Third Reich. "The point about really big business", Eric Hobsbawm drily observed, "is that it can come to terms with any regime that does not actually expropriate it, and that any regime must come to terms with it." In fact, the Nazis' elimination of the Communist Party in 1933 and their promise to do the same with elections and free trade unions and to defy Versailles and the League of Nations by re-arming was all profoundly attractive to the likes of Krupp, United Steel and IG Farben. At a meeting in February 1933 hosted by Dr Schach, Hitler's chief financial expert, Hitler and Göring announced their intentions. Krupp and others were enthusiastic in expressing their "gratitude for having given us so clear a picture". Dr Schach then passed the hat on behalf of the Party: "I collected three million marks," he recalled at Nuremberg…

With free trade unions out of the way, management felt much freer in dealing with its workforce: "Indeed, the fascist 'leadership principle' *[Führerprinzip]* was what most bosses and business executives applied to their subordinates in their own businesses, and fascism gave it authoritative justification" (Hobsbawm). If peace seemed initially preferable, once war had broken out, firms like IG Farben took full advantage of it: "Following close behind the troops, they dismissed Jewish employees and accepted Nazis on company boards in return for being allowed to take over non-German businesses" (Mazower).

In western Europe many businesses prospered during the war, as businessmen saw little point in not cooperating with the Germans. However, in the East the Germans and above all Göring's enormous Reichswerke HG took over everything they possibly could. By mid-1944 the Reichswerke HG, with over 400,000 employees from Austria to Russia, working in coal, mineral extraction, chemicals, armaments, iron and steel and other metals, and manufacturing in general, was probably the largest industrial conglomerate in the world. Göring attempted to take over western European industries as well, but experienced businessmen, bankers and very large firms such as Unilever and Philips saw the war as an opportunity to build on their long-established relationships, and he was less successful. Moreover, the *Wehrmacht* and even Hitler took the pragmatic view that as long as Belgian, Dutch and Danish industry continued to produce what the Germans wanted (about 20,000 Dutch firms accepted German contracts, for example), there was no need to interfere. After about 1940, increasing chaos and partial or piecemeal solutions in the absence of any long-term economic policy somewhat weakened Göring's position. But it is clear that the *Reichsmarschall* and former Luftwaffe ace would in peacetime have made an ace businessman.

p.144, *'History is to blame':* In the opening episode of *Ulysses,* the condescending English student of the Irish, Haines (cp. note on p.110, "He found he cared / and didn't care about do's/don'ts"), explains to Stephen Dedalus and Buck Mulligan, "We feel in England that we have treated you rather unfairly. It seems that history is to blame." This is, of course, one of the commonest of excuses in the guise of an explanation: "God, isn't he dreadful? [Mulligan] said frankly. A ponderous Saxon. He thinks you're not a gentleman. God, these bloody English. Bursting with money and indigestion. Because he comes from Oxford." Mulligan's "British Beatitudes" are well known: "Beer, beef, business, bibles, bulldogs, battleships, buggery and bishops." By adapting *The Odyssey* in the ways it does and at the time it did (1914–21), *Ulysses* implicitly and explicitly shows that there are other, more enlightened forms of 'heroism' than the military. In the Nighttown episode, Stephen addresses the Hue and Cry pursuing himself and Bloom:

STEPHEN: *(With elaborate gestures, breathing deeply and slowly)* You are my guests. The uninvited. By virtue of the fifth of George and seventh of Edward. History to blame....
PRIVATE COMPTON: He doesn't half want a thick ear, the blighter. Biff him, Harry.
LORD TENNYSON: *(In Union Jack blazer and cricket flannels, bareheaded, flowingbearded)* Theirs not to reason why...
PRIVATE CARR: *(To Stephen)* What's that you're saying about my king?...
EDWARD THE SEVENTH: *(Slowly, solemnly but indistinctly)* Peace, perfect peace...
PRIVATE CARR: *(To Stephen)* Say it again.
STEPHEN: *(Nervous, friendly, pulls himself up)* I understand your point of view, though I have no king myself for the moment... A discussion is difficult down here. But this is the point. You die for your country, suppose. *(He places his arm on Private Carr's sleeve)* Not that I wish it for you. But I say: let my country die for me. Up to the present it has done so. I don't want it to die. Damn death. Long live life!
EDWARD THE SEVENTH: *(Levitates over heaps of slain in the garb and with the halo of Joking Jesus, a white jujube in his phosphorescent face)*
>My methods are new and are causing surprise:
>To make the blind see I throw dust in their eyes...

BLOOM: *(To Stephen)* Come home. You'll get into trouble.
STEPHEN: *(Swaying)* I don't avoid it. He provokes my intelligence...
PRIVATE CARR: Here. What are you saying about my king?
STEPHEN: *(Throws up his hands)* O, this is too monotonous! Nothing. He wants my money and my life for some brutish empire of his. Money I haven't. *(He searches his pockets vaguely)* Gave it to someone.

p.147, **They wanted peace, not war, to have the last word:** The illusion that war can lead to any sort of lasting peace is at least as old as the 'Heroique Stanza'—thus named by Dryden in the title of his poem on the death of Oliver Cromwell—which *Stephanskirchen (1)* and *(2)* adapt to their own purposes: "Our former Cheifs", says Dryden, were all war-mongers—

> Warre, our consumption, was their gainfull trade,
> We inward bled whilst they prolong'd our pain:
> He fought to end our fighting, and assaid
> To stanch the blood by breathing of the vein.

In Shakespeare this futile self-deception dominates the words and deeds of assorted rulers, from Henry IV—the guilt-ridden initiator of approximately one hundred years of civil war—to the ruthless politico, Henry VII, who aspired to end them:

> In God's name, cheerly on, courageous friends,
> To reap the harvest of perpetual peace
> By this one bloody trial of sharp war.
>   *Richard III,* V.ii

p.147, **And yet Ernst Jandl, etc.**: Ernst Jandl (1925–2000) was a leading Viennese avant-garde poet and dramatist. The extraordinary story of his war-time experiences has recently been clarified by the publication of *Briefe aus dem Krieg* (Letters from the War, 2005), which illustrates how difficult—but not impossible—it was for young men in the wrong place at the wrong time to avoid fighting for Hitler. Although not primarily thought of as a war poet, Jandl's conscription into the German army in 1943, after finishing school, left its mark on his poetry and also his life. Cp. *after jandl*.

p.148, **Or what he'd done and not done—must have seen...**: Many examples of what the old man might have seen as a young soldier in the East have already been mentioned in these notes: the effects of political and historical anti-Semitism in Vienna, the Baltic states, Poland (by the end of 1942 public unease in Germany itself about the SS's—secret—'Final Solution of the Jewish Question' was being fed by soldiers returning from the East), and Romania and the Ukraine. Even one of the most notorious Ukrainian atrocities, at Babi Yar—a ravine near Kiev, where over 33,000 Jews were machine-gunned in a matter of days by the SS and Ukrainian guards—was in fact a 'punishment action' demanded by the *Wehrmacht* after delayed Soviet mines blew up some of the newly installed military administration of the city... Hilberg, in his classic work, lists numerous shootings and other war-crimes in eastern Europe which the *Wehrmacht* either demanded or was involved in, or at which soldiers were present as voyeurs (some of them taking photographs)—a practice which some officers attempted to prevent. As for the Russian campaign itself, its horrors will never be fully documented. The conditions in which Soviet prisoners of war had to be kept, for example, confounded even old and experienced soldiers: "So unbelievably many have starved to death", wrote one sixty-five-year-old former Wilhelmine officer in his diary in March 1942 of the 30,000 POWs he and his 200 men had to guard with neither sufficient provisions nor medical supplies nor proper accommodation: "Of millions of prisoners only a few thousands are capable of working... Many are ill with typhus and the rest are so weak and pitiful that they can't work in this state." As conditions behind the front continued to deteriorate, cases of cannibalism were dealt with by shooting the offenders ("The men there are beasts" was Hitler's comment—"a bestial degeneration of humanity *[Menscheitsentartung]*"...) Altogether, it took only a few months, in the winter of 1941–42 for the master race to allow more than two million Soviet POWs to perish in such crowded holding pens, out of sight and largely unrecorded. More than a million more died by the end of the war—most of them under *Wehrmacht* supervision. Small wonder that German generals themselves believed, as recent research has discovered, that "the *Führer* wishes for the decimation of the Slavic masses". Of course, such research might in general be less necessary, were it not for "the universal (and therefore 'banal') human tendency" noted above, to normalize what happened—as even slips of the tongue such as **"I was a long way east / Of here by then. And didn't see a thing..."** (p.140) unconsciously illustrate.

p.153, ***surfacetranslation (1)***: Jandl's own *oberflächenübersetzung,* on which this poem is based, is of Wordsworth's "My heart leaps up when I behold / A rainbow in the sky": *mai hart lieb zapfen eibe hold / er renn bohr in sees kai*, etc. The idea is varied somewhat in ***surfacetranslation (2)*** by using a (shortened) poem of Jandl's own as the 'original' and also by preserving its word-play—on

Philosophie—albeit with a different emphasis: *viel* means 'many' and *vieh* means 'pigs' (in the sense of disgusting people) or 'cattle'.

p.157, **otto's mops:** The German word *Mops* means pug-dog. In Jandl's poem, however, Otto *addresses* his dog as Mops—here taken to be his name for it.

p.162, **light and reft:** One of the 'thiggest contusions' of right and left was faked into the very name of the Nazi Party. After the Party had come to power in 1933 and the independent Left—the Communists and free trade unions—had been destroyed, there was much clamour for a 'second revolution', i.e. for a radical National *Socialism,* which would destroy the Right as well. The phrase "the second revolution" had been coined by Ernst Röhm, the Chief of Staff of the *ca.* two-million-strong SA. But Hitler's guiding political principle of exploiting rather than directly opposing powerful institutions—business, the Army, the President—led him, in June 1934, to purge the SA and remove Röhm entirely: see iv, *Death and Brandner Caspar,* 'Postscript'. For Hitler, Nazi socialist slogans had become no more than a means of keeping the masses (including six million unemployed) on his side on his way to power. And he in fact continued to woo the workers in one way and another… As for Jandl, he seems never to have been taken in by the Party's weasel words. While still at school, he had successfully avoided Hitler Youth meetings and become adept at keeping his head down. Even after conscription he managed—by taking every military training course available, pleading nervous disorders, and going AWOL (twice)—to get out of active service. Needless to say, some parts of this strategy were extremely dangerous but, wiser than his eighteen years, Jandl took every advantage he could of the growing disorder of the last two years of the war. Eventually, in November 1944, he was sent to the western front. This was, relatively speaking, a piece of luck since his plan was to defect if he possibly could, and on the eastern front no one defected to the Russians. As it was, he saw three months of front-line action before he managed to cross the line to the Americans without getting shot. Jandl later explained to his editor, Klaus Siblewski, that he had felt buoyed up through these adventures by his sense of himself as someone with poetry to write, on the one hand, and by his family on the other, to whom the *Letters* referred to above were addressed in such a way as to relieve them of worry, as far as was possible… After being sent by the Americans to POW camp at Stockbridge in England, he found himself more or less out of danger. He became camp interpreter and improved his English, which he then studied on returning to Vienna in 1946, where he worked as a grammar-school teacher until his writings permitted him to retire.

p.164, **i have nothing / to make a poem:** Ernst Jandl's writing is in many respects an act of existential anti-heroism, as this formulation of its contents indicates. Although he defected with flying colours, the war continued to affect both his physical and mental health. He described himself, with typical black humour, as a pessimist with a sense of black humour. By way of comment on his un- and even anti-poetic poetry, he explained that the war didn't sing. The section '*krieg und so*' ('war and all that') in his celebrated book, *Laut und Luise* (1966), gives some small hint of the horror and sheer word-destroying mechanical racket of the front. Elsewhere he wrote: "… he always had something to say, and he always knew one could say it in this way or in that way; and so he was never concerned with what he was saying but with how he said it, since there is no alternative to what one has to say but an unlimited number of possible ways of saying it. there are poets who say all sorts of things, and always in the same way. to write like this never interested him; because in the end there is only one thing to be said, but over and over again, always in new ways."

Without wishing to detract from Ernst Jandl's lifelong opposition of brilliant formal invention and pitch-black humour to the nothingness of everything, including the chaos of mechanized war, one can enter a plea as well for singing—not, perhaps, *of* but *over against* it. If things in themselves have (as *contents* implies) no inherent meaning but if human consciousness nevertheless gives them, with the help of one's ability to perceive, experience, think and express oneself, what meanings they appear to have, then when reality itself doesn't sing, can not the poet? Or can not anyone? And over against anything? After all, what W.B. Yeats wrote of old men in *Byzantium* is true, if less obviously true, of men and women of any age:

> An aged man is but a paltry thing,
> A tattered coat upon a stick, unless
> Soul clap its hands and sing, and louder sing
> For every tatter in its mortal dress.

p.164, ***Death and Dr Hornbrook:*** In Robert Burns's humorously ironic, tough-minded poem (which includes a self-portrait as a not-so-innocent by-stander), Death complains to the poet of being cheated of his victims, on the one hand, by the quack Dr Hornbrook's infallible medicines—against which his dart and scythe are helpless—and, on the other, by his activities as a poisoner:

> This night I'm free to tak my aith
>   That Hornbrook's skill
> Has clad a score i' their last claith,
>   By drap an' pill.

For example, bearing in mind Burns's wife's wry comment, "Oor Rab should hae had twa wives":

> A bonnie lass, ye kenned her name,
> Some ill-brewn drink had hoved her wame;
> She trusts hersel', to hide the shame,
>   In Hornbrook's care;
> Horn sent her off to her lang hame,
>   To hide it there.

> Etc.

p.164, **Franz, Ritter von Kobell:** Franz von Kobell (1803–1882) became a professor of mineralogy in Munich in 1826 but is nowadays mainly remembered for his verses and tales in Bavarian dialect. ***Die Gschicht von Brandner-Kasper*** is a ***Schwank*** or humorous narrative of the legendary practical-joker variety. A *Schwank* is also an unlikely or tall tale of any kind, or a theatrical farce.

p.166, **At nearby Gindlalm:** Gindlalm was and still is a *Wirtshaus* for hikers and locals as well as a working Alpine farm at the top of the path from Schliersee to Tegernsee. If one turns left after Gindlalm there is a path across and down to the other end of the Schliersee through a village called Neuhaus. As the war drew to a close with the unstoppable advance of the Red Army, Hans Frank, who, as the Nazi governor of much of Poland, had played host, as it were, to four of the six main killing centres of the Final Solution—not to mention his part in the wholesale slaughter of Polish civilians in the General Government (Poland itself and Polish culture were to disappear)—made an undignified run for it and ended up, with his family and closest entourage, at his villa in Neuhaus, which is nowadays a quiet resort. One has the impression that many top Nazis were adept at evading the reality of the war around them. In the former residence of the Polish kings at Wawel and in a private castle of his own near Kraków, whose Jewish population fell from 68,000 to 500, Frank had held court from 1941–45 with pomp and extravagance, surrounded by his family and numerous hangers-on, patronizing artists of all kinds, hosting concerts, and attending the opera. As one witness at Nuremberg said, Frank's court was "an oasis where no one noticed the war", and "even short-hand typists led a life such as one reads about in the Arabian Nights". Frank's fur-draped wife, Brigitte—herself a short-hand typist and her husband's former secretary—considered herself the 'Queen of Poland' and when the Americans arrived in Neuhaus to find the Franks holding court again among masterpieces by Leonardo, Rembrandt, Rubens, Dürer and others, which they had confiscated "for safe-keeping", she welcomed the end of hostilities and looked forward to a "normal life", confident she had done no wrong. At his trial in Nuremberg, her self-pitying, deluded and theatrical husband admitted some of his crimes—as witnessed by W.L. Shirer, who in *The Rise and Fall of the Third Reich* (1960) described him as "having become in the end contrite and, as he said, having rediscovered God, whose forgiveness he begged". Nevertheless, the Americans hanged him. The Café-Pension Bergfrieden, where the General Government had its last headquarters, is now a wellness centre.

p.169, **as drunk / As Tam o'Shanter:** Robert Burns's highly inventive, humorous and intelligent narrative poem, one of the finest of its age, became increasingly popular—together with his love-songs and other poems (though not, officially, his bawdy *Merry Muses of Caledonia*)— throughout the nineteenth century for reasons which have as much to do with the nature of Romanticism (its exaggerated interest in the 'primitive', in the supernatural, in almost any form of anti-rationalism) as with the actual qualities of Burns's writing. In fact, a hard-headed sense of reality distinguished Burns (as, later, Heine) from most of his contemporaries. From this point of view, one can read *Tam o'Shanter* as implicitly posing the question shortly to be asked by Brandner Caspar's grandson, **What really happened?** (p.171). All anyone *knew*, after all, was that Tam got drunk and came home late through very bad weather on Maggie, who lost her tail. As with Brandner Caspar's version of events, and those of Balthazar and Melchior later, the questions remain of who said who did what and why.

p.169, **To My Bed:** Much of this poem-within-the-poem has been borrowed from Burns's *Verses to My Bed*. Surprisingly, considering its subject—a stroke of Burnsian genius—*Verses to My Bed* is in English and not in his native lowland Scots. As usual, this cramps his style—which is perhaps some slight excuse for the changes here made as if by the persona on behalf of Brandner Caspar, a character who would have been much to Burns's taste.

p.173, **"What is truth?":** Amid the tangle of lies, deceptions and self-deceptions which we generally regard, or pretend to regard, as everyday communication—and then as history—certain individuals have always been remarkable for their refusal to play the game. As narrated in *John XVIII. 36–38,* when Jesus was questioned in the Roman judgement hall by Pilate as to whether he was the king of the Jews, he answered: "My kingdom is not of this world: if my kingdom were of this world, then would my servants fight… To this end was I born, and for this cause came I into the world, that I should bear witness unto the truth. Every one that is of the truth heareth my voice." It was in reply to this that Pilate asked him, "What is truth?" (cp. also, *No.3*, section 1, ii, 'Pontius Pilate's Wife, Procula…'). When Stephen Dedalus is questioned by Cranly towards the end of *A Portrait of the Artist as a Young Man* as to whether he felt sure that Jesus was not the Son of God, Stephen answers, "I am not at all sure of it… He is more like a son of God than a son of Mary." As for Pilate, he behaved like a son of Rome and, handing Jesus over to his accusers, washed his hands of him.

p.174, **With the death as well, some years before, / Of Georg, his firstborn:** If there had in fact been a Brandner family tomb at Gmund (cp. p.170), on the opposite side of the Tegernsee to Wiessee, its later inscriptions at that time might have informed the reader of the following dates of birth and death:

Traudl Brandner	1740—1794
Georg	1768—1799
Brandner Caspar	1724—1804 *(missing presumed dead)*
Balthazar	1745—1828
Toni	1770—1830
Melchior	1750—1840

If Toni returned from the war in 1805, Brandner Caspar's grandson was presumably born between then and about 1810. According to the *Postscript* (p.177), he died without issue in 1870, leaving von Kobell free to publish his own version of whatever happened.

p.179, **Case Studies, 1941–1945:** As its title implies, this section of the *Self-Portrait as…* keeps as close as may be to historical reality as represented by its main sources. In addition to the writings of Hilberg, Levi, Mazower, Shirer and others already mentioned, these include: Curzio Malaparte, *Kaputt* (no. *(vii)*); *Das Daimler-Benz Buch,* ed. A. Ebbinghaus, 1987 (no.s *(xiii)* and *(xiv)*); *Konzentrationslager Dokument F321,* ed. P. Neitzke and M. Weinmann, 1988 (no. *(xviii)*); and, above all, Claude Lanzmann's *Shoah* (no.s *(ix), (x), (xii), (xv)* and *(xvi)*). Moreover, the section as a whole owes a particular debt to W.G. Sebald for its passages in prose or what one might think of as the 'case histories' which follow each poem. If *after jandl* can be read as the white-collar worker's acknowledgement of the significance of his wife's remarks towards the end of *Stephanskirchen (1)*, i.e. as a portrayal of his own of another man's efforts to face the truth; and if *Death and Brandner Caspar* represents a consideration of how "thugs or rogues or fools" and others seem capable in general of explaining or justifying their crimes or other misdeeds both to themselves and those around them; *Case Studies* goes on to recreate or re-observe a series of real people in a direct attempt at last to break down, or rather *out of,* the state of denial regarding the works and words of the Second World War in which many or even most of us still find ourselves, as Sebald patiently and tirelessly demonstrates. Like Sebald as well, the section concentrates for the most part (though not only) on the 'Final Solution of the Jewish Question', as Hitler himself appears to have called it.

p.191, **but Daimler-Benz / was worse than Buchenwald:** By the end of 1944, an estimated 420,000 prisoners were working for the German war economy, and the SS and German industry were co-operating in their exploitation. Other firms which used forced labour were Heinkel, BMW, Krupp, Volkswagen, Siemens, Porsche... In *The Drowned and the Saved*, Primo Levi mentions that IG Farben actually owned Auschwitz-Monowitz.

p.194, ***diavoli neri:*** Dante's most extended treatment of devils is to be found in *Inferno,* Cantos XXI–XXII, where—perhaps by chance (if there is such a thing as chance in such matters)—the Hell of his poem resembles Müller's verbal and Lanzmann's visual descriptions of Auschwitz in a number of ways. More specifically, the mocking devils of Canto XXI are quoted by Primo Levi in ch.2 of *If This is a Man* as an obliquely ironic comment on the guard who epitomized Auschwitz in the words *"Hier ist kein warum".* As one might expect of an Italian author, there are many other allusions, direct and indirect, to Dante in Levi's writings. The great difference, of course, is that Dante took the view that the inmates of his Hell were tormented *justly:* that is, in Dante's mind at least, there was every reason "why" they should suffer.

p.195, **"Not now, Brigitte," he ordered: "Hans must wait…":** In spite (and perhaps because) of their intimacy with Hitler, the pretentious Frank and his uncultivated *Königin* (cp. note on p.166, "At nearby Gindlalm") were not popular in higher Nazi circles. Goebbels described the former in his diary as "half-mad" and noted caustically, "Frank does not govern, he rules"—hence, no doubt, the use of **Frank-Reich** (France), among Frank's peers, to refer to the *Generalgouvernement*… Frank's greatest enemy was Himmler who, by claiming (with Hitler's support) total responsibility for the Jewish question, was at liberty to ride rough-shod over Frank's authority. This irritated Frank intensely and he paid surprise visits to the death-camps of Belzec, Lublin-Majdanek and even Auschwitz (which was beyond his pale), only to be fobbed off. When he complained that he could get no detailed information as to what was going on, Hitler is said to have told him, "You can well imagine that there are executions going on—of insurgents. Apart from that, I do not know anything. Why don't you speak to Heinrich Himmler about it?"… The Franks appear at length in Curzio Malaparte's *Kaputt:* "[The Queen's] whole face was thrust toward the food heaped on precious Meissen plates, toward the scented wine glittering through Bohemian crystal, and on it, around her nostrils, quivered an expression of insatiable greed, almost of gluttonous rage… *Perhaps she was hungry?"*

p.198, **much has been discovered in the meantime:** Although Steinberg only gives his initial, "Dr K.", for example, is identified by Hermann Langbein (in *People in Auschwitz*) as Hans Wilhelm König, a young man who took his profession seriously: "On the other hand, König attempted to learn at the expense of the prisoners". Langbein describes König as otherwise courteous, intelligent, industrious and "not inhuman with regard to details". But "when he was no longer interested in the course of the disease, he sent his patient to the gas chamber".

As for **the likes of Mengele,** Dr Josef Mengele conducted painful examinations and sometimes multiple operations—many of them patently nonsensical—on twins and other children, with the aim of demonstrating racial characteristics. Mengele—like many other prominent Nazis, a man of ruthless personal ambition but no great ability—did not hesitate to kill such children if this suited his purpose. One notorious experiment involved dripping aggressive chemicals into children's eyes in order to change their colour to the 'ideal' Aryan blue.

The doctors at Auschwitz and other concentration camps were primarily supposed to attend to the medical needs of the SS. However, it soon became clear that such camps afforded unique conditions for medical research, in the pursuit of which the doctors were enthusiastically supported by Himmler, who in a letter to the egregious Dr Rascher of Dachau "personally assumed the responsibility for supplying asocial individuals and criminals who deserve only to die for [your] experiments" (this was one of the many letters signed in fact by Rudolf Brandt, Himmler's adjutant—see *(i)*). Rascher's field of investigation was into the effects of air pressure and lack of oxygen at high altitudes on behalf of the Luftwaffe. Many of his human guinea pigs died in unbearable pain as a result of experiments of almost incredible cruelty. Likewise with Rascher's experiments regarding the effects of extreme cold, in which he was assisted by two academics from the University of Kiel. A report was drawn up and a conference held on *Medical Questions in Marine and Winter Emergencies*, at which, in W.L. Shirer's words, "ninety-five German scientists, including some of the most eminent men in the field, participated, and though the three doctors left no doubt that a good many human beings had been done to death in the experiments, there were no questions put as to this and no protests therefore made." Shirer, who was present at the Nuremberg Trials, summed up this particular "tale of horror" as follows: "Although the 'experiments' were conducted by fewer than two hundred murderous quacks—albeit some of them held eminent posts in the medical world—their criminal work was known to thousands of leading physicians of the Reich, not a single one of whom, so far as the record shows, ever uttered the slightest public protest."

p.200, **a thousand Jewish women in Ravensbrück / could be shipped to Sweden:** In his 'Report to the WJC', Masur recorded his surprise at the absence of any personal passion in Himmler regarding the Jews. Himmler claimed always to have favoured expulsion but the world had refused to accept more Jewish refugees. The crematoria were solely a health and security measure, he insisted: "The treatment in the camps was severe but just." One gets the impression from Masur's report that Himmler believed his own lies—or some of them. Of the seven thousand women eventually released from Ravensbrück, for example, Mazower remarks: "They were the lucky ones. In Ravensbrück itself, the site of medical experiments, forced sterilizations and unspeakable acts of sadism, systematic gassing and other killing had been going on for several months"—as Himmler must have known.

p.200, **In twelve mad minutes twelve years of power imploded:** Himmler died, in spite of frantic efforts to pump his stomach, twelve minutes after biting on his cyanide capsule, on 23 May 1945, the gutter having come to power, in Alan Bullock's memorable words *(Hitler, A Study in Tyranny,* p.270) twelve years earlier, in 1933.

p.201, ***They sowed the wind, etc.:*** Cp. *Hosea VIII.7:* "For they have sown the wind, and they shall reap the whirlwind." Harris's statement of his mission as Commander-in-Chief of Bomber Command—a position to which he was appointed in February 1942—elevates himself, by implication, to the position not only of God's prophet, or approximate equivalent, but of His agent. This "rather childish delusion" is not helped by the insensitivity of the Biblical reference: Hosea was threatening the Jews themselves with destruction for their impiety in a blast of indignant righteousness resounding with such verses as "Israel hath cast off the thing that is good: the enemy shall pursue him", or "Israel is swallowed up: now shall they be among the Gentiles as a vessel wherein is no pleasure"… As luck would have it, the church at Stephanskirchen was empty when it was bombed, presumably by accident. A partly happy accident, then—whose absurdity, however, is entirely characteristic of the indiscriminate and more often murderous inaccuracy of any such war-time "whirlwind". Harris's strident self-assertiveness and fascination with destruction in general put one in mind of an ill-treated schoolboy with more talented brothers. In 1908, when he was sixteen, his father (who was in the Indian Civil Service) gave him the choice of army or colonies. He went to Rhodesia (Zimbabwe), where he flourished. Later he leap-frogged the army by joining the Royal Flying Corps and serving with distinction in the First World War. Back in the colonies, he cultivated an interest in bombing, first in India, then in Mesopotamia (Iraq, Syria) and Persia (Iran). In Mesopotamia, he was involved in developing the same sort of delayed-action bombs which were dropped together with high-explosive and incendiary bombs in the Second World War with the intention of blowing up rescuers and fire-fighters. While putting down Mesopotamian insurrections against the British with the help of such new devices, Harris famously remarked, "The only thing the Arab understands is the heavy hand." The lessons of his English schooldays were clearly not lost on him and, as a senior officer in Palestine in 1936, he recommended "one 250 lb or 500 lb bomb in each village that speaks out of turn". By the early 1940s these had become 4,000 lb and 8,000 lb bombs in their hundreds and the villages heavily populated German cities.

p.203, **"Just give them sufficient money // To keep them happy, Lord…":** This outburst of apparent cynicism (cp., however, "Just give me sufficient money // And please restore my health" from 'Lazarus'—"In fact, dear Lord, if you wouldn't mind"—in *From Now to Then,* p.22) will seem less unreasonable if one considers, for example, the effects of economic conditions after 1929 on the next two decades or so of history: "Would fascism have become very significant in world history but for the Great Slump? Probably not" (Hobsbawm, *Age of Extremes).* During the worst period of the Slump in 1932–33, 44% of German workers were unemployed. After the Nazis came to power in 1933, they succeeded by a wide variety of means (one of the most important of which was rearmament) in becoming the only Western government to eliminate unemployment as a major problem. The relative importance attached to money and genocide in the '30s and '40s can perhaps be gauged from the fact that when details of the Final Solution began to reach the outside world during 1941–42, "throughout the process of discovery, the findings, when published, were seldom front-page news" (Hilberg). In other words, almost everyone "lacked the frame of mind and sense of urgency to address the Jewish fate..."—whereas "The Slump was front-page news" *(Stephanskirchen (1),* p.142) as good as everywhere.

p.203, **'The Happy Warrior'**: Wordsworth's remarkable poem, *Character of the Happy Warrior* (1807), presents the career of the "man in arms" not only as a vocation but, potentially, as one of the highest. Endowed with "an inward light / That makes the path before him always bright", exercising "a power / Which is our human nature's highest dower"—namely, to control, subdue and *transmute* pain, fear and bloodshed—Wordsworth's soldier

> Finds comfort in himself and in his cause;
> And, while the mortal mist is gathering, draws
> His breath in confidence of Heaven's applause...

One is reminded, it may be, of the third of Eliot's *Four Quartets:* "So Krishna, when he admonished Arjuna / On the field of battle." And yet, as with the *Bhagavad-Gita*—which can similarly be viewed, up to a point, as an expression of spiritual enlightenment but, in the context of the *Mahabarata,* serves the predominantly worldly purpose of overcoming the hero Arjuna's resistance to slaughtering his relatives in battle *(TLS,* Letters, 8 Sept. 2011)—Wordsworth's alarming misapplication of great ideas illustrates by default the importance of a compassionate *ethical* basis for even the most 'enlightened' states of mind or modes of action. In this respect, it seems that Joseph Brodsky's diagnosis of "unenlightened self-interest" may sometimes in fact apply to beliefs or behaviour which *appear* to be the very opposite (cp. note on p.142, "The Jews were *different*, etc.", especially the last two paragraphs)... It was easier, perhaps, to deceive oneself then, in the English Lake District, than it ought to be in post-twentieth century Europe and America (where, however, variations on the early Christian idea of a 'just war' have been making a worrying re-appearance). Nevertheless, in less sheltered places than Grasmere, the early decades of the nineteenth century foreshadowed not only the disasters but some of the horrors of later history—as witnessed, for example, by Goya, who produced, between about 1810 and 1815 (i.e. only a few years after Wordsworth wrote his poem) his *Disastres de la Guerra* on the Spanish guerrilla war against the French. Whereas *Character of the Happy Warrior* simply fails to consider the morality or immorality—the justice or injustice—of either war in general or any war in particular, Goya confronts the viewer with scenes which compel him to do just that—and to answer or admit that he *cannot* answer the same question, inscribed beneath one of the series' cruellest images, as Primo Levi asked the guard in Auschwitz: *Por qué* (Why?)... The belief that any war should only be fought in self-defence—and as a last resort, when all else has failed—is at least defensible, although "justified" or "justifiable" might be a less inflammatory and self-congratulatory epithet than just "just". It goes—or ought to go—without saying that the wholesale murder of civilians, or 'total war', is nothing but wholesale murder and, as such, indefensible.

p.204, ...**gave rich and poor** / **The *Wirtschaftswunder*:** As Sebald and others have pointed out, forgetting (cp. **we *must* deceive ourselves, forget...**) was one of the prerequisites of the *Wirtschaftswunder,* as was the more or less deliberate cultivation of insensibility. In his quietly unnerving way, Sebald also lists: "the scrapping of outdated industrial complexes—an operation performed with brutal efficiency by the bomber squadrons—but also something less often acknowledged: the unquestioning work ethic learned in a totalitarian society, the logistical capacity for improvisation shown by a [war] economy under constant threat, experience in the use of 'foreign labour forces', and the lifting of the heavy burden of history that went up in flames between 1942 and 1945..." *(Air War and Literature).*

Much of the power of Sebald's writing derives from his unflinching ability to confront his readers with the sort of historical and psychological realities they might prefer to look away from even while looking, as he carefully puts it, at the same time as he calmly disarms most forms of objection with unanswerable arguments. As regards forgetting in general, though, Sebald himself seems sometimes to forget that the more or less consciously deceptive or self-deceptive variety is not the only one. Borges' little story, *Cain and Abel,* for example, in which the brothers cannot remember who killed whom, presents another argument which, if not unanswerable, is persuasive in its brevity: "Forgetting *is* forgiving." In day-to-day life, this may overlap with the implications of Yeats's vision in *The Second Coming:* "The darkness drops again...". Or, as Emily Dickinson—a poet profoundly (self-)endowed with that "peculiar honesty, in a world too frightened to be honest" which Eliot found in Blake—unforgettably wrote of remembering / forgetting:

> There is a pain—so utter—
> It swallows substance up—
> Then covers the Abyss with Trance—
> So Memory can step
> Around—across—upon it—
> As one within a Swoon—
> Goes safely—where an open eye—
> Would drop Him—Bone by Bone.

p.206, "**It seems 131 towns and cities** / **Were bombed...**": From about 1940 onwards support for an all-out bombing campaign had been growing in the RAF and Churchill sent a much-quoted letter to Beaverbrook in the summer of that year hoping for "an absolutely devastating attack by very heavy bombers from this country on the Nazi homeland". In October the War Cabinet pronounced that "the civilian population around the target areas must be made to feel the weight of the war". This was already a weakening of the high principles with which the British had entered the war: shortly before the fighting began, Neville Chamberlain had instructed Bomber Command to restrict its activities to "legitimate military targets" which were to be "capable of identification". He told the House of Commons that the Air Ministry would "never resort to the deliberate attack on women and children, and other civilians, for the purpose of mere terrorism". However, by 1941 the Germans were at the height of their power and there was almost nothing the British *could* do apart from bomb. In February 1942, shortly before Arthur Harris became C-in-C of Bomber Command, so-called area bombing was approved by a Cabinet decision "to destroy the morale of the enemy civilian population and, in particular, of the industrial workers". The idea of area bombing—usually under cover of darkness—had developed because efforts at bombing specific targets were found to be suicidal by day, on account of highly effective German defences, and almost totally inaccurate by night. Voices were raised in protest on moral grounds at every stage, resulting in what has been called a "massive official war of lies": "In some ways area bombing was a three-year period of deceit practised on the British public and on world opinion" (Martin Middlebrook, *The Battle of Hamburg,* 1980). Churchill himself referred to the campaign as "moral bombing"—a formulation which continues to defy belief. But the nature of Harris's task seems to have been clear to him from the start and, after the tremendous success of 'Operation Gomorrah' or 'the Battle of Hamburg' (as Harris himself vaingloriously named it—together with the Battle of Berlin and the Battle of the Ruhr), he grew openly irritated with Churchill's unwillingness to endorse his tactics in public: "The aim of the Combined Bomber Offensive," he wrote, "should be unambiguously stated [to be] the destruction of German cities, the killing of German workers, and the destruction of civilized life throughout Germany." Or, more pugnaciously still, "the destruction of houses, public utilities, transport and lives, the creation of a refugee problem on an unprecedented scale, and the breakdown of morale both at home and at the battle fronts by fear of extended and intensified bombing, are accepted and intended aims of our bombing policy. They are not by-products of attempts to hit factories." The bombing of Hamburg in July 1943, resulting in the great *Feuersturm* (the word was coined to refer to it) of the night of the 27/28th—*die Katastrophe,* as the inhabitants of Hamburg still call it—was capable at the time of being defended, at least, as a strategic necessity. But 'Operation Thunderclap', or the utter destruction of fifteen square miles of the heavily populated historic centre of Dresden—one of the most beautiful cities in Europe—in February 1945 seems to have worried even Harris, who first of all opposed it as not worthwhile and later defended himself in *Bomber Offensive* by writing, "I know that the destruction of so large and splendid a city at this late stage of the war was considered unnecessary even by a good many people who admit that our earlier attacks were as fully justified as any other operation of war. Here I will only say that the attack on Dresden was at the time considered a military necessity by more important people than myself." Churchill attempted to disown Harris after the war, but earlier he had found himself caught in a trap of his own making: the government and the semi-controlled press had glorified 'Bomber' Harris and his aircrews, and it was impossible to get rid of him publicly even when he as good as refused to concentrate on industrial targets and kept 'browning' one city after another. Churchill had initiated the bombing of German civilians in order to destroy their morale and he knew, of course, from the beginning what was meant by this. The bother over Dresden seems to have worried him as well, however, and he sent a now notorious telegram (dated 28 March) to the British Chiefs of Staff and the Chief of the Air Staff: "It seems to me that the moment has come when the question of *bombing German cities simply for the sake of increasing the terror, though under other pretexts,* should be reviewed. Otherwise we shall come into control of an utterly ruined land… The Foreign Secretary has spoken to me on this subject and I feel the need for more precise concentration upon military objectives such as oil and communications behind the immediate battle-zone, rather than on *mere acts of terror and wanton destruction, however impressive"* (my italics). These "acts of terror" eventually resulted in the deaths of over 400,000 German civilians, if one finds that "impressive"—not to mention the sixty-out-of-a-hundred British airmen who were lost in the operations, leading Harris's own men to nickname him 'Butcher'or 'Butch' Harris.

p.206, **My own 'synoptic, artificial view'**: So called by Sebald *("einen synoptischen, künstlichen Blick", Luftkrieg und Literatur,* p.33) because he attempts to go beyond the inevitably partial accounts of individual eyewitnesses to offer a more general view of the bombing of Hamburg, put together by himself. **Out of Niemandsland** is indebted again—as is Sebald—to Martin Middlebrook's pioneering work, *The Battle of Hamburg,* quoted above. As one would expect, many estimates and details vary or are disputed, but the first and worst fire-storm of the war seems to have developed because of the unusually dry and warm weather, the accurate concentration of the bombing in one area, and the virtual impossibility of fighting the great number of fires which were started simultaneously by the lethal combination of high-explosive 'blockbusters' of up to 4,000 lb followed by incendiary bombs.

p.208, **"I got no further."**: Or "That was a way of putting it", as Eliot put it in *East Coker* (1940), shortly before asserting that "The poetry doesn't matter" (cp. note on p.132). East Coker is a village in Somerset from which Eliot's seventeenth century ancestors had fled because of religious persecution to the New World, and in whose churchyard he saw "old stones that cannot be deciphered" marking graves which may have been those of even earlier, forgotten forebears… The Biblical quotation in **Out of Niemandsland** is from *Genesis XIX.24–28.* The problem of *how* to approach in writing such unimaginable events as the bombing of Hamburg is perhaps unresolvable, and "every attempt / … a different kind of failure". Nevertheless, in praising Hans Erich Nossack's description of the bombing in *Der Untergang* (The End), which was first published in 1948, Sebald says, "he was the only writer of the time to try recording what he actually saw as plainly as possible." *Der Untergang,* Sebald continues, is unique even in Nossack's own work. Moreover, "The ideal of truth inherent in its entirely unpretentious objectivity, at least over long passages, proves itself the only legitimate reason for continuing to produce literature in the face of total destruction. Conversely, the construction of aesthetic or pseudo-aesthetic effects from the ruins of an annihilated world is a process depriving literature of its right to exist."

p.210, **As 'fire-gel' flared and clung—a form of napalm:** Some survivors of the bombing have always claimed that phosphorus was used, particularly in the second phase of the attack, but this has been professionally disputed—for example, by the Dresden explosives expert, Thomas Langer, in Sebastian Dehnhardt's documentary film, *Das Drama von Dresden* (ZDF, 2005). Langer uses the words *Brandgel* and *Feuergel* for the variety of incendiary which he believes was dropped (napalm itself had already been invented and named in the USA). Dehnhardt's documentary ends with a service of atonement in the Dresden *Frauenkirche,* which had at last been restored after its virtual destruction in the bombing. At about the same time, the British historian, Frederick Taylor, from whose book, *Dresden: Tuesday, February 13, 1945,* some of the quotations in these notes derive, said in an interview with *Der Spiegel:* "I personally find the attack on Dresden horrific. It was overdone, it was excessive and is to be regretted enormously." *Das Drama von Dresden* is not a great film. However, it includes some extraordinary testimony from survivors, and this part of the poem is indebted in particular to the memories and words of Gerda Birnbaum, Helmut Camphausen, Ursula Elsner, Werner Hanitzsch, Eleonora Kompisch, Leandro Marton-Karoly, Günther Reichel, Johannes Süß.

p.211, **His own self-portrait claimed:** Gray's *Elegy* is plainly enough—as the 'self-portrait as...' here claims—a self-portrait in a country churchyard:

> The curfew tolls the knell of parting day,
> The lowing herd winds slowly o'er the lea,
> The ploughman homeward plods his weary way,
> And leaves the world to darkness and to me.

On the other hand, Gray's identity within the poem is highly artificial and it is tempting, since the completed *Elegy* was not published until he was in his mid-thirties, to read it as a 'self-portrait as a young poet' in the country churchyard and then, towards its close, '...as a *dead* young poet'—a fascinating variation on the genre, rescued from proto-Romanticism not only by the degree of its artifice but by more than a suggestion of self-mockery:

> Here rests his head upon the lap of earth,
> A youth to fortune and to fame unknown...

Gray's poem is otherwise remarkable for its rejection of the belligerent assumptions which lay behind Dryden's two famous poems—on the death of Cromwell and *Annus Mirabilis*—in this verse-form, "which I have ever judg'd more noble, both for the sound and number, than any other Verse in use amongst us". If the lot of those buried in the country churchyard forbad greatness—"Some mute inglorious Milton here may rest, / Some Cromwell guiltless of his country's blood"—it never tempted them either to make calculated use of terror, like Cromwell in Ireland:

> nor circumscribed alone
> Their growing virtues, but their crimes confined,
> Forbad to wade through slaughter to a throne,
> And shut the gates of mercy on mankind...

p.212, *'Wo wird einst des Wandermüden / Letzte Ruhestätte sein?':* The first two lines of Heine's *Wo?* (Where?), inscribed on his gravestone in Montmartre, Paris. The poem is translated in *Words in the Dark* (p.114).

p.212, *'How you take it':* A quotation from *The Tempest* (II.i.77), used also as the epigraph of the final subsection of 'The Dance of Death' in *No.3* (p.280).

p.213, **As for what really happened:** Modern Biblical scholarship tends to the view that Jesus would have been unlikely to rebuke Martha for her hard work and hospitality and that the thirty or so years of oral tradition between his life and Luke's account of it have somewhat upset the balance of what he meant. Even so, the story of Mary and Martha comes immediately after that of the Good Samaritan *(X.25–37)* and Luke may well have intended to (re-)emphasize in this way the importance of the spiritual as well as the ethical life... The Mary of the story has been identified in later Christian tradition with Mary Magdalene and she and Martha with the sisters of Lazarus, and though there is no evidence in support of these assumptions, the poem also makes them. At the end of ch.VII, Luke describes Mary Magdalene washing Jesus's feet with her tears and anointing them with oil. When Simon the Pharisee objects that she is a sinner, Jesus replies: "Her sins, which are many, are forgiven, for she loved much." To Mary herself he says, "Thy faith hath saved thee; go in peace" (vv. 47, 50). In other words, in Jesus's view, Mary was instantaneously saved *by herself*, albeit with his help, as Satan instantaneously fell: "I beheld Satan as lightning fall from heaven" *(Luke X.18)*.

p.213, **Many, it's true, see work / As domination. Little Caesars:** Cp. the episode at the office of the *Irish Freeman* in *Ulysses* in which Professor MacHugh (a Dublin classicist) declares, "I speak the tongue of a race the acme of whose mentality is the maxim: time is money. Material domination. *Dominus!* Lord! Where is the spirituality? Lord Jesus! Lord Salisbury. A sofa in a westend club." In the discussion towards the end of *A Portrait of the Artist as a Young Man*, referred to above (in note on p.173, " 'What is truth?' "), Cranly observes to Stephen Dedalus, "—It is a curious thing, do you know, ... how your mind is supersaturated with the religion in which you say you disbelieve." And the same was true of Joyce. In *Ulysses,* MacHugh has already been rude about the Roman mentality, which he compares to the English:

> – What was their civilization? Vast, I allow: but vile. Cloacae: sewers. The Jews in the wilderness and on the mountaintop said: *It is meet to be here. Let us build an altar to Jehovah.* The Roman, like the Englishman who follows in his footsteps, brought to every new shore on which he set his foot (on our shore he never set it) only his cloacal obsession. He gazed about him in his toga and he said: *It is meet to be here. Let us construct a watercloset.*
> – They were nature's gentlemen, J.J. O'Molloy murmured. But we have also Roman law.
> – And Pontius Pilate was its prophet, professor MacHugh responded.

Roman civilization was the context in which Luke's version of Jesus's life was written as well as of the life itself. When, on the night of 18 July AD 64, a fire broke out in Rome which burnt for a week and destroyed half the city, rumour blamed the Emperor Nero, who, "to divert suspicion from himself, looked for a scapegoat. His choice fell on the Christians, because, as Tacitus tells us..., they were already 'detested for their outrageous practices'" (G.B. Caird, *The Gospel of St Luke).* By the time of Nero, the Christians had been harried both by the Jews, whom the Romans had for the most part treated with tolerance, and by their pagan neighbours, who saw their religion as "*antisocial* and *different"* (Caird, my italics)—not to say *unpatriotic.* As the grim persecution of the Christians which followed gradually abated, Luke addressed his gospel to a high-ranking Roman civil servant named Theophilus with the aim of showing not only that the representatives of Rome in Judaea had found Jesus innocent of any crime but that he had been "a figure of nobility, grace, and charm", whose teaching inspired the same qualities in those who followed him.

p.214, **He asked which part of things, though treasured, corrupted / On earth:** Cp. "Lay not up for yourselves treasures upon earth, where moth and rust doth corrupt,... But lay up for yourselves treasures in heaven... For where your treasure is there will your heart be also" *(Matthew VI.19–21).*

p.214, **both parts are good:** At approximately one o'clock in the morning in Skin-the-Goat Fitzharris's cabman's shelter, Leopold Bloom discusses "the money question, which was at the back of everything, greed and jealousy, people never knowing when to stop", as opposed to Jewish practicality and the necessity of work—to which Stephen, still recovering from the excesses of Nighttown, manages to respond, "Count me out, … meaning to work". Stephen and Bloom are, in this respect, a sort of modernist Mary and Martha. Stephen's words surprise Bloom, who takes it for granted that "All must work, have to, together.—I mean, of course, … work in the widest possible sense. Also literary labour, not merely for the kudos of the thing." He sees this as a form of patriotism:

> You have every bit as much right to live by your pen in pursuit of your philosophy as the peasant has. What? You both belong to Ireland, the brain and the brawn. Each is equally important.
> – You suspect, Stephen retorted with a sort of half-laugh, that I may be important because I belong to the *faubourg Saint Patrice* called Ireland for short.
> – I would go a step further, Mr Bloom insinuated.
> – But I suspect, Stephen interrupted, that Ireland must be important because it belongs to me.

In spite of Stephen's eloquence and Bloom's uncomprehending clichés, one can fairly easily imagine the latter, in later years, remarking to the former, as Johannes Fest remarked to his son Joachim (cp. note on p.141, "He'd volunteered …, etc."), "You weren't wrong, but I was the one who was right." And if this inverts the referents, so be it. Another version of the same relationship was proposed by Jesus himself in answer to the question, "Is it lawful for us to give tribute to Caesar, or no?"—namely, "Show me a penny. Whose image and superscription hath it? They answered and said, Caesar's. And he said unto them, Render therefore unto Caesar the things which be Caesar's, and unto God the things which be God's" *(Luke XX.22, 24–25)*.

p.214, **right work:** 'Right Means of Livelihood' is the fifth branch of the Buddha's Noble Eightfold Path Leading to the Cessation of Suffering. In the Buddha's teaching, the *karma* of each individual's moral life leads to—or results in—a more or less enlightened or benighted spiritual life: see note on p.215, *"Who are those who love themselves? and who do not love themselves? Etc."*. The third branch of the Eightfold Path is 'Right Speech' and the fourth is 'Right Action': cp. **we need to believe / In what we do, etc.** … The Buddha's Eightfold Path is the fourth of his Four Noble Truths—of which more in *No.3*, section 15, ii ('Siddhartha and Others').

p.214, **We need to absolve / Ourselves from our 'devices':** Cp. note on p.139, "The German landscape Primo Levi / Found 'rich and civilized'", which alludes to the same passage in the General Confession in *The Book of Common Prayer* ('Morning Prayer' and 'Evening Prayer'): "Almighty and most merciful Father; We have erred, and strayed from thy ways like lost sheep. We have followed too much the devices and desires of our own hearts…"

p.214, **As the Son / Of Man, he neither lost nor won:** Jesus himself seems to have been fond of such conundrums, which bear a relationship to the *mantras* and *koans* of other religions. Memorable examples recorded by Luke are:

> Woe unto you when all men shall speak well of you *(VI.26)*.

> Give to every man that asketh of thee; and of him that taketh away thy goods ask them not again *(VI.30)*.

> For whosoever will save his life shall lose it; but whosoever will lose his life for my sake the same shall save it *(IX.24)*.

> And, behold, there are last which shall be first, and there are first which shall be last *(XIII.30)*.

Of course, he could also speak with admirable directness:

> Take heed, and beware of covetousness: for a man's life consisteth not in the abundance of the things which he possesseth *(XII.15)*.

Opus 3, No.3: From Outsight to Insight

p.215, **From Outsight to Insight:** *OED* defines "outsight" as "Sight of that which is without; perception of external things; faculty of observation or outlook." For the purposes of *Opus 3*, "outsight" is taken to consist of perceiving / understanding / coming to terms with / accepting in order to act on the world as it is or things as they are, including the nature and needs of others. Outsight is, therefore, an essential component of any conscious or meaningful ethical life. The two 'autobiographical' sections of *No.2* have already presented (among other things) their personas as attempting in one way and another to achieve outsight more fully or comprehensively, leading in the end—in *Mary and Martha*—to 'insight' or the spiritual life. Other personas inhabit the pages of *From Outsight to Insight*, which is likewise concerned with the relationship of the ethical to the spiritual.

p.215, *Who are those who love themselves? and who do not love themselves? Etc.:* According to the law of *karma*—or moral cause and effect—a man is punished *by* his sins, not *for* them, and rewarded by his virtues. In traditional Buddhist teaching, in other words, it is the individual who is responsible for the state of his soul.

p.217, *"It is choice or intention that I call* **karma**, *etc."*: Cp. the preceding note. To all intents and purposes, *karma* is indistinguishable from choice. In the *Digha Nikaya* the four causes of wrong-doing are said to be: greed, in the widest sense *(tanha)*, hatred, ignorance and fear. All too often, the *Anguttara Nikaya* also observes (III.415), "inflamed by greed, incensed by hate, confused by delusion, overcome by them, obsessed in mind, a man chooses for his own affliction, for others' affliction, for the affliction of both, and experiences pain and grief." The epigraph from the *Samyutta Nikaya* on the title page emphasizes the corollary that a man is rewarded by and not for his virtues.

p.217, **After Rilke: 'Abishag':** Of the two poems translated in 'The Death of King David', Heine's *'König David'* (p.222) was published in *Romanzero* (1851) and Rilke's *'Abisag'* in *Neue Gedichter* (1907–8). The transferral of 'Abishag' from the emotional/physical context of *The Death of Innocence* (p.116) to the more ethically oriented *From Outsight to Insight* changes the meaning of the poem somewhat, whose centre of gravity shifts from the girl to the old man, as the remainder of the section emphasizes. In the chronology of the life of David *(ca.* 1040–971 BC), Heine's poem comes shortly after Rilke's, and I have linked the translations with three Heinesque variations on Rilke, relating to the struggle for power before and after the king's death as narrated in *1 Kings I–II*.

p.219, **... for that adulteress:** As King Saul's envy and fear of David grew, his behaviour became irrational to the point of psychopathic. He married Michal again to a rival of David's *(1 Samuel XXV.44),* from whom David then claimed her back *(2 Samuel III.13–16).* Saul had taken to flinging a javelin at David, when the evil spirit was upon him, while the latter was playing his harp. It was after one such incident that Michal—who seems to have loved David to begin with—helped him escape out of a window *(1 Samuel XIX.8–12).* David married and had children with six other wives while Michal was living with her other husband *(2 Samuel III.1–5).* Her mockery of his ecstatic dancing before the ark of the Lord *(2 Samuel VI.16–23)* seems to have resulted in David's ensuring that she "had no child unto the day of her death"… The story of David's eldest son Amnon's rape of his half-sister Tamar and consequent murder—with David's connivance—by her brother Absolom is told in *2 Samuel XIII,* and that of David's eliminating the last of Michal's relatives in *2 Samuel XXI.1–9.*

p.220, **He'd swallowed Nathan's soppy story:** The famous story of David's spying from the roof of his house on Bathsheba at her ablutions, falling in love with her and then giving instructions to "General Joab" (see *After Heine: 'King David')* to dispatch her husband Uriah to the forefront of the battle at Rabbah—"that he may be smitten and die"—is told in *2 Samuel XI.* At the beginning of *2 Samuel XII,* the prophet Nathan tells the king of a very rich man's stealing a poor man's only lamb: "And David's anger was greatly kindled against the man; and he said to Nathan, As the Lord liveth, the man that hath done this thing shall surely die… And Nathan said to David, Thou art the man." David had already married Bathsheba, but the child she conceived while still Uriah's wife died after seven days. She then bore him Solomon—quite possibly during the grisly slaughter of the Ammonites which David seems to have indulged in after the sack of Rabbah (see *Solomon*): "And thus did he unto all the cities of the children of Ammon" *(2 Samuel XII.31).*

p.222, **But first, with God's help, peace must be established:** Solomon's utterly ruthless establishment of the kingdom, as recommended by David, is described in *1 Kings II.* For some reason, Solomon's early reputation for wisdom—"gilder of guile with charm"—has obscured the fact that he eventually angered and alienated the Lord. Some idea of his greed and excessive luxury can be gained, for example, from *1 Kings X.14–23*. As for his sensuality, or uxoriousness, Solomon is explicitly condemned for permitting himself to be led by the nose "by his strange wives" in *1 Kings XI.1–8*. Not long after, the kingdom was in serious trouble…

p.222, **After Heine: 'King David'**: As Heine's poem clearly indicates, *Romanzero* was a post-Romantic work whose author already regarded the idea of the Hero as defunct or as a dangerous falsification of history. As early as *Ideas: The Book of Le Grand* (1827), which deals among other things with the Napoleonic wars, Heine had ironically declared what a fine idea it would be if he were to write a national epic celebrating "all those heroes out of whose rotting corpses worms are known to have crawled—and claimed to be their descendants". In the opinion of Heine's biographer J.L. Sammons, *Romanzero* was "too modern for German ears at that time". One of Heine's most powerful personas in it is that of the diseased beggar Lazarus, lying at the gate of the wealthy Dives (see 'Lazarus' in *From Now to Then*). Rilke, on the other hand, preferred the company of well-off patrons and (especially) patronesses, and imagined himself in royal, aristocratic, heroic or vatic roles. For all his great gifts, he had little interest in what one might call everyday morality. David mattered for Rilke because he was a poet and a king. In the sixth of his *Duino Elegies* (1912–13 / 1922) he celebrates "Karnak the conquering king", Samson, the mother of Samson, and the mothers of other David-like "Heroes". In the words of one of the most able translators of the *Duino Elegies,* Patrick Bridgwater, the Hero of the sixth Elegy, "akin to those who die young and the ancient Greeks, is above all Rilke as he wished to be and sometimes felt himself to be". And yet, while Heine is one of the most interesting and perceptive political and social commentators of the nineteenth century, Rilke, according to W. Leppmann *(Rilke: A Life)*, "was a non-political man who could wax enthusiastic about this issue or that and about one statesman or another"—including, notoriously, in 1926, Benito Mussolini… All of which constitutes, in the context of *From Outsight to Insight,* sufficient reason why the poems in this section 'progress' from Rilke to Heine, and not *vice versa*.

p.223, **Pontius Pilate's Wife, Procula…**: The only mention made of Pilate's wife in the Bible is in *Matt. XXVII.19:* "When he was set down on the judgment seat, his wife sent unto him, saying, Have thou nothing to do with that just man: for I have suffered many things this day in a dream because of him." A number of legends have grown up around this shadowy figure. The poem selects from and adds to them—and adds as well to what we know about her husband. Its main Biblical source is *John XVIII–XIX*—a brilliant but in places cryptic account of what amounted to Jesus' show-trial. The famous incident of Pilate's washing his hands—he was evidently something of a show-man in general—is from *Matt. XXVII.24*.

p.223, **your church / Or synagogue**: The very first Christians were all Jewish, of course—and much is made in *Acts XI–XII* of Peter's acceptance of the first Gentiles into the church at about the same time as Pilate's wife, according to the poem, arrived back in Rome. Peter himself was probably in Rome *ca.* AD 42, but earlier groups of Christians are generally thought to have formed around Jewish travellers—in particular those present in Jerusalem six weeks after the Crucifixion for the major Jewish feast of Pentecost *(Acts II.10* mentions "strangers of Rome,

Jews and proselytes"). According to *Acts II.41,* "about three thousand souls" were baptized during Pentecost, many of them "devout men, out of every nation under heaven" (v.5). The fact that most of these nations were also under Rome contributed as well to the rapid spread of the Christian message. Shortly after, a further five thousand were baptized *(IV.4)* and then "multitudes" *(V.14, etc.).* According to *Acts VIII.1* "a great persecution against the church which was at Jerusalem" broke out after the stoning of Stephen—which would have encouraged others to leave, taking the new movement with them.

p.224, **This Emperor, claiming he's a god:** Among Caligula's many lunacies—which led to a number of failed conspiracies against him, one of which may have half-poisoned him, making matters worse—he wished or rather hoped to be worshipped as a living god and even as the father of the gods, Jupiter. Jews were tactlessly accused of not honouring him, causing disputes and riots from Alexandria to Jerusalem. He planned to have a statue of himself erected in the Temple at Jerusalem, but the Governor of Syria managed to delay this for a year until Caligula eventually lost interest in what could easily have led to a serious uprising.

p.225, ***Then said Jesus, Father, forgive them:*** The first of what are traditionally known as the Seven Last Words from the Cross. The following quotations inserted into the poem from the New Testament include the remaining six. None of the Last Words is found in all the Gospels. They are presented here in their traditional order apart from the last two, which rearrange the texts slightly so as to end with the earliest of the Gospels, *Mark (ca.* AD 65–75). *John* was probably written about ten years later.

p.226, **the half-truth (and half-lie) that the Jews / Were not allowed to judge the likes of Jesus:** *John XVIII.31* has presented something of a puzzle to commentators: "Then said Pilate unto them, Take ye him, and judge him according to your law. The Jews therefore said unto him, It is not lawful for us to put any man to death…" This was not in fact the case, certain offences under Jewish law being punishable by stoning. Procula's version of events provides an at least imaginable explanation of how this bit of the story got into *John.*

p.226, ***Poor Malchus' ear:*** When Jesus was taken prisoner in the Garden of Gethsamane, one of his disciples, attempting to defend him, cut off the ear of one of the high priest's servants with his sword. *John XVIII.10* says that the disciple was Simon Peter and that the servant's name was Malchus. *Luke XXII.51* says Jesus healed him.

p.233, **Francesco Bernadone:** St Francis was born in Assisi in 1181/82 and died there in 1224. The addressee of the (fictional) Mayor of Gubbio's letter, Bishop Guido II of Assisi, died in 1228, shortly after his protégé was canonized.

p.233, **The lad / He taught to feed and release them:** The source of this anecdote is the *Fioretti di San Francesco,* ch. XXII. This famous collection of tales emphasizing the 'Spiritual' as opposed to the organizational (or 'Conventual') aspects of St Francis' order, dates from around 1325 to 1350. At about the same time as the (originally Latin) *Fioretti* were written, Pope John XXII, weary of

Franciscan polemics and of assuming financial responsibility for the order, ruled that the quintessentially Franciscan notion of evangelical poverty *("la sua donna",* as Dante spoke of her—cp. note on p.3, *"Credette Cimabue ecc."*) was untenable not only juridically but as the highest form of the imitation of Christ. No one knows whether the *Fioretti* were a Spiritual reaction to these rulings, which are passed over in silence, although they stunned and divided the order... While a number—or even most—of the *Fioretti* are in the realm of fairy-tale rather than history, some of them, such as ch. XXII, ring remarkably true—at least in part. Another of these is ch. XXI *(How St Francis converted the very fierce wolf of Gubbio),* on which the poem as a whole is based.

p.234, **the holy martyrs / He worships:** Assisi was well known for its third-century martyrs, after one of whom, San Rufino, the cathedral was named. St Francis was said by his early biographers to have conceived a strong desire for martyrdom himself and taught the brothers that they should always seek it. Born in the first century of the Crusades, Francis made three attempts to reach the Holy Land, finally arriving in Egypt in 1219, when, far from becoming a martyr—although his position was dangerous in the extreme—he impressed the Sultan profoundly with both his personal presence and teaching.

p.235, **As his father was:** St Francis' father was Pietro Bernadone, a wealthy merchant about whom little is known apart from what is narrated by the hagiographers, who present his alleged avarice, anger and pride as a uniformly black background against which the saint can shine. Pietro indulged his son's youthful excesses—at least to begin with. The process of conversion may have begun when Francis, at the time a flamboyant and even riotous young man-about-town, was seized by guilt after refusing alms to a beggar while selling cloth in his father's shop. As his father's only son, he was presumably expected to take over the family firm but, while praying in the ruinous church of San Damiano, outside Assisi, after his first visit to Rome in 1204/05, seemed to hear the voice of Christ telling him to repair his church. He then took some of the expensive fabric in which Pietro dealt and sold it, together with his horse, at the market in Foligno. Legally speaking, this was theft and Pietro reacted by taking him to the episcopal court, where he presumed that the Bishop—himself an extremely rich, litigious and imperious person—would support him.

p.235, **With Papal blessings reaped in Rome:** With the Bishop's encouragement, Francis set off to Rome with a small band of brothers in 1209/10, hoping to gain an audience with the Pope. This hope would almost certainly have gone unfulfilled if Guido had not been in Rome already and arranged for him to see Innocent III, who—as impressed by Francis as practically everyone was who met him—gave the brothers his blessing and permission to preach repentance and beg for alms. In 1223, Honorius III fully confirmed the Franciscan Rule.

p.238, **A ragged crowd of so-called brothers:** Resentment at the friars' practice of begging for alms seems to have begun in Assisi itself, where wealthy citizens joined the fraternity and publicly renounced their possessions. The admiration which this initially inspired turned sour when such formerly well-off brothers started begging for what was clearly a portion, however small, of the possessions of others. Bishop Guido seems to have mediated in this dispute and, according to

Michael Robson, who devotes an entire chapter to him in *St Francis of Assisi—The Legend and the Life* (1997), listened with understanding to Francis' argument that not only was he imitating Christ, who was likewise (he claimed) a beggar, but that if the friars had possessions they would need to defend them. Article VI of the *Second Rule* states categorically: "The brothers are to own nothing, neither place, nor house, nor anything at all; but as 'strangers and pilgrims' in this world, serving God in poverty and humility, they are to go out begging for alms without shame, because for us our Lord Jesus Christ took the form of a poor man in this world." Guido doubted whether the absolute renunciation of possessions could work in practice, but he made no attempt to impose his thinking on the fraternity, which grew with extraordinary rapidity. The Mayor mentions a General Chapter of 2,000 brothers at Assisi. In the *Fioretti* there is one of 5,000 (ch. XVIII), which was regarded as an exaggeration at one time but as plausible today. In spite of John XXII's ruling a hundred years later—the papacy having had enough by then of paying for the order—the *Fioretti* takes Francis' ideal of poverty for granted throughout, including a sermon by the saint himself on "the measureless treasure of most holy poverty" (ch. XIII).

p.239, **Their great *palazzi's* raised doors:** An architectural curiosity of Gubbio is that many of the older buildings, in particular those built by merchants, have a smaller, narrower door, two or three feet from the ground, beside their main door. These *'porte dei morti'* (doors of the dead) can look sinister and inhospitable. The most likely explanation of them is that they were for addressing unknown or un-wanted visitors in relative safety and from a dominant position… Francis' love-affair with Lady Poverty was doubtless intended to counter not only the greed which arose from the new commercial life of the cities but the alienation from one's neighbour which accompanied it. That this was the beginning of the modern world goes without saying.

p.240, **Frate Ginepro:** The *Life of Brother Juniper* ('Ginepro') is usually included in editions of the *Fioretti*. As well as giving his clothes away, Ginepro was famous for distributing vestments, books and other objects out of the churches to any who asked for them. Francis' extreme behaviour was usually meaningful, as when (in the incident mentioned earlier by the Mayor) he humbled Brother Rufino by ordering him to preach naked in the cathedral of Assisi—and then joined him (*Fioretti*, ch. XXX). But Ginepro's was far less so. Nevertheless, Francis himself rejoiced in mockery and tribulation, which is part of the meaning of the very first sentence of the *Fioretti*: "We must first consider that the glorious St Francis, in all the acts of his life, modelled himself on Christ."

p.243, **Lilies that fester etc.:** In a short but important note in *PN Review 100*—"an introduction to all my poetry, if you wish"—the Anglo-American poet of the Age of Aids, Thom Gunn, remarks on "the idealizations and the contempt" found so often in Renaissance poetry. His examples are Wyatt and Donne, but he could just as well have adduced Shakespeare's *Sonnets*, in which the (inevitable?) fall from idealization to contempt—including self-contempt—is particularly evident. In the context of *Sonnet 129* ("Th'expense of spirit in a waste of shame / Is lust in action"), "heaven" is primarily ironic. And yet the phrases "A bliss in proof" and "A joy proposed" in the preceding lines ensure that the word's religious connotations are felt as well… By *Sonnet 144*, the Young Man and the Dark Lady can be understood as representing the conflict *within* the poet as much as the two people he is in love with:

> Two loves I have, of comfort and despair,
> Which like two spirits do suggest me still;
> The better angel is a man right fair,
> The worser spirit a woman coloured ill.
> To win me soon to hell, my female evil
> Tempteth my better angel from my side,
> And would corrupt my saint to be a devil,
> Wooing his purity with her foul pride.
> Etc.

"To fall in love," wrote Borges of Dante and Beatrice, "is to create a religion with a fallible god"... Thom Gunn, as the author of *The Man with Night Sweats,* suggests that what we might benefit from instead is a love poetry "of mere truth, without fudging".

p.243, *"Per una ghirlandetta":* It is a matter of conjecture who Ladies such as the Fioretta of this extract actually were, but any or all of them may have constituted the "short-lived vanity" of which Beatrice speaks with withering scorn in her diatribe against Dante's behaviour after her death in *Purgatorio XXXI*. Dante has entered the Earthly Paradise, where he finally encounters Beatrice again, but she reprimands and humbles him for not coming to her sooner, enumerating the errors of his ways and accusing him of infidelity:

> "No girl or other short-lived vanity
> Ought to have weighted down your wings
> To wait for further arrows…"

When Beatrice forces him to confess, he stammers and weeps… As good as caught out in this way by his own idealization of Beatrice, Dante lowers his eyes, humiliated:

> As children, speechless with shame, their eyes
> Fixed on the ground, admitting they were wrong
> And sorry for what they've done, stand listening,
>
> I stood and listened.

Beatrice then makes him look at her, until

> The nettle of repentance stung me so
> Badly that what I'd once loved most in others
> Became an object and a source of hatred…

p.244, *(Rime XIV):* Thus numbered in M. Bardi's *Società dantesca italiana* edition of the complete *Rime,* this *canzone* is also the first—though not the first poem—in the *Vita nuova,* where it is elaborately presented by Dante as a new start in which he will no longer speak of himself and his own inadequacies but find beatitude in praising Beatrice. Dante's prosimetrical work (to use an *obs. rare* epithet from *OED)* is an exercise in poetics as well as in 'autobiography' and poetry itself—and so in some respects a precursor of *Then and Now.*

p.244, **Ladies who live in the knowledge of love… / An angel in the fullness of God's knowledge:** Throughout the *Vita nuova,* Dante lays much emphasis not only on keeping one's love a secret from others (except, in his case, from "a certain group of ladies") but also on the arcane and ineffable nature of love, such that he uses the same word *("intelletto")* in the first lines of the first and second stanzas of this poem to refer, respectively, to the ladies' knowledge (of love) and to the all-comprehending mind of God. The idealized and religious nature of Dante's love and Beatrice's virtue—or, more accurately, her very being—is everywhere apparent in this prelude to the *Divina commedia,* and the *Vita nuova* ends with a sigh or *"peregrino spirito"* which emanates from Dante's heart until, gazing at Beatrice in glory, it speaks "in subtle words I did not understand", after which "a marvellous vision appeared to me and I saw things which made me propose to speak no more of this blessed one before I could do so more worthily…" After the humiliating scene in the *Purgatorio* referred to above, Beatrice acts as his guide through the *Paradiso,* until her apotheosis in Canto XXXI, when she suddenly disappears from his side—to reappear above him in one of the circles of the celestial Rose. For Borges, paraphrasing Dante in *Beatrice's Last Smile,* "the azure firmament is no farther from the lowest depths of the sea than she is from him". Dante gazes at her on high: "There, in an aureole of reflected glory, is Beatrice; Beatrice, whose gaze used to suffuse him with intolerable beatitude; Beatrice, who used to dress in red; Beatrice, whom he thought of so constantly that he was astonished by the idea that some pilgrims he saw one morning in Florence had never heard speak of her; Beatrice who once refused to greet him; Beatrice, who died at the age of twenty-four; Beatrice de Folco Portinari, who married Bardi… Dante prays as to God, but also as if to a longed-for woman:

> 'O Lady, in whom my hope is strong,
> And who for my salvation condescended
> To leave a track through Hell…'

Beatrice looks at him a moment and smiles, then turns away towards the eternal fountain of light."

p.247, **That woman / Who shuns my love:** As with the *"Fioretta mia bella"* of subsection i, no more is known of the subject of Dante's so-called *rime petrose* or 'stony verses'—of which there are four altogether—than is contained in the poetry itself. She may or may not be the same person as the *"pargoletta"* (young girl) of *Rime LXXXVII–LXXXIX,* with whom he appears to have fallen passionately in love and whom Beatrice may also be referring to in the lines from *Purgatorio XXXI* translated above. If **that unfeeling block / Of loveliness** was in fact the *pargoletta,* she was permitted, before he turned against her, to explain in *Rime LXXXVII* that

> I came from heaven, and there I shall return
> To give my joyful light to others.

p.248, ***The Carpenter's* 'Cook's Tale'. Or: *Blindman's Buff*:** The opening lines of *Blindman's Buff* have been approximately taken over (by the Master Carpenter who turns out to be telling the story) from Chaucer's unfinished *Cook's Tale*. Chaucer's own Carpenter is one of a group of five guildsmen not allotted a tale in *The Canterbury Tales*. The guildsmen have brought with them on the pilgrimage a ribald and somewhat unappetizing Cook (suffering from a dry scabbed ulcer on his shin) who is inspired by the scurrilous humour of *The Reeve's Tale*—*"Ha! ha! quod he, for Christes passion, / This millere hadde a sharpe conclusion…"*—to tell one of his own… Chaucer's idea was that his thirty pilgrims should tell two tales on the way to Canterbury and two coming back, but only about a fifth of these had been written by his death or disappearance some time after 5 June, 1400—the last known reference to him as alive. As far as *The Cook's Tale* is concerned, Chaucer may have intended to complete or rewrite what he had started. However, the Cook himself introduces it as *"a litel jape that fil in oure citee",* and if it was in fact the case that Chaucer had some such Boccaccian tale as *Decameron* IX,v—on which *Blindman's Buff* is very loosely based—in mind for the Cook, he may well have abandoned it as too similar in theme (a rather heartless practical joke or revenge story) to *The Miller's Tale* and *The Reeve's Tale* which precede it. At any rate, the Master Carpenter is no *"cherl"*—as Chaucer evidently thought the Cook was—and is here presented as turning the *"litel jape"* into more than a *"cherl's tale"*. He is also presented as a friend of Chaucer's and as picking up the threads of the latter's *Cook's Tale* ten years or so after his disappearance, around the time that Henry IV had become so ill—some said as a punishment for murdering Richard II—that he had been compelled to leave the day-to-day government of the country to the future Henry V and had retired to Lambeth Palace where his comrade-in-arms, Thomas Arundel, whom the Carpenter believes to have been Chaucer's arch-enemy, was still Archbishop… But, of course, the tale—like those of Boccaccio and Chaucer himself—is fiction rather than history and takes anachronistic and other liberties of the imagination with whatever really happened.

p.248, *"Ella, rispostogli, il cominciò a guatare…":* "She, having returned his greeting, began to gaze at him…" In Boccaccio's tale, Calendrino—the *"modesto pittore"* (as Vasari called him) who is the butt of several other practical jokes in *The Decameron*—falls in love, while working on the frescoes at Camerata, near Florence, with a girl who turns out to be a local prostitute. His colleagues, Bruno and Buffalmacco (cp. 'The Chest' in section 10, *Three Fables Ancient and Modern*), first of all encourage Calendrino's infatuation and then arrange to have his wife, Tessa, catch him with the girl *in flagrante delicto*. Monna Tessa's furious onslaught leaves Calendrino badly scratched, torn and bleeding, and she drags him off home to Florence with his tail between his legs—where, to the great amusement of his friends, he is vexed and humiliated day and night *("il dì e la notte molestato ed afflitto")* by his wife's reproaches… Of course, Chaucer had told tales of this sort himself. His overall approach to the subject of love, however, differs from Boccaccio's in its moral sensitivity—as well as from Dante's and Petrarch's (whose writings he had also studied) in its openly sexual nature and realistic refusal to idealize the beloved (cp. notes on p.16, *The Convent Garden* and p.17, "God knows I've wept, etc."). In fact, if we take "love poetry" to include poetry *about* love, Chaucer had already fulfilled Thom Gunn's requirement of "mere truth, without fudging" by the end of the fourteenth century.

p.248, **before he'd fully served / his time:** Apprenticeships lasted seven years—which explains, if it does not excuse, the virulence of Perkin's later desire to pay his master back.

p.250, **Buridan—/ first loved, then dumped, in Paris by Queen Jeanne:** Cp. note on p.40, "And where's the queen who ordered her guard / To tie up Buridan etc."

p.257, ***"My sone, keep wel thy tonge":*** The Carpenter is here quoting from one of Chaucer's fables, *The Manciple's Tale*, in which Mercury's pet crow tells tales on his master's unfaithful wife, as a result of which he kills her. Mercury then hates and punishes the crow…

p.262, **Chaucer—for he it was:** Some of the details of *The Carpenter's* 'Cook's Tale' from this point on are derived from F.N. Robinson's edition of *The Works of Geoffrey Chaucer* (1933, 1957)—to which everyone who reads Chaucer is indebted. Robinson notes the curious anomaly whereby "far from giving any information about his literary work, contemporary documents do not once betray the fact that he was a man of letters". A number of more recent scholars have drawn attention as well to how little we know of the last year or more of Chaucer's life, after the accession of Henry IV in September 1399. Chaucer seems to have died some time between 5 June 1400 and, possibly, 1402, but there is no clear evidence as to how or where; nor did he leave a will, which has been described by a leading historian of the period as puzzling, to say the least, for a man of his standing. On the other hand, there is only circumstantial evidence relating to the death of King Richard himself… Perhaps not very surprisingly, deciphering or uncovering who said and did what seems to be no easier when it comes to medieval England than with more recent falsifiers of history—cp. *No.2*, 'Self-Portrait as a White-Collar Worker (4)'… Some historians (as in T. Jones *et al.* in *Who Murdered Chaucer?*, 2003) now take the view that the traditional version of events, according to which Henry Bolingbroke, wishing to do no more than reclaim his inheritance, felt obliged to relieve the country of an unpopular, incompetent, morally flawed and foolish Richard, was largely the (intended) result of Lancastrian propaganda and/or pressure—as were contemporary chroniclers' descriptions of the usurpation as a bloodless revolution. As everyone knows from Shakespeare, Henry was Richard's cousin and had grown up amid the extraordinary political tensions of Richard's minority before getting himself exiled in 1398 because of his mysterious—and still unexplained—quarrel with Thomas Mowbray. His return from exile in 1399 may in fact have been more of a calculated and ruthless political *coup* than Shakespeare had any way of knowing. According to this hypothesis, at least some of the calculation stemmed from the former Archbishop of Canterbury, Thomas Arundel, whom Richard had exiled for treason in 1397 and who could easily have planned the deposition in Paris together with Henry. Arundel, at any rate, returned with Henry's party and marched with them through England, bribing and threatening others to join the rebellion. He at once reinstated himself as Archbishop of Canterbury, in defiance of the Pope as well as Richard… For Shakespeare's historically somewhat inaccurate but nevertheless brilliantly perceptive view of the period which included the last few years of Chaucer's life, one has only to turn to his sequence of five plays: *Richard II, 1 Henry IV, The Merry Wives of Windsor, 2 Henry IV* and *Henry V*. Interestingly, Shakespeare seems to have been almost as antipathetic towards Henry IV as are modern historians. If his attitude towards Richard is more ambivalent, he presents both kings as the slaves of history (the oxymoron is Tolstoy's, cp. *From Now to Then,* p.7)—deceiving themselves, as well as others, in different ways. Shakespeare quite clearly saw the deposition not only as a catastrophe in itself but as setting off a whole chain of catastrophic events... *The Carpenter's* 'Cook's Tale' alludes as well to *Measure for Measure,* whose plot involves similar elements. The fall and redemption of Angelo (as one may think of it) is remarkable for taking place in a Vienna peopled largely by Londoners, including a descendant of the Carpenter's 'Pompey'— whose real-life equivalent no one will convince me Shakespeare had not encountered at the Boar's Head in Eastcheap.

p.262, **Retractions:** As F.N. Robinson says, there are many instances more or less parallel to Chaucer's *"retracciouns"*, and he provides a short list, from St Augustine to Tolstoy, which "might easily be extended". Apart from this obviously ancient literary convention, there was also something of a rash of religious recantations—particularly by Oxford intellectuals—around 1400, relating to the (heretical) teachings of John Wyclif and the spread of Lollardy. Archbishops Courtenay and then Arundel, in particular, were keen on getting both Church and laity back in line—and it has been suggested that Chaucer's retractions together with his thoroughly orthodox ***Parson's Tale*** (a sermon in prose on Confession and the Seven Deadly Sins) were written under duress.

p.262, *"he was a good felawe, etc.":* This passage from the *General Prologue,* describing the Shipman, is here applied by the Carpenter to the "former smuggler", Pompey.

p.263, **what Henry was up to:** There is no way of knowing, of course, exactly when Bolingbroke— with or without the support of Arundel—started thinking about a *coup,* but the peace-loving Richard, who modelled his relatively enlightened Renaissance court on such as Robert of Anjou's, where Boccaccio had spent his youth (see also *No.1,* 'A Giotto Triptych', v), had long been unpopular with his war-mongering barons. To make matters worse, some of the more prominent of these had exercised unusual power (while squabbling over it among themselves) between Richard's accession in 1377 and his coming of age in 1389. Henry's humorless and vindictive mind may in fact have been mulling a rebellion over for some time before his actual exile... But whatever his thoughts were, his consequent usurpation and regicide provided, needless to say, sufficiently dramatic raw material for Shakespeare's subtle portrayal of this particular revenger's tragedy. Possibly all tyrants are soft-centred and/or mad: hence their indomitable and self-destructive need to assert their authority. At any rate—as Henry almost confesses in Shakespeare's play—uneasy lay the head that stole Dikkon's crown.

p.263, **I'd worked on Chester quire:** The carving of the stalls in Chester cathedral dates from around 1380 and is considered some of the finest medieval woodwork in Europe. As full of devils as it is of angels, this delicate but not cheerful piece of work has been likened to an enormous crown of soaring thorns. As for the Master Carpenter's meeting Chaucer **on the pilgrimage,** the *General Prologue,* as Robinson says, "is usually associated with 1387". However, "There has been much speculation as to what suggested to Chaucer the idea of a pilgrimage. He may, of course, have been describing an actual experience, or more than one": i.e. the pilgrimage on which the Carpenter and Chaucer met is here imagined as dating from not long after the completion of Chester quire.

p.263, **not least by knocking clerics in his rhymes:** Chaucer had also written excellent poems of impeccable piety—such as *The Man of Law's Tale, The Clerk's Tale, The Prioress's Tale* and *The Second Nun's Tale.* However, these are probably earlier work and not quite so well known even now as *The Pardoner's Prologue, The Friar's Prologue and Tale, The Summoner's Prologue and Tale, The Shipman's Tale, The Canon's Yeoman's Prologue and Tale,* in all of which clerics are unforgettably held up as "scroungers, thieves or wealthy hypocrites…".

p.263, **he rented a new place etc.:** This was a fine old tenement and not a bolt-hole. Even so, Chaucer could have claimed whatever protection the sanctuary of Westminster Abbey might have afforded, had he wished to—although there was no certainty that the King or Arundel would not violate it, as they had done on more than one occasion.

p.264, **Free-thinking speech became a thing of the past:** The earlier fourteenth century appears to have been an era of relatively free thought, typified by the proto-Protestant John Wyclif and the Lollards with their radical criticism of the Church's vast wealth and pursuit of political power. While there had always been criticism of the Church from within, one of the reasons for this "crisis of faith", as it has been called, was very possibly the Black Death (cp. note on p.16, *The Convent Garden,* especially the second paragraph). Wyclif and the Lollards, at any rate, had been blamed for the Peasant's Revolt of 1381, and the Church had already done battle with Oxford Wyclifite theologians in the 1380s. After the accession of Henry, the freedom to say what one thought came to an abrupt and ruthless end. King Richard had been consistently opposed to the Continental practice of burning heretics and other needlessly cruel or terrifying punishments such as hanging, drawing and quartering. However, the 1401 statute *De Haeretico Comburendo* stated that heretics were to be "burnt before the people in a conspicuous place; that such punishments may strike fear into the minds of others…" And before the law had even been passed, one William Sawtre had the unenviable distinction of being the first Englishman to be burnt in public at Smithfield. "After this terrible example," wrote one chronicler, "other accomplices of his recanted their heresies in person at St Paul's Cross." After Chaucer's death the repression continued, until in 1409 Archbishop Arundel published his *Constitutions,* which have been described as "one of the most draconian pieces of censorship in English history". With all the thoroughness of the Inquisition, "Every warden, head, or keeper of a college or principal of a hall or hostel", for example, "shall inquire diligently every month at least in the college, hall or hostel over which he presides whether any scholar or inhabitant of any such college, hall or hostel, has held, defended, or in any way proposed any conclusion, proposition, or opinion, sounding ill for the Catholic faith or good customs." And so on.

p.265, ***"Ther is namore to seye, etc.":*** The Carpenter here cuts and pastes assorted passages from *The Canterbury Tales* as if Chaucer had quoted and adapted his own lines in his narration of the painter's story. His main sources are *The Shipman's Tale, The Miller's Tale, The Reeve's Tale* and the Host's words at the end of *The Pardoner's Tale.*

p.267, **like snails:** In another story about Calendrino, *Decameron* VIII, iii, the painter dreams of getting rich quick—"without having to daub walls all the time, like a lot of snails..." The Boccaccian tale which Chaucer couldn't place is of course *Decameron* IX,v—"a fine / If heartless story" *(The Chest, p.334)*—which might have been expected to appeal to the author of *The Merchant's Tale, The Reeve's Tale,* etc.. But for all the tough-mindedness and realism of his later writings—particularly, as noted already, on the subject of love—Chaucer's sense of compassion *("For pitee renneth soone in gentil herte")* was his great step forward—one which, in innumerable forms and variations, Shakespeare himself was later to follow, from *Titus Andronicus* at the very beginning of his career to Prospero's words to Ariel at its end:

> Hast thou, which art but air, a touch, a feeling
> Of their afflictions, and shall not myself,
> One of their kind, that relish all as sharply
> Passion as they, be kindlier mov'd than thou art?
> Though with their high wrongs I am struck to th' quick,
> Yet with my nobler reason 'gainst my fury
> Do I take part: the rarer action is
> In virtue than in vengeance: they being penitent,
> The sole drift of my purpose doth extend
> Not a frown further.

p.268, **The Dance of Death (after 'Totentanz der Stadt Basel'):** The Dance of Death, or *Danse macabre,* developed as a genre in various parts of Europe after the arrival of the Black Death from Asia in the mid-fourteenth century (cp. note on p.16, *The Convent Garden*). Over the next hundred years or so the ravages of late medieval war also contributed to its grim imagery. The *Basler Totentanz,* consisting of paintings and accompanying rhymes, dates from around 1440 and was originally a fresco on the 60-metre-long cemetery wall of the *Predigerkirche*. The work was 'renovated' several times and copied at the beginning of the seventeenth century and again in 1770. Because of its deteriorating quality it was eventually destroyed in 1805, although some fragments have been preserved. Apart from their effective juxtaposition of two complementary quatrains, the Basel poems are mostly plain and often cumbersome and I have frequently elaborated on them. However, I have preserved the original order of the poems, replacing the Painter and the Painter's Wife with the Poet and the Poet's Wife. I have also excluded the Jew, Pagan and Paganess—which leaves perhaps only the Usurer as obviously *punished* by Death. Otherwise, the emphasis (as was common) is on the inevitability of Death's usually unexpected and mocking arrival. Ingmar Bergman's masterly extension of the genre, *The Seventh Seal* (1957), shows the Church's efforts to present death by plague as a punishment for one's sins—believed by some, but not by others—as well as the terrible arbitrariness of when and where death actually struck. Even so, there is a sense in which Bergman's characters create their own futures—and the innocent, for example, escape for a time...

The *Basler Totentanz* includes some introductory verses, entitled *'Der Prediger Spricht...'* ('The Preacher Speaks...'), which are markedly inferior to the rest of the poem. In fact, they incompetently contradict the Dance itself, which shows no more respect for prelates than for anyone else. The introduction looks forward to the Day of Judgement, when the dead shall awake again and be eternally punished or rewarded for their deeds,

> While those who have worked for God as a teacher—
> Hear, o hear the word of the Preacher!—
> Shall shine like a star in the firmament,
> Rewarded world without end. Amen.

The *Totentanz* proper—very possibly by another poet or poets—offers no such 'eternal' solution to the fact that everyone dies. On the other hand, the realism and rough-and-ready humour with which its verses (and once its paintings) present what awaits us all can certainly be understood as a way of coming to terms with and even accepting it. Or, as the Buddha more tersely put it: "The world is led by mind."

p.280, *"...how you take it!"*: *The Tempest* II.i.77. *Pace* the Arden (1961) edition, which remarks, "The sense is not at all clear...", the meaning of Sebastian's comment on Gonzago's "widow Dido" *(viz.* "What if he had said 'widower Aeneas' too? Good Lord, how you take it!") is clearly enough related to one of the play's main themes: i.e. things depend on how you take them. Shakespeare's dramatic irony in putting these and other ironic remarks in the mouth of one the tempest's most helpless victims is complex but effective.

p.282, **I wrote my troubled Life etc.:** Benvenuto Cellini (1500–1571) wrote his *Life* between 1558 and 1562, when it breaks off abruptly... The first part of this poem is a translation and the second an adaptation of the opening sonnet of *La vita*.

p.282, **to wreak such vengeance:** Cellini admits in *La vita* to having killed three men in acts of vengeance. Moreover, during the so-called Sack of Rome (1527), when the Emperor Charles V laid siege to the Vatican itself, he distinguished himself as a gunner on the battlements of Castel Sant' Angelo, deriving much pleasure from his success in slaughtering the enemy with an assortment of weapons. Cellini was a member of Clement VII's household, and the Pope, who had also retreated to the castle, absolved him in person of "all the murders I had ever perpetrated or should ever perpetrate in the service of the Apostolic Church".

p.282, ***Rota sum etc.:*** Cellini paraphrases this motto as "Wheresoever the wheel of Fortune turns, Virtue stands firm." His father was, among other things, a gifted musician. His wish that Benvenuto should become primarily a musician caused intense conflict both between them and also in Cellini himself, since he loved and respected his father—who was almost as stubborn as his son, however... Giovanni died of the plague which raged in Florence in 1527, having successfully persuaded Benvenuto to leave until the worst was over.

p.283, **'That devil Benvenuto etc.':** Said of Cellini by Paul III's predecessor, Clement VII, who was a great admirer of his work but with whom he repeatedly quarrelled over money. Before Paul III fell out with Cellini as well, he said (of one of his murders—an act of calculated revenge),

"Men like Benvenuto, unique in their profession, stand above the law." No doubt he saw himself—likewise unique in his profession—as standing above the law. The difference, though, was that, whereas this had always been true of Popes, Cellini's sort of extreme individualist was a relative newcomer.

p.283, **Who mind St Peter's pence:** Money was, of course, promised to Cellini—but seldom forthcoming. When in fact paid, he was paid too little. His outspoken and violent temperament made him enemies at the Papal court, who indulged in back-stabbing. At last, one of his workmen, feeling badly treated by Cellini, alleged that his master had stolen some Papal jewels during the Sack of Rome, and still had them. This "piece of malice", Cellini says in *La vita,* "succeeded at once because of the avarice of Pope Paolo da Farnese". Arrested and imprisoned, he was able to prove he had stolen nothing. But the Pope had now turned against him and refused to set him free.

p.283, *... cruel orders for my death, etc.:* Ugolini was at first well-disposed towards Cellini, being "aware how greatly I had been wronged". He turned furiously against him when Cellini, putting his own interest before the Castellan's trust and authority, broke his parole and, by climbing down the sheer walls of the castle, succeeded in escaping. However, he was soon recaptured. The Castellan suffered from an illness involving periodic hallucination. At the top of the Castel Sant'Angelo is an enormous statue of an angel. Hence, perhaps, the Castellan's obsession, recorded by Cellini, with bats, birds, and flying, as well as Cellini's own visions, *de profundis,* of angelic forces at work in his favour *(La vita* I. cxviii–cxxii). Hearing of this, the Pope "sent word—as one who had no faith either in God or aught beside—that I was mad". He then consigned Cellini to the Castellan, shortly before he died of his illness, to do with as he pleased: "I will let him put that Benvenuto to death in any way he likes, for he is the cause of his death, and so the good man shall not die unrevenged." When the Pope heard of Ugolini's change of heart, he "took it very ill indeed".

p.284, **he kept my Caterina / To serve him:** Pagolo Micceri was one of Cellini's Italian workmen in Paris, where he lived from 1540–1545 after the Cardinal of Ferrara had arranged his release from prison. The Cardinal, whom Cellini had met on his first trip to France in 1537, knowing that King Francis I wanted him back, entertained the Pope extravagantly, got him happily drunk, persuaded him to release his obstreperous prisoner, and whisked Cellini away in the middle of the night before Farnese sobered up and changed his mind. Shortly after, Cellini was back in France, working for the King in person… Cellini's version of Pagolo and Caterina's story is given in *La vita* II. xxviii–xxxv. Once he had finished the work Caterina was modelling for—one of his very finest, the *Nymph of Fontainebleu*—he lost interest in her and her husband entirely.

p.285, **After his great escape:** Ascanio, who was apprenticed to Cellini at the age of ten, here forgets that his 'father''s actual escape was not so glorious (see above). He is remembering how Cellini had accomplished the virtually impossible by climbing single-handed out of Castel Sant'Angelo, setting "all Rome in an uproar, for they had observed the bands of linen fastened to the great keep of the castle, and folk were running in crowds to behold so extraordinary a thing" *(La vita* I.cxi). Anyone who has seen the towering walls of Castel Sant'Angelo will appreciate that this was indeed a "great escape"… Ascanio is here imagined as having returned in the late 1560s to his native village.

p.285, **He's ill. I'll wait. See Perseus then:** Cellini worked on his *Perseus* from 1545 to 1554, when it was exhibited to the public. He eventually died after repeated bouts of illness in 1571, having worked for Cosimo de' Medici in Florence after leaving Ascanio and his other apprentice, Pagolo Romano, in Paris. He left France in 1545 largely because of difficulties caused by the King's mistress, Madame d'Etampes, who disliked him intensely. Like other powerful people in his life, she obviously felt that Cellini treated her with insufficient respect.

p.285, ***one single foe:*** Cellini, who quickly made as many enemies in Florence as in Rome and Paris, has just overcome the temptation to attack his rival, Baccio Bandinelli, in a public place. Bandinelli was a predictable but reliable mediocrity who, until Cellini arrived, dominated the art of sculpture in Duke Cosimo's Florence, Michelangelo having left for Rome some years before. He was a favourite of the Duchess, Eleonora di Toledo, who grew to dislike Cellini (whom she clearly saw as an upstart) almost as much as had Madame d'Etampes—whereas Agnolo Bronzino (1503–1572) immortalized her in his portraits. Bronzino, nevertheless, was one of the few contemporaries whom Cellini rated as highly as himself. He also painted 'allegorical portraits', of which the young **Duke… as *Orfeo*** is perhaps the most remarkable. This strange and unsettling picture is analysed at length by Maurice Brock in his fine monograph (2002) on Cosimo's court painter…

p.285, **Perseus, for Cosimo, stood / For law and order:** Perseus slaying the Gorgon was the increasingly autocratic Duke's idea, for the Loggia dei Lanzi on the Piazza della Signoria… *"Un sol / Giovin ch' all' ali"* (a lonely young man with wings) is a quotation from one of Bronzino's four sonnets in praise of the statue… After much "haggling", as Cellini calls it, the Duke agreed to pay him 3,500 crowns—perhaps a third or a quarter of the statue's real value. The money came in dribs and drabs and 500 crowns were still unpaid when Cellini died. John Pope-Hennessy *(Cellini,* 1985) comments: "Reading through [Cosimo's account-books] it seems a miracle that in this context any work of genius could have been produced." Cellini admits in *La vita* to realizing too late "that [Cosimo] was more a merchant than a duke" and imagining "I had to do with a prince, and not with a commercial man". Of course, he had to do with a prince in the Machiavellian sense : see head-note to 'Jove's New World' in *No.1*. It is no exaggeration to say that, while Cellini's individualism was relatively new in the sixteenth century, Cosimo de' Medici as a thorough-going materialist—"the philistine Duke", Pope-Hennessy calls him—is recognizably our contemporary.

p.286, ***Mona Fiore:*** Cellini names his housekeeper at the time of the casting of Perseus in 1549 as Mona Fiore da Castel del Rio, but little is known of her. It was once thought that she might be the same person as the woman he secretly married in 1562 after she had born him a daughter, although she is named differently in other documents. During the dramatic events of the casting—which came perilously close to catastrophe—Mona Fiore had played a crucial role by getting him back on his feet after "battling thus with all these untoward circumstances, I could at last bear up no longer, and a sudden fever of the utmost intensity attacked me…" *(La vita* II.lxxv). But Cellini's account of the casting as a whole has an air of fiction about it, and the poem treats 'Mona Fiore' as his wife, dubious though this may be historically. His wife, at any rate, bore him three daughters, two of whom survived, and in 1569—the date of the poem—a son, who also survived.

p.286, ***his final claim for his Crucefix:*** The Crucefix—which Pope-Hennessy describes as Cellini's greatest work and "the supreme marble sculpture of its time"—was briefly exhibited on its completion in 1562. The statue was based on a wax model made while Cellini was still a prisoner in Castel Sant'Angelo in 1539 after a vision of the sun forming itself into a Christ on the Cross. Bronzino might have seen it again in 1570 when it was valued, disgracefully, at the Duke's request, by Cellini's rival, Ammanati, at 700 crowns—less than half of what Cosimo had agreed to pay for it five years earlier, when it had been removed to his private chambers in the Palazzo Pitti. Cellini himself had priced it at 2,000 crowns.

p.287, ***Nor was I able to find out the reason for the evil plight I was in:*** Cellini's plight could indeed be described as "evil". Its reason was presumably that Cosimo saw him as his employee, but (enough being enough of art, though never of money) was unwilling to pay for further masterpieces when various collaborative projects were on offer (for example, the choir of the cathedral). However, he did not want the status which great art-works still bestow on their owners to be enjoyed by anyone else, and actively blocked the possibility of Cellini's working elsewhere, particularly in Paris and Rome. The despotic Duke no doubt took pleasure as well in exercising his power—in this case over a great artist with whom he had rarely seen eye to eye. For all his insights into Cosimo's character, Cellini seems to have had difficulty believing that he would sacrifice art to materialistic values in this way. But this appears to have been what happened.

p.287, ***Bandinelli's sack / Of melons:*** The sculptor's *Hercules and Caccus*—still in the Piazza della Signoria—was heavily criticized from the start. Cellini lists its defects in *La vita* II.lxx. **Giorgetto** was his scornful name for Giorgio Vasari, whom he regarded with contempt. Vasari was strongly in favour of collaborative projects, of which the parsimonious Duke too often approved: "The fruit of this unenlightened trade unionism," Pope-Hennessy says, "can be seen all over Florence today." He also says that Vasari's posthumous reputation as a painter is due to his facility and as a writer to his assiduity. The latter is not, of course, to deny his usefulness (cp. notes to 'A Giotto Triptych' in *No.1).*

p.288, ***Vitzliputzli:*** A popular corruption of *Huitzilopochtli*, the Aztec god of war, found in the German puppet play of Dr Faustus, where he is associated with Mephistopheles. Huitzilopochtli's temple was in the centre of the Aztec capital, Tenochtitlán, and captured enemy warriors were sacrificed to him. Unsurprisingly, Heine made no attempt to fit "Tenochtitlán" into the metre of the poem (first published in *Romanzero)* on which this section of the work is based—whereas "Vítzlipútzli" may have suggested it. The translation is generally somewhat looser than others in *Then and Now.* It also omits a *'Präludium'* of eighty lines, apart from the first two, here printed in italics.

p.288, **Cortez was his brazen name:** The *conquistador,* Hernando Cortez, after the sort of setbacks described in the poem, defeated the Mexican Aztecs conclusively at the fall of Tenochtitlán in 1521. Cortes founded Mexico City on the site of the former capital after he had laid it waste. The poem adapts historical events to suit its purposes, and from about the end of the second subsection modulates into fiction.

p.294, **That great Briton, Henry Martin:** This must be John Martin (1789–1854)—a well-known Romantic painter much given to epic subject-matter, who was derided as much as praised at the time. Heine (who had written about him in *Lutezia)* presumably gets the name wrong deliberately.

p.301, **For it's said the realm's destroyers / Shall be men like bearded beasts:** When the Spanish first arrived towards the end of the fifteenth century, there were an estimated seventy to ninety million Aztecs, Incas and Mayas living in central America. One hundred and fifty years later, only three and a half million survived. This is not to mention the six million Carib, Taino and Arawak people who originally lived on the Caribbean islands. Very little remains of their history since all were massacred or died, as did the Aztecs, of European diseases, especially smallpox. A few words of Taino origin have survived: hammock, barbeque, hurricane…

p.302, **As a devil… // Stifle their benumbed sensations:** These four stanzas expand on two in the original, which could be more closely translated:

>   My long-term aim is
> To begin a new career—
>
> As a devil. By persuading
> Them I AM—a God-be-with-us—
> I, their bitterest enemy, shall
> So possess these unbelievers
>
> Till their torments drive them mad:
> Phantoms I shall send to shock them—
> Constant whiffs of hellish sulphur
> Shall intimidate and mock them.

The additional stanzas have been smuggled into the poem in the subversive spirit of Heine's original… Generally speaking, there is no equivalent in nineteenth century English literature of Heine's brilliantly clear understanding of the motivations, nature and consequences (even the long-term consequences)—in short, the *karma*—of European colonialism. In his chapter, 'Consolidated Vision', in *Culture and Imperialism* (1993), Edward Said demonstrates that, on the contrary, "There were hardly any exceptions to the overwhelming prevalence of ideas suggesting, often ideologically implementing, imperial rule." The likes of Ruskin's now infamous *Inaugural Lecture* at Oxford in 1870 were typical of British thinking on this subject:

There is indeed a course of beneficial glory open to us, such as was never yet offered to any poor groups of mortal souls. But it must be—it *is* with us now, 'Reign or Die'. And if it shall be said of this country, *'Fece per viltate il gran rifiuto'*, that refusal of the crown will be, of all yet recorded in history, the shamefullest and most untimely. And this is what she must either do, or perish: she must found colonies as fast and as far as she is able, formed of her most energetic and worthiest men;—seizing every piece of fruitful waste ground she can set her foot on, and there teaching these her colonists that their chief virtue is to be fidelity to their country, and that their first aim is to be to advance the power of England by land and sea: and that, though they live off a distant plot of ground, they are no more to consider themselves therefore disenfranchised from their native land, than the sailors of her fleets do, because they float on distant waves. So that, literally, these colonies must be fastened fleets;… and England, in these her motionless navies (or, in the true and mightiest sense, motionless *churches,* ruled by pilots on the Galilean lake of all the world), is to 'expect every man to do his duty'; recognizing that duty is indeed possible no less in peace than war; and that if we can get men, for little pay, to cast themselves against cannon-mouths for love of England, we may find men also who will plough and sow for her, who will bring up their children to love her, and who will gladden themselves in the brightness of her glory, more than in all the light of tropic skies…

And so on, until "under the green avenues of her enchanted garden, a sacred Circe, true Daughter of the Sun, she must guide the human arts, and gather the divine knowledge, of distant nations, transformed from savageness to manhood, and redeemed from despairing into peace".

Heine, of course, regarded any such spiritual mission with a jaundiced eye:

Den König Wiswamitra

The great king Vishwamitra
Is marching off right now
Through non-stop war and suffering
To capture Vasishta's cow.

Oh, great king Vishwamitra,
You are an ox—and how—
To go on warring and suffering,
All for the sake of a cow!

In the ancient Indian religious epic, the *Ramayana,* Vishwamitra tried to capture the holy cow of the priest-king, Vasishta—which had it in its power to endow its owner with all the wealth of the world… At any rate, in nineteenth century Europe, it came about—according to Said—that "Whenever a cultural form or discourse aspired to wholeness or totality, most European writers, thinkers, politicians and mercantilists tended to think in global terms. And these were not rhetorical flights but fairly accurate correspondences with their nations' actual and expanding global reach."... As regards the thorough-going imperialism of Ruskin's contemporary Tennyson, for example, Said presents a list of "the quite staggering range of British overseas campaigns, all of them resulting in the consolidation or acquisition of territorial gain, to which Tennyson was sometimes witness, sometimes (through relatives) directly connected...". Quoting Tennyson's infamous remark that he was all for putting up with no nonsense from the Afghans, Said goes on to observe that what the Victorian era, including its writers, saw was "a tremendous international display of British power virtually unchecked over the entire world. It was both logical and easy to identify oneself with this power"... George Orwell, who viewed huge empires such as the British or the French as "in essence nothing but mechanisms for exploiting cheap colonial labour", would have agreed. On the other hand, he was manifestly wrong, as we now know, to imply (in his 1939 essay, *Not Counting Niggers*) that the British Empire was worse than Hitler's Germany a) because it was bigger, and b) because "It is not in Hitler's power... to make a penny an hour a normal industrial wage; it is perfectly normal in India, and we are at great pains to keep it so." Of course, it was Hitler's intention and, for a time, in his power, to do a lot worse. A great admirer of the British Empire, he had hopes, at least to begin with, of an agreement with London on how to divide the world. But, in spite of the racial discrimination, forced labour and (when necessary) ruthless brutality, which the two imperialisms had in common, there was a difference. Whereas the official or mainstream British intention was not only to subjugate and exploit but *(pace* Heine) to civilize and, eventually, to liberate, "It was this promise of eventual (if always tenuous) political redemption that Nazism decisively rejected... Based upon the immutable truths of racial hierarchy, Nazism was a doctrine of perpetual empire, for the only alternative it envisaged to domination was oppression and national death" (Mazower, *Hitler's Empire).* No matter how much writers such as Ruskin, Tennyson and others may now seem to have ignored or misunderstood the true nature of European colonialism, in other words, what they said could never have included Raul Hilberg's third anti-Semitic policy in Europe, which was annihilation (cp. headnote to 'Princess Sabbath' in *No.1),* whereas what the Nazis said culminated in it.

p.304, *"The Concord of this Discord":* The plays referred to in *Shakespearean Sonnets* have been loosely grouped into genres, the first of which is (early) comedy. Although not exactly in the order in which Shakespeare wrote them, the groups progress approximately from earlier to later. Within each subsection, the order is in fact that in which the plays were written (as far as this is known), apart from the 'history plays' (see below)... Very briefly, my idea was to write a sonnet for each play, using one of the characters to add a thought or two not actually in it as a sort of commentary or variation on its themes (a few lesser works, in part by other authors, have been omitted)... References are to the Arden Shakespeare (second series).

p.305, **Love feeds, chameleon-like, on air:** Valentine and Proteus both claim to be in love with Silvia but change their minds at critical points in the play about which of them should have her... The belief that the chameleon could nourish itself on air was widespread (at the end of II.i, Valentine's servant, Speed, says "though the chameleon Love can feed on the air, I am one that am nourished by my victuals; and would fain have meat"). As for the **wretched cur,** Crab, the fact that his master—Proteus's servant, Launce—takes upon himself the punishment of his dog for misbehaving under Silvia's father's dining-table signifies more, in this context, than comic relief…

p.309, **As second brother turned St Nicholas' clerk:** Poins describes himself to Prince Hal (in *2 Henry IV*, II.ii) as "a second brother", i.e. a younger son without inheritance and thus dependent on his wits. St Nicholas was the patron saint of children and travellers, among others—hence of vagabonds and, by the sixteenth century, of highwaymen. The phrase "St Nicholas' clerks" is used to refer to Falstaff *et al* in *1 Henry IV*, II.i. Although an occasional companion of Falstaff and friend of Prince Hal, Poins accompanies neither of them to help put down the rebellions with which Henry IV's reign was constantly troubled…

p.309, **If I can't persuade Anne's father to approve / Of me:** As a former companion of "the wild Prince and Poins", Master Fenton has been forbidden to court Anne Page by her father, a gentleman of Windsor. But Fenton (like Falstaff) is "out at heels", and plans to marry Anne in secret…

p.311, ***1-3 Henry VI*, etc.:** This play (or plays) and *Richard III* were written before the others in this subsection—towards the beginning of Shakespeare's career, around 1589–1591. However, Shakespeare seems to have thought of the 'history plays' (with the possible exception of *King John*) as a group, and presenting them in historical order makes sense in this case. In fact, the remaining five plays were *written* in historical order, and form a 'sequence' in themselves.

p.311, **At Towton even I lost heart:** The Battle of Towton (Palm Sunday, 1461) has been described as "probably the largest and bloodiest ever fought on English soil". An estimated 26,000 died on the battle-field… As Geoffrey Hill noted in his 'essay' on 'Funeral Music' in *King Log*, "One finds the chronicler of Croyland Abbey writing that the blood of the slain lay caked with the snow which covered the ground and that, when the snow melted, the blood flowed along the furrows and ditches for a distance of two or three miles…". The 'King-maker' Warwick fought on the Yorkist side and benefited from their victory, which established Edward IV on the throne and forced Henry and his followers to withdraw to Scotland. Dissatisfied with Edward, he restored the former king—who, after Warwick's death in battle, was finally murdered in the Tower of London by the future Richard III.

p.312, **Half of my great-grandfather's lands were lost, etc.:** This was because Buckingham's great grandfather, Humphrey de Bohun, Earl of Hereford, Essex, and Northampton, died without a son but with two daughters, one of whom married the future Henry IV. When Richard became king, half of the Bohun possessions were thus already the property of the crown and remained so. Richard's offer (III.i.194) of the earldom of Hereford to Buckingham as a reward for his (unscrupulous) services in helping him to become king would therefore have returned the lands to a direct descendant of their original owner. But Buckingham hesitates, fatally, when Richard demands of him as well the deaths of Edward IV's two young sons, the 'Princes in the Tower', and by the end of IV.ii, Richard is no longer in the giving vein…

p.313, **The Friar plotted to free us // From biting error:** When Hero, daughter of the Governor of Messina, is wrongly suspected of being unfaithful to her future husband, Count Claudio, he and his friend, Prince Pedro of Aragon, publicly accuse her in the church on her wedding-day. The Friar who was to have married her suggests that her cousin Beatrice, Benedick and her family give out that she has died. When the truth emerges, Claudio repents of his heartlessness and he and Hero are married…

p.314, **Self-love is not the only love which tastes / Its fancy food with a sick appetite:** In I.v, Olivia tells her steward Malvolio, "You are sick of self-love, Malvolio, and taste with a distempered appetite". Later, Malvolio—because of false information fed to him by his enemies in Olivia's household—falls absurdly in love with her. As for Viola's opinion of love in the remainder of this stanza, cp. Shakespeare's own sonnets to the Dark Lady, for example, *Sonnet 137*, which begins:

> Thou blind fool, Love, what dost thou to mine eyes
> That they behold and see not what they see?

Sonnets of this contemptuous and embittered sort are indeed the 'darker' side of the disguises and mistaken identities of Shakespearean comedy.

p.314, *All's Well That Ends Well*—**Helena:** Helena cures the King of France—who is suffering from an apparently fatal illness—by means of a prescription left her by her father, a famous physician. The King rewards her by inviting her to choose her husband and she names Bertram, the young Count of Rossillion, who unwillingly marries her. Bertram immediately goes to Italy and serves in the Duke of Florence's army, writing to Helena that she may only claim him as her husband on two conditions… Shakespeare's source is *Decameron* III, ix, *All's Well* being his principal adaptation of Boccaccio. In Boccaccio's original, the heroine is simply rewarded for her "remarkable persistence and intelligence by getting her husband back". Moreover, "from that time forth he loved her and held her in the greatest esteem"…

p.315, **To stand aside … seemed right:** The Duke, on pretence of travelling, leaves the stringent Angelo to restore respect for laws against unchastity which he has neglected to enforce. When Angelo sentences Claudio to death, his sister Isabel pleads for him until Angelo offers to let Claudio live if she will "love" him. The Duke, disguised as a friar, implements a ruse to make Angelo think she has complied. Angelo orders Claudio's death even so, but the Duke prevents it. In the end, Angelo's guilt is exposed and the Duke marries Isabel…

p.318, *Julius Caesar*—**The Poet Phaonius:** Phaonius' only appearance in the play is when, aware that Brutus and Cassius are quarrelling, he bursts in on them with a rhyme, much to the amusement of Cassius and annoyance of Brutus, who drives him away… Shakespeare himself refers to this character as, simply, "a Poet". He is named (as Marcus Phaonius, a cynic philosopher) in Shakespeare's main source for *Julius Caesar*, Sir Thomas North's translation of Plutarch, *The Lives of the Noble Grecians and Romans.*

p.319, ***Troilus and Cressida:*** This is not, of course, a Roman play. However, the Trojans fight in "the high Roman fashion"—and, after the fall of the city, Aeneas was to cross the Mediterranean, as in Virgil, to become Rome's founder. In *Coriolanus* I.viii, Hector—who is as good as murdered, in *Troilus and Cressida,* by the degenerate Achilles—is said to be of Caius Martius' "bragg'd progeny", indicating that Shakespeare was conscious of the connection. In fact, although less of a sequence than the history plays, this group of plays might also have been presented (instead of in the order in which they were written) in their historical order—namely, *Troilus and Cressida, Coriolanus, Julius Caesar, Antony and Cleopatra.*

p.320, **At least their bastards fear / My greatness now:** Cleopatra had three children by Antony. After Antony and Cleopatra had committed suicide, Octavius ordered that the elder brother and **Caesarion**—Cleopatra's son by Julius Caesar—should be killed. Antony's wife, Octavia—Octavius' sister—bore him two children... As the first Emperor and sole ruler of Rome and her territories, *Gaius Julius Caesar Octavianus* changed his name to *Imperator Caesar Divi Filius Augustus.* The Senate also gave him the title of **Princeps Civitatis** ('first Citizen of the State').

p.321, **"... born at sea, buried at Tarsus, / And found at sea again":** Convinced that his wife died after bearing their daughter Marina in a storm at sea, Pericles later comes to believe that Marina has died as well, and relapses into months of silence on board his ship. All three are at length reunited as a result of Marina's courage and integrity.

p.322, ***Cymbeline*—Iachimo:** Iachimo bets with Imogen's husband that he can seduce her. He fails, but her husband—tricked into believing he was successful—orders her death. Although this order is not carried out, both presume that it has been. Later, when they meet again, Imogen's husband forgives Iachimo... Shakespeare's source for the wager story and the character of Iachimo in *Cymbeline* was almost certainly *Decameron* II, ix, at the end of which Iachimo's equivalent, Ambrogiuolo of Piacenza, is punished in the way described (**Once I was smeared with honey, etc.**). Boccaccio shares Shakespeare's fascination with questions of revenge and punishment but not, foreseeably, with reconciliation. In the last scene of *Cymbeline*—one of Shakespeare's greatest achievements—Cymbeline declares that ***Pardon's the word to all...***

p.324, ***Mine are all fools. Or liars on the make:*** Poets appear or characters write verses in a number of Shakespeare's plays. In practically all cases the poets are as described or their poetry foolish. Shakespeare's own 'Poet' in *Julius Caesar* is, as Brutus says, "a jigging fool" and Cinna is so ineffectual as to get himself killed by the Plebeians... An exception is Gower, who serves as the Chorus in *Pericles,* one of Shakespeare's main sources being *Confessio Amantis,* Bk 8. The metre forbids but others could obviously be added to Shakespeare's "few"—Ovid, Seneca, Ben Jonson...

p.325, **Oliver Cromwell lay buried and dead:** The poem relates to the Cromwell-motif which runs through *From Now to Then,* and to the theme of atonement or reconciliation in *From Outsight to Insight...* Most of the details in the first seven stanzas are derived from Christopher Hill, *God's Englishman,* and Antonia Frazer, *Cromwell, Our Chief of Men.* The final stanza is quoted as an 'old rhyme' by Hill (p.243). The remainder of the poem has been assembled from various sources, such as Ovid, *The Tempest*, Coleridge, folk-tales, hagiographical motifs…

p.325, **King Oliver's head looked down:** Before his installation as Lord Protector, Cromwell was offered the crown, which he refused. Nevertheless he was popularly known as 'King Oliver'—and, as Antonia Frazer remarks, "almost immediately preparations were set in hand to invest the new Protector with what were at least the trappings of royalty, even if the title was sedulously denied".

p.326, **His favourite daughter:** Cromwell's favourite daughter was Elizabeth (Bettie), who died at the age of twenty-nine in 1658. Cromwell failed to recover from her death and less than a month later died himself.

p.326, **a twangling isle:** Cp. *The Tempest*, III.ii:

> Be not afeard; the isle is full of noises,
> Sounds and sweet airs that give delight and hurt not.
> Sometimes a thousand twangling instruments
> Will hum about mine ears; and sometimes voices,
> That, if I then had wak'd after long sleep
> Will make me sleep again; and then, in dreaming,
> The clouds methought would open, and show riches
> Ready to drop upon me; that, when I wak'd,
> I cried to dream again.

These lines are the more effective for being uttered by Caliban.

p.328, ***Three Fables Ancient and Modern:*** The title alludes to Dryden, whose translations are quoted in all three parts of this section: cp. note on p.27, "The clouds dispell'd, etc." Dryden's subtitle for his own *Fables Ancient and Modern* is "Translated into Verse from Homer, Ovid, Boccacce and Chaucer: with Original Poetry". In some respects, Dryden was extending a long tradition—including works by Chaucer and Shakespeare—of adapting classic authors of the sort he mentions. His book was unusual, however, in *naming* and discussing its sources and in its deliberate addition of "Original Poetry". The 'translations' themselves remind one of Bach adapting Vivaldi for the organ (BWV 593 etc.) or Mozart adapting Bach for strings (KV 404a etc.)—except that Dryden turned this 'unoriginal' (proto-Modernist?) way of writing into a far-reaching genre or broad channel for his own or anyone's originality.

p.329, **Philemon, wake up. Look! The gods are gone, etc.:** The stanza-form of this poem is derived from that of Dante's *canzone, "Quantunque volto, lasso! mi remembra",* in which he laments (in ch. XXXIII of *La vita nuova*) the death of Beatrice. The second stanza of the poem *("ne la seconda mi lamento io"* as he emphasizes—"in the second part of the poem it is I who lament") may be translated as follows:

> Gradually a sound is heard, among my sighs,
>   Of deeper pity and pain,
> Which keeps on crying for the peace of Death.
> My great desire for her thus turns my eyes
>   To him who stopped her breath—
> By whose unsparing cruelty she's slain.
> For she, whom we shall never see again,
> Whose beauty is departed from our sight,
> Has now become a beauty of the spirit
>   Spreading Love's light-filled merit
> Through Heaven. She greets the angels with its light—
> Whose high and subtle intellects discern
> With wonder how Love's gentle colours burn.

Thus Dante idealizes the death of Beatrice, whereas Ovid's old couple simply do their mundane best. On her way from the second and third stanzas of *"Donne ch'avete intelletto d'amore"* (cp. section 3, *From 'Dolce stil nuovo'...*) to the heart of the *Divina commedia* Beatrice becomes, in *"Quantunque volto, lasso!", "spiritual bellezza grande"* (literally, "great spiritual beauty"). Baucis and Philemon, on the other hand, end up as a limetree and an oak, with their roots in the ground… The formal principle in *Baucis and Philemon,* as elsewhere in *Then and Now,* is related to that described in an interview by Joseph Brodsky whereby "the ancient form" is invested "with a qualitatively new meaning"—for example, by diversifying one's ideas or "through the unpredictability of the content; by what you are going to stuff these familiar lines with", as he says in his essay on Auden's *September 1, 1939,* in *Less Than One*. Classic or traditional forms all have their own associations (or 'echoes'), in other words, which can contribute to one's overall meaning.

p.330, **It seems we all "receive but what we give"**: Coleridge's phrase is quoted from *Dejection—An Ode* , five lines of which are slightly adapted in *From Now to Then* as an epigraph for 'Fragments of a Juvenilium':

> I may not hope from outward forms to win
> The passion and the life, whose fountains are within.
>
>   O Wordsworth! we receive but what we give,
> And in our life alone does nature live:
> Ours is her wedding garment, ours her shroud.

'Fragments of a Juvenilium' is one of a number of poems in *Then and Now* whose personas are bedevilled by the sort of "tensions and double-binds" which Baucis and Philemon have succeeded in outliving. As for Coleridge's poem, it usefully corrects Wordsworth's idea of Nature and is true as far as it goes. Like most Romantic art, though, it may also be thought to lay too much emphasis on how one *feels*. What one does, in other words, is at least as important, and can change how one feels. Baucis and Philemon, in the end, are content because of what they *do*.

p.331, *"Those to whom evil is done, etc.":* Quoted from W.H. Auden's *September 1, 1939*. These deservedly famous lines on "what has driven a culture mad" are praised by Brodsky in *Less Than One* for "their breathtaking simplicity".

p.333, **The Chest:** This poem is an adaptation of *Decameron* VIII, viii and IV, ix, which present two different solutions to the problem of adultery, neither of which could be described as Christian. Boccaccio's main interest in *The Decameron* was in a good story, and he was happy enough to approximate to one morality or another, depending presumably on his sources as well as his temperament (cp. notes to *Boccaccio in Florence*, 'The Dream' etc., in *No.1*). In the process of adhering to this or that morality—or none in particular—Boccaccio sometimes illustrates unintentionally the common limitations or inadequacies of what we may like to think of as our ethics. Even on Day Ten, when he attempts (by way of an inspiring conclusion) to present ten stories about more principled people, his characters are for the most part more concerned with sexual or other politics (their reputations and social standing) than with Dantean issues of sin and virtue. However, if Boccaccio in *The Decameron* strayed too far in one direction, it has in the meantime become at least conceivable that Dante's *"triste* contraption" (Wallace Stevens' idea of the future status of *The Divine Comedy*) strayed too far in the other. Ideas of good and evil clearly vary from culture to culture and, even within particular cultures, change over time. For example, usury, homosexuality and extramarital sex, once Christian sins, are now permissible, to say the least. Sin matters and doesn't matter, in other words. Doesn't but also does matter, it should be emphasized, nevertheless. Regardless of how many differences there may be between then and now—or China and Peru—relative good and evil remain good and evil.

p.334, **a fine / If heartless story—*No. 5, Day 9:*** The two "well-known painters", Bruno and Buffalmacco, have been transferred from *Decameron* IX, v to those parts of *The Chest* which adapt VIII, viii: cp. note on p.248, *"Ella, rispostogli, il cominciò a guatare"*. Their story in *The Chest* is thus imagined as taking place some time after Calendrino's humiliation in IX, v.

p.336, **The sea, the sky, and Venus on a shell, etc.:** The description of the two sides of the chest is based partly on Chaucer's account of the temples of Venus and Mars in *The Knight's Tale*, *ca.* ll.1918–2050.

p.337, **The fatal day, the appointed hour was come, etc.:** The italicized passage is from Dryden's translation of Aeneas' description to Dido of the fall of Troy in *Aeneid* Bk.II.

p.342, **His zealous men fulfil, etc.:** Adapted from the execution of Melanthius and the unfaithful servants in Pope's translation of *The Odyssey*, Bk.XXII. The other italicized passages at this point are based on the end of Bk.XXI and beginning of Bk.XXII, in which Ulysses draws his bow and begins to slaughter the suitors.

p.349, **Tancredi, prencipe di Salerno:** The story of Tancred and his daughter has been told in many forms by many authors, beginning (in the West, at any rate) with Boccaccio, whose version in *Decameron* IV, i (quoted here) is typically direct and unadorned. According to Herbert G. Wright,

Boccaccio in England (1957), *Decameron* IV, i has been translated or retold at least fifteen times in English alone. Dryden's version in *Fables Ancient and Modern,* while purporting to be a translation, practically doubles the length of the story. "The treatment of Italian themes belongs to the tradition of England through the efforts of Chaucer and Shakespeare," Borges wrote, and Dryden doubtless saw himself as adding to what his illustrious predecessors had achieved. He was certainly aware, at any rate, that many of Chaucer's stories derived from Italian sources. His additions to *Decameron* IV, i mainly intensify the incestuous atmosphere and increase the suspense, but he also makes Sigismonda, as he calls her, less bold and more respectable, in particular by having her organize a priest to marry her to Guiscard "before they took their full Delight"… *Tancred's Daughter,* obviously, takes a different approach again from Dryden's—that of the ballads—its main models being *Helen of Kirkconnell, Earl Mar's Daughter,* and *The Unquiet Grave.*

p.351, **Peter Bell the Fourth:** This section consists of a re-make or re-write—about a third of the length of the original—of Wordsworth's *Peter Bell. A Tale,* which was rewritten in the form of parody (by Shelley, among others) in Wordsworth's own lifetime. Unlike the parodists' versions, however, *Peter Bell the Fourth* is as much a tribute as a critique and uses what it can of Wordsworth's original…

p.351, *"Peter Bells, one, two and three, etc.":* The first of these, "the antenatal Peter", is a mockery of Wordsworth's idea that "Not in entire forgetfulness, / And not in utter nakedness, / But trailing clouds of glory do we come / From God who is our home" *(Intimations of Immortality…).* The second is an "evil cotter / And a polygamic Potter" in the world of the living; while the third "is he who has / O'er the grave been forced to pass… / Damned eternally in Hell—/ Surely he deserves it well!"… Needless to say, Shelley has little or no appreciation of Wordsworth's ability to "think into the human heart", as Keats expressed it in a letter—an ability which is the source of some of his finest and most lasting poetry… Shelley destroys as well the melancholy beauty—one might almost say 'stoicism'—of Wordsworth's stanza, which is profoundly suited to the (best of) the poem's subject-matter, by rhyming its first line with its third and fourth. In Wordsworth's own stanza *(abccb),* the first line remains unrhymed, as does the second until the fifth. The stanza only resolves or pulls itself together, in other words, in its last two lines, and the *b* rhyme has a distant, unexpected feel to it in comparison with the standard or 'normal' *abab* quatrain. To give Shelley his due, the stanza's subtle sadness was not to his purpose. It is also one of the reasons why Wordsworth's attempts at humour in the first two hundred lines or so of his poem fail so signally.

p.352, **He was a churl as rough and rude / As any hue-and-cry pursued:** In three hard-hitting stanzas on *Peter Bell* in *Don Juan* (III. xcvii-c), Byron (like Shelley) objects to Wordsworth's "scumlike" subject-matter—to the "vulgar brain" of such "Jack Cades / Of sense and song"… This is, of course, the Byron whose advice on waking with a hangover was "Ring for your valet—bid him quickly bring / Some hock and soda-water…" (II. clxxx). It is also the Byron who tended to sink into sentimentality or Byronic Heroism when approaching without the defence of irony such Wordsworthian subjects as "our tears, our mirth, / Our common hopes and fears." He was thus able to see only "trash" by a "blockhead" in Wordsworth's poem. More justifiably he mocks the bathos of Wordsworth's feeble attempts at the sort of light-hearted humour of which he himself was (without question) a past master.

p.356, I'll do what the ass would have me do: Cp. note on p.330, "It seems we all 'receive but what we give'", on the relative importance of what one feels and what one does. Confronted with the ass and the situation in which he finds himself, Peter could equally as well have ignored them and continued on his way—"Whether to buy or sell, or led / By mischief running in his head…". As it is, Wordsworth strikes a fine balance in this case between what Peter feels and what he does, and the course of *action* he decides on changes his life.

p.363, (after Grimms' *Märchen*, No.15): As said already in connection with *Gretl Braun Remembers Her Sister, Eva* (cp. note on p.97, *The Grandfather's Tale (1)*), not all *Märchen* are equally edifying. In No.15 a witch is burnt alive and her possessions requisitioned… Moreover, **The Witch was the Jew-in-the-Bush's wife** alludes to a little-read anti-Semitic *Märchen*, No.110.

p.364, And so they married: Ideas of what constitutes incest vary from society to society and even from state to state. In the UK, for example, there is no legal impediment to a step-brother and -sister marrying, since there is no blood relationship between them. The Church of England requires, however, that they should not have been brought up as brother and sister under the same roof from early childhood, which is clearly a socio-religious rather than genetic prohibition. Not that this renders it meaningless…

p.365, *Thou shalt remain, in midst of other woe / Than ours, a friend to man*: The form of *A Brief Prelude (3)* first of all approximates towards and then departs from the ten-line stanza of *A Grecian Urn*, which Keats used again in *On Melancholy* and *On Indolence*. *Ode to a Nightingale* has a short eighth line and *To Autumn* (in accordance with autumn's "ripeness to the core") adds an eleventh. In these great poems of 1819, Keats showed distinct signs—particularly in their emphasis on art and artifice, including the artifice of their own style—of becoming a quite different sort of poet from his Romantic contemporaries… Keats had been thinking, when he came to compose his odes, about the form of the sonnets he occasionally dashed off—and questioning both the Petrarchan and Shakespearean rhyme-schemes. His few experiments with other possibilities are no great success, but the rhyme-scheme of most of his odes *(ababcdecde,* with variations in the sestet) feels very much like a condensed sonnet with both Shakespearean and Petrarchan elements. Together with their content, this "makes it impossible", to adapt a sentence of Borges', "for the reader to lose sight of irreality, one of art's requisites". The formal exception among Keats' odes is the first of them, *To Psyche*, whose content, however, is of particular interest. The entire poem is a highly wrought or 'irreal' construct, not unrelated (of course) to life but standing over against and with implications for it. The active creativity of its final stanza, for example, is a far cry from the passive tendencies of Wordsworth and Arnold, as remarked on in *A Brief Prelude (1) & (2)*:

>   Yes, I will be thy priest, and build a fane
>   In some untrodden region of my mind,

> Where branchèd thoughts, new grown with pleasant pain,
>> Instead of pines shall murmur in the wind:...
> And in the midst of this wide quietness
> A rosy sanctuary will I dress
> With the wreathed trellis of a working brain,
>> With buds, and bells, and stars without a name,
> Etc.

Of *To Psyche* he wrote in a letter, "… [the poem] is the first and only one with which I have taken even moderate pains—I have for the most part dash'd off my lines in a hurry—this I have done leisurely—I think it reads the more richly for it and will I hope encourage me to write other things in even a more peaceable and healthy spirit." He goes on to describe the Classical content of his poem. His other five odes are similarly filled with Classical allusions—to a degree unimaginable in Wordsworth and Coleridge, for example.

p.365, **Two very early memories:** The dog-Latin of Joyce's medical student which is used as an epigraph for *A Brief Prelude (1)* (p.107) refers to *"Liverpoolio"*, whereas the setting of the Merseyside sections of the sequence—as here becomes apparent—was in fact the Wirral. Not that there was much difference in the 1950s, when both sides of the river were in a state of post-war decay and dilapidation. Such was less the case (if I remember rightly) with **Port Sunlight**, however.

p.367, ***King Richard swinging his chains:*** In Peter Hall's 1964 production of *Richard II* at Stratford, David Warner memorably swung his chains about him in a vain but courageous attempt to prevent Exton and his servants from murdering him… As for the **Film Club,** Shakespeare's Roman plays are particularly fraught with moral issues regarding how one should live one's life, as in its minor way is *Scott of the Antarctic* (why *race* Amundsden in the first place?). In *Casablanca,* Rick refuses to compete with Laslo for Ilsa, although he might have won her… And so on.

p.368, ***Guido, I wish that Lapo, you and I:*** A condensation into Keats' stanza-form of Dante's sonnet to Guido Cavalcanti. 'Lapo' was a contemporary poet, Lapo Gianni. The conventions of courtly love do not permit Dante to name his beloved—hence the square brackets… Not long after writing his light-hearted fantasy, both he and Cavalcanti were exiled from Florence: cp. Cavalcanti's famous *canzone*, *"Perch' i no spero"*, the first stanza of which is translated in *From Now to Then* (p.68).

p.369, **His first magnolia bloomed … at Villa Camerata, Florence:** Cp. *A Brief Prelude (1),* xix. The *"ostello* where he'd worked" is in fact called Villa Camerata, whereas the Camerata where Calendrino came to grief (cp. note on p.248, *"Ella, rispostogli, il cominciò a guatare"*) is a village near Fiesole… As for **Massetto's way / With nuns etc.,** cp. *No.1,* 'The Convent Garden', p.19, ("Asleep one morning by the great magnolia,…") and note on p.17, "God knows I've wept, etc."

p.369, **Also sat looking there at Botticelli's / Vision of Spring:** The book in question, *L'opera completa del Botticelli* by Gabriele Mandel (1967), lists a number of the older *"ipothesi attendibili"* (hypotheses worthy of attention) concerning *La primavera*... The figures and setting of the picture have been interpreted in many ways. In *Botticelli* (2006), Hans Körner presents the case for seeing all nine figures as representing Botticelli's view of the various aspects of human sexual relations—from Zephyrus' rape of the nymph Chloris on the right of the picture, who (according to Ovid's *Fasti*) then became his wife, Flora, to Cupid's aiming his arrow at one of the Three Graces, who looks longingly at (her future husband?) Mercury on the left, the proceedings as a whole being presided over from the centre by Venus in person. That the painting was almost certainly intended for the marriage of a member of the Medici family in 1482 does not prevent the artist from including in his Garden of Love **natural forces tense / with violence**. After all, as the next poem expresses it, **Pictures leave us free / ... to interpret what (for us) they mean.** Anyone wishing to do so can read the 'natural force' of Zephyrus, for example, as sublimated or transmuted into the more acceptable power of 'love'. Or not.

p.371, ***From Outsight to Insight: Nine Poems After Rilke—The Turn:*** Although Rilke rarely deals with the sort of outsight which concerns itself directly with moral issues, all statements of any kind relate to or imply an ethic—in Rilke's case, the individual's right to live a contemplative life of inner freedom, which in some of his poems is such that danger or enmity or death itself can scarcely affect or reduce it. His idea of 'outsight', in other words (cp. note on p.215, *From Outsight to Insight (No.3,* title page)) was mainly oriented towards the individual's observation of the world—and of himself as part of it—in order to maximize his 'insight' or ability to transform reality in this sense. As he said of wishing to die his own death, "I don't want the doctors' death—I want to have my *freedom*" (my italics—cp. note on p.122, *At Rilke's Grave*). Rilke's limitations (cp. note on p.222, *After Heine: 'King David'*) are obvious—his egocentricity and self-importance (which in his life could be downright ruthless), his glorification of heroic individuals, his lack of interest in almost everyone's everyday life (the world of work, for obvious example, but also family life and other social and political realities)—and it would, of course, be wonderful if his poetry had been as capable of ethical as of emotional and spiritual acumen. But we had better be grateful for the superlative poetry he wrote, of which the poems in *Opus 3* are a small though outstanding selection. The original texts—to which I can only hope my translations do justice—of all but *The Turn ('Wendung')* and *From 'Sonnets to Orpheus (I.1)'* are to be found in *Neue Gedichter*.

p.371, **We never saw or heard the numinous head:** The semi-anonymity or impersonal nature of the ancient Greek torso which the poem takes as its starting point is typical of what one might think of as Rilke's post-Romantic pursuit of the subjective into virtually objective regions of emotional and spiritual observation. As he noted in 1920, "Art can proceed only from a purely anonymous centre." There are many sorts of art, of course, but Rilke's remark is clearly relevant to other poets than himself—for example, Homer or Shakespeare. And there are ways as well of producing at least an effect of anonymity, as a sort of antidote to Romantic egocentricity, including one's own—for example, translation. Others to be found in *Then and Now* are: quotation, story-telling, the use of personas, dramatic monologue, and (most pervasively) the many traditional metres and stanza-forms—including, by now, 'free' verse of one sort or another—which "have been around longer than any poet... because they are themselves equivalents of certain mental states (which include ethical states)—or contain the possibility of curbing a certain state…" (Brodsky, *On 'September 1, 1939' by W.H. Auden*).

p.377, **Siddhartha and Others:** Siddhartha Gautama lived about 2,500 years ago (?563 BC–?483 BC) among the Sakya people in the northern Ganges basin, presumably in their capital Kapilavatthu, now Lumbini. He became the Buddha (the Awakened One) at the age of thirty-five and thereafter travelled and taught throughout the region, accompanied by monks from the monastic order *(sangha)* which he founded. The originals of the two poems translated from Rilke in this subsection are also to be found in *Neue Gedichter*.

p.377, **I, Channa:** This poem is loosely based on several sections, especially §5–§8, of the *Jataka* (a collection of legends about the former lives and life of the Buddha) translated from the Pali by Henry Clarke Warren in *Buddhism in Translations*, as well as a number of discourses by the Buddha himself included in that book (e.g. §71 'The Noble-craving Sermon' and §74 'The Four Intent Contemplations')… Borges remarks in his essay *Forms of a Legend*—about later variations on the Buddha's life—"The chronology of India is unreliable; my erudition is even more so…" And I had better admit at once that the second part of Borges' sentence is true as well of *I, Channa*. On the other hand, one of the ways in which art is analogous to life is that all of us in our everyday lives make what use we can of the little that we know about most subjects—and Borges adds, "it would not surprise me if my history of the legend was itself legendary"… As for the first part of his remark, we are in the (for Westerners) odd position of having a better idea of what the Buddha taught than of which century he lived in. However, the basic facts of his biography as narrated in the poem are now thought to be more or less historical and true in substance if not in detail…

p.378, **my position as an *arhat*:** Strictly speaking, an *arhat* was a monk who had achieved enlightenment. Since Channa admits—in fact, he insists—that he was not enlightened, he must have been some sort of "honorary *arhat*", as he describes himself later (p.383)… Borges points out in another essay, *Personality and the Buddha*, that "there is no lack in the legend and in the history of the Buddha of those slight and irrational contradictions that are the signs of egocentrism—the admission of his son Rahula into the order at the age of seven, contradicting the very rules established by him; the choice of a pleasant place for his hard years of penitence" etc. The elevation of Channa to arhatship and other aspects of his relationship to Siddhartha in the poem correspond with and build on this perception, which Borges himself, though, considered misleading—the Buddha had no personality in the Western sense. However, ideas of personality and enlightenment (or anonymity—cp note above on "We never saw or heard the numinous head") are not necessarily exclusive of one another, and there is no need to idealize a man such as Siddhartha Gautama, although the Buddhist scriptures tend to do that. What he understood and practised anyone could understand and practise—or such was his teaching. He was no god or even 'hero', but one who sought to live as fully as possible the life of the spirit.

p.378, **a wise ascetic:** Ascetics, or homeless wanderers, or spiritual strivers—some of them *sadhus* (teachers)—were not uncommon in the Ganges basin before the Buddha himself renounced the world. Their beliefs were Upanishadic (leading to Hinduism proper) and, later, Jainist. Their aims were more or less as Channa describes them in the course of the poem. The Buddha eventually rejected them in favour of his 'Middle Way' between extreme austerity and sensual indulgence.

p.379, **a widow screamed etc.:** The practice of *sati* (or *suttee*) is very old, though when and why it spread have been debated without consensus. It has been noted that the Buddha had nothing to say on the subject—but comment would have been unnecessary. He certainly condemned suicide, though not all cases of *sati* were voluntary.

p.382, **One player tuned his *veena*:** A *veena* is a lute-like instrument still played in India. The Buddha's comment is based on the Pali *Sona Sutta*, Sona being a monk and former musician whose austerity went too far, in the Buddha's opinion. The *veena* was Sona's instrument, which the Buddha used to illustrate his Middle Way.

p.382, **Brahmans and Warriors, Husbandmen and Servants:** Indian society at the time of the Buddha was divided into these four main hierarchical classes or 'estates'. The Buddha's teaching disputed the superiority of Brahmans in particular, and officially all ***bhikkhus*** (monks) were equal. In theory, even a layman could become enlightened. The estates were in fact under pressure as well from the rise of cities and commerce, but Brahmanical theorists managed to preserve their basic structure and, by adding to it, eventually created the Hindu caste system—also related to people's occupations. Many Indians still see society in terms of the original four estates, and Buddhism gradually declined in India from about 700 AD, moving to other more compatible South-East Asian cultures.

p.383, **his Eightfold Path:** The Noble Eightfold Path Leading to the Cessation of Suffering is the fourth of the Buddha's Four Noble Truths, discussed in H.C. Warren, §74, and in the *Samyutta Nikaya*, for example (cp. note on p.214, "right work"). In 'The Noble-craving Sermon' (§71), the Buddha describes his first steps in the direction of these Truths. In Michael Carrithers' translation *(The Buddha,* 1983): "Why, since I am myself subject to birth, ageing, disease, death, sorrow and defilement, do I seek after what is also subject to these things? Suppose, being myself subject to these things, seeing danger in them, I were to seek the unborn, unageing, undiseased, deathless, sorrowless, undefiled supreme surcease of bondage, the extinction of all these troubles?" The First Noble Truth, then, states that life is suffering *(dukkha)*; the Second that the cause of suffering is craving or greed *(tanha*—literally, thirst) or clinging; the Third that the disease of suffering has a cure; the Fourth that this cure is the Eightfold Path of right understanding, motivation, speech, action, means of livelihood, effort, concentration and meditation… Needless to say, this is an extremely brief account of a complex subject on which countless pages have since been written, beginning with the Pali scriptures themselves, which were first committed to parchment three to four hundred years after the Buddha's death. The Buddha, it will be noticed, sees the ethical life (or 'conduct')—the first five or six steps of the Eightfold Path—as leading to or enabling the spiritual life of the last two or three steps—i.e. as the reverse of how Arnoldian Christianity and many if not most tendencies in Christian thinking generally see them (cp. note on p.109, "Milton ... viewed Christian dogma / as a form of science"). To put it very simply, the life of the spirit, as he understood it, cannot be led with a guilty conscience. The law of *karma*, as described by Channa, says that bad deeds punish the doer and good deeds reward him, one of the rewards being freedom from guilt.

p.385, **And I praise / our other path, etc.:** Channa's physicality is no less (ancient) Indian than the Buddha's celibacy—as the Tantra technique of *karmamudra*, the temple carvings and myths of Shiva, his wife Parvati and others, and the *Kama Sutra,* are alone enough to indicate. The attempt to exclude the body from our idea of the soul can result in ugly tensions—"to put it mildly", as Channa says: cp. note on p.29, "He believed the Fall / ... caused Adam's fleshly lusting". In Christian religious thinking as reflected in the arts in general, the beloved tends to be idealized and/or lusted after and despised (as, for example, in section 3, *From 'Dolce stil nuovo'...)*—presenting the lover with irresolvable double-binds... No doubt the Buddha's ability to meditate transcended these sorts of tension. Celibacy was, for him, in other words, no problem. But for many it is—or would be—and Buddhism's tendency to prescribe it is one of the religion's more questionable aspects.

Most Westerners are likely to have trouble as well with the Buddha's idea of the soul or self's reincarnation in a higher or lower form as a result of one's past life or lives—which placed a new emphasis on what was, apparently, already a very ancient Eastern belief. Collections of Buddhist writings, from Warren's (excellent) *Buddhism in Translations* to Donald S. Lopez' (irritating) *Buddhist Scriptures,* make it clear from the beginning that Buddhism is *based* on reincarnation—and that the ultimate aim of meditation is to escape from the cycle of rebirth by extinguishing life itself, since life is suffering... If we take the Buddha's observations as a form of psychological and social analysis, however, rather than as a religion "which aims at the destruction of all views,... at the extinction of craving, at detachment, at stopping, at *nirvana*" *(Majjhima Nikaya* I.22), there is a very great deal to be learned from them. Although desire in itself is not greed or obsessive thirst *(tanha)*, but is indispensable to life, it can all too easily *become* greed or thirst and so create suffering in ourselves, in others, and in the world in general. Desiring *too much*—craving or grasping / clinging—is certainly one of the commonest causes of suffering, especially when compounded with ignorance. The Buddha's observation of the misery which attitudes such as 'the more the better' invariably cause is psychologically impeccable, and his Eightfold Path can (with perseverance) lead to the reduction of such misery, to say the least... His inclusion of the conduct of the laity—who gained 'merit' by good behaviour and alms-giving—was one of his system's greatest strengths. Buddhist morality *(sila)* is based on the four 'Brahma *viharas'*: i.e. the four 'great virtues', which cause harm neither to oneself nor to others: *maitri* or *metta* (loving-kindness to all), *karuna* (compassion, sorrow for the sufferings of all), *mudita* (joy in the good of all), *upekkha* (forgiveness of all). As William Empson, who cultivated a lifelong interest in Buddhism, once observed, no one has been burned alive in the name of the Buddha: "This was the teaching that went across all the east of Asia and only by touching a country made it strong. It seemed beautiful, it seemed safe, it seemed a new way of living and a good one and it bore fruit for millions of men" *(The Complete Poems,* ed. J. Haffenden, p.151).

p.386, ***Buddha in Glory:*** Two of the Buddha's many titles are 'Light of the World' and 'Radiant One'. He taught that those who had attained enlightenment "do not repent the past nor brood over the future. They live in the present. Hence they are radiant" *(Samyutta Nikaya* I.5).